RMB Towards Internationalization

RMB Towards Internationalization

Siwei Cheng
Research Center on Fictitious Economy and Data Science,
Chinese Academy of Sciences, China

World Scientific
NEW JERSEY • LONDON • SINGAPORE • BEIJING • SHANGHAI • HONG KONG • TAIPEI • CHENNAI

Published by

World Scientific Publishing Co. Pte. Ltd.
5 Toh Tuck Link, Singapore 596224
USA office: 27 Warren Street, Suite 401-402, Hackensack, NJ 07601
UK office: 57 Shelton Street, Covent Garden, London WC2H 9HE

Library of Congress Cataloging-in-Publication Data
Cheng, Siwei.
RMB, towards internationalization / Siwei Cheng.
pages cm
Includes index.
ISBN 978-9814644655
1. Renminbi. 2. Foreign exchange--China. 3. Money--China. I. Title.
HG3978.C434 2015
332.4'560951--dc23
2014040805

British Library Cataloguing-in-Publication Data
A catalogue record for this book is available from the British Library.

人民币国际化之路
Originally published in Chinese by China CITIC Press

In-house Editor: Qi Xiao

Typeset by Stallion Press
Email: enquiries@stallionpress.com

Preface

After the Asian Financial Crisis broke out in 1997, I began to pay attention to the fictitious economy, including exchange rate issues. In 1999, I came up with a three-step strategy for exchange rate reform: moving first from pegging dollar to pegging a basket of currencies, and finally to free convertibility. After that, I carefully studied and researched exchange rate system reform, RMB convertibility, capital account liberalization and financial system reform. After the subprime mortgage crisis triggered the global financial crisis in 2007, I wrote a paper entitled "The Next Step after RMB Exchange Rate System Reform — To Establish a Flexible Dual Target Zone of RMB Exchange Rate" and submitted it to the central government leaders. With instructions "Please send to Premier Wen Jiabao for review" written by President Hu Jintao, the paper was subsequently sent by Premier Wen to Vice-premier Wang Qishan for comment and the People's Bank of China for reference. The paper was at last included in the third volume of my 2009 book *Economic Reforms and Development in China*, and also published in the first and the second issues of the magazine *Economic Affairs* in 2010, gaining some influence.

In July 2009, the Chinese Academy of Sciences (CAS) Research Center on Fictitious Economy and Data Science (where I worked as the chief director) undertook a project funded by the National Natural Science Foundation of China (NSFC) on research related to reform of the RMB exchange rate system. I served as the project's general superintendent. The project was completed in the beginning of 2011 and we submitted the following five reports: (1) "An Analysis on the Selection and Key Factors of an Exchange Rate Regime"; (2) "Research on International Experience: The Relationship between the Sequencing of Exchange Rate Regime Reform, Opening of the Capital Account, and Financial Development"; (3) "The Evolution and Evaluation of the RMB Exchange Rate Regime"; (4) "The Construction of a RMB Currency Basket Index"; and (5) "Exchange

Rate Policies and Management — The Important Issue of Constructing a RMB Exchange Rate Target Zone".

RMB internationalization has become a hot topic recently. The 12th Five-Year Plan examined and approved by the National People's Congress (NPC) in March 2011 proposed that the capital account should be gradually made convertible. This gave me the idea to write a monograph compiling all my research and thinking over the years. With the support of my students, and based on my initial paper, it took me over one year to complete this book — *RMB: Towards Internationalization.*

This book has eight chapters. Chapter 1, as the overview, discusses the essence of RMB internationalization from the perspectives of objectives, methods and processes. It also expounds three issues: exchange rate regime reform, RMB convertibility, and capital account liberalization. The chapter explores how all these relate to the internationalization of the RMB. In addition, it proposes that RMB internationalization should be achievable in ten years and offers a timetable to reach this goal.

Based on arguments I made in 1998 about the fictitious economy, Chapter 2 analyzes six problems related to the exchange rate. It also introduces and discusses new views about issues such as the transition to a fiat currency (after a regime is divorced from the gold standard and gold convertibility), dual purchasing power theories, fiat currency effects on capital flows, effects of the fictitious economy on inflation, the politics of exchange rate tools, and the selection of an exchange rate.

Using recent cross-country statistics on exchange rate arrangements published in the *Annual Report on Exchange Arrangements and Exchange Restrictions* (AREAER) by the International Monetary Fund (IMF), Chapter 3 discusses changes in the international exchange rate regime after the financial crisis. It gives an empirical analysis of various factors that affect exchange rate arrangements.

As Japan, Chile, Poland and Singapore have already converted to free-floating exchange rate regimes, we adopt these four countries as case studies. Chapter 4 discusses China's exchange rate regime reform and capital account liberalization through analysis of these countries' experiences. In each of the four cases, we examine the relationship between the sequence of exchange rate regime reform, capital account liberalization, and financial development.

Chapter 5 discusses the evolution of the RMB exchange rate regime in six different phases, analyzing and commenting on the background, measures and effects of exchange rate regime evolution at each phase.

Chapter 6 concludes with an equilibrium exchange rate determination theory, as well as a theory for selecting real effective exchange rate (REER) weighting factors. This includes estimations for factors influencing the RMB exchange rate and the magnitude of its undervaluation. It also calculates weights for a currency basket and constructs a RMB REER index by using an international competitiveness model. In addition, it utilizes an equilibrium real exchange rate model to calculate a RMB equilibrium exchange rate and exchange rate index. These are intended to provide guidance on a central rate target zone for the RMB.

Chapter 7 discusses the implications and trends of capital account liberalization, commenting on methods for measuring and comparing capital account openness across major countries. It further reviews the process of opening China's capital account from 1992 to 2012, using the actual scale of capital flows, financial market indicators and related analysis of savings-investment data.

Chapter 8 analyzes and discusses approaches to implementing RMB internationalization in four different areas: currency circulation, currency settlement, currency investment and reserve currency management.

Some chapters are written based on my general idea. Under my guidance, my students contributed to these chapters by collecting documents, processing data and writing the draft. They are Yang Haizhen, Li Ping, Long Wen, Li Ziran, Guo Kun, Xiong Yuan, Jing Zhongbo, Zhou Zhou, Dong Huiyan, Wang Xuan, and Cao Dingmu, among others. After my checking and revising, these chapters were finalized. So the book can be said to be finally completed by me based on the collective work. As a result, the book uses "we" to represent the collective work while it uses "I" to indicate my own opinion, where appropriate.

RMB internationalization is a complicated issue. Although the book manages to combine thesis with argument, qualitative analysis with quantitative analysis, statistical inference with case studies, reductionism with holism, there still exist shortcomings. Criticism and suggestions are welcome.

Cheng Siwei
October 9, 2013, in Beijing

Contents

Chapter 1

RMB Internationalization Is an Irreversible Trend

1.1 Introduction

In recent years, with China's rapid economic development and rising international status, the RMB's exchange rate has aroused much concern at home and abroad. There are several reasons for this.

First, since China adopted the reform and opening up policy 34 years ago, its economy has turned more export-oriented and its dependency on foreign trade (exports' and imports' share of GDP) has risen sharply from 9.7% in 1978 to 47% in 2012 (after hitting a record high of 67% in 2006). Changes in exchange rates can therefore significantly affect not only the prices of Chinese commodity exports, but also the performance and structure of its foreign trade, and even China's overall economic growth.

Second, because of China's comparative advantages — including abundant human resources and lower prices — its foreign trade has grown from a deficit of USD$1.14 billion in 1978 to a surplus of USD$231.1 billion in 2012. Such a long-term imbalance in imports and exports has caused increasing trade frictions and put more pressure on the RMB to appreciate.

Third, due to China's rapid economic growth, huge market potential, high quality and low-priced human resources, fine infrastructure facilities and favorable investment environment, China is becoming increasingly attractive to foreign investors. Average annual investments flowing into China's non-financial sector have soared from USD$1.956 billion in 1985 to USD$111.7 billion in 2012. Numerous world-famous multinational companies in China now are clearly taking the RMB exchange rate into consideration when making investment decisions.

Fourth, the foreign trade surplus plus the net inflow of foreign capital has resulted in a continued capital and current account surplus. These have built up China's foreign exchange reserves, which expanded from

USD$167 million at the end of 1978 to USD$3.3116 trillion by the end of 2012. While such huge foreign exchange reserves enhance China's economic strength, they may also pose risks due to exchange rate fluctuations.

Fifth, China's overseas investment has been surging in recent years. In 2012, non-financial foreign direct investment grew 28.6% year on year to USD$77.2 billion, posing new challenges to the RMB exchange rate and China's foreign exchange management mechanisms.

Sixth, as the income of China's urban and rural residents continues to increase, ever greater numbers of people are purchasing imported goods and travelling abroad. Changes in exchange rates affect the RMB's international purchasing power and thereby the behaviors and structure of Chinese citizens' consumption.

Lastly, the effect of the RMB exchange rate on China's fictitious economy should also be noted. The exchange rate influences cross-border, short-term capital flows, financial asset prices, inflation and deflation trends, and other factors affecting China's economic stability and security. Thus, the RMB exchange rate is a major issue that involves the national economy and people's livelihood. Any policy recommendation dealing with the exchange rate calls for discretion.

Since 2003, China's economic development, further opening up and increasing national strength have all put its exchange rate in the spotlight. The United States, Japan and other developed countries have all demanded appreciation of the RMB. At the G7 Summit in the spring of 2003, Japan accused China of using the undervalued RMB to dump cheap products on the international market, causing deflation in the international community. Later, United States congressmen claimed that cheap Chinese exports to the United States had resulted in higher unemployment rates in the US, a huge trade deficit, and even economic stagnation. Some in the US Congress even threatened to impose a 27.5% tariff on imported Chinese products through legislation, unless the RMB could be appreciated by 30% to 40%. Some foreign media reports also added fuel to the fire, which severely affected RMB exchange rate expectations and placed even greater pressure on RMB exchange rates and the international balance of payments.

On July 21, 2005, China launched reforms in the RMB exchange rate mechanism. These were based on market supply and demand, with reference to a currency basket, allowing the RMB to fluctuate within a certain range. The changes promised to enhance the exchange rate's flexibility through market mechanisms. Since then the RMB's exchange rate against the US Dollar has been increasing and, by the end of 2012, the exchange rate against the US Dollar had reached RMB6.2855 to USD$1, with an accumulative appreciation range of 32%. Although the RMB exchange rate against the US Dollar has dipped from time to time, the RMB is still expected to remain strong against the US Dollar. At the same time, the pressure of RMB appreciation can also be felt against the Euro and the Yen. In the short run, factors such as China's rapid economic development and the double-digit surplus in its international balance of payments will linger, China's high dependence on foreign trade will continue and the export-oriented economic structure formed by large-scale foreign direct investment (FDI) in China will remain unchanged. Thus external pressure on the RMB exchange rate will continue apace. Although a currency's exchange rate, exchange rate mechanism and related policies should be determined by the state that issues the currency, given that the exchange rate of the RMB affects the global economy, external pressures from Western countries cannot be ignored. Judging from the trends, China will endure great pressure for RMB appreciation in the long term, during which time it must exercise careful consideration and discretion.

It should also be noted that economic globalization and regional integration have made the circulation of production factors much easier than before, enabling optimized allocation of resources in real economies. To make this happen, fictitious economies (corresponding with real economies) must also go global: The internationalization of financial markets is necessary. With the faster and larger scale of international capital flows in recent years, financial markets in different countries have grown closer than ever and the global financial market can be affected by even slight changes within countries. It is fair to say that no country can achieve economic development with a completely closed financial market, which means further globalization of financial markets should be promoted.

A globalized financial system also means that financial turmoil in one economy can spread to the rest of the world, from fictitious economies to real economies, and finally lead to a global crisis. The global financial crisis — caused by the US subprime mortgage crisis — has indicated the need to reform international financial mechanisms to make them more responsive to current needs. China, as a developing country with a total economic output and trade volume second only to the US, is contributing 10% to the global gross domestic product, 9% to global trade volume, and a quarter to global economic growth. Therefore, it should have a say in the international financial market and play a more significant role in restoring the international financial order. However, to make this happen, China must further deepen reform of the RMB exchange rate regime, enable free convertibility of the RMB, open up the capital account in an active, but steady way, and promote the internationalization of the RMB.

1.2 The Implications of RMB Internationalization

As the name implies, an internationalized currency can circulate and be transacted internationally, with no set borders. It would offer traditional functions, such as being a store of value, a medium of exchange, a unit of pricing, and a generally accepted means of payment in the international market.

So far, most studies on RMB internationalization are conceptual, and many valuable results have been obtained. However, this book holds that, from a scientific and management perspective, analysis of the implications of RMB internationalization should include its goals, means and processes. That is, RMB internationalization is simultaneously a goal, a means, and a process.

1.2.1 *The Ultimate Goal of RMB Internationalization*

China, as a major developing country, is playing an increasingly significant role in global politics and the global economy. Thus an internationalized RMB should be standing side by side with the US Dollar and the Euro in the international currency system.

First, in the future, the RMB should be convertible within and outside of China. Consumers will have access to RMB accounts in foreign banks and use RMB-based credit and debit cards outside of China and small amounts of RMB cash on special occasions.

Second, RMB will be used as a unit of pricing in international trade (which may or may not involve China as a participant).

Third, in international trade settlements, RMB will be used as a currency of payment. In some international trade activities, even if RMB is not a denominated currency, the payment can be settled in RMB with consensus between buyers and sellers.

Fourth, RMB will be used in international investment and financing. This means that, besides greenfield investment and cross-border acquisitions in the real economy, RMB will also be used in various financial assets and their derivatives in the fictitious economy, including stocks, bonds, bills, insurance policies, guarantees, futures, options, forwards, and swaps, etc.

Fifth, the RMB can serve as an international reserve currency. Alongside its use by governments and central banks in foreign exchange markets, the RMB should also play a role in Special Drawing Rights (SDR).

It should be noted that China's current economic volume ranks third after the European Union and the United States. Because of its large population, resource shortages and unique political system, it is difficult for China to establish mutual trust with most developed countries. And because China's society, economy, technology and culture remain relatively underdeveloped, its financial system lacks competitiveness. Even with a fully convertible RMB, China still has a long way to go. According to the "2013 RMB Internationalization Report" released by the International Monetary Institute of Renmin University of China on June 16, 2013, the RMB Internationalization Index (RII) was only 0.87, as compared to 52.34 and 23.60 for the US Dollar and the Euro, respectively. This book holds that, with favorable international conditions and successful domestic reforms, the internationalization of the RMB can be achieved within ten years. But for the RMB to become a fully internationalized currency, it may take 20–30 years, if not longer, and calls for careful planning, phased goals, great efforts and step-by-step implementation.

1.2.2 *The Internationalization of the RMB Is a Key Step in Achieving China's Goal of Strategic Development*

At its 18th National Congress, the Communist Party of China again specified China's goal of strategic development. China will strive to build a comprehensive, well-off society by 2020 and a prosperous, democratic, highly civilized, harmonious modern socialist country by 2049. RMB internationalization is thus more of a way to deepen reforms and further open up, rather than a goal in and of itself.

The past half century has witnessed rapid development in the fictitious economy, with finance as its backbone. The total volume of the world's fictitious economy (including the market value of stocks, bond balances, as well as the notional amounts outstanding financial derivatives) exceeds USD$800 trillion. In certain developed countries, the real economy only contributes 50% to GDP. After breaking free from the gold standard system and gold convertibility, currencies are now issued according to state credit, which enables developed countries to "bully" developing countries financially. Unlike centuries ago when capitalist countries had to literally rob their colonies and poverty-stricken countries of labor and natural resources, today, to get the same economic benefits, all they need to do is purchase products and energy resources in their own currency from underdeveloped countries. These payments, in the form of foreign reserves, can only be spent on technology license and high-tech products produced by developed countries (with many restrictions). The rest can only go to financial products such as state bonds. In this way, foreign reserves acquired by developing countries actually flow back into the developed countries.

China, the largest developing country nowadays, also has the largest foreign exchange reserves, which stood at USD$3.3116 trillion at the end of 2012. However, due to the low level of the RMB's internationalization, China's spending is in many ways restricted. For example, in the case of a strong RMB, export contracts denominated and settled in RMB would benefit China's export enterprises. But in 2012, only RMB350 billion of cross-border trade settlement was made in RMB (accounting for 17.5% of the annual total). Another example is FDI. In 2012, the actual utilized FDI in non-financial investments registered USD$111.7 billion, of which only RMB253.58 billion (36.1%) was made in RMB. Of the USD$77.2 billion in non-financial overseas direct investment, only RMB30.44 billion (6.3%) was made in RMB. Moreover, in 2012, international bonds and notes denominated in RMB accounted for only 0.27% of the world's total (International Monetary Institute, Renmin University, 2013). In addition, only a few countries (such as Cambodia) have incorporated RMB into their foreign exchange reserves, and the SDR cannot at present be exchanged for RMB. Therefore, China's foreign exchange reserves are mostly used to buy foreign bonds. This means China is supporting the economic development of other countries at the expense of its own wealth: The average yield on US bonds is only 4% as compared to the 8% average return on investment. Moreover, China has to bear any losses caused by foreign currency devaluation on those reserves. However, China has no better alternatives at the time being.

Although the RMB is the sovereign currency of the largest developing economy, it is somehow invisible in the international monetary system, not to mention in the international allocation of financial resources. With favorable conditions such as a stable political environment, relatively rapid economic development, balanced foreign trade, stable currency value and abundant foreign currency reserves, China should make efforts to achieve internationalization of the RMB and become a more active player in international financial markets and the international monetary system in general. Only in this way can China take the initiative in international economic competition and acquire a higher international status.

An internationalized RMB can also help promote China's domestic financial reform and promote sound and rapid economic development. China still needs to further open its financial sector, improve efficiency, and strengthen competitiveness, which will be made easier with an internationalized RMB.

First, China should reform its exchange rate regime. Although China claims to base its current exchange rate regime on market supply and demand with reference to a basket of currencies, the currency is still heavily managed. Likewise, although China allows the exchange rate to fluctuate within a certain range, no real fluctuations have been observed during its appreciation. It appears to still maintain a "soft" peg to the USD. According to the 2009 IMF report titled "Revised System for the Classification of Exchange Rate Arrangements", China's exchange rate regime is classified as a "conventional fixed peg arrangement" under a "soft peg", which, according to our research, actually functions more like a "hard peg". In the 2011 version of the report, China was placed under a "crawl-like arrangement". Indeed, both the 2009 and 2011 reports classified China's monetary policy framework as using the USD as an "exchange rate anchor". The internationalization of the RMB will make China's exchange rate regime more market-oriented and more reliant on a basket of currencies. Its transparency and flexibility will grow, and its dependence on the USD will gradually fade away.

Second, an internationalized RMB can promote market-oriented interest rate reform. With the internationalization of the RMB, China is bound to relax controls on interest rates so that domestic and foreign commercial banks can arrange their funds according to supply and demand at home and abroad. In this way, capital efficiency will increase and arbitrage space will shrink. In addition, the marketization of interest rates can facilitate the design and launch of offshore RMB financial products, expand the scale of RMB in circulation on overseas financial markets and open more channels for RMB recycling. Although China has lifted controls on the upper and lower lending rate limits, as well as on the threshold of deposit interest rates, the upper limit of deposit rates is still under government control.

Third, an internationalized RMB can facilitate reforms in China's commercial banks. A more internationalized RMB will drive the RMB deposit and loan business of China's commercial banks. Although the amount of deposits may vary with expectations on RMB exchange rates (when the expectations go up, deposit will grow and loans will shrink; when the expectations go down, the opposite will occur), increasing demand for RMB from offshore markets will maintain increases in the total amount of deposits and loans. In addition, with increasing RMB transactions in offshore markets and higher credibility, the intermediary business of China's commercial banks' overseas branches will grow, and RMB derivatives will also be developed. In the face of fierce competition, these overseas branches will have to improve efficiency, provide better services, innovate and expand their business scope.

Fourth, an internationalized RMB can promote the reform of China's capital markets. The RMB capital account will further open up with higher demand for the internationalization of the RMB. This will, on the one hand, allow foreign-funded companies to be listed on China's A-share market and thus force domestic listed companies to improve their performance, On the other hand, this will also allow foreign institutional and individual investors to enter China's capital market, resulting in the decline of the B-share market. Moreover, with greater usage of RMB in offshore markets, China will have to facilitate RMB recycling through various methods (including issuing RMB bonds), thus helping to establish a multi-level capital market and increase the proportion of direct investment.

Fifth, an internationalized RMB will make China's monetary policy more flexible and independent. While the RMB is not internationalized, China needs abundant foreign currencies as reserve assets to guard against a potential currency risks or financial crisis. This explains China's present huge foreign exchange reserves. However, such reserves have also deprived China of the flexibility and independence it needs to enforce monetary policy. Huge reserves have brought several complications. First, the RMB20 trillion funds outstanding for foreign exchange have contributed to oversupply in the broad money supply (as measured by M2). As of the end of 2012, China's M2 balanced at RMB97.42 trillion, with a record high ratio to GDP of 188%. Secondly, to maintain the value of its foreign exchange portfolio, China spends a large proportion of its foreign exchange reserves on US bonds, which further pegs China's monetary policy to the USD. Moreover, China has to bear the consequences if the USD weakens against the RMB. With a more internationalized RMB, the RMB exchange rate formation mechanism would be more rational. China's imports and exports would be more balanced, the growth in its foreign exchange reserves would slow down, and foreign exchange reserves would be more diversified. These changes would free China to formulate more flexible and independent monetary policies.

Sixth, an internationalized RMB can improve China's financial system supervision. RMB internationalization will not bring about "laissez-faire" regulation. Rather, regulators will have to step up their efforts. Right after the Asian Financial Crisis, the author pointed out that "only by keeping things under control can China let go of some restrictions" (Cheng, 1999). In the past decade since China opened up its current account (in 1996), its financial regulatory institutions have spared no efforts in providing better service, and the results are showing. In the 40 capital items under seven major divisions of the IMF's *Annual Report on Exchange Arrangements and Exchange Restrictions* (IMF, 2012), 14 items of China's are now "basically convertible" and another 22 are "partially convertible". RMB internationalization will continue to help China build a legal, rational, moderate and effective financial regulatory system. Meanwhile, financial regulatory bodies will have to strengthen information exchange and cooperation with customs, tax, and foreign trade authorities, to achieve "comprehensive supervision and mixed operation".

But RMB internationalization has its pros and cons. There are people in China opposing RMB internationalization, citing four major concerns, each tied to potential risks. First, RMB internationalization may weaken China's ability to regulate the national economy through monetary policy, making it more difficult to guard against speculative capital flows and imported inflation. Second, it may increase the volatility and fluctuation frequency of exchange rates, adding to the difficulty of macro control and reducing the profits of import and export enterprises. Third, RMB globalization may reverse China's current "double surplus" in its international balance of payments, thus burdening China with a heavy debt. The fourth concern is that China's financial institutions may have difficulty surviving and developing in the face of fierce international competition. It is fair to say that none of these concerns are groundless. But in the larger picture, as long as China persists in reform and opening up and pushes forward in internationalizing the RMB in an active and prudent manner, an internationalized RMB in the future will bring more benefits than harm. In addition, we should guard against protectionism. A minority may try to protect vested interests, continue to take advantage of the financial system's present defects, spread rumors, or even attempt to protest against RMB internationalization.

1.2.3 *RMB Internationalization Is a Gradual Process*

RMB internationalization can only be realized through the gradual interaction between China's domestic financial reform (internal forces) and the international financial system (external forces) rather than solely through China's own wish and single-handed efforts. From a scientific perspective, the complexity of interactions between members in a system, as well as the mutual influence between a system and its external environment, will push the system to evolve in a certain direction. The process of RMB internationalization suggests the following rules and patterns.

First, the RMB's internationalization originated in cross-border trade. After reform and opening up, the Chinese government gradually opened up border trade, allowing residents within 20 kilometers of the border on either side to exchange and trade goods on government-approved markets within permitted quantities. In early 1992, the State Council approved 13 open cities on the border, including Heihe, where certain enterprises were allowed to carry out small-scale trade activities with neighboring countries in border areas. Some of China's provinces and autonomous regions have been engaged in small cross-border trade activities with a variety of neighboring countries, including Vietnam, Laos, Myanmar, India, Nepal, Pakistan, Kazakhstan, Kyrgyzstan, Tajikistan, Russia, North Korea, and Mongolia, etc. With a stable exchange rate and a trend towards further appreciation, the RMB is more and more frequently used in cross-border payments, which has further promoted its cross-border flow. However, the scale of such flows is relatively small and mostly in the form of cash instead of credit or RMB account transfers.

Second, the rapid growth of foreign trade can facilitate cross-border RMB flows. With the growth of China's foreign trade sector and increasing numbers of foreign-funded enterprises, the clamor for the Chinese government to relax trade exchange restrictions had been growing ever louder. The requests were answered by the Chinese government in 1994. In fact, as China's foreign exchanges became increasingly frequent, restrictions on foreign exchange settlement by individuals were lifted back in 1991. On December 21, 1996, China formally accepted Article VIII of the IMF and made RMB convertibility possible under the current account.

Since China became a member of the WTO in 2001, it has experienced rapid growth in foreign trade, a surge in its foreign trade surplus, and expanding foreign exchange reserves. With rising demand for RMB and market expectations of RMB appreciation, many neighboring countries and regions have allowed RMB into circulation and established exchange facilities. Banks have started to accept RMB deposits and other RMB transactions. Moreover, the RMB has even been used in settling cross-border trade.

On April 8, 2009, the State Council executive meeting decided to launch a pilot cross-border RMB trade settlement program in Shanghai, Guangzhou, Shenzhen, Zhuhai and Dongguan. On July 2, 2009, China's six government authorities jointly issued the "Method for Managing RMB Trade Settlement Pilot Program", which marked the official launch of the pilot program. On June 22, 2010, the People's Bank of China (PBOC), Ministry of Finance, Ministry of Commerce, General Administration of Customs, State Administration of Taxation and the China Banking Regulatory Commission jointly issued "Notice on the Relevant Issues Concerning the Expansion of RMB Settlement in Cross-border Trade Pilot Program", which expanded the pilot program from four cities including Shanghai and Guangdong Province to 20 provinces (autonomous regions and municipalities), including Beijing. At the same time, overseas coverage was expanded from Hong Kong, Macao and ASEAN countries to all parts of the world. The "Notice" also specified the business scope to be covered: cross-border trade in goods, trade in services and other RMB settlements under the current account. On June 21, 2011, the PBOC released "Notice on Specifying Issues Concerning Cross-border RMB Business", which made clear how to use RMB settlement for FDI. On August 23, 2011, the RMB cross-border trade settlement program was expanded to the whole country. So far, the policy barrier to RMB cross-border trade settlement has been cleared. But because China's capital account is not yet open, the percentage of RMB settlement in cross-border trade is still very low, at only 10%.

Third, the RMB is increasingly used for personal use in foreign countries. Since the reform and opening-up, the number of Chinese citizens traveling to and studying in foreign countries has surged, and foreign exchange administration authorities have also gradually relaxed control over foreign exchange swaps and foreign currency deposits by individuals. Because of the stable exchange rates for the RMB, sellers in some countries and regions are willing to accept RMB payment; for Chinese travelers, paying with RMB can help them avoid losses resulting from exchange rates fluctuations. Thus the use of RMB for direct transactions in overseas markets is gaining wider adoption. Such direct transactions, at a small scale and cash-based, were first limited to some of the neighboring countries and regions, as well as Hong Kong, Macao and Taiwan. But as outbound travel heated up, the RMB is now widely and officially used in many countries. The introduction of China Unionpay has also expanded the scope of RMB payment. As of early 2013, China Unionpay service is available in 141 countries and regions outside China.

Fourth, there are increasing investment demands from both businesses and individuals. With China's growing economic strength and with increasing economic globalization, the Chinese government made the decision to "go global" in 1997. The goal was to encourage strong domestic enterprises to make investment and set up factories abroad, so as to tap local markets and make use of local resources. But since the RMB was not fully convertible, Chinese enterprises had to convert RMB into USD or other convertible currencies before making their investments, which not only exposed both sides to the risk of fluctuations in exchange rates, but also added to Chinese enterprises' financial burden (due in part to transaction costs, like conversion fees). Therefore, in government-led foreign investment and government-funded projects, the foreign party was expected to accept payment in RMB. With the expansion of the cross-border trade RMB settlement pilot program, domestic institutions became more eager to directly invest in RMB overseas. To this end, in 2010, the PBOC carried out the RMB overseas direct investment pilot program based on the principles of controllable risks, stability, and orderly expansion. The project gained widespread popularity among enterprises and banks. In January 2011, the PBOC issued the "Method for Managing RMB FDI Settlement Pilot Project", which facilitated banks, financial institutions and other domestic institutions' overseas direct investment RMB clearing business, as well as Chinese enterprises' FDI in the real economy.

With the strengthening of China's financial sector and increases in household wealth, financial institutions, businesses' and citizens' demand to invest directly in the fictitious economy has been growing. In June 2007, the PBOC lifted restrictions on mainland financial institutions to issue RMB bonds in Hong Kong. In 2009, the issuers expanded to include the Ministry of Finance and Hong Kong banks' mainland subsidiaries. In 2010, the restrictions were furthered eased to include average companies and international financial institutions. On March 28, 2012, the State Council approved the implementation of the "Overall Program of Comprehensive Financial Reform Pilot for Wenzhou City". On November 23, 2012, Wenzhou city government released the "Implementation Plan for

Comprehensive Financial Reform Pilot for Wenzhou City", which contained 12 detailed directives, including "to carry out the individual foreign direct investment pilot program". Other cities such as Shanghai and Tianjin are also seeking opportunities to try out individual FDI pilot programs, which include RMB or foreign currency cross-border remittances, direct investment, financing, clearing and financial market investments.

In summary, the degree of RMB internationalization depends on China's attitude and the acceptance of the RMB worldwide. To enhance the popularity of the RMB, China must further deepen reforms, continue to open up, maintain the sound and rapid development of its macro economy, strive to improve the financial markets and the financial system, maintain a relatively stable exchange rate, explore more ways for RMB investment, and constantly enhance confidence in the RMB as a viable international currency. Moreover, China should work to create the necessary conditions for RMB internationalization. Important steps include making efforts to promote the reform of the RMB exchange rate system, gradually achieving convertibility in the capital account, and moderately opening up the capital account.

1.3 Reforms in the RMB Exchange Rate Regime and RMB Internationalization

An exchange rate regime encompasses the principles, methods and arrangements and stipulations of an authority in controlling and managing the exchange rates of its currency. Reforms in a country's exchange rate regime are a prerequisite for the internationalization of its currency. The RMB is no exception to this. The RMB exchange rate regime consists of two parts: institutions and mechanisms. Therefore, during the reform period, China needs to study how to arrange the determination of specific exchange rates over time. Moreover, it has to study the course and driving forces of the evolution of the exchange rate regime, and how to head towards its goals while maintaining policy guidance and strong management.

In order to specify meaning of the word "regime", this book adopts the IMF official term "exchange rate arrangement", which is defined as the relationship between domestic currency and foreign currency. Thus, an exchange rate arrangement falls into the category of institutions (structures), which are relatively stable over a certain period but can gradually evolve in the long run.

1.3.1 *Major Factors That Influence Exchange Rate Arrangements*

Many factors can affect exchange rate arrangements. They vary with political, economic and financial developments and from country to country. Therefore, the exchange rate arrangement is a very complex matter. Considering different factors, economists may draw dramatically different conclusions when it comes to guidance on an exchange rate arrangement. Most of them may take a static partial equilibrium perspective while leaving out changes in or interactions between various factors. Therefore, their conclusion may be reasonable from a static point of view but cannot stand if realistic, dynamic interactions are taken into consideration.

The transition to a new exchange rate arrangement is a dynamic and evolutionary process, and should be studied from short-, medium- and long-term perspectives, keeping in mind that the outcomes in one time horizon may not apply to the other two.

In the long run, the exchange rate arrangement is mainly affected by the coordination between the exchange rate regime and economic policy. Fixed or pegged exchange rates between two countries require that the countries' economic factors achieve simultaneous development, which is impossible. Therefore, no country or region can stick to a pegged exchange rate system for a long period of time. That is to say, particular exchange rate arrangements may only meet the needs of a particular country during a specific period of time, though for most countries their exchange rate arrangements will eventually become relatively stable.

In the medium term, the main factors affecting exchange rate arrangements are the economic and financial features of a country. These include the scale of its economy, the openness of the economy, the government's ability to exert macroeconomic control over the country, the degree of trade concentration, interest rate marketization, the domestic money supply, and the government's preferences on exchange rate policy.

In the short term, major factors affecting exchange rate arrangements are a country's borrowing power, financial vulnerability, ability to sustain shocks from capital flows, its government's credibility, investors' expectations, and the presence (or absence) of financial panics.

Thus, the choice of exchange rate regime is a very complex issue, involving both a government's choice of policy and a country's specific circumstances. Therefore, studies on reforming the RMB exchange rate regime should not only analyze China's economic characteristics and policy objectives but also take into account the international economic situation and the decisions made by other countries in regards to exchange rates.

1.3.2 *Conclusions from an Empirical Analysis of Exchange Rate Arrangements*

The following conclusions can be drawn from the results of an empirical study and relevant theories:

(1) A country's exchange rate regime must follow its level of economic development.
(2) As a country's economy develops, it should adjust its exchange rate regime to adapt to changing demands. Static exchange rate arrangements are misplaced and go against the real evolution of exchange rate regimes.
(3) Adjustments and changes in an exchange rate regime should be made gradually, according to objective economic laws and actual needs.
(4) The reform of an exchange rate regime is highly dependent on the openness of capital projects and the financial market. To maintain stability in the macro economy and foreign exchange markets and avoid imbalances, sufficient foreign exchange reserves must be maintained during the reforms. According to past experience, the exchange rate regime reform is usually done in the following way. First there is a fixed exchange rate system (including a "pegged" exchange rate system, adjustable pegs, crawling peg, and/or basket peg). Then there is the floating, interval-bound exchange rate regime (including the crawling band exchange rate system and the target zone exchange rate regime). Finally, as reforms deepen, a floating exchange rate regime takes place, which moves from a managed floating exchange rate regime to a free floating exchange rate system.
(5) Although most countries and regions with internationalized currencies have adopted a floating exchange rate regime, there are exceptions. For example, Denmark still sticks to a soft peg, while Chinese Hong Kong is following a hard peg exchange rate regime. Thus, the use of a floating exchange rate system to promote the internationalization of RMB is not a prerequisite.
(6) Although the exchange rate regime of China from 2008 to 2009 could be categorized as a "soft peg", based on an analysis using an overall discriminant function with global data, it is disposed towards behaving like a "hard peg". According to a rough estimation, when GDP per

capita reaches USD$15,000, conditions for China to steer towards a free floating exchange rate regime will be ripe. Before that time, however, a managed floating exchange rate regime will be necessary during the transitional period.

1.3.3 *The Direction of China's Exchange Rate System Reform*

On July 21, 2005, China began to implement a managed floating exchange rate regime based on market supply and demand, with reference to a basket of currencies. Such reform increased the flexibility of the RMB exchange rate and facilitated its appreciation. However, shortcomings of China's existing exchange rate system still remain and further reforms are needed. Favorable conditions should be created for the full convertibility of the RMB.

From being pegged to the USD to being pegged to a basket of currencies, China's exchange rate regime has moved forward from a fixed exchange rate system to a floating exchange rate system. This follows with the rapid development of China's export-oriented economy and growing financial strength. However, in the reform of the RMB exchange rate regime, China is still facing many difficulties and unfavorable conditions, such as arbitrage-seeking capital inflows resulting from expectations about RMB appreciation, domestic institutions' poor endurance of exchange rate fluctuations and lack of experience in currency risk management, as well the strong market impact from any potential exchange rate policy adjustment. In addition, given China's imperfect market mechanisms and government control over trade, investment, and interest rates, the prices formed under such conditions cannot represent true market supply and demand. It is obvious that China cannot implement a completely free floating exchange rate regime overnight, but it should take the initiative to move towards such goal in a gradual way.

According to the domestic and international environment, and with reference to various exchange rate arrangements, the author proposed a "flexible exchange rate target zone system" in 2009, which can be a sound choice for China at this stage (Cheng Siwei, 2009). The exchange rate target zone is a range for exchange rate fluctuations, set by monetary authorities who pledge to intervene in the foreign exchange market to maintain the exchange rates within said range. The exchange rate target zone system involves several components: a central exchange rate at the center of the target zone, a band around said central rate, transparency about the target zone from monetary authorities, a monetary policy for market intervention, and certain means and willingness on the part of the monetary authorities to intervene when necessary.

With the capital account not yet fully open, an RMB exchange rate target zone regime would be more active than the current regime which is in reference to a basket of currencies. A target zone regime would not only benefit from the stability of the present RMB exchange rate, but also give room for exchange rate adjustment, thus enjoying the advantages of both fixed and free floating exchange rate systems. In that case, expectations of RMB appreciation would be determined by market supply and demand rather than some officials' remarks or the amount of foreign exchange assets purchased by monetary authorities. The monetary authorities can set the central exchange rate of the target zone with reference to the equilibrium exchange rate, measured by scientific methods, and the central bank can step in when the market exchange rate reaches the upper or lower limits. The "honeymoon effect", brought by the exchange rate's target zone management mechanism (i.e., when the exchange rate approaches the upper or lower limits, expectations of appreciation or depreciation push the exchange rate lower or higher than that in a free floating system), can also help stabilize the exchange rate. This dynamic would give full play to the market, facilitate effective allocation of resources and stabilize market regulations in the exchange rate regime. This option can also avoid speculation and questioning regarding the currency basket, instead providing reasonable interpretations of government regulation of the RMB exchange rates. Effectively the target zone regime would prevent or at the very least reduce frictions with external economies.

The "flexibility" proposed by the author can be realized via the following three aspects.

First, there can be dual target zones. When determining the exchange rate target zone, monetary authorities can set hard and soft exchange rate target zones. The hard target zone refers to a relatively stable zone with high transparency and a narrow floating band, maintained by the monetary authorities through market intervention. The soft target zone, on the other hand, also with a narrow band, is not open and can be determined and corrected by the monetary authorities according to the balance of international payments as well as domestic and international economic conditions.

Second, the target zone can be expanded. Instead of fixed boundaries, the target zone can expand with the deepening of China's financial reform and the internationalization of RMB until the boundaries are eliminated and full convertibility of RMB is achieved.

Third, the target zone can be adjusted. The central exchange rate of the target zone is relatively fixed, but it can be adjusted in line with international financial fluctuations and domestic inflation.

To establish an RMB exchange rate regime centered on a target zone, the upper and lower limits of the RMB exchange rate target zone should first be determined. If the zone is set too narrowly, it may fail to reflect the market demand for flexibility in the exchange rate; if it is too wide, on the other hand, the trading sector and the stability of capital flows may be undermined. As Yang and Wang (2008) see it, although most European monetary systems adopt the $\pm 2.25\%$ range and a few follow a $\pm 6\%$ exchange rate target zone, China is still a developing country with many financial variables. Thus a range of $\pm 5\%$ is appropriate. However, this figure lacks legitimate proof. Wang (2007), based on analysis of historical data, suggests that the upper and lower limits of the target zone should be the equilibrium exchange rate plus twice its variance. Thus the band of the target zone would be four times the equilibrium exchange rate variance. However, Wang did not give a specific value. Using a least squares method, Guo (2007) conducts a regression analysis of China's exchange rate data from 1990 and 2005. Guo finds that the nominal exchange rate always fluctuates within $\pm 15\%$ of the equilibrium value, therefore this band should be set as the RMB exchange rate target zone. However, such band may be too wide for the initial phases of policy reform.

The "flexible RMB exchange rate target zone regime" proposed by the author consists of both hard and soft exchange rate target zones. The hard target zone is determined by market demand and supply, and is generally free of government intervention. The soft target zone, on the other hand, can be adjusted through market intervention by monetary authorities. As China's market-oriented exchange rate reform deepens, the above-mentioned target zones can be expanded gradually in three stages until the RMB is freely convertible.

When first established, the two exchange rate target zones should be controlled within a narrow range, allowing Chinese businesses to adapt and monetary authorities to perfect their management methods as well as gain experience. At this stage, the central bank (the PBOC) should gradually give up direct intervention, and monetary policy tools such as reserve requirements, the discount rate and open market operations should be used in regulating the foreign exchange market. Only in special circumstances should direct interventions (in the form of injecting foreign currency or RMB to the market) be used. In 2011, the author suggested a ±1% hard target zone, which is reliable based on the standard deviations of the RMB against the USD, EUR and JPY (0.50, 0.60 and 0.33 respectively) from July 2005 (after the reform) to May 2009 (Ding, Ding, Wang and Li, 2009). With recent progress in exchange rate reform and the opening of capital account items, the band can be enlarged to ±3–5%. The soft target zone, on the other hand, can be set at ±8–10% of the central exchange rate, so as to guard against large and abnormal exchange rate fluctuations.

When adjusting the exchange rate target zone, China can expand the hard target zone in small steps to ±10–15% and the soft target zone to ±15–20%, proceeding in step with the gradual opening of the capital account and marketization of the exchange rate.

In the next stage, China should continue to expand the hard and soft target zones in greater steps, with the former expanding more than the latter. In this way, the two zones will ultimately converge into a single exchange rate target zone with a ±30% band width. After this convergence, China will move the RMB to full convertibility.

Another key issue in establishing an exchange rate target zone regime is determining the central exchange rate — choosing a central foreign currency and the RMB exchange rate against it.

The central currency should be determined according to a country's foreign trade situation, and can be one or a few (in a basket of) foreign currencies. With the integration of the global economy, more and more countries will chose a basket of foreign currencies as their central currency. When deciding on which currencies to place in the basket (as well as their weighting), a country usually takes into consideration its imports and exports, foreign investment, and foreign debt. But usually the USD, EUR and JPY (G3) are on the top of the list. The author agrees that a basket of currencies should be adopted in the establishment of a RMB exchange rate target zone, so as to truly reflect China's foreign trade, balance of payments, and the international purchasing power of the RMB. Based on China's actual situation, two currency baskets are suggested here. The currency basket in a narrow sense only contains currencies of China's four most important foreign trade partners (whose unilateral/bilateral trade volume far exceeds that of other countries or regions), namely the USD, EUR, JPY and KRW. The currency basket in a broad sense also could include the GBP, AUD, SGD and INR. In both broad and narrow senses then, the RMB exchange rate index can thus be established.

Generally, it is believed that the central exchange rate of an exchange rate target zone should be the equilibrium exchange rate, or the actual exchange rate when both balanced international payments and full employment are achieved. The author believes that the equilibrium exchange rate should not serve as the central exchange rate when the exchange rate target zone has just been established, for two reasons. First, China still cannot launch a widely recognized RMB equilibrium exchange rate model. Moreover, using the equilibrium exchange rate as the central exchange rate will affect the relative stability of the RMB exchange rate and therefore threaten the steady transition from an exchange rate based on a currency basket to an exchange rate target zone. When adjusting the target zone, China can move the central rate towards the equilibrium exchange rate according to specific circumstances, so as to move the entire target zone. When the exchange rate target zone is to be abolished, the central exchange rate will approach (and eventually converge with) the equilibrium exchange rate. As China deepens its reform, opens up its market, and improves its socialist market economic system, its foreign market, featuring a simple structure and monopoly by the central bank, is bound to undergo changes. Only when companies and banks are given full play in their market activities can the RMB exchange rate be determined by supply and demand, or can the central exchange rate of the proposed target zone approach the equilibrium exchange rate.

1.4 RMB Convertibility and RMB Internationalization

Currency convertibility refers to the right enjoyed by a country's residents to convert the local currency into foreign currencies based on certain exchange rates. According to the level of intervention of the central bank or the government, currency convertibility can be divided into three types: fully convertible (when there are no restrictions or limitations on the amount of currency that can be traded on the international market), partially convertible (when certain restrictions are placed on the purposes and amount of currency that can be traded) and nonconvertible. In fact, because of insufficient foreign exchange reserves and pitfalls in financial systems, most countries impose certain restrictions on the purposes and amount of currency to be traded. But generally, residents can freely convert their national currency into foreign currencies in the country, while the residents' overseas assets in the form of foreign currencies and their overseas transactions with foreign currencies are restricted.

According to different purposes, the international convertibility of a currency is usually divided into current account convertibility and capital account convertibility.

Current accounts items are accounting identities which record frequent domestic and foreign economic transactions. They include the foreign trade balance (including foreign exchange income from exports and foreign exchange spending on imports), non-trade transfers (including income and expenditure of trade in services, individual income and investment returns), as well as current transfers (including one-way transfers of funds or goods among countries).

Zhou (1995) points out that current account convertibility can give the economy more freedom, promoting domestic output by improving production input and acquiring advanced technology. Meanwhile, it can also simplify import procedures and increase the variety of imported goods and services, both of which benefit consumers. There are also indirect benefits such as the positive effects of import competition on domestic production efficiency and guidance on investment allocation from relative prices on the international market. But such merits also come with costs. First, since it requires a short-term real exchange rate lower than the long-term equilibrium exchange rate, current account convertibility would raise the relative prices of imported products (including important production inputs and capital goods). Second, to maintain balance in the current account means either exacerbating exchange rate instability or placing greater pressure on the authorities to adopt policies and measures that balance international payments rather than focusing on domestic economic stability.

Overall, the benefits of current account convertibility far outweigh the costs. For this reason, now many countries including China have accepted the provisions of Article VIII in "Agreement of the International Monetary Fund": "No member shall, without the approval of the Fund, impose restrictions on the making of payments and transfers for current international transactions; no member shall engage in, or permit any of its fiscal agencies to engage in, any discriminatory currency arrangements or multiple currency practices; each member shall buy balances of its currency that have been recently acquired as a result of current transactions." This article's directives thereby promote current account convertibility.

The capital project, also known as the capital account, refers to a country's capital and financial account for its international balance of payments. The capital account records international or cross-region transfers of financial assets. In the international balance of payments, the capital account is divided formally into the capital account and financial account. The former includes capital transfers, and foreign trade of non-production, non-financial assets; the latter covers all foreign transactions that change the ownership of an economic entity's assets and liabilities, including direct investment, portfolio investment, other investment forms, and reserve assets. According to the explanation provided in the "Ancillary Provisions" of "Regulations on the Foreign Exchange System of the People's Republic of China" published in 2008, "capital account transactions refer to the increase and decrease of assets and liabilities in the balance of payments as a result of inflow and outflow of capital, including direct investment, loans and portfolio investment, etc."

Quirk and Evans (1995) define capital account convertibility as the removal of restrictions, tax and subsidies on cross-border capital transactions. Jiang (2002) defines it as "the lifting of restrictions imposed on the currency exchange, foreign payments and transaction in capital account transactions, which enables free movement of capital". Since capital account convertibility is a process, it is also known as "capital account liberalization" (Jiang and Zhu, 2004).

The State Council's 1993 "Decisions of the State Council on the Reform of Financial System" states: "The long-term goal of the reform in China's foreign exchange management system is to achieve RMB convertibility." Although conditional RMB current account convertibility was realized in 1994 and full convertibility in the current account was achieved in 1996, China has been cautious with RMB convertibility in the capital account, considering the perplexing pros and cons. The pros are as follows. First, capital account convertibility can develop a currency's functions from a tool in trading to one that can be used in settlement, investment and reserves, improving its presence in overseas markets. Second, it can promote the free flow of capital around the world, facilitate optimal allocation of resources and improve efficiency. Third, it can boost foreign investors' confidence in the domestic market and encourage inflows of private foreign capital, which can make up for a lack of savings and foreign exchange in developing countries, thus promoting economic growth. Fourth, it can improve local technology and management skills. Fifth, it generates greater investment returns and reduces risks by enabling local residents to explore more investments channels.

The possible disadvantages of capital account convertibility are as follows. First, it may result in greater volatility in the exchange rate, as free flows of capital will change foreign exchange supply and demand. (This explains why most countries with capital account convertibility adopt a floating exchange rate regime). Second, it may impact the domestic economy, since the majority of cross-border capital flows may not only affect the domestic economy through exchange rate changes, but also allow profits through a variety of speculative means, which could undermine domestic economic and financial stability. Third, it may cause economic and financial instability, especially in small economies with underdeveloped financial markets and imperfect financial mechanisms. For developing countries, therefore, the benefits of capital account convertibility may be offset by these negative effects.

Making the right decisions can be tough given the complicated pros and cons inherent in capital account convertibility. But in the overall picture, to adapt to economic globalization and financial integration, China's capital account convertibility is imperative. In March 2011, China's National People's Congress pledged to achieve capital account convertibility in the "Development Plan for the 12th Five-Year Plan Period". While enjoying the benefits of greater openness, China will also have to continue reforming its financial system to guard against possible risks.

Wang (2010) holds that greater convertibility in a currency can boost the internationalization of that currency in two ways. First, greater convertibility can give more opportunities for cross-border transactions using the currency. The currency convertibility under the current account requires that a country buy balances of its currency that have been recently acquired via transactions. Therefore, currency convertibility under the capital account means a country should buy balances of its currency that have been recently acquired as a result of all transactions. This can promote the use of the currency in cross-border transactions and extend the functions of the currency from trade to investment, storing value, etc. Second, currency convertibility will encourage foreign countries to hold a country's currency and therefore make it more internationally acceptable. Without currency convertibility under the capital account, the currencies held by other countries can only be used for recurring transactions (due to a lack of investment channels). In contrast, with currency convertibility under capital account, the currencies held by other countries can generate more returns through investments in financial markets, which can add to the popularity of the currency.

1.5 Capital Account Liberalization and Internationalization of the RMB

Capital account openness — placing no restriction on cross-border transactions (or any measures that can affect the costs of such transactions) — is a gradual relaxation of capital controls to ultimately achieve a freely convertible currency, thereby allowing residents and non-residents to hold cross-border assets and engage in cross-border asset transactions. In its *Annual Report on Exchange Arrangements and Exchange Arrangements 2010* (IMF, 2010), the IMF defined capital controls as: a country's authorities banning capital flows; requiring approval for capital flows, authorization and notification; multiple interventionist currency practices; discriminatory taxes; and reserve requirements or authority-imposed penalties.

In its *Annual Report on Exchange Arrangements and Exchange Restrictions 2011* (IMF, 2011), the IMF divides capital accounts into seven major categories and 40 sub-items. The seven categories are: capital and money market instruments, derivatives and other trading instruments, credit operations, direct investment, direct investment liquidation, real estate transactions and personal capital flows. The report also includes explicit summaries of the annual changes made by each member state in regards to capital account restrictions and records such restrictions in every sub-item.

Capital account convertibility (i.e., openness) is a prerequisite for, but not equivalent to, capital account liberalization (i.e., the greatest degree of openness). The latter calls for the total cancellation of restrictions on trade and any related measures that may increase the costs of capital transactions such as "transaction taxes and subsidies", in addition to the liberalization of "exchange and payment" and capital flows. Moreover, capital account liberalization requires a single exchange rate or non-discriminatory exchange rate arrangement (though not necessarily a floating exchange rate).

Thus, although capital account convertibility is the basis of capital account liberalization, they are not equal. It's still possible that, with convertible capital accounts, some countries may pose restrictions on the ways, number and directions of transactions under certain capital accounts, for the sake of maintaining economic and financial security, keeping monetary policies independent and/or protecting their own country's interest.

Also, opening the capital account does not mean lifting controls of every sub-item under the capital account. Rather, it is a gradual process. In the IMF's *Annual Report on Exchange Arrangements and Exchange Restrictions 2012* (IMF, 2012), it listed all its members' various controls over their capital accounts in that year, showing that virtually none of them had completely opened their capital account. About 75% of the 192 surveyed member states had controls over securities trading, direct investment and real estate transactions in the capital market, with special terms on commercial banks, other credit institutions and institutional investors. Over 50% imposed restrictions on their capital market instruments, collective investment securities and financial credit.

Even the United States, though known for its capital account openness, still imposes some restrictive regulations on some of the sub-items of its capital account according to its macroeconomic development and risk appetite. These include control over securities transactions and derivative tools in the capital market and restrictions over direct investment, real estate transactions, etc.

According to the 40 sub-items of the current account under seven major categories in the *Annual Report on Exchange Arrangements and Exchange Restrictions 2011* (IMF, 2011), and based on China's existing laws, regulations and policies, the Survey and Statistics Department of the PBOC (2012) divided the above-mentioned 40 items into "convertible", "basically convertible", "partly convertible" and "non-convertible". As of the end of 2011, there were 14 items under the "basically convertible" RMB capital account (with fewer restrictions but subject to registration or approval), which mainly involve credit derivative transactions, direct investment, direct investment, liquidation, etc. The 22 items under the "partially convertible" RMB capital account (subject to strict access control or quota control) mainly involve the bond market, stock market trading, real estate transactions and personal capital transactions. The four "non-convertible" items include the participation of non-Chinese citizens in the domestic capital market, trust fund market and trading derivative tools. No items are fully convertible After analyzing China's capital account openness from 1992 to 2012 using actual capital flows indicators, financial market indicators, and savings-investment-relationships, this book concludes that despite the gradual opening of China's capital account in the past 20 years, in general China's capital account is still not open enough.

The pros and cons of capital account openness need to be weighed. It can facilitate free capital flows and optimized allocation in the world market, so that China can attract foreign investors, especially strategic investors, with its broad market, stable economic environment, inexpensive high-quality human resources and good infrastructure. The value of Chinese enterprises will increase with more resources in capital, market and management provided by foreign strategic investors, and China's economic growth will be further promoted. It can also help Chinese enterprises go global by gaining access to markets and resources, to improve technology and management, and to spread their risks around the world through investing abroad. It can aid China's economic restructuring and industrial upgrading through the international transfer of industries. Finally, it can promote reforms in China's financial system, help China strive for innovations when facing challenges, and enhance its international competitiveness.

Opening the capital account will facilitate Chinese enterprises and individuals investing in offshore financial markets. At the same time, it will allow foreign investors to invest in China's financial markets with their RMB, thereby encouraging them to hold and use RMB in the long term. Moreover, China should improve and broaden the channels for RMB recycling through providing high-quality services for exchange and settlement of RMB, so that foreign investors are willing to use RMB for invoicing and settlement, and so foreign governments are willing to use the RMB as a reserve currency. In this way the internationalization of the RMB can be further promoted.

One concern of opening the capital account is that it may greatly enhance the scale and speed of cross-border capital flows, leading to a possibly significant impact on interest rates, exchange rates, and the demand for currency. In addition, it would place Chinese enterprises in fiercer competition with international firms. Excessive inflows of speculative capital inflows may exacerbate economic fluctuations and push up domestic prices, including the prices of financial assets. Moreover, huge capital flight may even cause a financial crisis, as insufficient foreign exchange reserves and financial misconduct combine to squeeze the financial system. To this end, China must adjust the pace and intensity of opening the capital account based on the endurance of its financial system and the capacity of its financial supervision institutions while maintaining stability in the macro economy and abundant foreign currency reserves.

In 2012, the IMF presented its latest views regarding capital account convertibility. When a country's financial system and financial development have reached a certain level, opening the capital account will bring enormous benefits. But for countries with immature financial systems, opening the capital account will only introduce huge risks. Therefore, timing is important. Based on experiences from the recent financial crisis, even for developed countries with an open capital account, huge and volatile cross-border capital flows carry significant risks. Still, countries inflicting long-term restrictions on capital flows may benefit from prudent capital account openness. To avert risks and shelter the country from possible external shocks, both the procedure and pace of opening China's capital account call for careful planning and step-by-step implementation.

Many studies have been conducted by domestic and foreign scholars on the sequencing of opening the capital account. Dong, Guan and Ming (2010) have reviewed and commented on some of the research, while Yin (2013) and Ma and Liu (2013) have given suggestions on the sequencing itself. A research team from the Survey and Statistics Department of the People's Bank of China (2012) suggests that, generally, opening the capital account should follow several rules: "Inflows before outflows, long-term before short-term, direct before indirect, and institutions before individuals." Short-, medium- and long-term arrangements have also been made for China's capital account to open in the next decade.

Based on these studies, it is fair to say the following sequencing of capital account liberalization is appropriate. Controls on long-term capital flows should be lifted before short-term capital flows, which should be followed by liberalizing financial services transactions related to capital transactions and foreign exchange transactions, then financial services transactions unrelated to capital transactions, and finally foreign exchange transactions unrelated to capital transactions. In terms of investment, restrictions on FDI should be eased first, followed by easing of restrictions on foreign indirect investment. Controls over capital inflows should be eased before those over capital outflows. Restrictions on securities investment should be lifted before those on bank loans. Controls over capital markets, including the stock market and the bond market (from government bonds to corporate bonds) should be eased before controls over the financial derivatives market and the asset-backed securities (ABS) market. Controls over local citizens' overseas trade should be eased before controls over domestic transactions by foreign citizens.

1.6 Timetable for the Internationalization of RMB

As mentioned above, the internationalization of the RMB is an irreversible trend. The Chinese government should seize the opportunity and take effective measures, so that in a decade, the RMB can grow into the third largest currency in international settlements and payment after the USD and the EUR. Hopefully, the RMB will account for over 5% in SDR and 10% in total reserve currencies, with an internationalization index of over 15%.

To achieve this goal, China needs to push forward reforms in the exchange rate mechanism, RMB convertibility, the capital account, and the financial system. Based on the ten-year goal of RMB internationalization and the author's experience (Cheng, 1999, 2002, 2003, 2006a, 2006b, 2009, 2012), the following timetable is recommended.

2014–2015

(1) A flexible exchange rate target zone system based on a broad RMB basket exchange rate index will be established. The band of the target zone will be set at ±5%, and the central rate's unilateral exchange rate against the USD will be between RMB6.0 and RMB6.5.

(2) Transfer restrictions on domestic enterprises' overseas investment will be lifted to encourage Chinese enterprises to "go global"; restrictions on domestic enterprises and individuals' purchase and sale of real estate overseas will be relaxed. To facilitate foreign investment, procedures for foreign capital inflows with tangible business activities will be further simplified based on "Stipulations on Foreign Reserves Management of Foreign Investors' Direct Investment in China" released on May 11, 2013 by the State Administration of Foreign Exchange. Transfer restrictions on direct investment liquidation will be basically removed and control over immigrants' asset transfers to China will also be eased.

(3) "Negative list" management for foreign investment will be conducted. Foreign investment restrictions will be explicit and targeted, rather than implicit and blanket. Any economic sector that is not open will be specified as such. All management measures for foreign capital inconsistent with national or Most Favored Nation (MFN) treatment, or those imposing restrictions on business performance and executives, are to be listed.

(4) Upper limits for interest rates on large-denomination time deposits will be lifted. Certificates of deposit (CD) will be reintroduced. A deposit insurance system will be established. The current inter-bank bond market and exchange bond market will be combined and all stock trading will be conducted in exchanges. Short-term (three to six months) national bonds will be issued with open market operations, so as to improve China's bond maturity structure. Bond issuance by local governments and enterprises on domestic and foreign markets will be further regulated.

2016–2017

(1) The boundaries of the exchange rate target zone will be expanded to ±10%.
(2) Transfer limits on Chinese enterprises' overseas investment will be removed. Transfer limits on Chinese individuals' investment in foreign securities will be eased.
(3) Foreign enterprises and individuals will be allowed to invest in the A-share and bond markets. Control over loans applied by companies engaged in trade will be relaxed. Chinese enterprises and individuals will be allowed to invest in overseas securities markets.
(4) Upper limits of the interest rate for small-denomination time deposits will be lifted. The B-share market will be integrated into the A-share market. The SME sector of the Shenzhen Stock Exchange will be split, and one part will be incorporated into the motherboard of A-shares while the other into Growth Enterprise Market (GEM). Open market operations using bonds will replace open market operations using notes.

2018–2019

(1) The exchange rate target zone will be widened to ±15%.
(2) Transfer limits on domestic residents' overseas investment will be basically canceled. Transfer limits on commercial credit will be basically canceled.
(3) Commercial banks will be allowed to issue capital market funds overseas. Businesses and individuals will be allowed to invest in overseas capital markets. Foreign enterprises and individuals will be allowed to invest in the domestic capital market.

(4) Upper limits for interest rates on demand deposits will be lifted. The China Securities Regulatory Commission (CSRC), China Banking Regulatory Commission (CBRC) and China Insurance Regulatory Commission (CIRC) will be integrated into a single new financial regulatory body.

2020–2021

(1) The exchange rate target zone will be expanded to $\pm 30\%$.
(2) Transfer limits on financial credit will be basically canceled. Restrictions on immigrants' transfer of assets to foreign countries will be eased.
(3) Businesses and individuals will be allowed to trade financial derivatives on overseas markets. Foreign enterprises and individuals will be allowed to trade immovable properties in China. The financial derivatives and ABS market will be opened up.
(4) Commercial banks will be allowed to engage in the securities and insurance businesses (mixing operations together).

2021–2023

(1) A floating exchange rate system will be in use.
(2) Transfer limits on all capital accounts will be basically canceled and the RMB will be convertible.
(3) The capital account will be basically open, but certain controls will still be in place on stock market transactions, money market instruments, collective investment securities, derivatives and other trading tools, financial credit, guarantees, warranties and standby financing instruments, real estate transactions, and other projects. FDI will still be managed with the "negative list" approach. On certain occasions, temporary control measures can still be used in managing some open capital accounts.
(4) Reforms in the financial system will be basically completed, yielding an international, market-oriented system.

At the same time, China should also play an active role in the reform of the international monetary system, helping to further improve the structure and operational mechanisms of the IMF, adjust the structure of SDR, and strive for a status in the international monetary system that is commensurate with China's economic strength.

Bibliography

In English

IMF (2009). *Annual Report on Exchange Arrangements and Exchange Restrictions.* Washington D.C.: IMF.

IMF (2010). *Annual Report on Exchange Arrangements and Exchange Restrictions.* Washington D.C.: IMF.

IMF (2011). *Annual Report on Exchange Arrangements and Exchange Restrictions.* Washington D.C.: IMF.

IMF (2012). The Liberalization and Management of Capital Flows: An Institutional View. Nov. 14. Washington D.C.: International Monetary Fund.

Quirk P. J. and Evans O. (1995). *Capital Account Convertibility: Review of Experience and Implications for IMF Policies.* IMF Occasional Paper 131.

In Chinese

Cheng S. W. (1999). Overall Analysis and Perspective of East Asia Financial Crisis. In *Analysis and Perspective of East Asia Financial Crisis.* Beijing: Democracy and Construction Press, 1–50.

Cheng S. W. (2003). System Analysis and Adjustment Suggestions for China Stock Market. In *Diagnosis and Treatment: Explain China Stock Market.* Beijing: Economic Science Press: 1–46.

Cheng S. W. (2006a). *On Financial Reform by Cheng Siwei.* Beijing: China Renmin University Press.

Cheng S. W. (2006b). Target and Main Measures for the Reform of China's Commercial Banks. In *Process and Key Points: on the Reform of China's Commercial Banks.* Beijing: Economic Science Press: 1–37.

Cheng S. W. (2008). Strategic Thinking on Development of Chinese Monetary Market. In *Cultivation and Supervision: Relates to Chinese Monetary Market*. Beijing: Economic Science Press: 1–46.

Cheng S. W. (2009). *Research on Economic Reform and Development of China.* Beijing: China Renmin University Press: 261–311.

Cheng S. W. (2012). *The U.S. Financial Crisis: Analysis and Inspiration.* Beijing: Science Press.

Ding Z. J., Ding J. P., Wang Hui and Li D. P. (2009). Reform of RMB Exchange Rate: Four Years of Trials and Hardships. *China Foreign Exchange*, 13: 10–14.

Dong Z. Y., Guan H. and Ming Y. (2010). The Specific Sequence of Capital Account Opening: Enlightenment to the Policy Choice of China. *Technoeconomics & Management*, 6: 144–149.

Guo J. J. (2007). *Analysis on RMB Exchange Rate Target Zone based on Sticky Price Target Zone Model.* Hunan University.

Jiang B. K. (2002). *Study on RMB Capital Account Convertibility.* Working Paper, Financial Research Institute of Fudan University. IFS-WP2002-002.

Jiang B. K. and Zhu Y. G. (2004). Study on Opening of Capital Account: an Analytical Framework based on Internal and External Equilibrium. *Studies of International Finance*, 04: 12–19.

Ma J. and Liu L. N. (2013). Capital Account Opening Order and RMB Cross-Border Flow. International Financing, 3: 49–53.

Research Center for International Monetary Research, Renmin University (2013). *RMB Internationalization Report 2013.*

Research Group of Financial Survey and Statistics Department, People's Bank of China: Sheng S. C. (2012). The Conditions to Accelerate the Opening of Capital Account in China Becomes Basic Mature. *China Finance*, 5: 14–17.

Wang Q. H. (2007). Empirical Research on Construction of RMB Exchange Rate Target Zone System. *Finance and Economy*, 4: 17–20.

Wang S. T. (2010). The International Experience of Currency Convertibility and Internationalization. *Rural Finance Research*, 11: 44–47.

Yang M. and Wang S. (2008). Analysis on the Path of Constructing RMB Exchange Rate Target Zone. *Economic Tribune*, 12: 40–44.

Yin J. Z. (2013). The Opening of Capital Account during the RMB Internationalization. *Journal of Financial Development Research*, 3: 20–24.

Zhou X. C. (1994). RMB towards Convertibility. *International Trade*, 5: 7–12.

Chapter 2

Exchange Rates under the Perspective of Fictitious Economy

The fictitious economy, as the counterpart to the real economy, is composed of both the economic activity related to the allocation of fictitious capital (mainly through financial platforms), and the resultant complexity of the various relationships arising from this activity. As a special commodity that serves as a universal medium of exchange, currency has many functions including as a measure of value, medium of exchange, means of payment, store of value, and as a world currency in the commodity economy. It plays an important role in both real and fictitious economic activity. According to the theory of the fictitious economy, we can observe the RMB exchange rate from the following six aspects.

2.1 The Transition to Fiat Currency

In the history of currency development — and especially since the gold standard was first adopted in Britain in 1821 — gold has played the role of guaranteeing the widespread issuance of currencies. The gold standard gradually became popular in European and American countries and, in 1870, became the basis of currency in global circulation. After WWI, the original standard gradually became the Gold Exchange Standard. Later, after WWII, the US set the minimum USD price for foreign central banks' purchasing and selling of gold, prompting major European countries to stipulate that their currencies could be freely exchanged for gold or US Dollars in international payments. But since 1971, when the US ceased exchanging gold for dollars at a fixed price (USD$35 per ounce) in international payments, US Dollars and other currencies became the basis of the world monetary system. This brought the official role of gold in international exchange to an end. As a result, money has been completely "de-pegged" from gold, and cannot be freely exchanged for gold at a fixed price. Since then, currency has been issued according to a country's total credit, and exists as fiat money.

As a universal equivalent, currency is a special commodity with the function of measuring value. It can be compared with other commodities in quantity: The value of a commodity is first transformed into a price expressed by currency, and subsequently can be exchanged with other commodities. In this way, the direct trade by barter is replaced by trade mediated through currency. Thus, currency gains the function of mediating exchanges.

When currency is pegged to gold, it directly represents the social labor embodied in gold. When money and gold are "de-pegged", money itself is virtualized to some extent. Since fiat money itself is only a piece of paper, it only has value through the support and credit of the government that issues it as currency. Thus, people can no longer determine the value of the currency by "referencing" a fixed value, but instead must indirectly measure its value through its purchasing power. Since there is no global system by which a currency's quantity automatically defines its value (in contrast to the Gold Exchange Standard which tethered a currency's value to a definite supply of gold), the purchasing power of a currency is decided by the relationship between the supply of the currency and the supply of real economic outputs (mainly commodities and services).

Thus, the purchasing power of a country's currency can be conceptualized as:

$$\mathrm{P}_i = (\mathrm{C}_i + \mathrm{S}_i)/\mathrm{M}_i.$$

In the formula above, P_i stands for the purchasing power of Country i, C_i for total commodities of Country i, S_i for the total services of Country i; and M_i for the total currency of Country i. The reciprocal of P_i is the general price level of Country i.

When a currency is de-pegged from gold, the supply of the issued currency in a country is no longer constrained by the supply of gold or the country's gold-equivalent currency reserves, but by the government's decision. Also there is no longer a common measurement basis for all countries' currencies, so exchange rates become unfixed, which is also a form of currency virtualization.

De-pegged from gold, a fiat currency is only issued based on a government's credit, which means political factors will influence the country's currency exchange rate. When a country enjoys a stable political and social environment, the exchange rate will likewise be stable. Yet when there are severe international economic problems and/or social unrest, the foreign exchange market will reflect the turmoil, leading to volatile exchange rate fluctuations. Therefore, the stability of the political environment determines the stability of exchange rates.

2.2 Two Kinds of Purchasing Power for Currency Exchange Rates

In recent years, with China's fast economic development, continuously increasing economic size, and gradual improvement in international status, the RMB exchange rate has drawn more and more attention from the international community. Therefore, because the RMB exchange rate and value are crucial for China's economy and the people's livelihood, we must be prudent on this issue.

One option for determining exchange rates is the concept of equilibrium exchange rates. Research on equilibrium exchange rates seeks to find a benchmark for rate fluctuation, so as to decide whether the current rate is imbalanced, and in such a case to take measures to avoid exchange rate risks. Equilibrium exchange rates can also be used to predict future trends in exchange rates. At present, the mainstream theories on equilibrium exchange rates include purchasing power parity (PPP), based on price, as well as various methods based on macroeconomic equilibrium (Yang and Zhong, 2012). PPP is the most widely accepted and used. Because PPP-based measures of the RMB exchange rate show the currency to be seriously undervalued, many foreign and domestic scholars advocate for RMB appreciation. However, there are limitations in applying PPP to calculate equilibrium exchange rates. In particular, PPP makes no strict distinction between domestic purchasing power and international purchasing power. I revise and improve PPP, deriving a theory of "dual PPP". This dual PPP theory conforms better to economic principles, and caters to China's national conditions so as to provide a more effective theory for determining China's equilibrium exchange rate. I believe that, when using this theory to decide the RMB exchange rate, we should distinguish two kinds of purchasing power: international purchasing power and domestic purchasing power. Further, we should not simply determine the RMB exchange rate by PPP alone.

2.2.1 *PPP and Its Limitations*

PPP has its origin in the work of 19th century economist David Ricardo, and was improved and systemized by Gustav Cassel, a Swedish economist, in his 1922 book *Money and Foreign Exchange after 1914*.

PPP theory holds that the exchange rate between different countries is decided by the ratio of their price levels, which can be expressed as the composite price index of a basket of goods and services. The price level in a country reflects the purchasing power of that country's issued currency. Therefore, exchange rates can be understood as the ratio between the two currencies' purchasing powers in their corresponding countries. When a currency's purchasing power decreases (for instance, when currency inflation occurs) the exchange rate of its currency will decrease (as expressed in an indirect quotation on a foreign exchange). To put it simply, people's demand for domestic and foreign currency fundamentally result from their demand for domestic goods, foreign goods, and/or labor. In essence people's demands for different currencies can be understood as an expression of their demand for the purchasing power of a currency, and currency exchange is in fact the exchange of different currencies' purchasing powers. Based on this understanding, the ratio between different currencies, or the exchange rate, can be expressed by a purchasing power calculation — the PPP.

PPP can be divided into Absolute PPP in its static form and Relative PPP in its dynamic form. Absolute PPP is the exchange rate as determined by two countries' total price levels in a specified time. Its formula is:

$$e = \frac{EP^*}{P}.$$

In this formula P^* stands for the foreign commodity prices, P stands for the domestic commodity prices, E stands for the nominal exchange rate, e stands for real exchange rate.

Relative PPP is a dynamic form that incorporates inflation into its calculation. It is the change of exchange rate in a specified period, where the difference between the two countries' inflation rates determines the rate's movement. The formula is:

$$e' = p - p^*.$$

In this formula e' stands for the rates of exchange rate changes, $p - p^*$ stands for the Inflation rate differential between the two countries. It means that from the relative PPP theory perspective, the rate of change of the

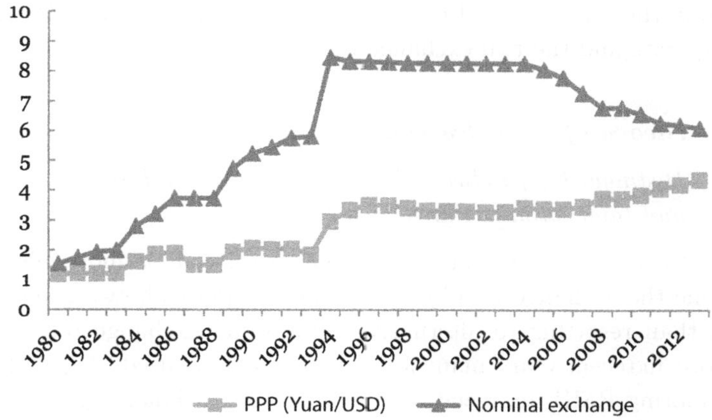

Figure 2.1: Comparison of Nominal RMB Exchange Rate and PPP-derived RMB Exchange Rate[1]

exchange rate is equal to the inflation rate difference between the two countries.

PPP theory has been criticized for its many limitations. Figure 2.1 shows the nominal RMB exchange rate and the equilibrium exchange rate, calculated according to PPP theory. There is noticeably large deviation between the two rates. Therefore, PPP theory is of little help in determining the equilibrium exchange rate, and can only act as an indicator when real exchange rates greatly deviate from the equilibrium exchange rate.

Usually, PPP explains the changes in exchange rates simply from the perspective of the currency's domestic purchasing power, leaving out many other factors such as labor productivity, cost of production, international capital flows, degree of marketization, national income, dependence on foreign trade, trade structure and politics. In particular, PPP theory fails to distinguish between domestic purchasing power and international purchasing power. PPP-based calculations of the equilibrium exchange rate do not show the different influences of these two purchasing powers on the exchange rate. Moreover, PPP is based on the comparison between aggregative price indexes of a group of articles of the same kind and quality across two different countries. Yet the construction of these indexes is different across countries. When building a price index, different countries usually give different weights to the same kind of goods or services.

[1]The PPP data in the figure is the RMB exchange rate level under PPP theory worked out by RMB nominal exchange rate and PPP conversion factors.

Therefore, these factors lead to huge differences between the PPP-derived exchange rate and the real exchange rate.

2.2.2 *Theory of Dual Purchasing Power*

2.2.2.1 *Distinguishing Between Domestic Purchasing Power and International Purchasing Power*

From both an economic and a policy perspective, it is more effective to determine the exchange rate by examining differences between purchasing powers than resorting to alternative equilibrium exchange rate theories. Therefore, in recent years, many foreign scholars have used PPP as the basis for promoting RMB appreciation. Some Chinese scholars agree with this choice. In June 15, 2004 when I discussed the RMB exchange rate with Fred Bergsten and other scholars at the Institute for International Economics in Washington D.C., US, I proposed that it is necessary to distinguish two purchasing powers — international purchasing power and domestic purchasing power — and that we should not simply use PPP as the basis to determine the RMB exchange rate. I believe that PPP at present is not suitable for determining the RMB exchange rate, mainly because, as long as the RMB cannot be exchanged freely, there will exist differences between international purchasing power and domestic purchasing power. The RMB exchange rate is mainly determined by the Chinese government. Although it reflects the supply–demand relationship to some extent, it only represents the international purchasing power of the RMB (i.e., the value of the RMB) when it is used to purchase foreign goods and labor. Yet PPP is based on a currency's domestic purchasing power. China differs greatly from Western countries in terms of its degree of marketization, composition of its price index, its foreign trade structure, labor productivity, etc. There are also non-economic differences. Therefore, the exchange rate worked out by PPP cannot truly and fully represent the value of goods and labor bought in China when a Western currency is converted to RMB.

A feature of currency virtualization (i.e., fiat currency) is that the currency itself gradually becomes a tradable good (Cheng, 2009). In other words, currency exchange is a legitimate kind of economic exchange. When the currency is de-pegged from a gold standard, the exchange of a domestic currency for a foreign currency is essentially an exchange of purchasing power — the domestic currency's purchasing power for that of the foreign currency's purchasing power. Purchasing power is the reciprocal of the general price level, so domestic purchasing power can be expressed as the reciprocal of the price index. Since different countries use differently structured price indexes to represent domestic purchasing power, in theory the exchange rate calculated from PPP is different from the equilibrium exchange rate. International purchasing power is measured by exchange rates, or the purchasing power of some amount of foreign currency bought by some amount of domestic currency. Yet each currency has its own "domestic" and "foreign" contexts, giving it two distinct purchasing powers. Traditional PPP theory overlooks the influence of these two purchasing powers, which explains the huge differences between a PPP-derived equilibrium exchange rate and a real exchange rate.

Figure 2.2 shows the relationship between domestic and international purchasing powers. Assume there are two countries — Country A and Country B — each with their respective currencies a and b. The upper half of Figure 2.2 shows the currency exchange under the gold standard system, and the lower half shows the currency exchange under a floating exchange rate system. Under the gold standard, the two currencies are pegged to gold, which forms a relatively fixed exchange rate between a and b. However with a floating exchange rate, the two currencies are de-pegged from gold and are instead exchanged directly on the foreign

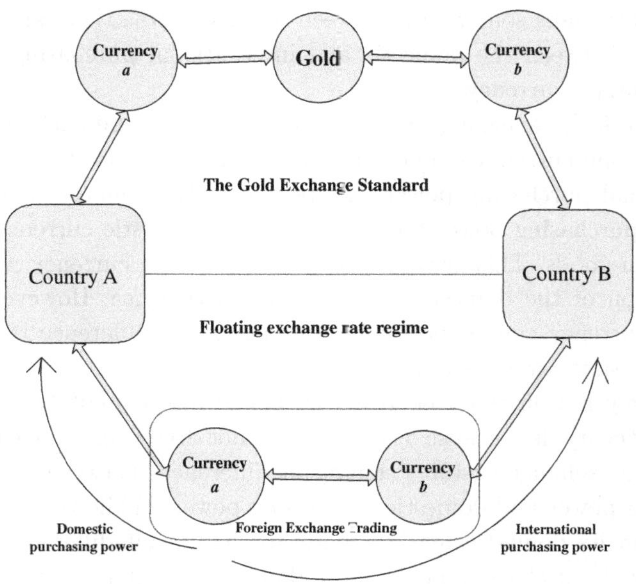

Figure 2.2: Two Purchasing Powers

currency market. Under the floating exchange rate system, the supply–demand relationship in the foreign currency market alone determines the exchange rate. Take currency *a* in Country A as an example. The purchasing of goods and labor in Country A using currency *a* forms the domestic purchasing power of currency *a*. Currency *a* can also be exchanged for currency *b* (so as to purchase goods and labor in Country B) according to the exchange rate in the foreign exchange market. This cross-border exchange indirectly forms the purchasing power of currency *a* in Country B (i.e., its international purchasing power). Currency *a* thus embodies two purchasing powers: its domestic purchasing power (expressed in domestic exchange) and its international purchasing power (expressed in cross-border exchange).

The purchasing power of a currency is the combination of its international and domestic purchasing powers. It should not be expressed solely by its domestic purchasing power. Only in extreme situations can the two be conflated. For example, if a country's degree of foreign trade dependency is zero, the exchange rate has nothing to do with domestic purchasing power. But, if the foreign trade dependency degree is 100%, the domestic purchasing power is equal to its international purchasing power. Only this time the exchange rate is equal to the exchange rate level that determined by conventional PPP. Since the foreign trade dependency of every country falls somewhere between 0% and 100%, there are inevitable differences between the domestic and international purchasing powers of every country's currency.

Theoretically speaking, when two currencies can be exchanged freely, and when one currency's domestic purchasing power is stronger than its international purchasing power, the people in the country with stronger domestic purchasing power tend to hold more domestic currency and buy less foreign goods. This greater demand of domestic currency will lead to appreciation of the domestic currency, and vice versa. However in cases where a currency cannot be freely exchanged, the difference between the two purchasing powers is difficult to narrow.

The key reason that the RMB exchange rate cannot be determined by PPP theory is because the RMB is not freely exchangeable. This lack of free exchange sustains significant differences between international purchasing power and domestic purchasing power. While the RMB has to circulate in its domestic market there are significant differences between international purchasing power and domestic purchasing power, which maintains its domestic purchasing power, it also has to flow through the international foreign exchange market, in exchange for foreign currency, which creates its international purchasing power to buy foreign goods and service. On the one hand, since China has a large foreign trade surplus and huge foreign currency reserves, the RMB is faced with international pressure to appreciate (its international purchasing power is increasing). On the other hand, the RMB faces inflation in China (its domestic purchasing power is decreasing). This divergence — external appreciation outside China and internal depreciation within China (Cheng, 2007) — exactly demonstrates the two different purchasing powers of the RMB.

2.2.3 *Main Factors Driving Differences Between the Two Purchasing Powers*

2.2.3.1 *The Degree of Foreign Trade Dependency*

The two purchasing powers are different, yet connected: If a country has no foreign trade and only relies on domestic supply and consumption, then its currency will only circulate domestically (only buying domestic goods and labor). Its currency's purchasing power is thus fully embodied in the currency's domestic purchasing power, which has no relationship to an exchange rate. Indeed, any change in the exchange rate will not influence the currency's domestic purchasing power. However, if a county is totally dependent on foreign trade, its domestic currency will only be used to buy foreign goods and labor. This means its currency's international purchasing power will fully embody and exactly equal its overall purchasing power. Its purchasing power can thus be expressed by its exchange rate. Following this, it can be found that the relationship between domestic purchasing power and international purchasing power is positively correlated with a country's degree of foreign trade dependency (Cheng, 2009). But each country falls somewhere between the two extremes exampled above. No country's currency is determined solely by either domestic or international purchasing powers. Therefore, it is incomprehensible to determine the RMB exchange rate using PPP theory, as any PPP-derived equilibrium exchange rate only expresses domestic purchasing power and does not reflect differences between international and domestic purchasing powers. Therefore, to determine the RMB exchange rate, it is necessary to consider the relationship between the two purchasing powers so as to correctly work out a reasonable equilibrium exchange rate between currencies.

2.2.3.2 *Foreign Trade Structure*

Foreign trade structure is another reason why PPP cannot correctly calculate the equilibrium exchange rate. When working out exchange rates using PPP, we have to first determine a commodity basket — including consumer goods, raw materials and services — and then compare the basket's price levels across different countries. But in fact, not only are the compositions of every commodity basket different across countries, but the foreign trade structures of each country are different as well. While the prices of imported goods are determined by international purchasing power, the prices of domestic goods are determined by domestic purchasing power. Tables 2.1 and 2.2 show the top ten commodities in terms of value among China's import and export in 2012.

From the tables we can see that the export commodities are mainly consumer goods, whereas the majority of imported goods are bulk raw materials. Since Chinese people's basic consumption relies little on imported goods, the commodity basket is less sensitive to the exchange

Table 2.1: Volumes of China's Top Ten Exported Goods in 2012 (Accumulative Value in a Year, USD$10,000)

1. TV, radio and wireless telecommunications equipment accessories	18,531,779.30
2. Telephone sets	15,914,498.70
3. Clothes and accessories	9,577,553.40
4. Color TV sets (including complete sets and parts)	8,298,723.10
5. Bikes	8,102,451.30
6. Automatic data processing equipment and parts	6,258,790.50
7. Toys	5,343,483.80
8. Power-on and off protection circuits equipments and parts	5,148,378.20
9. Steel	4,882,397.60
10. Handheld wireless phones and car-mount radio telephones	4,681,187.70

Table 2.2: Volumes of China's Top Ten Imported Goods in 2012 (Accumulative Value in a Year, USD$10,000)

1. Crude oil	22,066,591.60
2. Iron ore and its concentrate	9,560,535.20
3. Automobile and automobile chassis	4,757,102.20
4. Plastic in primary form	4,618,629.30
5. Unwrought copper and copper products	3,858,679.70
6. Soybeans	3,498,803.00
7. Refined oil (from customs)	3,299,299.50
8. Steel	1,780,506.70
9. Airplanes	1,569,170.20
10. Waste copper	1,486,209.80

rate (international purchasing power) than are the baskets of developed countries in Europe and America. This contributes to large differences between the PPP-derived exchange rate and the real exchange rate.

2.2.3.3 *Labor Cost: The Root Reason for Distortions in the Big Mac Index*

The Big Mac Index is an unofficial index published by *The Economist.* At its core, it is an application of PPP theory. The Big Mac Index assumes that McDonald's Big Mac hamburgers, sold all over the world, are of the same value. The equilibrium exchange rate between two countries is thus obtained by dividing the price of a Big Mac in one country (the first currency) by the price of a Big Mac in another country (the second currency). This value is then compared with the actual exchange rate. If it is lower, then the first currency is under-valued (according to PPP theory) compared with the second. Conversely, if the first currency is higher, then it is deemed over-valued. For example, a Big Mac burger in China is sold at RMB15.5, whereas in the US it is USD$4.07. The exchange rate between the RMB and the USD worked out by the Big Mac Index then is 1:3.8. But the real exchange rate is 1:6.2. According to the Big Mac Index, the RMB is thereby under-valued by 38.7%.

That is a mistaken conclusion, however, because the Big Mac burgers sold in the two countries cannot possibly be of the same value. As Parsley and Wei (2007) have pointed out, in calculating the cost of a Big Mac hamburger, non-tradable components such as labor, rent and electricity amount to up to 55% to 64% of the total cost. The prices of non-tradable components by definition do not converge in the same manner as do the prices of tradable components. That is, non-tradables do not follow the Law of One Price (Zheng, 2009). In China, labor costs are low, and represent the majority of a Big Mac hamburger's cost. Therefore, while the cost of the tradable goods in a Big Mac will converge (via the law of one price), the low labor costs will still lower the overall cost of a Chinese Big Mac. In other words, the Big Mac burger made in China has a different value from one made in the US. Therefore, the Big Mac Index's assumption of the Law of One Price is wrong. Further, to decide whether the RMB is over or under-valued according to the Big Mac Index is groundless. According to the index's logic, only when Chinese workers command the same salary as workers in the US will the RMB be correctly valued, which is ridiculous. Besides, it is simplistic and irrational to use the price of one product to represent the general price level of an entire country.

2.2.4 *Other Factors Affecting the Exchange Rate*

There are other factors that affect an exchange rate. If the exchange rate is affected by the relationships among people and the influence of the surrounding environment on people's behaviors, it is also affected by people's confidence and anticipation of future changes in value. For example, people's anticipation of currency appreciation will encourage many to hold more of it, in an attempt to profit from the appreciation. This behavior creates more demand for the currency, causing further appreciation, and, subsequently, even greater demand.

A country's balance of payments will also cause fluctuations in the exchange rate. The balance of payments is a country's accounting of all economic and financial transactions between itself and the rest of the world. The influence of a country's balance of payments on an exchange rate essentially represents the supply–demand relationship between the currencies of two countries. When there is a trade surplus in one country, it means that the total sum of exported goods and labor from another, foreign country is larger than the sum of imported goods and labor from that foreign country. While a trade surplus requires a net import of foreign currency to finance, a trade deficit, in contrast, requires a net export of foreign currency. However, since a foreign currency usually cannot freely circulate in a domestic market, a net import of it will increase demand for local currency (conversely a net export of foreign currency will increase the demand for foreign currency). When the trade surplus and the supply of foreign currency increases, the local currency will appreciate and the foreign currency will depreciate (and the opposite will occur under a trade deficit).

A country's base interest rate also influences its exchange rate. In fact, the difference between two interest rates causes the transnational flow of international hot money. For example, assume a case of two countries with mutually free capital flows: Country A, with a higher interest rate, and Country B, with a lower interest rate. The hot money in Country B will flow to Country A, seeking higher profits in the latter. But to facilitate this flow, the hot money in Country B has to be exchanged (a sale of the currency of Country B) to buy the currency of Country A. Since the exchange of a huge amount of hot money will drive demand for Country A's currency, the currency will appreciate. At the same time, Country B's currency will depreciate.

In sum, traditional PPP theory is based on a currency's domestic purchasing power. However the RMB has not yet been made freely exchangeable. There are also big differences between China and Western countries in their degree of marketization, the composition of their price indices, their foreign trade structure, labor productivity, etc. There are further many non-economic differences. Therefore, a PPP-derived exchange rate cannot objectively represent the RMB's purchasing power to buy goods and labor in Western countries (when exchanged at market rates for a Western currency). I do not think PPP is totally without use or unreasonable, but we have to take into consideration all kinds of political and economic factors. Only then we can truly decide the rational level of the RMB exchange rate.

2.3 Transnational Capital Flows Gradually "De-coupled" from the Real Economy

2.3.1 *Global Capital Flows*

According to the International Monetary Fund (IMF), international capital flows can be categorized into foreign direct investment (FDI, including equity capitals, reinvesting profits, other capitals, etc.), foreign portfolio investment (FPI, including stocks, bonds, financial derivatives, etc.), and foreign other investment (FOI, including long-term and short-term credits, loans, currencies, deposit, and untraded stocks, bonds, insurances, pensions, etc.).

With the development of financial markets all over the world, the loosening of capital flows, and the advancement of information technology, financial trades can occur continuously 24 hours a day and huge amounts of capital can travel tens of millions of kilometers in a second. All these factors encourage the increasing scale of transnational capital flows and drive the trend for short-term capital flows.

In particular, because of capitals' nature to seek profits, the sign of transnational capital flows "de-coupling" from the real economy is more obvious. Such a change is much faster than changes in real economy, and capital tends to be virtualized. Since 2009, global FDI has averaged at USD$1–2 trillion a year. But according to IMF estimates, there is a pool of capital worth trillions of USD — partly controlled by securities investment funds and hedge funds looking for profits from short-term exchange rate

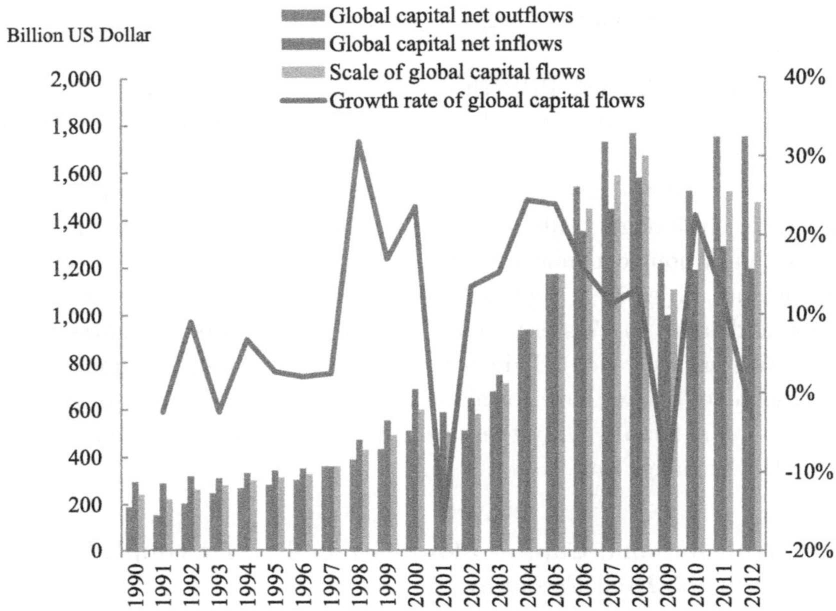

Figure 2.3: Global Capital Flows, 1990–2012

and interest-rate changes — that seeks arbitrage opportunities in the world financial market almost every day.

Since the 1990s, there have been two trends in global capital flows.

First, the overall scale of global capital flows[2] is increasing (Figure 2.3). The total scale of global capital flows in 2012 was USD$1.38 billion — an increase of USD$4.2 billion — making 2012 the third time the world has seen negative growth in global capital flows since the 1990s. The previous two times were in 2001 (caused by the burst of the dotcom bubble in the US) and in 2009 (caused by the financial crisis in the US). The negative growth in 2012 was mainly due to a remarkable slowdown in global economic growth caused by the European sovereign debt crisis.

Second, in terms of categories of capital flow, since the 1990s the overall scale of FDI, FPI and FOI have all steadily grown. However, both the scale and growth of FDI has been smaller than those of FPI and FOI. Meanwhile, their growth rates are much higher than that of global trade. The data

[2]The definition of global capital flows is from the World Economic Outlook. Global Surpluses; World net capital import = Global Deficits; the scale of global capital flow = (World net capital export + World net capital import)/2.

shows that from 1995 and 2012, the growth rates in the overall scale of FDI, FPI and FOI reached about 10%, 12% and 22% respectively, whereas the growth rate of global trade was only around 7%. It should be pointed out that since 1990, merger and acquisition (M&A) investment accounted for over 50% of FDI in most years. In 2007, global FDI reached a peak of USD$1.83 trillion including USD$1.64 trillion M&A trade that accounted for 89.6%. Since about 80% of all M&A trade is related to changes in equity structure instead of green field investment, M&A capital in fact may not directly flow into the real economy.

Therefore, while the scale of global capital flows are constantly increasing, this transnational capital is mainly seeking arbitrage opportunities in capital markets and does not directly provide goods or services for the real economy.

2.3.2 *The Current Situation of China's International Capital Flows*

In China, the overall international capital flows in the past 30 years have shown distinctive features in different periods (Figure 2.4). Small scale and

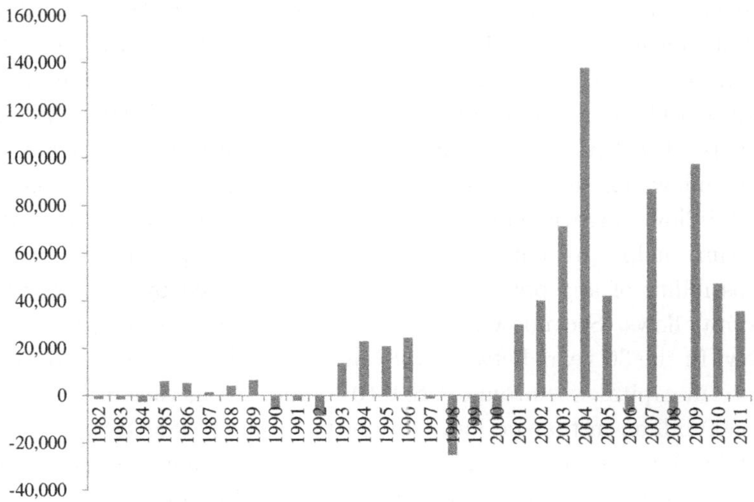

Figure 2.4: Net Capital Flows in China (billion USD)

Data source: Annals of Mathematical Statistics on China's Balance of Payments from the State Administration of Foreign Exchange.

Note: Positive figures mean capital inflow, and negative figures mean capital outflow.

small fluctuations from 1982 to 1992 suggest a lack of confidence from international investors regarding China's early reform and opening up. During the period between 1993 and 1996, because of the unification of exchange rates in 1994 and the free exchange of the RMB in the current account in 1996, capital flows to China reached a net inflow of more than USD$10 billion. Between 1997 and 2000, due to the Asian Financial Crisis, capital flows reversed to a net outflow as the country experienced severe capital flight. Since the turn of the 21st century, with China's entrance into the WTO, continuous reform of the exchange rate system, the loosening of capital controls, and in particular China's steady economic development, it returned to a net inflow on a scale much larger than in the 20 years prior to reform and opening up. In 2006, FDI and FPI in China rapidly increased, leading to a net inflow of capital. In 2007, with the rapid increase of FDI, private capital flow increased to a net inflow. The global financial crisis, originating from the subprime crisis in the US, resulted in a net outflow of capital in 2008. However, since 2009, when China's economy took the lead in the global recovery, private capital flows have again returned to a net inflow. This back-and-forth trend demonstrates that, as the Chinese market becomes more international, the capital stock in China experiences huge inflows and outflows in line with international events.

Regarding term structures, in the past 30 years the capital flows to China have had the following features. First, long-term capital was generally a net inflow. Before 1992 the scale was only a few billion USD, and since 1993 it has been increasing, keeping around USD$40 billion. In 2007 it reached USD$124.87 billion, which is the first time that long-term capital inflows exceed a USD$100 billion. The large amount of long-term capital inflows greatly supports China's economic growth, and at the same time helps prevent difficulties in balance of payments, stemming the possibility of any potential financial crisis caused by a rapid reversal in capital flows. Second, China's short-term capital is in general a net outflow. In the 30 years between 1982 and 2012, the average net outflow of short-term capital was around USD$10 billion. Altogether, it totaled over USD$300 billion in that period. Only in five years (1985, 1989, 2003, 2004 and 2009) did it reach a net inflow. From 1985 to 1989 it was the beginning period of reform and opening up in China when the foreign trade volume was small, the securities market was just established, and domestic financial institutions were not well internationalized. Thus, the net inflow of over USD$1 billion in short-term capital had little influence on China's economy. In 2003 and 2004, due to the anticipation of RMB appreciation, short-term capital reached a large amount and turned to net inflows. Particularly in 2004, the net inflow of short-term capital reached USD$80.885 billion — more than any other year in the prior 28 years. In 2009, China's steady economy during the economic crisis attracted huge capital inflows.

In terms of kinds of foreign capital, FDI, FPI and FOI all enjoyed vast increases. FDI has had considerable inflows since 1993, steadily growing from USD$3.385 billion in 1995 to USD$41.67 billion. After 1997, due to the Asian Financial Crisis, there were temporary outflows, but this trend reversed in 2002 and the following decade has witnessed rapid growth. Between January 2001 and December 2012, FDI in China amounted to a total of USD$884.2 billion and the average monthly year-on-year growth exceeded 10%. During this period, because of the 2008 financial crisis in the US and the widespread sovereign debt crisis in Europe, 2009 and 2012 had negative growth. As for FPI, net inflows and outflows have alternated since 1993. The five years between 1993 and 1997 saw a net inflow. Later, due to the Asian Financial Crisis, these changed to a net outflow until 2003, when net inflows again returned. The government's reform in the division of equity resulted in brief outflows in 2005 and 2006. Then, in the six years after 2007, the country saw net inflows. By the end of 2012, the net capital inflow reached USD$47.8 billion. Finally FOI, seen from the balance of payments account, includes all the financial transactions except for direct investment and portfolio investment. It can be classified into four kinds: trade credits, loans, currency and deposits, and other assets and liabilities. If the FOI balance is negative, it means China's international liabilities are increasing. Since 2001, China's foreign debt scale has been increasing, and the proportion of the scale of short-term foreign debt is increasing too. In the end of 2012, the balance of foreign debt was 3.7 times that at the end of 2001, reaching USD$737 billion. The balance of short-term foreign debt was USD$540.9 billion, accounting for 73%. The short-term foreign debts between 2001 and 2012 accounted for 63% on an average.

Along with the long-term net inflow of transnational capital, China's foreign reserves have sustained steady growth. In terms of scale, China's foreign reserves have skyrocketed since 1994. By the end of 2012, they totaled USD$3.31 trillion, about 60 times those of 1994, 20 times those of 2000, and four times those of 2005. In the end of February 2006, foreign reserves reached USD$853.7 billion, exceeding Japan's reserves and ranking first in the world — a status that has been kept hitherto. In the end of October the same year, they exceeded USD$1 trillion for the first time. Then, in less than 3 years, in the first half of 2009, foreign reserves exceeded USD$2 trillion. By the end of 2009, they exceeded the total of all G7 countries, amounting to USD$2.4 trillion. At the end of the third quarter of 2011, they were more than USD$3 trillion. Finally, by June 2013, China's foreign reserves reached USD$3496.686 billion. Thus foreign reserves increased annually by 22.63% on an average between 1994 and 2000, and close to 35% annually in the decade after 2001.

Based on the above analysis, it can be found that, since the 1990s, China has experienced rapid growth in capital flows both in scale and across different categories. This is closely related to China's constantly increasing economic strength and deepening reform and opening up. Meanwhile, capital flows are increasingly influenced by global economic events. Such influence was very obvious during the Asian Financial Crisis, the 2008 US financial crisis, and the European sovereign debt crisis.

Despite this growth, we can see that China's international capital flows are also decoupling from the real economy. This is evidenced in several ways. Firstly, capital flows tend to be short-term, and there is increasingly more short-period fluctuation in transnational capital flows. Take the year 2012 as an example. In the first quarter, capital and financial projects totaled a surplus of USD$56.1 billion, rising from a deficit of USD$29 billion in the previous quarter. In the second and third quarters, net capital outflows reached USD$41.2 billion and USD$51.7 billion, respectively. The fourth quarter witnessed a surplus of USD$20 billion. Secondly, the scale of FPI and FOI has increased remarkably faster than that of FDI; the fluctuation ranges of FPI and FOI have likewise been larger than FDI. Thirdly, hot money has flowed in and out of the country. Errors and omissions in national accounts can, to some extent, reflect the flow direction of hot money. Between 2002 and 2008, the balance of China's errors and omissions were in credits, indicating the possibility of hot money inflows. Since 2009 however, with the spread of the US subprime mortgage crisis, there has been a loss of capital mobility, so the balance of China's errors and omissions are in debts, suggesting some measure of capital outflows.

2.3.3 *Analyzing the Influence of Transnational Capital Flows on Exchange Rates*

Generally speaking, in a fixed exchange rate system, continuous inflows of foreign capital will increase a country's demand for and the mobility of currency. In order to keep a fixed exchange rate, the government has to intervene through selling local currency and buying foreign currency.

Usually this would over-value the local currency, weaken domestic companies' export competitiveness, and probably result in a trade deficit that weakens the balance between the current account deficit and capital account surplus. When a current account deficit reaches a certain degree and the economic environment worsens, international capital inflows will stop and capital may escape from the country. Once this balance is upset, the exchange rate of the local currency will decrease. The Asian Currency Crisis in the 1990s was a typical example of this. In contrast, in a floating exchange rate system, constant foreign capital inflows will lead to appreciation of the exchange rate, increasing the current account deficit and there by tending to keep the country's balance of payments in equilibrium.

Scholars also have conducted numerous empirical studies on the influence of international capital flows on exchange rates. Many of them offer empirical evidence on the relationship between "the stability of exchange rates and free capital flows", as proposed in the "Impossible Trinity" (Frankel, 1999; Summers, 2004; Bordo, 2004). Their conclusions suggest that the free flow of capital will affect the stability of a country's exchange rate. The studies of Obstfeld (1984) and Cohen (2012) show that, following the liberalization of capital accounts, capital flows will lead to real appreciation of the local currency in the short term and, at the same time, a current account deficit will result in both real depreciation of the local currency and increasing foreign debt. Elbadewi and Soto (1994) divide the capital flows of Chili into four parts: short-term capital flows, long-term capital flows, portfolio investment and direct investment. They find that short-term capital flows and portfolio investment have no influence on the equilibrium real exchange rate, yet long-term capital flows and FDI will lead to considerable appreciation. The studies of Kosteletou and Liargovas (2000) and Combes *et al.* (2012) show that changes in the real exchange rate of major countries (the US, Japan, etc.) that adopt floating exchange rates drive changes in FDI. In contrast, in countries with fixed or quasi-fixed exchange rates, the real exchange rate and FDI are strongly correlated. The studies of Huang (2009) and Wang *et al.* (2012) show that FDI inflows have had a remarkably positive influence on the appreciation of the RMB.

Therefore, the influence of capital flows on an exchange rate is complicated. In terms of transnational M&A, in theory, huge amounts of foreign capital inflows acquired by the host country will lead to appreciation of the local currency, which will further increase the cost of future M&A, ultimately decreasing foreign capital inflows. Yet in reality, if the influence of increased M&A costs caused by local currency appreciation is not a significant factor in the host country's comparative advantage of attracting foreign capital, then foreign capital inflows will not decrease. Besides, short-term capital flows tend to be "virtualized", which also increases the complexity of the international capital flows' influence on the exchange rate. That is, the "virtualized" short-term capital actually commands capital amounting to hundreds times its own value, much of which will be invested in foreign reserve markets, stock markets, futures markets and financial derivatives markets with high risks, high returns, and short cycles. Any concentration of speculative activity is usually a vulnerability in a country's economy, because speculative flows do not follow the logic and rules of the real economy. Instead, speculation is mainly determined by many irrational factors, hence the mass, disordered and unpredictable transnational capital flows on record, which have a huge impact on the country's exchange rate.

In fact, changes in exchange rates and transnational capital flows have a complicated relationship. On the one hand, mass transnational capital inflows will usually appreciate the local currency and increase the exchange rate; on the other hand, the anticipation of an increasing exchange rate will speed up transnational inflows of capital. Against the background of international capital flows determining foreign exchange transactions, foreign exchange is regarded as an asset, and the exchange rate as its price. A change in a currency's exchange rate in the foreign exchange market is caused by the whole market's evaluation of the value of this currency; market anticipation and investor confidence play a crucial role. Like comparative advantage in the real economy, big countries like the US with trade deficits have comparative advantage in fictitious assets in the fictitious economy. The comparative advantage of fictitious assets is based on investor confidence, which comes from the country's overall economic strength and its currency's status. The US enjoys an absolute leading position in the global economy and the US Dollar has replaced gold to become the "currency of a big country" with the best secured credit. Therefore, the US can keep its trade deficit without worrying about imbalances in its domestic economy.

China put an end to the dual exchange rate system for the RMB in 1994, and set up an interbank foreign exchange market to carry out a managed floating exchange rate system. In 2005, the second exchange rate system reform was carried out to build a managed floating exchange rate system based on market-determined supply and demand, adjusted according to a basket of currencies.

Although after 1996 the nominal RMB to USD exchange rate remained stable, in terms of the real exchange rate, the RMB actually appreciated against the USD between 1996 and May 1997 due to changes in the two countries' price levels. Later, because of the Asian Financial Crisis, the RMB's general trend until February 2003 was one of depreciation. During this period, the capital flows in China mainly resulted in a net outflow. While in 2001 and 2002 capital flows saw a net inflow, the imbalance was not large. After March 2003, due to the rapid recovery of China's price level, the real exchange rate of the RMB against the USD appreciated by a large margin. The appreciation by the end of 2003 was an increase of 9.28% compared to February 2003. Huge levels of foreign capital entered China in 2003 and 2004. The foreign reserve balances at the end of 2003 and 2004 saw a year-on-year increase of over 40%. After the exchange rate reform in July 21, 2005, the RMB to USD exchange rate rapidly appreciated. By December 2012, the exchange rate of the RMB rose from RMB8.1/USD$1 to RMB6.3/USD$1, accumulative increase of 22.4%. But there was a sudden depreciation in December 2011 when the exchange rate reached the trading limit floor set by the PBOC for a consecutive 11 trading days. This reflected the fact that the free flow of transnational capital in China had become a new and significant influence on the RMB exchange rate. 2009 and 2011 witnessed negative year-on-year growth of FDI, which to some extent slowed the appreciation trend of the RMB.

Therefore, the appreciation and depreciation pressures on the RMB exchange rate are closely related to international capital flows. The huge capital inflows and outflows during recent years, in particular, have had huge impact on the RMB exchange rate.

2.4 The Ever-Increasing Scale of the Fictitious Economy

Along with the development of the world economy, information technology, and financial innovation, the scale of financial markets in countries all over the world (especially developed countries) have expanded rapidly. Particularly pushed by the burst of the dotcom bubble in the US between 1997 and 2000, the fictitious economy (based on the transactions of fictitious capital such as stocks, bonds and financial derivative products) also saw rapid expansion. By the end of 2012, the over-the-counter (OTC) trade balance of global stock market values, outstanding bond balances and financial derivative products had totaled USD$752.063 trillion, about ten times the world's total GDP. Among this, the market value of stocks reached

USD$53.2 trillion, outstanding bond balances USD$85.7 trillion, and the total open interest derivative contracts USD$623.6 trillion. Of this, 77.41% was related to interest rates, 10.65% related to exchange rates, 3.96% to credit default swaps (CDS), 0.99% to equity, 0.41% to commodity contracts, and 6.58% to other financial assets.

The average daily nominal transaction volume in the global foreign exchange market is as much as over USD$4 trillion — or about 50 times the world's average annual real transaction volume. That is to say, only 2% of the capital flowing in the world every day is actually used in international transactions.

Transnational financial activities are the process of choosing investors and financiers all over the world under the same "game rule" and with the same financial instruments. Among all the financial markets in all areas, different kinds of financial markets are connected, so capital not only can flow in a certain kind of market, but also can move quickly between different kinds of markets. Therefore, the boundaries between "long-term capital" and "short-term capital" are blurring, just as the distinction between "international finance" and "domestic finance" is gradually dissolving. Since the links between financial markets are much closer, risk transference is more rapid. A small action can set off a chain of events.

After the 1970s, with the development of financial innovation, financial derivative markets were created in the US, Britain and other countries. Such markets can be categorized into two kinds. One is the market composed of financial derivatives issued by banks, called OTC transactions (though most of these transactions are made through telephone networks). The massing of financial derivatives has changed the operation model of the whole banking industry. Transnational banks are developing into "all-round" banks, with rapid growth in off-balance sheet activities. The other kind is the visible market organized by financial futures transactions. The currency derivatives traded in derivative markets include forward contracts, currency and exchange rate swaps, life interest rate agreements, financial futures and options, etc. The role of these currency derivatives is as hedges, but they can also become a high risk speculative tool. In 2007, the financial crisis was caused by America's subprime mortgage crisis, which itself was mainly due to the hyperinflation of financial derivatives related to residential mortgage loans (Cheng, 2011).

In contrast to the rapid expansion of the fictitious economy, the proportion of the real economy in any country's gross output (usually expressed in GDP) has been declining, which has attracted much attention from Chinese scholars. However, there is little literature to define the boundary between the real and fictitious (or "virtual") economy. For example, in 2004, Liu and Wu explored the relationship between the two, using GDP to represent the real economy and the stock markets in Shanghai and Shenzhen to represent the fictitious economy. Yet such a definition has its limitations in that the statistical standards for both economies are different and there is little comparability between the two.

In National Economic Accounting, the common system used in the world is the System of National Accounts (SNA). SNA uses GDP to represent a country's economic output. The System of Material Product Balance (MPS) was previously used in the Planned Economy System (represented by the former Soviet Union). MPS only accounts for materials production, and regards areas like education and health care as non-material production, which are not included. The Planned Economy System uses MPS volume data to present the total production of a country's real economy, i.e., the scale of the social wealth created by the real economy. Other industries, such as education, health care, catering and the accommodation industry, and government services, are regarded as the general services industry. They are considered consumption of the real economy, i.e., the volume of services exchanged from the social wealth created in the real economy. The financial services industry and real estate industry, which can "directly make money through money", are regarded as the representation of the fictitious economy.

According to MPS, and in reference to the ISIC/Rev.4 and GB/T 4754-2002, the industries in Table 2.3 are defined under the category of the real economy, so the GDP data in SNA are converted into MPS volume data, to show the scale of production in a country's real economy.

Table 2.3: The Standard for Defining Industries in the Real Economy

GB/T 4754-2002	ISIC/Rev.3
Farming, forestry, animal husbandry, sideline production and fishing	Farming, forestry, fishing, and animal husbandry
Extractive industry	Extractive industry
Manufacturing industry	Manufacturing industry
Production and supply industries for electricity, gas and water	Public utilities
Construction industry	Construction industry
Wholesale and retail trade	Wholesale trade
	Retail trade
Transportation, storage, and postal industries	Transportation and storage industry

Table 2.4: The Proportion of MPS, the General Services Industry, and the Fictitious Economy in GDP (%)

	The US		China	
	1980	2012	1980	2010
Real economy				
MPS	49.9	35.1	87.4	70.5
General services industry	34.1	44.7	8.8	18.7
Virtual economy	16	20.2	3.8	10.8

When the value of all the industries in Table 2.3 is added up, we arrive at MPS volume data that presents the scale of material production in the real economy. Except for the industries included in the MPS, other industries in the real economy are regarded as the general services industry, providing non-material services such as education, health care and public management. Therefore, MPS, the general services industry and the fictitious economy's output together compose the general economic output of a country.

After defining the boundaries for MPS, the general services industry, and the fictitious economy, Table 2.4 summarizes the proportions of these three industries in GDP for China and the US. It shows that, compared with 1980, the proportion of MPS to GDP in both China and the US decreased considerably, whereas those of the general services industry and fictitious economy increased. Non-material production sectors and the fictitious economy made increasing contributions to GDP. This is in line with the fact that the fictitious economy has been increasing in recent years.

Using the definition above, Figure 2.5 shows the proportions of the real economy in GDP for the US and China respectively. Both the US and China saw a decreasing proportion of the real economy in GDP in recent years. The proportion in the US decreased from 89.5% in 1947 to 79.8% in 2012, and that in China from 96.2% in 1980 to 89.2% in 2010. The data from these two countries indicates a considerable decrease in both the proportion and contribution of the real economy to GDP. Correspondingly, the fictitious economy has been increasing, thereby increasing its contribution to GDP.

Applying a similar accounting method, we use the added value of the financial services industry, real estate industry, and leasing industry to represent the scale of the fictitious economy, analyzing the development of the fictitious economy in China and the US (see Figure 2.6). Although there is a gap in the fictitious economy between China and the US, the

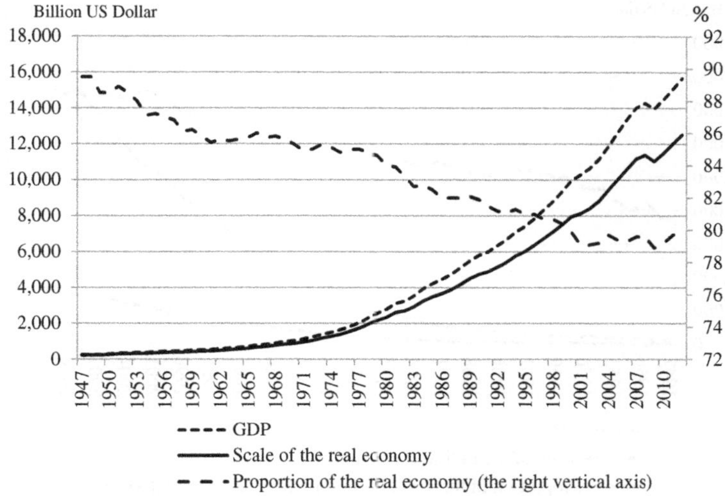

(a)

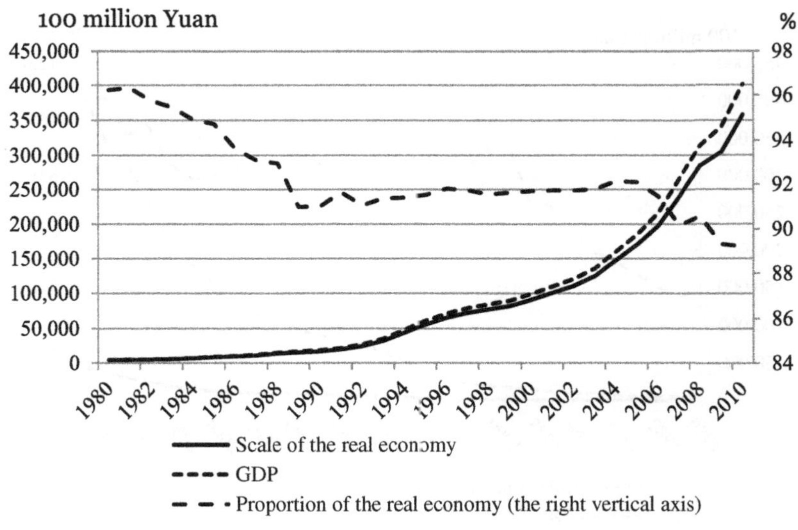

(b)

Figure 2.5: (a): The Proportion of The Real Economy in GDP for the US; (b): The Proportion of the Real Economy in GDP for China[3]

[3]Due to the limitation of statistics, the added value data of China's industries is only till 2010.

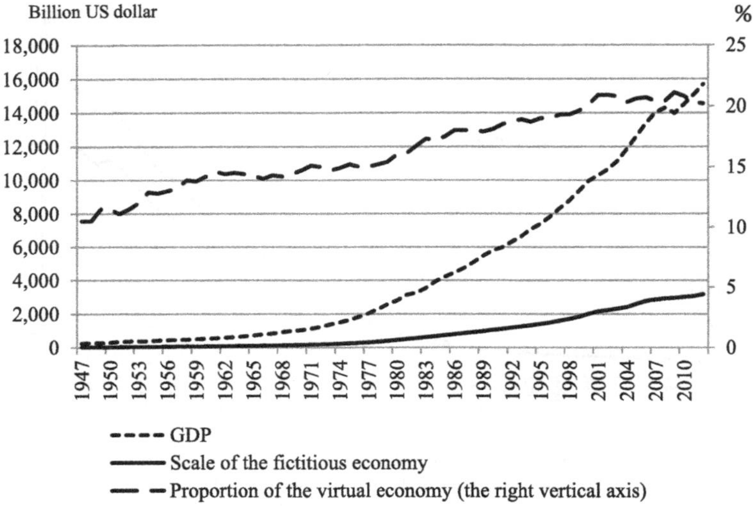

(a)

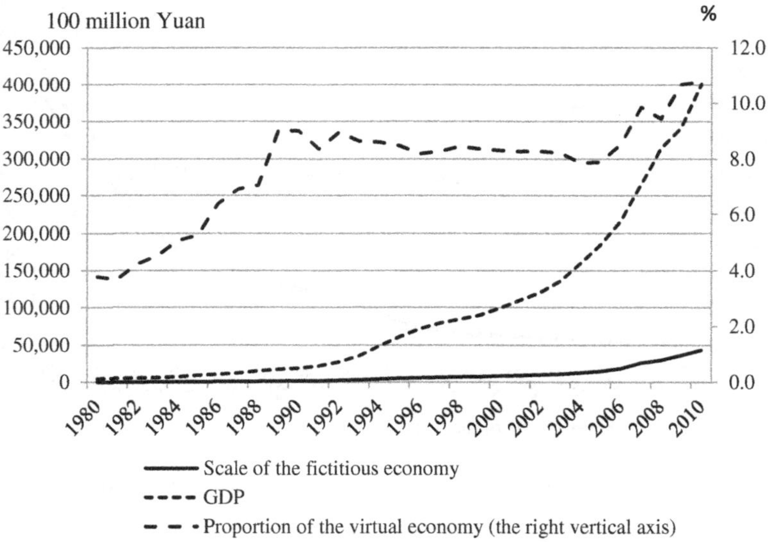

(b)

Figure 2.6: (a): The Proportion of the Fictitious Economy in GDP for the US; (b): The Proportion of the Fictitious Economy in GDP for China

recent years have seen a rapid development of the fictitious economy in both countries. In terms of the contribution of the fictitious economy to GDP, it increased in the US from 10.5% in 1947 to 20.2% in 2012, and in China from 3.8% in 1980 to 10.8% in 2010.

With the expansion of the fictitious economy, financial derivative products related to exchange rates have also rapidly developed. According to BIS data, by the end of 2012, outstanding exchange rate derivatives totaled USD$6.74 trillion, representing 47.1% of foreign exchange swaps, 37.8% of currency swaps, and 15.1% of foreign exchange options. With insufficient supervision, these financial derivative products cannot fulfill their intended role as hedges against risks. Instead, they will become speculative tools in foreign exchange markets. Some hedge funds, with their huge strength, affect the financial systems in some countries and regions, causing severe financial turmoil.

2.5 Exchange Rates Has Become a Tool for Political Competition

After a currency transitions to a fiat system, the exchange rate is usually not an objective reflection of prices. Instead, it has become a comprehensive reflection of contesting interests: the fight among different interest groups within a country for their own interests, and the fight and compromise among different countries for advantageous trading conditions. That is to say, the exchange rate is the result of strategic games at both the international and domestic levels of a country (Li, and Li 2007). Studies by foreign scholars also support this view. Around the reform of China's exchange rate system in 2005, apart from China, many countries in the world had their currencies pegged to US Dollars or dollarized, yet they were not criticized for manipulating their exchange rate by Western countries. Thus, putting pressure on the RMB exchange rate and demanding that it fluctuate and appreciate was only a means used by the US to heal its domestic political wounds (O'Driscoll and Hoskins 2004). This section will illustrate the important influence of international and domestic political factors on exchange rate changes, and how an exchange rate has become a tool for political ends.

2.5.1 *International Political Competition Involving Exchange Rates*

In the fictitious economy, since the exchange rate can only reflect the domestic purchasing power of local currency, exchange rates among different currencies will fluctuate with the rise and fall of countries' economic power. Yet, when a currency is de-pegged from gold, its exchange rate is no longer determined by the production and value of gold, so it provides the government with the power to adjust the exchange rate according to its needs. At the same time, governments can use the exchange rate as a policy tool to maximize their interests in their current account or capital account, making the adjustment of the exchange rate a competition among governments. Theoretically speaking, if related countries start from general interests to adjust international exchange rates, there will be a Pareto effect when all parties involved attain satisfactory results. Exchange rates are not merely an economic phenomenon, but also a political phenomenon. Their determination and fluctuation are influenced by people's nature: seeking their own interests and avoiding losses. Different people, interest groups, and countries will try to influence exchange rate policy in order to maximize their own interests. Exchange rates can be tuned to maximize interests, so that the adjustment of exchange rates becomes a competition. Exchange rates thereby transform from a simple economic issue to a tool in a broader political contest.

2.5.1.1 *Trade Disputes*

A long-term trade deficit in a country (i.e., where exports total more than imports) will lead to losses for export companies, a withering of export industry, and increasing unemployment. But a trade deficit usually happens because of the different trade structures, industry structures and labor prices in different countries, and cannot be changed in the short term. To achieve a faster remedy, many countries depreciate their currency to put pressure on their trading partners. They may hope to rapidly increase the price advantage of their exports by shifting the cost of adjustment to their trading partners.

Since the 1980s, the situation described above has existed among developed countries. Between 1981 and 1985, with the decreasing exchange rate of the Japanese yen relative to the increasing rate of the US Dollar, Japan's exports increased rapidly — an increase of 74% over those of the US — and created a Japan–US trade surplus. Against this backdrop, the US advocated a meeting in New York's Plaza Hotel on September 22, 1985. It was attended by finance ministers and central bank governors from the G5 (US, Japan, Germany, France and Britain). The meeting aimed to coordinate the exchange rate policy among the G5 to better reflect the economic development of the respective countries, and to change the payments imbalance in various countries' current accounts. Through negotiation, the G5 reached the Plaza Accord, which coordinated joint action to gradually decrease the exchange rates of all major currencies against the US Dollar.

The Plaza Accord was the first case in which wide international action was taken to coordinate exchange rates. It reached its expected results in a short period. Central banks in most countries began to dump the US Dollar and to buy the Yen and Deutschemark. Within a week after the Plaza Accord, the US Dollar depreciated by 8% against the Yen and 6% against the Deutschemark. By the end of December 1986, the Dollar depreciated by another 20% against both the Yen and Deutschemark. At that time, related countries believed that, leaving Dollar depreciation unchecked would have adverse effects on their countries' economic development. Therefore, in 1987 the finance ministers of the G6 (the G5 plus Canada) reached the Louvre Accord, which agreed to limit the fluctuation of exchange rates within a certain range, and to intervene when it exceeded such a range. But after the meeting, the US did not keep its promise to reduce its deficit. Especially after the stock market crash in October 19, 1987, the US government was only concerned with its domestic economic problems, leaving the depreciation of the Dollar unchecked. The Louvre Accord became a dead letter agreement. The constant appreciation of the Yen became a major factor of in Japan's economic bubble. When the bubble burst in 1991, Japan became trapped in a long-term recession.

2.5.1.2 *Debt Dilution*

Another international competition involving exchange rates is that of debt dilution. A country can dilute its debt (denominated in its local currency) through currency depreciation. Take the debtor–creditor relationship between China and the US as an example. Figure 2.7 shows that by July 2013, the foreign debt of the US had totaled USD$5590.1 billion, a year-by-year increase of 20%. Among this, China held up to USD$1277.3 billion, accounting for 22.85% of the total. Still, China is holding increasingly more US debt. Since China is currently the largest creditor of the US, the stability of the exchange rate of the RMB against the USD is crucial for hedging China's dollar assets. In recent years, the constant appreciation of the RMB against the USD has amounted to a depreciation in China's dollar assets and, consequently, a severe loss.

With the development of China's foreign trade, China's foreign reserves are increasing year by year. Figure 2.8 shows that about 40% of China's

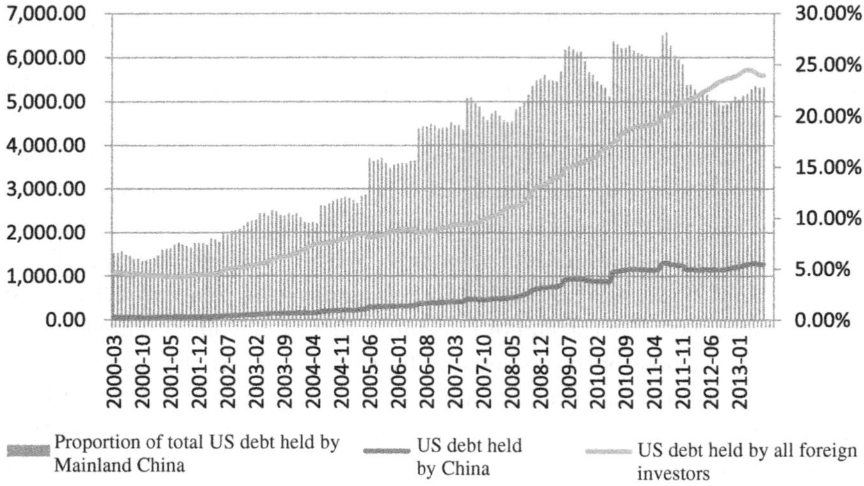

Figure 2.7: Total Foreign US Debt and China's Holdings

Data source: Wind Database.

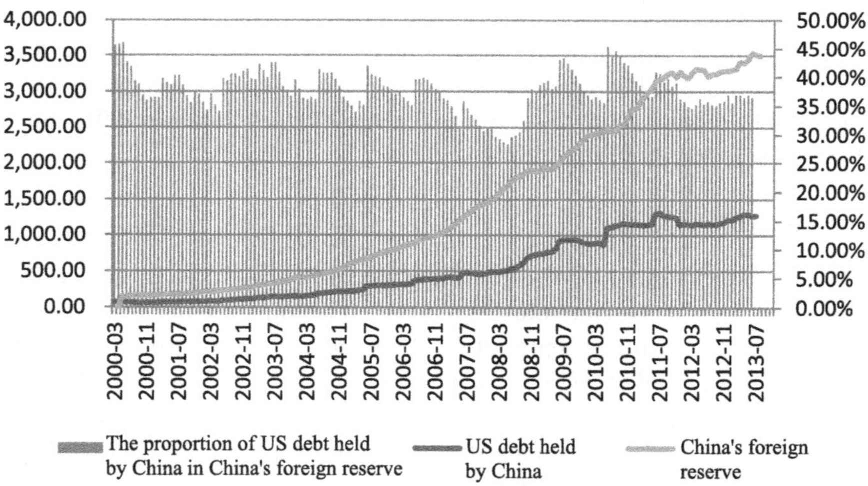

Figure 2.8: The Proportion of US Debt Held by China in China's Foreign Reserves

Data source: Wind Database.

foreign reserve assets are held in US debt. By June 2013, the accumulated foreign reserves in China had totaled USD$3496.686 billion and kept a rapid average yearly increase of 23.82%. By June 2013, the US foreign debt held by China accounted for 36.49% of China's total foreign reserves. Such a figure peaked at 45.31% in June 2010. This means that China lent nearly half of its foreign reserves to the US. If there is a large fluctuation in the exchange rate, credit will shrink considerably, which will bring a great loss to China. Since the re-launching of China's exchange rate reforms in 2005, the RMB to USD exchange rate has maintained an average yearly appreciation of about 3.4%. Based on such a rate, China's holdings of US debt are shrinking by USD$24.06 billion a year, on an average.

2.5.1.3 *National Strategy*

National strategy is a country's general guiding plan to safeguard its sovereignty, territory, ensure its national security, and promote its national economic, cultural and technological development. Such a strategy can be achieved through a combination of national resources and strength in politics, economics, culture, science and technology, military and psychology based on both international and domestic conditions. Viewing the exchange rate from the perspective of national strategy, we find that the exchange rates are in fact a tool for political strategy among different countries — effectively political bargaining counters in international competition. From this perspective, there are two reasons why one country puts pressure on another through exchange rates. One is that a country wants to make demands through its exchange rate, so that the other country is forced to make concessions in other areas. The other reason is to hinder the economic development of the other country.

With the development of China's economy, the view of the "China threat" has appeared in Sino-US relations. Many institutions, such as the US–China Economic and Security Review Commission of the US Congress, are always advocating the "China threat", always criticizing China by labeling it a "exchange rate manipulator", and seek to influence the US Congress to enact laws to respond to the RMB exchange rate issue. This is, in fact, a misunderstanding of and prejudice towards China's economic development. China is still a developing country, with its per capita GDP ranking under 100th in the world and its technology and education still relatively backward. Thus, the so-called "China threat" and mislabeled "responsibility" of China are in fact misunderstandings of, and effectively prejudice against, China. Exchange rates are a sovereign right. China's exchange rate has to be decided by China itself. China has to keep the RMB exchange rate stable at a reasonable and balanced level. Putting pressure on the RMB cannot solve the problem of a trade deficit between China and US, nor can it help solve the unemployment problem in the US (Li *et al.*, 2010).

History has told us that we should not regard exchange rates only as an economic or financial issue, but also as a political issue. For example, after the breakout of the East Asia Financial Crisis in 1997, facing pressure from Western countries to depreciate the RMB, China stuck to the principle that exchange rate management is a sovereign right, and adhered to the stability of the RMB exchange rate. This decision helped many East Asian economies pull through the crisis and subsequently won praise from many East Asian countries. After 2003, China again was under constant pressure from Western countries to appreciate the RMB. This required China to take actions and make decisions according to the situation, weighing both advantages and disadvantages.

People of insight draw experiences from the competition among exchange rate policies and have realized that it is very difficult to achieve a reasonable coordination between many countries participate — especially when there is great power gap between most countries and the US. So it is better to coordinate countries in a region to form a joint force that can compete with the US, reducing the impact of fluctuations in the US Dollar exchange rate and ensuring financial stability in the region. This is the main reason why the Euro was created. It can be predicted that, with the development of regional integration, financial integration among countries in a region will increase. A new example is that, in the beginning of 2006, the Asian Development Bank announced the conception of the Asia Currency Unit (ACU), based on the weighted average of 15 currencies across China, Japan, South Korea and ASEAN countries.

2.5.2 *The Domestic Political Competition over Exchange Rate Policy*

When a currency is virtualized, the exchange rate not only becomes a tool for political contest between countries, but also between domestic interest groups.

Traditional research-based theoretical frameworks on exchange rates have a common limitation, in that they regard exchange rate changes and system adjustment as being a one-way process a government's top-down adjustment while neglecting other political influences, such as the competition among interest groups and other political lobbies. Seen from the perspective of these domestic factors, exchange rate policy is actually a competition between domestic interest groups and a tool in political campaigning. Therefore, through studying how exchange rate policy has become a tool for domestic political competition, we can further realize Western countries' true purpose in putting pressure on the RMB exchange rate.

2.5.2.1 *Political Campaigning*

Exchange rates in some countries will change considerably before an election. The reason why political campaigns can influence exchange rates is because rate changes can directly affect imports and exports. Currency depreciation before an election can rapidly reverse a trade deficit, promote export industries, increase employment and consumption, and generally boost the economy. Providing these benefits can increase votes. Therefore, candidates for political office all want to use exchange rates as a tool to increase their votes among their constituencies. For example, the RMB exchange rate is usually the target of politicians during American presidential elections. Before the election on November 6, 2012, Republican candidate Romney criticized China as an "exchange rate manipulator" that caused dramatic increases in unemployment in the US. He announced that, if elected, he would legally name China a "exchange rate manipulator" the very day of his inauguration. Romney criticized Obama, stating that he "was not brave towards China", because the US Treasury Department postponed the semi-annual Currency Report after the G20 finance ministers' meeting, failing to meet its commitment to "conduct negotiation" on China's exchange rate. However, in fact Romney just wanted to win more support from his Ohio constituency (where there are many labor unions) through his remarks.

From Obama's election campaign we can see that, if he was elected, he would be committed to creating more jobs in his next term to control the high unemployment rate. This meant that the Obama administration would increase protection for some weak industries, and try to solve the problem of a trade imbalance, including taking a tougher attitude towards the RMB exchange rate and keeping pressure on China. In his election agenda, Obama stressed "the importance of obeying international economic rules" to express his tough attitude towards the RMB exchange rate. But since Obama's successful election, the US has taken no action on the exchange rate issue. This also proves that exchange rates have become a tool for political campaigning. Bonomo and Terra (2005) found that in some countries where the number of employees in the non-tradable goods sectors is much larger than that in the tradable goods sector, the ruling party will appreciate its currency during an election to win the vote from its primary constituency (in the non-tradable goods sector). However, since the tradable goods sector contributes more to a government's tax revenue, the ruling party will depreciate the currency after it wins an election to develop that sector.

2.5.2.2 *Political Factions*

The influence of political factions on exchange rates mainly exists in countries with two-party or multi-party systems. The influence of political factions on exchange rate is different from that of political campaigns.

Political factions can exert influence on exchange rate policy because different factions or leaders of factions have different ideologies. Previous research suggests that the ideology of ruling parties or political factions can be divided into two kinds: left-wing and right-wing (Alesina, 1987). Left-wing and right-wing political factions have different ideologies, so their views and propositions on exchange rate policy are different. Since different scholars have different criteria for distinguishing left-wing and right-wing ideologies, and the situations in different countries vary considerably, a simple division between left-wing and right-wing cannot include all political views. But generally speaking, left-wing groups prefer to intervene in the economy through micro control, so their exchange rate policy is more likely to be in the form of the central bank's direct intervention, or intervention in a trading partners' exchange rate through diplomacy. The right-wing trusts more in the market's independent regulation of the economy, and right-wing governments will usually not intervene in exchange rates (Li, 2011).

Table 2.5 shows Brazil's exchange rate system and politics between 1990 and 2005. We can see that the exchange rate system under the left-wing government is relatively conservative, with greater government control and intervention. In contrast, the policies of the right-wing government are usually liberal, with less intervention from the government.

2.5.2.3 *Interest Groups*

Interest groups are social organizations driven by a common interest and purpose. Interest groups were first created in the manufacturing industry in the US. They evolved from all kinds of manufacturer associations, and

Table 2.5: Brazil's Exchange Rate System and Politics 1990–2005

Year	Exchange Rate System	Degree of Democratization	Electoral System	Political Leanings
1990	Managed floating	Open election	Proportional representation system	Left-wing
1991–1993	Conservative crawling peg	Open election	Proportional representation system	Left-wing
1994	Managed floating	Open election	Proportional representation system	Left-wing
1995–1997	Conservative crawling peg	Open election	Proportional representation system	Right-wing
1998	Forward-looking crawling peg	Open election	Proportional representation system	Right-wing
1999–2001	Independent floating	Open election	Proportional representation system	Right-wing
2002–2005	Independent floating	Open election	Proportional representation system	Left-wing

Data sources: IMF; the official website of the Inter-Parliamentary Union: www.ipu.org; Lv Y. C. and Zhou J. N. (2004); and Kuang M. and Wang H. (2007).

gradually developed from regional organizations to national ones. Interest groups do not necessarily have great wealth, but have strong lobby capacity, and organize lobbies to directly affect government policy to benefit their interests. For example, in the US interest groups have great influence. According to statistics, there were 17,644 national interest groups in the US in 1983, 60% of American adults belonged to at least one interest group, and over half of Americans thought that the government is "largely controlled by a few interest groups that are only concerned by their own interests" (though this figure was only 21% in 1980).

In recent years, the American economy has been consistently sluggish with both its trade deficit and fiscal deficit increasing. Most manufacturing industry has been severely affected and unemployment has been increasing. The US unemployment rate in 2003 alone reached 6.4%, among which nearly 90% was from the manufacturing industry. At the same time, China had been the US's largest deficit trading partner for three consecutive years, which further pushed the American manufacturing interest groups to target the RMB exchange rate. The American interest groups led by the National Association of Manufacturers and the AFL-CIO began direct and indirect lobbying of the executive branch and members of Congress to put pressure on the RMB exchange rate, hoping to ease domestic unemployment pressure by restraining China's exports. To pressure the RMB exchange rate, interest groups usually opt for three tactics: lobbying the American executive branch to put pressure on RMB exchange rate; lobbying the legislative branch to enact laws; and using the judicial branch (Zeng, 2013).

For this purpose, interest groups need the executive branch to push RMB appreciation onto the bilateral agenda of the two countries, or to enact laws to express their demands through members of Congress. For a successful lobbying effort, interest groups have to approach executive officials or members of Congress to express and carry out their favored policy through direct or indirect influence (Zeng, 2013).

(1) Direct Lobbying

Interest groups directly referred reports pressuring for RMB exchange rate appreciation to government officials or members of Congress, made public announcements, sent letters or emails, and arranged face-to-face talks. Tables 2.6 and 2.7 show some examples of American interest groups' direct lobbying.

(2) Indirect Lobbying:

There are many indirect means of lobbying: influencing members of Congress to press the government; propaganda to guide public opinion; lobbying the constituency to influence members of Congress; and forming alliances to enlarge influence. Table 2.8 shows some examples of interest groups' pressuring government through members of Congress.

In the previous part, I discussed interest groups' influence on interest rates. But different interest groups have different preferences. The Frieden Matrix (Table 2.9) can clearly show different interest groups' preference for various interest rates.

It can be seen from the Frieden Matrix that producers of export-oriented goods prefer a low-value, low-flexibility exchange rate. A low exchange rate can increase the competitiveness of exported goods, and low flexibility can ensure that the exported goods are less influenced by any fluctuation in the exchange rate. Producers of domestic tradable import goods hope that a low exchange rate can increase the competitiveness of their goods compared relative to other imports. For outward investors, a high exchange rate can help them buy more foreign assets. Also they prefer low flexibility, so as to avoid losses caused by exchange rate fluctuations. While providers of non-tradable goods and service are not directly influenced by the exchange rate, appreciation of the local currency

Table 2.6: Examples of American Interest Groups' Lobbying Administrative Departments 2003–2010

Time Period	Target of Lobby	Tactics	Lobby Groups	Message
January 2003	Treasury Secretary Snow	Letters	National Association of Manufacturers, Coalition for a Sound Dollar	Asking the Treasury Department to press China, Japan, Taiwan of China, and South Korea to stop using currency manipulation to promote their export.
September 2003	Treasury Secretary Snow	Letters	Coalition for a Sound Dollar	Pressing the Treasury Department to make it a primary goal to stop Asian countries' so-called currency manipulation, especially the devalued RMB.
September 2004	Office of the US Trade Representative	Submit appeal report	AFL-CIO, China Currency Coalition	Criticizing the RMB as undervalued by 40% and demanding that the Coalition conduct a 301 Survey on China's currency manipulation according to US domestic trade law.
November 2005	Treasury Secretary Snow	Make announcement	National Association of Manufacturers, AFL-CIO	Expressing disappointment towards the Treasury Department that it did not define China as currency manipulator, and asking the Treasury to take necessary measures via the IMF to solve the problem of China's currency manipulation.
October 2008	Office of the US Trade Representative	Testify at a Congressional hearing	China Currency Coalition	Criticizing China for not fulfilling its commitments to the WTO.
January 2010	Commerce Secretary Gary Locke	Email	Committee to Support US Trade Laws	Asking the Commerce Department to investigate whether China's exchange rate practice is a special export subsidy, according to US domestic laws and international law.

Data source: Cao (2013).

Table 2.7: Examples of Ways American Interest Groups' Lobby Members of Congress 2003–2010

Time Period	Target of Lobby	Tactics	Lobby Groups	Message
September 25, 2003	US–China Economic and Security Review Commission	Testify at congressional hearing	AFL-CIO	Criticizing China's devaluation of the RMB exchange rate by 40% to promote exports as against WTO rules; and urging the government to take actions including appealing to the WTO to solve the problem.
February 3–5, 2005	US–China Economic and Security Review Commission	Testify at congressional hearing	China Currency Coalition	Undervaluation of RBM is an important reason for the huge trade deficit between the US and China; urges for solution.
April 14, 2005	House Ways and Means Committee	Testify at congressional hearing	National Association of Manufac-turers	It is difficult to compete with China's low wage, and impossible to compete with unfair trade.
November 29, 2005	House of Representatives	Letters	AFL-CIO	Urging the House to support the Chinese Currency Act of 2005
January 30, 2007	Ryan and Hunter	Letters	China Currency Coalition	Expressing thanks to two members of Congress who had long-term concern about China's currency, and supporting the Fair Currency Act of 2007 initiated by them.
October 26, 2007	Senate manufacturing task force	Testify at congressional hearing	China Currency Coalition	Criticizing China's manipulation of the RMB exchange rate, and asking the Congress to take actions to cope with the crisis.
April 22, 2010	Senate Finance Committee	Testify at congressional hearing	Fair Currency Alliance	Explaining the relationship between China's exchange rate policy and the Sino-US trade imbalance, and criticizing China's manipulation of exchange rates.
November 16, 2010	Senators	Letters	AFL-CIO	Asking senators to support the Currency Reform for Fair Trade Act (H.R.378) passed by the House.

Data source: Cao (2013).

Table 2.8: Examples of Pressurizing the Executive Branch via Members of Congress, 2003–2011

Time Period	Target of Lobby	Tactics	Members of Congress	Contents
July 31, 2003	President Bush	Letters	16 members of Congress led by Schumer and Manzullo	Asking the president to urge the Treasury Department, the State Department, and the USTR to take more powerful actions to correct the RMB devaluation.
October 30, 2003	President Bush, Treasury Secretary Snow and Trade representative Zoellick	Letters	Riegel and Lhevinne	Asking the executive branch to take further steps in regards to China's currency manipulation.
September 30, 2004	President Bush and Trade representative Zoellick	301 Appeal	30 members of Congress led by Lhevinne and Schumer	Asking the government to support the China Currency Coalition's 301 appeal request
November 5, 2009	President Obama	Letters	45 M.H.R including Ryan and Murphy	Asking President Obama to support the Currency Reform for Fair Trade Act 2009 (H.R.2378/S.1027) approved by Congress.
February 26, 2010	Commerce Secretary Gary Locke	Letters	15 senators including Schumer and Graham	Asking the Commerce Department to accept American companies' appeal to investigate whether China's exchange rate practices are a special export subsidy.

(Continued)

Table 2.8: (*Continued*)

Time Period	Target of Lobby	Tactics	Members of Congress	Contents
March 15, 2010	Treasury Secretary Geithner, Commerce Secretary Gary Locke	Letters	130 members of Congress including Mitchard and Ryan	Urging the Commerce Department to apply US antidumping duty laws to investigate China's currency manipulation, and asking the Treasury Department to define China as an exchange rate manipulator in its semi-annual report.
August 4, 2010	President Obama	Letters	11 Senators including Brown and Snowe	Suggesting to the President to urge executive departments such as the Commerce Department to actively support American companies' appeals, and to investigate whether China's exchange rate manipulation is a special export subsidy.
January 18, 2011	President Obama	Letters	31 Members of Congress including Murphy and Wisky	Asking the President to talk with President Hu Jintao about the losses of the US steel industry caused by behaviors that violate trade laws, such as the RMB devaluation.

Data source: Cao (2013).

Table 2.9: Interest Groups' Favored Combination of Interest Rates

	Preference of Interest Rate's Flexibility	
	Low	High
Preference of Interest Rate		
Low	A. Producers of export-oriented trade	B. Producers of domestic tradable import goods
High	C. Outward investors	D. Providers of non-tradable goods and services

Data source: Liu and Jin (2012).

can increase the prices of their goods, which is generally against their interests.

2.6 The Problem of Exchange Rate Arrangement

The fictitious economic system and the real economic system are closely connected. The Fictitious economic system is produced from the real economic system, and is dependent on it. Because of their close connection, the risks to the real economy, such as excessive inventory, rapid decline in foreign trade, bankruptcy, etc. can all be transferred into (and thereby destabilize) the fictitious economy. The direct risks to the fictitious economy — such as dramatic falls of stock index, plunging real estate prices, soaring bad debts of banks, and a huge depreciation of the currency — will also have severe effects on the real economy. Today when finance has become the core of an economy, the real economy cannot operate without the fictitious economy. Therefore, if the real economy is regarded as the hardware in economic system, then the fictitious economy is the software. As an important part of the fictitious economy, an exchange rate arrangement has a huge impact on domestic prices of commodities, capital flows, foreign trade and foreign reserves.

2.6.1 *The Debate between Fixed and Floating Exchange Rate Arrangements*

The evolution of the international exchange rate system shows that the arrangement of exchange rates is a dynamic one full of changes. As early as the 1950s when the Gold Exchange Standard system dominated by the US Dollar prevailed, there was argument about which was better: a fixed or floating exchange rate. Scholars represented by Kindieberger advocated a fixed exchange rate, holding that a floating exchange rate will cause instability in the exchange rate. Other scholars represented by Friedman argued that a floating exchange rate is "not necessarily an unstable exchange rate". Even if the exchange rate is unstable, it is due to instabilities in international trade. Indeed, while a fixed exchange rate is nominally stable, it can prolong and enhance the instability of other factors.

After WWII, many decision makers believed that one of the reasons for the unstable world economy between WWI and WWII was the prevalence of flexible exchange rates and the widespread competitive depreciation of currencies. Thus, a fixed exchange rate was instituted through the Bretton Woods system. Yet with the collapse of the Gold Exchange Standard system in 1971, currency was made fiat. This increased the difficulty in choosing an exchange rate arrangement and intensified the debate.

Supporters for fixed exchange rates believe that a fixed exchange rate has the following advantages (Pilbeam, 1998).

Firstly, a fixed exchange rate can provide the best international trade and investment environment, avoid risks, promote international trade and increase investment, so as to bring considerable benefits to a country. The fluctuation of an exchange rate will increase uncertainty in international economic activities. In particular, the financial markets in many developing countries are not well-developed, and lack tools such as forward transactions to avoid risks, so there will be negative risk effects from an unstable currency, limiting economic and financial development.

Secondly, a fixed exchange rate can prevent the abuse of currency policy. Under the fixed exchange rate system, expansionary monetary policy will lead to reserve capital flight, and finally pose a threat to the maintenance of the fixed exchange rate. If the government has to depreciate its currency, the public would regard it as mismanagement of the economy. Therefore, a fixed exchange can bar government from the temptation to adopt an expansionary economic policy.

Thirdly, a fixed exchange rate is good for promoting international cooperation. Countries that adopt a pegged exchange rate usually promise to take necessary measures to adjust their economy once the current currency parity is under pressure. Yet under a floating exchange rate system, due to the lack of agreement to restrain exchange rates, all countries will put domestic objectives first, so governments are more likely to use a floating exchange rate to carry out the beggar-thy-neighbor policy of competitive depreciation. Therefore, a fixed exchange rate is beneficial for all countries' economic development, and can bring a more stable international economic order.

Fourthly, speculation under a fixed exchange rate system is usually stable. Because speculators anticipate the stability of a fixed exchange rate, the arbitrage gap will be reduced when there is a difference between the real exchange rate and parity. Besides, under a fixed exchange rate system, government intervention will erase uncertainty in the minds of market traders about exchange rate policy and promote rational market behavior. In comparison, market traders' anticipations are usually irrational, whereas rational traders may not know the correct exchange rate model with uncertain conditions, so unstable speculations prevail under a floating exchange rate system (for want of a firm government commitment to a target rate). Driven by herd behavior, speculators usually adopt a strategy of buying stocks at rising prices and selling at falling price. Competitive speculators even deliberately create exchange rate volatility so as to make profits from it. This will certainly lead to increasing instability in a floating exchange rate system.

On the other hand, advocates for a floating exchange rate system have determined numerous advantages of floating exchange rates (Artus and Young, 1979; MacDonald 1988; Pilbeam, 1998).

Firstly, a floating exchange rate is not necessarily an unstable exchange rate. Even when the exchange rate is unstable, this is mainly because of an unstable economic basis for international trade. While a fixed exchange rate is nominally stable, it can prolong and enhance the instability of other economic factors. Besides, an unstable exchange rate is the sign of an unstable basic economic structure (not the reverse). The official exchange rate cannot help any imbalance in the economy's structure, but instead can only make it more difficult to adjust.

Secondly, a floating exchange rate can ensure a balance of international payments. In a floating exchange rate system, if a country has an unsustainable current account deficit, it can simply allow the exchange rate to adjust and let its currency depreciate (adjusting one variable). Yet in a fixed exchange rate system, it has to change the currency supply to adjust the price system, which involves adjustment of many variables. Apparently, the former adjustment is faster and costs less. Especially when there is sticky price adjustment, the advantage of a floating exchange rate is more obvious.

Thirdly, a floating exchange rate can ensure the autonomy of monetary policy. In a floating exchange rate system, monetary policy is independent from exchange rate policy. The exchange rate can adjust on its own to achieve external balance, while monetary and fiscal policy can be focused on achieving a domestic balance. Moreover, in a floating exchange rate system, a country can protect itself from foreign inflation. If the price level in a foreign country is increasing, with the role of PPP, the local currency will appreciate against the foreign currency, which will deter inflation from the foreign source. In this way, a government can independently formulate policies for domestic economic stability and development. In contrast, with a fixed exchange rate system, the increase in the foreign price level can bring a corresponding increase in the domestic price level, exposing the country to external shocks.

Fourthly, a floating exchange rate is conducive to economic stability. When there are external shocks, appreciation and depreciation of the exchange rate can adjust international payments and the whole economy without any special policy or any enforcement measure. Yet with a fixed exchange rate system, any imbalance in international payments is usually solved through special government policy, which may cause delays and sometimes are ineffective.

Fifthly, speculation in a floating exchange rate system is stable. Speculators buy low and sell high so the gap between high prices and low prices of foreign currency narrows, reducing fluctuation in market prices. Furthermore, with a floating exchange rate, since the exchange rate is adjusted all the time and the government does not promise to maintain a certain exchange rate, it is difficult for speculative money to find opportunities when the exchange rate is clearly overvalued or devalued. At the same time, speculators have to take on the risk of a reversal in the exchange rate, adding to their overall risk. Therefore, in a floating system, private speculators will actually push the exchange rate towards an equilibrium rate.

From the analysis above, it can be found that there is no clear answer to which kind of exchange rate system is superior. Their advantages and disadvantages, shown in comparison, apply to different economic contexts and times. So while the inherent features of different exchange rate systems are important, many other factors have to be taken into consideration in choosing an exchange rate system.

2.6.2 *The Dilemma of Maintaining Exchange Rate Stability or the Independence of Monetary Policy under the Condition of Capital Controls*

The argument between a fixed exchange rate system and a floating exchange rate system involves determining the ultimate target of policy. With an open economy, if maintaining the stability of the exchange rate is the major target, then a country should give up its independent monetary policy and adopt a fixed exchange rate. If reducing the influence of exchange rate changes on the real economy is the major target, then the country should give up the stability of the exchange rate and adopt a floating exchange rate system. Some economists have tried to explore an exchange rate system that combines the advantages of the two, yet it has proven to be difficult to achieve (e.g., by Mondale and other economists). The problem is encapsulated in the Trilemma theory of exchange rate arrangement.

The fundamentals of the Trilemma theory are found in Meade's Conflict and the Mundell–Fleming Model (M–F Model). In the 1950s, the British economist Meade (1953) formulated the "dilemma" between international capital flows and a fixed exchange rate system — that is, one of the premises of a fixed exchange rate system is capital controls. On such a basis, in the 1960s Mundell (1963) and Fleming (1962) came up with the M–F Model. The Model, adopting a short-term demand analysis and bringing in the factors of foreign trade and capital flows, analyzes the different roles of monetary policy and financial policy in both fixed and floating exchange rate systems in an open economy. The assumptions of the model are: (1) totally open finance, i.e., an open current account and capital account; (2) free capital flows, i.e., full replacement between domestic and foreign currencies and securities; (3) output deciding demands, and full flexibility of output supply; (4), a small-scale domestic economy that has no influence on foreign interest rates and price level; (5) a stable interest rate in a given period; and (6) that depreciation of the local currency can improve the current account. With these assumptions, if a fixed exchange rate system is chosen, then monetary policy cannot help to stabilize the economy (having no influence on income and employment). If a floating exchange rate system is chosen, financial policy cannot stabilize the economy. Therefore, the M–F Model already embodies the Trilemma of three elements — free capital flows (or open financial markets), a fixed exchange rate and independent monetary policy (or adjusting currency supply to achieve the required level of interest rate). The dilemma implies that only two of these choices can be chosen, thereby fixing the third choice.

The M–F Model laid the foundation for Western exchange rate theory. Later, plenty of research has been focused on extending or revising the assumptions and developing the model. Krugman (1979) and Frankel (1999) developed the M–F Model into the "impossible triangle" model, and came up with the combination of "half independent and half stable".

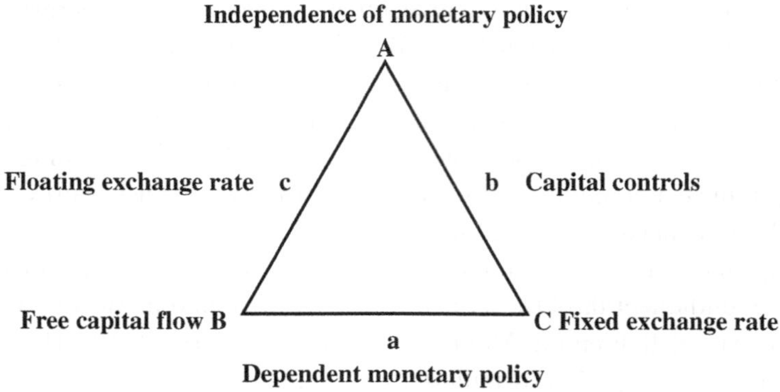

Figure 2.9: Trilemma

The Trilemma can be vividly illustrated by the "impossible triangle". As Figure 2.9 shows, the three vertexes of the triangle represent the three policy targets mentioned above.

"A" for independence of monetary policy, "B" for free capital flows, and "C" for a fixed exchange rate. The three sides represent the contrary situations of those represented by their corresponding vertexes: *a* for dependent monetary policy, *b* for capital controls, and *c* for a floating exchange rate. The triangle provides three possible combinations of a country's economic policy. Each policy can only be formed by two vertexes and the side between them.

According to the Trilemma theory, the combinations of a country's economic policy are as follows.

(1) Independent monetary policy A + free capital flows B + floating exchange rate *c*. Such a policy seeks independence for monetary policy and free flows of capitals, so gives up a fixed exchange rate system. In this combination, the government adopts a floating exchange rate system and freely allows capital inflows and outflows. It makes timely use of monetary policies, such as interest rate adjustments, to change overall domestic demand, and to fulfill domestic economic goals such as full employment, curbing inflation, and economic growth. At the same time, it can ease the shock from foreign capital flows on local currency to ensure the security of the domestic economy. But the country has to take on the uncertainty brought about by a floating exchange rate and higher costs.

(2) Independent monetary policy A + fixed exchange rate C + capital controls *b*. Such a policy combination seeks an independent monetary policy

and a fixed exchange rate, but restrains the flow of capital. The government can effectively control all kinds of transnational capital flows and forms a completely closed capital market, so as to remove the influence of the international capital market on domestic interest rates and also rule out the possibility of a shock brought about by currency speculation. The government can also freely use all kinds of flexible domestic economic policies to make timely and effective adjustment to the economy, but at the cost of strict capital controls.

(3) Free capital flows B + fixed exchange rate C + dependent monetary policy a. In this situation, the capital market is completely open, and adopts a fixed exchange rate. This will render domestic monetary policy ineffective. The domestic interest rate is not decided by supply and demand in the domestic currency market. Because capital can flow freely, minor changes in domestic interest rates will lead to interest rate arbitrage between domestic and foreign capital. Ultimately, domestic and international interest rates converge. The main cost is that the government has to give up a flexible monetary policy to adjust overall domestic demand and to keep a stable economy. For example, when there is inflation in the domestic currency, the government has to increase the interest rate to ease the situation, but at the same time this will bring capital inflows, which will put great pressure on the local currency to appreciate. In order to maintain a fixed exchange rate, the government has to sell local currency and buy foreign currency until the domestic and foreign interest rates are the same. Thus, monetary policy tends to be ineffective.

The Trilemma theory shows that, for any country, it is impossible to realize three objectives at the same time: free capital flows, a fixed exchange rate system and an independent monetary policy. A country may only choose two of these goals. For example, once a country allows free capital flows, it has to make a choice: whether to give up the independence of its monetary policy to maintain a fixed exchange rate, or to keep the independence of its monetary policy by allowing a floating exchange rate. This is because under the condition when the three objectives are satisfied, if the central bank in a country adopts an easy monetary policy, it will decrease local currency interest rates, raise capital outflows, and depreciate the currency. In order to maintain the stability of the exchange rate, the central bank has to intervene in the foreign exchange market, selling foreign currency and buying local currency, which will lead to an increasing local currency interest rate, and hence invalidate the monetary policy.

As a practical example, many Asian countries including Thailand and the Philippines during the 1997 Asian Financial Crisis, were under attack from huge amounts of hot money directed by George Soros. The countries experienced a massive devaluation in their currencies' exchange rates. Their central banks, in order to maintain the stability of their exchange rates, used foreign reserves to intervene in the foreign exchange market. Yet the scale of their foreign exchange markets was still not enough compared with the hot money. Finally, when their foreign reserves were used up, they could only let the massive devaluation of exchange rates continue unchecked. Their fixed exchange rate system collapsed, which further triggered a crisis of international payments. This example proved that any country can only choose one side of the impossible triangle when making its economic policy. The US, for instance, for a long time has allowed free capital flows and has maintained an independent monetary policy, but at the cost of an unstable exchange rate for the US Dollar.

Although the Trilemma is sound in theory, in practice there are more than three combinations of economic policy. In many cases, capital account controls and the exchange rate system are not absolutely open or controlled, but exist in a compromised state and are adjustable. Take Japan as an example. It has made many compromises in the practice of its economic policy. Before the 1970s, Japan adopted a fixed exchange rate system with strict capital controls and a highly protective policy towards its financial markets. Yet after WWII, its economic development triggered its first reform in its exchange rate system. Between 1971 and 1980, Japan's fixed exchange rate system was changed to a floating one with a controlled capital account. After the 1980s, Japan experienced stable economic development and adapted to a free floating exchange rate system, followed by Yen appreciation. In the beginning of this period, capital account controls were still kept. By the end of 1990s, when the new foreign exchange rate law was implemented, Japan had a liberal capital account. At the same time, with the development of its financial market, its interest rate was gradually marketized, and the financial markets began to open.

2.6.3 *The Trilemma in China*

As mentioned above, the theoretical framework of the Trilemma is based on a series of simplified presuppositions, including small countries and open economies. For China, a big developing country that is not totally open, although the Trilemma points out that the setting of the RMB exchange rate, management of capital flows and monetary policy are closely connected, it is still a research question whether the Trilemma can really apply to China.

Chinese scholars have also done some research on developing the Trilemma theory. For instance, Yi and Tang (2001) proposed the Extended Triangle Hypothesis, which features intermediate regimes. Shen and Shi (2002) tried to expand the impossible triangle model to a tetrahedral one by introducing the local currency's international debt capacity as a variable in the model, proving that the impossible triangle model is a special case of the tetrahedral model. On this basis, they hold that the choice of exchange rate system is a dynamic process and is simultaneously in coexistence with (and leans towards conversion to) many possible exchange rate systems, according to multiple factors. Li and Li (2009) proved in theory that, for capital flows, the optimum combination of exchange rate and monetary policy lies in the middle ground of the Trilemma. China should, they suggest, find a balanced point in this middle ground, so as to minimize overall losses inherent to an open economy. Yu (2009) held that we can choose a combination of policies, since in an equilateral triangle, the total perpendicular distances from any vertex to three sides equal to the height. The perpendicular distances can represent the degree of interdependence of monetary policy, the degree of capital flow controls, and the degree of exchange rate fluctuation. The model, as applied to China, is a combination of independent monetary policy, an increasing fluctuation in the exchange rate, and a gradual easing of capital controls. Weng and Zhang (2009) created an "expanded Trilemma" by drawing a line parallel to the base line: The upper smaller triangle represents the policy combination of "limited capital flows + independent monetary policy + managed floating exchange rate".

In my opinion, the three vertexes of the impossible triangle in the Trilemma actually represent three extreme situations: an absolute stable exchange rate, total control over capital flows and a completely independent monetary policy. But China has usually adopted a compromise during different periods, according to the needs of each particular situation.

Between 1994 and 1996, China's economic growth rate exceeded 10%. The economy was overheated, and there was an abnormal phenomenon of internal depreciation (increasing domestic inflation) and external appreciation (increasing exchange rate) of the RMB. Usually, during inflation the RMB would depreciate externally, but international payments surplus and market anticipation of an increase in the RMB's exchange rate led to a sustained appreciation. The rapid increase of foreign reserves brought fast increases in M2, causing conflict with the monetary policy objective of curbing inflation. In such circumstances, to reduce the pressures of inflation and to stabilize the price level, it is necessary to implement tighter monetary policy. But tight monetary policy would lead to a larger international payments surplus, further adding pressure for RMB appreciation. In order to ease this pressure, it was necessary to ease monetary policy, increase domestic needs and imports, and reduce the trade deficit. But with these measures, it was difficult to control inflation. So to achieve both a stable exchange rate and monetary policy goals, the government had to appropriately relax capital controls. Thus, at the end of 1996, China completely opened its current account.

Between 1997 and 2000, the aftermath of the Asian Financial Crisis gradually affected China, starting from the beginning of 1998. In May 1998, China's capital account had its first deficit since 1993. Due to the increasing gap between the relatively high RMB interest rate and relatively low US interest rates, domestic companies and individuals found strong motivations to hold foreign currency. Foreign reserves decreased dramatically, and the RMB faced great pressure towards depreciation. At the same time, there was deflation in China's economy (Cheng, 2002). At this time, to promote fast economic development and ease deflation, it was suggested that China adopt an easy monetary policy, which could lead to RMB depreciation and affect the surrounding Southeast Asian countries by creating a new round in the currency crisis. Instead, to maintain the stability of the RMB exchange rate, it was necessary to adopt a tight monetary policy and increase capital flow controls.

Between 2003 and 2007, after China's 2001 entry into the WTO, its foreign trade increased rapidly. In particular, its exports saw huge increases alongside large current account surpluses. The economic growth rate of China's economy was over 10%, and reached 13% in 2007. However, the economy was overheating and the abnormal phenomenon of internal depreciation and external appreciation occurred (Cheng, 2007). In order to reduce the pressure of inflation and stabilize the price level, it was necessary to adopt a tight monetary policy. But a tight monetary policy led to an even larger international payments surplus and, thus, more pressure for RMB appreciation. In the face of a "double surplus" of international payments, in order to keep a stable RMB exchange rate, the central bank was forced to intervene by sterilizing foreign reserves. However constant, large international payments surpluses greatly weakened the effectiveness of sterilization. Domestic excess liquidity further increased the pressure for inflation. Therefore, China eased its financial control of its capital accounts, such as QFII. Moreover, since July 21, 2005, China began a managed floating exchange rate system based on market supply and demand, adjusting it in reference to a basket of currencies. This reform in fact eased the target of maintaining the stability of the RMB exchange rate and facilitated gradual RMB appreciation.

In early 2008, to cope with overheated economic growth, China adopted a tight monetary policy. But because of the expansion of the financial crisis — triggered by the US subprime crisis — China's monetary policy was forced to reverse, becoming a moderately loose monetary policy. In 2009, total bank credit increased by RMB9.6 trillion. This policy lasted until 2012, and was changed to a more prudent monetary policy in 2013. At the same time, the reform of the RMB exchange rate stagnated for a period. On June 19, 2010, the PBOC announced the re-launching of exchange rate system reform. The 18th National Congress of the Communist Party of China clearly put forward a plan to realize the convertibility of the RMB capital account. The opening of the capital account is an issue a country has to face alongside its economic development and integration into the world economy. It is an inevitable demand of all-round participation in global competition. In particular, when the current account is convertible, with the deepening of reform and opening up, the effectiveness of capital flow controls will continue to decrease. The opening of the capital account is an inevitable result of a country's economic globalization. It is a long-term objective for China's exchange rate management system to realize the total convertibility of the RMB, including the current account and the capital account. Of the 43 capital trading accounts delineated by the IMF, nearly half of the capital account transaction types in China are basically unlimited or have few limits. Over 40% have significant limits and only over 10% are under strict control. In terms of FDI, China's degree of openness is even sometimes higher than some developed countries. China's capital inflows are very large. At the end of 2012, China's foreign debt balance (excluding Hong Kong, Macau and Taiwan) reached USD$736.9 billion. This figure was only USD$184.8 billion in 2001 when China entered the WTO. On the other hand, capital outflows are increasing year by year. In 2012, the net amount of China's outward FDI (OFDI) totaled USD$87.8 billion. Between 2002 and 2012, China's OFDI increased for a consecutive ten years, and OFDI in 2012 increased 17.6% compared with 2011. The scale of capital flows increased constantly, basically forming a pattern of bi-directional transnational capital flows. It is becoming more difficult for China to control its capital account, which is of course an inevitable result of China's gradual opening of the account. Therefore, from a long-term perspective, it is China's inevitable choice to realize free capital flows.

In today's open economy, economic globalization is deepening, and the economy of every country is increasingly more connected with the wider world economy. If a country wants to ease its capital control and realize free capital flows, while also maintaining the independence of monetary policy, it can only choose a floating exchange rate system. If the RMB is to be internationalized, it requires opening of the capital account and free capital flows. Since China is a big country, during the process of the RMB's internationalization it has to maintain the independence of its monetary policy, which decides the necessity of reforming the past rigid exchange rate system. The current reform of exchange rate system will create favorable conditions for the internationalization of the RMB.

Bibliography

In English

Alesina A. (1988). Credibility and Policy Convergence in a Two-party System with Rational Voters. *The American Economic Review*, 78(4): 796–805.

Artus J. R. and Young J. H. (1979). Fixed and Flexible Exchange Rates: A Renewal of the Debate. *IMF Staff Papers*, 26(4): 654–698.

Bonomo M. and Terra C. (2005). Elections and exchange rate policy cycles. *Economics & Politics*, 17(2): 151–176.

Bordo, M. D. (2004). Exchange Rate Regimes for the 21st Century: A Historical Perspective. *Proceedings of OeNB Workshops*, 64–89.

Cohen B. J. (2012). The Benefits and Costs of an International Currency: Getting the Calculus Right. *Open Economies Review*, 23(1): 13–31.

Combes J. L., Kinda T. and Plane P. (2012). Capital Flows, Exchange Rate Flexibility, and the Real Exchange Rate. *Journal of Macroeconomics*, 34(4): 1034–1043.

Elbadawi I. and Soto R. (1994). Capital Flows and Long-Term Equilibrium Real Exchange Rates in Chile. Policy Research Working Papers 1306. Washington D.C.: World Bank.

Fleming J. M. (1962). Domestic Financial Policies under Fixed and under Floating Exchange Rates. *Staff Papers-International Monetary Fund*, 9(3): 369–380.

Frankel J. A. (1999). No Single Currency Regime Is Right for All Countries or at All Times. NBER Working Paper No. 7338.

Frieden J. A. (1991). Invested Interests: the Politics of National Economic Policies in a World of Global Finance. *International Organization*, 45(04): 425–451.

Friedman M. (1953). The Case for Flexible Exchange Rates. In Friedman M., *Essays in Positive Economics*, 159–205. Chicago: University of Chicago Press.

IMF (1993). *Balance of Payment* Manual, 5th edition. Washington D.C.: International Monetary Fund.

Kindleberger C. P. (1972). The benefits of international money. *Journal of International Economics*, 2(4): 425–442.

Kosteletou N. and Liargovas P. (2000). Foreign Direct Investment and Real Exchange Rate Interlinkages. *Open Economies Review*, 11(2): 135–148.

Krugman P. (1979). A model of balance-of-payments crises. *Journal of money, credit and banking*, 11(3): 311–325.

Macdonald R. (1988). *Floating Exchange Rates: Theories and Evidence.* London: Unwin Hyman.

Mundell R. A. (1963). Capital mobility and stabilization policy under fixed and flexible exchange rates. *The Canadian Journal of Economics and Political Science/Revue canadie'ned'Economiqueet de Science politique*, 29(4): 475–485.

O'Driscoll Jr G. P. and Hoskins L. (2004). China: Just Say No to Monetary Protectionism. *Free Trade Bulletin*, 6: 15.

Park Y. C. and Wyplosz C. (2008). Monetary and Financial Integration in East Asia: The Relevance of European Experience. *Economic Papers 329*, Directorate-General for Economic and Financial Affairs, European Commission.

Parsley D. C. and Wei S. J. (2007). A Prism into the PPP Puzzles: The Micro–Foundations of Big Mac Real Exchange Rates. *The Economic Journal*, 117(523): 1336–1356.

Pilbeam K. (1998). *International Finance*, 2nd edition. London: Macmillan. Obstfeld M. (1984). Balance-of-Payments Crises and Devaluation. *Journal of Money, Credit and Banking*, 16(2): 208–217. Summers L. H. (2004). The US Current Account Deficit and the Global Economy. *Per Jacobsson Foundation Lecture.* Washington D.C.: Per Jacobsson Foundation.

In Chinese

Asian Development Bank. (2000). *Monetary and Financial Integration in East Asia.* Beijing: Economic Science Press.

Bai Q. X. and Liu G. (2010). The Root Causes of the Game of the China–US Exchange Rate, Process and Impact. *Wuhan Finance Monthly*, 2010(009): 4–8.

Cao X. J. (2013). Analysis of Ways American Interest Groups Press for RMB Appreciation. *Foreign Affairs Review*, 2: 30–46.

Cheng S. W. (2002). Deflation Theoretical Analysis and the Practical Problems of China. Reproduced in *Causes and Countermeasures: Dialysis China's Deflation.* Beijing: Economic Science Press.

Cheng S. W. (2003). *Fictitious Economy Theory.* Beijing: Democracy and Construction Press.

Cheng S. W. (2005). Probing into the Details of Fictitious Economy. *Management Review*, 17(1): 3–8.

Cheng S. W. (2007). A Simple Explanation of China's Current Three "Abnormal" Financial Phenomena. *Financial News*, First Edition.

Cheng S. W. (2009). *Economic Reform and Development in China*, Beijing: China Renmin University Press.

Cheng S. W. (2010a). The Next Step of the RMB Exchange Rate Regime Reform to Establish a Flexible Exchange Rate Target Area with Double Layer (I). *Economic Affairs*, 1: 4–10.

Cheng S. W. (2010b). The Next Step of the RMB Exchange Rate Regime Reform to Establish a Flexible Exchange Rate Target Area with Double Layer (II). *Economic Affairs*, 2: 4–14.

Cheng S. W. (2011). *Analysis and Enlightenment of American Financial Crisis.* Beijing: Science Press.

Cheng S. W. (2004). Deflation Theoretical Analysis and Practical Problems Facing. *China Science Technology Daily*, 11-0078.

Gu Y., Gao T. M. and Fu X. W. (2008). RMB Exchange Rate Equilibrium Level and Short-term Fluctuations under the Background of International Capital Flows. *Journal of Financial Research*, 5: 1–13.

Hashimoto T. L. (1997). *Japan's Economic — The 20th Century System and the Japanese Economy.* Shanghai: Shanghai University of Finance and Economics Press.

He X. Q. (2006). American Interest Groups and Pressure of RMB Appreciation. *Contemporary Asia-Pacific Studies*, 3: 50–57.

Hu T. and Zhang S. M. (2006). The Mechanism Analysis of the Relationship between the China Interest Rate Marketing and Its Exchange Rate. *Finance and Economy*, 9: 70–73.

Huang S. (2006). The Research of RMB Exchange Rate Factors and Trend. *Special Zone Economy*, 11: 12–14.

Huang Z. G. (2009). Foreign Direct Investment, Trade Surplus and the Exchange Rate. *The Journal of World Economy*, 4: 3–14.

Jiang B. K. and Li H. D. (2006). Theoretical Literature Review of Equilibrium Exchange Rate. *Contemporary Finance & Economics*, 2: 44–50.

Jiang B. K. and Mo T. (2009). A Modification of Balassa Exchange Rate Theory. *Journal of Financial Research*, 10: 1–6.

Jiang M. Z. (2013). *Interest Groups and the U.S. Exchange Rate Policy Adjustment.* Jilin: Jilin University Press.

Jin Z. X. (2000). The Interaction between China's Exchange Rate, Interest Rate and Balance of Payments: 1981–1999. *The Journal of World Economy*, 23(9): 19–24.

Kong L. Z. and Qi B. Y. (2010). The Exchange Rate Interval Decision Based on AHP Target Rate. *Journal of Educational Institute of Jilin Province*, 10: 136–137.

Kuang M. and Wang H. (2007). Political Factors that Affect Exchange Rate Regime Choice — Empirical Analysis of Emerging Markets in East Asia and Latin America. *Studies of International Finance*, 10: 26–33.

Li C. and Li Y. (2009). Institutional Arrangement of China's Economy According to the Non-Corner Solutions of Trilemma. *Journal of Xi'an University of Finance and Economics*, 22(3): 10–16.

Li Z. G. and Li T. (2007). Political Analysis of China–US Exchange Rate Debate. *Journal of Graduate School of Chinese Academy of Social Sciences*, 3: 72–77.

Li Z. L. (2011). Politics and Exchange Rate: The Political Economy Analysis of RMB Appreciation. *World Economics and Politics*, 9: 136–155.

Li Z. R., Cheng S. W., Zu L., Zhang J. and Wang S. Y. (2010). Can RMB Appreciation Really Reduce the US Unemployment Rate. *Journal of Financial Research*, 8: 68–80.

Liu J. M. and Wang G. Z. (2005). A Study of Exchange Rate Theory on Fictitious Economy Theory Perspective. *Economic Theory and Business Management*, 1: 24–30.

Liu T. and Jin H. F. (2012). Political Economic Study on Exchange Rates: A Literature Review. *World Economic Papers*, 1: 106–120.

Lv Y. C. and Zhou J. N. (2004). *Guide to the World States — Brazil*. Beijing: China Social Sciences Press.

Shen G. B. and Shi J. C. (2002). Choice of Exchange Rate Regime: Impossible Triangle and Its Extensions. *World Economy*, 10: 3–9.

Song G. X. and Sheng Y. F. (2003). 1980s the Revelation from the International Exchange Rate Coordination. *Economic Herald*, 2003(10): 54–56.

The United Nations Conference on Trade and Development. World Investment Report (2008–2012), http://www.unctad.org. 2009: 09–12.

Wang S. H. and Hu F. (2007). China's Short-term International Capital Flows: The Present Situation, the Flow Path and Factors. *The Journal of World Economy*, 7: 12–19.

Wang X. G., Fan C. L. and Dai F. (2012). An Empirical Study of the Effect of the Structure of China's Foreign Exchange Capital Flows Towards the Real Effective Exchange Rate, *Journal of Financial Research*, 4: 71–82.

Wei H. (2002). The Views of American Scholars about China's Socialist Market Economy both the Left Wing and Right Wing. *Theoretical Reference*, 1: 008.

Wen J. D. (2005). The Research of Purchasing Power Parity of RMB. *Journal of Financial Research*, 4: 44–56.

Weng G. M. and Zhang G. Q. (2009). Further Understanding of the Trilemma Theory. *Times Finance* 04: 27–29.

Xu J. J. and Wen X. Q. (2007). Summary of PPP Theory. *Commercial Times*, 29: 33–34.

Yang C. J. and Zhong N. H. (2012). PPP and Equilibrium Exchange Rate. *Journal of Financial Research*, 1: 36–50.

Yi G. and Tang X. (2001). A Theoretical Foundation for the "Corner Solutions" Hypothesis of Exchange Rate Regimes. *Journal of Financial Research*, 08: 5–17.

Yu Y. D. (2012). Short-term Capital Flows Exacerbate Renminbi Exchange Rate Fluctuations. *China Securities Journal*, 2012-02-03A04.

Yu L. (2009). The Independence of China's Monetary Policy from the View of "Trilemma". Times Finance, (06): 6–7.

Zeng X. J. (2013). The path analyze of pressure that American interest groups put on RMB appreciation. *Foreign Affairs Review*, 2: 30–46..

Zhang K. (2008). Impact of International Capital Flows on the RMB Exchange Rate. Xi'an University of Technology Ph.D. dissertation.

Zhang Q. S. and Kong L. Z. (2010). Exchange Rate Determination Based on the Power of Paradigm. *Economic Research Journal*, 45(3): 104–113.

Zhang X. P. (1999). Theories and Models of RMB Equilibrium Exchange Rate. *Economic Research Journal*, 12: 70–77.

Zhang X. P. (2000). The Latest Evolution of Purchasing Power Parity and Its Application in the RMB Exchange Rate. *The Journal of World Economy*, 9: 10–18.

Zheng L. S. (2009). Hamburgers and RMB Appreciation. *Teahouse for Economists*, 6: 68–72.

Zhou D. E., Qiu C. and Jia R. D. (2011). The Research of RMB Exchange Rate Movements and the International Balance of Payments. *Prices Monthly*, 8: 84–87.

Zhou X. P. (2006). Political Economy of Exchange Rate Policy in Latin America — Comment on Political Economy of International Finance. *Social Sciences Abroad*, 3: 008.

Zhu M. N. and Liu L. (2010). Short-term International Capital Flows, Exchange Rates and Asset Prices — An Empirical Study Based on Data after the Exchange Rate Reform. *Finance & Trade Economics*, 5: 5–13, 135.

Zou W. W. (2010). *Historical Development and Policy Game of China–US Economic and Trade Relations*. Chengdu: Southwestern University of Finance and Economics Press.

Chapter 3

The Choice of Exchange Rate Arrangement — Empirical Analysis

The exchange rate arrangement is an important part of a government's exchange rate policy. It provides an institutional framework of specific measures to influence exchange rate changes. Under different exchange rate arrangements, the government should follow different rules to realize a balanced economic target, indicating the central position of the exchange rate arrangement in national exchange rate policy.

3.1 Changes in the Classification of Exchange Rate Arrangements

3.1.1 *Changes in the International Exchange Rate Regime*

In the last 60 years, the international exchange rate regime has transformed from the adjustable or exogenous fixed exchange rate regime under the Bretton Woods system to a mixed exchange rate regime under the so-called "Jamaica System". During the process of international exchange rate changes, the International Monetary Fund (IMF) has also transformed from a mutual-aid organization tasked with maintaining a fixed exchange rate regime among member countries, providing financial aid for deficit countries, and building a multilateral payment system into the current monitoring organization responsible for safeguarding international financial stability. To adapt to changes in the international economic climate and exchange rate regime, and taking into consideration that the international exchange rate regime should play a guiding role, the IMF has been continuously adjusting its classification methods for exchange rate arrangements. From 1950 to 1978, the IMF compiled its *Annual Report on Exchange Rate* (ARER) and, since 1979, it has compiled the *Annual Report on Exchange Arrangements and Exchange Restrictions* (AREAER). In these two annual report series, amounting to 63 annual reports from 1950 to 2012, the IMF has classified the exchange rate arrangements of each member country based on set methods.

3.1.1.1 *The Adjustable Fixed Exchange Rate Regime under the Bretton Woods System*

In July 1944, 44 Allied nations attended the International Monetary Conference in Bretton Woods, New Hampshire, United States. During the conference, the *Bretton Woods Agreement* was officially passed, building the international monetary system upon the Bretton Woods system framework. The Agreement included: (1) The United States would link and peg the Dollar to gold, promising that each central bank could exchange dollars for gold at the rate of USD$35 per ounce of gold; (2) other currencies were linked to the Dollar at a fixed rate and each government promised to freely exchange their currency with the Dollar, with their monetary authorities maintaining exchange rates within plus or minus 1% through intervention in their foreign exchange markets; (3) the IMF would arrange and monitor each country's exchange rate for compliance with the new adjustable fixed exchange rate regime under the "dollar-gold" standard. Only when member countries experienced a "fundamental imbalance of payment" were they authorized to adjust their currency's fixed parity with the Dollar.

Since the 1960s, however, America has become powerless in maintaining the fixed exchange due to the increasing pressure of capital outflows. In fact, starting from 1960, America's gold reserve has been less than its external floating debt. Moreover, financial innovation intensified both in breadth and depth and each government started to loosen capital controls, forming a trend of financial liberalization. At last, under the attack of a large amount of international short-term, speculative capital flows, the adjustable fixed exchange rate regime under the Bretton Woods system became mired in difficulties. On August 15, 1971, US president Nixon announced the end of gold-to-dollar convertibility. Delinking the Dollar from gold meant that a major pillar of Bretton Woods collapsed. On March 19, 1973, due to the continuous devaluation of the Dollar and a series of crises, six European Economic Community (EEC) countries decided to allow their currencies to float. This marked the end of the dollar-centric adjustable fixed exchange rate regime, the gold standard, and the Bretton Woods system in general.

3.1.1.2 *Mixed Exchange Rate Regime under the Jamaica System*

During the IMF interim committee meeting, held in Jamaica in January 1976, attending countries passed the *Jamaica Agreement*, which created a new floating exchange rate regime From that time, the international monetary system started to embrace the Jamaica System. According to the *Jamaica Agreement*, IMF member countries are free to choose their own exchange rate arrangements. In particular, IMF member countries can: (1) link currencies with the IMF's Special Drawing Rights (SDRs), other major currencies or a basket of currencies (excluding gold); (2) establish currency cooperation arrangements; (3) maintain their chosen exchange rate arrangements, including floating exchange rates. The Jamaica System was innovative in its understanding of exchange rate regimes, espousing two policy directives. "First, seek exchange rate stability through basic monetary policies and financial policies instead of pegging. Second, the floating of an exchange rate should be a process strictly monitored by the IMF" (Edwards, 1996).

Unlike the fixed exchange rate regime under the gold standard or the adjustable fixed exchange rate regime the Jamaica System is basically a uniform and complete international exchange rate regime. Each country chooses an exchange rate regime based on their specific economic situation (their internal and external economic environments) and other relevant factors. Therefore, the international exchange rate regime under the Jamaica System is a mixed exchange rate regime that offers a co-existence of multiple exchange rate arrangements while also attending to regional monetary cooperation. For example, developed countries basically have adopted a floating exchange rate regime, and others, like those belonging to the European Monetary System (EMS), have adopted a combined floating exchange rate regime. However a majority of developing countries have adopted a fixed or pegged exchange rate regime, with some even forming a common monetary zone (as in the case of the African Financial Community or CFA) and others opting for a floating exchange rate regime.

3.1.2 *Study of IMF Exchange Rate Arrangement Classifications*

3.1.2.1 De jure *Classification*

Before the 1990s, the IMF's classifications of exchange rate arrangements had not caused much debate. Each government registered their exchange rate policies and regimes with the IMF. This cooperation with the IMF, and subsequent classification of a country's exchange rate arrangements, has become a statutory method and is based on data made public by each participating government. This method is known as *de jure* classification.

The advantage of the *de jure* classification system lies in its authoritative data, the wide scope of countries it covers, its use over a long time span and its frequent and timely updates. Moreover, if a country follows its statutory exchange rate regime, then that regime can be treated as a good reference indicator of the future performance of its exchange rate. However, the *de facto* exchange rate regime implemented by each country is not reflected by the *de jure* classification. First, countries announcing implementation of a pegged exchange rate regime always implement (in order to strengthen their export competiveness) additional monetary devaluation policies not in conformity with the definition of a fixed exchange rate regime. Further, due to changes in the exchange rates of pegged currencies, their exchange rate regimes behave more closely to flexible exchange rate arrangements. Second, countries announcing implementation of a floating exchange rate regime frequently intervene in the exchange market due to fear over currency trends or to control inflation, making their exchange rate regimes behave similar to pegged exchange rate arrangements. For example, Obstfeld and Rogoff (1995) found out that without considering capital controls, only six major economies had adopted the pegged exchange rate regime over a six-year period. In addition, Reinhart and Rogoff (2004) pointed out that after the 1980s, over half *de jure* floating exchange rate regimes were actually pegged regimes and nearly half of *de jure* pegged exchange rate regimes were floating regimes (Wei and Wang, 2011).

3.1.2.2 De facto *Classification*

After the 1990s, the contrast between the *de jure* and *de facto* exchange rate classifications gradually became acute. The issue of classification caused frequent debates. In response, in 1999 the IMF started to adopt the *de facto* classification method based on the *de jure* exchange rate regime of each member country. This involved classifying exchange rate arrangements based on the policy intentions of monetary authorities and the degree of flexibility in a currency's exchange rate. The IMF segmented the original classifications into three categories and eight sub-categories, collected data exchange rate policies announced by each government, and also considered each government's real policy intentions (Wei *et al.*, 2011).

Since 1999, the international economic situation and financial order have been transforming, especially since the 2008 financial crisis, which caused great changes in the international economic environment. To adapt to these changes, and taking into consideration that the international exchange rate regime should play a guiding role, the IMF has been continuously adjusting its classification methods of exchange rate arrangements. We have analyzed 12 AREAERs compiled by the IMF from 1999 to 2010 and found that the IMF made micro adjustment to the *de facto* classifications in 2007 and greatly revised the *de facto* classification in 2009. Specifically, they reorganized the original three categories (and eight subcategories) into three categories plus one other category (with ten subcategories in all). What is worth mentioning is that, since 2001, the IMF has classified both the monetary policy frameworks of member countries and their exchange rate arrangements. The IMF thought doing so would be conducive to evaluating the impact of exchange rate arrangement choices on monetary policy independence, ultimately displaying how different exchange rate arrangements are compatible with one monetary policy framework.

The IMF's *de facto* classification is only a representative of various *de facto* classification schemes. In fact, the boundaries between different exchange rate regimes are not very clear and many researchers have put forward alternative classification schemes, such as Bubula and Otker-Robe's scheme (2002), Ghosh's consistent classification (Ghosh *et al.*, 2002), RR natural classification (Reinhart and Rogoff, 2004), DLM mixed classification (Dubas *et al.*, 2005), LYS classification (Levy-Yeyati and Strurzenegger, 2003, 2005) and CD classification (Coudert and Dubert, 2004). Due to different theoretical assumptions, classification schemes and the measurement factors of various *de facto* classifications, their results differ greatly. In actual study, researchers always choose a proper exchange rate arrangements based on their research content. And when there is no proper choice, they provide their classification results as merely basic research. Compared with *de jure* classifications, these *de facto* classifications can theoretically reflect the real-world situation, however, they are classified ex post facto based on statistical methods, especially exchange rate performance, and therefore they are not appropriate in analyzing future trends of exchange rate arrangements.

The current *de facto* classifications have their own characteristic advantages and disadvantages. Among these, the IMF's *de facto* classification is the most authoritative with the best most continuous data. The

IMF's AREAER provides annual updates on both *de jure* and *de facto* classifications. As for other *de facto* classifications, the PR classification data series has been updated to 2007, LYS classification has received no updates since October 2005 and other classifications have all stopped updating their data series. Users must themselves compile and calculate data series on these classifications (Levy-Yeyati, 2006; Levy-Yeyati and Sturzenegger, 2003, 2005). But since the IMF's *de facto* classification is greatly dependent on officially announced exchange rate policies, it is subjective and is difficult to apply consistently to judging different countries in different time periods.

(I) 1999–2008 IMF *De facto* Classification

Due to flaws in the original exchange rate arrangement classification and the birth of the Euro (starting from January 1, 1999), the IMF has proposed new classifications based on *de facto* exchange rate regimes instead of officially announced exchange rate arrangements. The following explains the categories (Shen and Liu, 2001):

(1) Arrangements with no separate legal tender (NS): The currency of another country circulates as the sole legal tender or the member belongs to a monetary or currency union in which the same legal tender is shared by the members of the union, including dollarization and currency union.
(2) Currency board arrangements (CBAs): A monetary regime based on an explicit legislative commitment to exchange domestic currency for a specified foreign currency at a fixed exchange rate, combined with restrictions on the issuing authority to ensure the fulfillment of its legal obligation.
(3) Other conventional fixed peg (FP) arrangements: The exchange rate may fluctuate within narrow margins of less than $\pm 1\%$ around a central rate, including a peg to a single currency at a fixed rate, a peg to a currency basket and a peg to SDR.
(4) Pegged exchange rate within a horizontal band (HB). The value of the currency is maintained within certain margins (fluctuation of at least $\pm 1\%$ around a fixed central rate), such as the ERM under the EMS.
(5) Crawling pegs (CP). The currency is adjusted periodically in small amounts at a fixed rate or in response to changes in selective quantitative indicators.
(6) Exchange rates within crawling bands (CBs). The currency is maintained within certain fluctuation margins, and the central rate or

margins are adjusted periodically at a fixed rate or in response to changes in selective quantitative indicators.

(7) Managed floating (MF) with no predetermined path for the exchange rate. The monetary authority attempts to influence the exchange rate without having a specific exchange rate path or target. Indicators for managing the rate include the balance of payments position, international reserves, parallel market developments and automatic adjustments.

(8) Independent floating (IF). The exchange rate is market-determined, with any official foreign exchange market intervention aimed at moderating the rate of change and preventing undue fluctuations in the exchange rate, rather than at establishing a level for it.

(II) The IMF's Latest *De facto* Classification, 2009

The IMF put forward the latest exchange rate arrangement classifications in 2009, dividing international exchange rate regimes into three classes and one residual term (ten categories in all): Hard peg exchange rate regimes (including NS and CBAs); soft pegs (including conventional pegs, stabilized arrangements (SAs), CP, and crawl-like, pegged exchange rates within HBs); floating exchange rate regimes (including floating exchange rates and free floating (FF) rates); and residual term regimes (other managed exchange rate arrangements) (Habermeier, 2009; Ding and Sun, 2009).

3.2 The IMF's Latest *De facto* Classification Study

3.2.1 *New and Old* De facto *Classifications*

According to the AREAER compiled by the IMF, the new and old *de facto* classifications from 1998 to 2009 are listed in Table 3.1. For clarity, Section 3.2 studies the IMF's exchange rate regime classifications. All years mentioned in this section refer to years in the AREAER.

3.2.1.1 *1999–2008 IMF* De facto *Classifications*

From 1999 to 2008, the IMF divided exchange rate regime classifications into three categories, eight sub-categories in all based on exchange rate flexibility: Hard peg exchange rate arrangements (including NS and CBAs); soft peg exchange rate arrangements (including conventional pegs, pegged exchange rates within HBs, CPs and CBs) and floating exchange rate arrangements (including MF with no predetermined exchange rate target and IF), as shown in Figure 3.1.

Table 3.1: IMF Exchange Rate Regime *De facto* Classifications

IMF Exchange Rate Arrangements Classification from November 1998 to January 2009 (micro adjustment in 2007)	IMF Exchange Rate Arrangements April 2009 till Today (the latest *de facto* classification)
I. Hard Peg Exchange Rate Arrangements	**I. Hard Peg Exchange Rate Arrangements**
Exchange Arrangements with NS (1) The currency of another country circulates as the sole legal tender or the member belongs to a monetary or currency union in which the same legal tender is shared by the members of the union, including dollarization and currency union. (2) CBA. A monetary regime based on an explicit legislative commitment to exchange domestic currency for a specified foreign currency at a fixed exchange rate, combined with restrictions on the issuing authority to ensure the fulfillment of its legal obligation.	(1) Exchange Arrangements with NS. Unchanged. (2) CBA. Unchanged.
II. Soft Peg Exchange Rate Arrangements	**II. Soft Peg Exchange Rate Arrangements**
(3) FP. The exchange rate may fluctuate within narrow margins of less than ±1% around a central rate, including peg to a single currency at a fixed rate, peg to currency basket and peg to SDR of combined currency. Each country's currency exchange rates are calculated at some certain accepted currency units. The currency exchange rates would be basically fixed or the government would promise to limit the rate fluctuation within small range (less than ±1%). (4) Pegged exchange rate within HB. This differs from the third group in that the fluctuation band is wider than 1%. (5) CP. The currency is adjusted periodically in small amounts at a fixed and predetermined rate or in indicators [around a central exchange rate of within ±1% (Sun, 2004)].	(3) FP. Unchanged. (4) SA. These entail a spot market exchange rate that remains within a margin of 2% for six months or more (with the exception of a specified number of outliers or step adjustments), and is not floating. The required margin of stability can be met either with respect to a single currency or a basket of currencies. In addition, the arrangement requires that the exchange rate remains stable as a result of official action and exchange rate fluctuation caused by government intervention must be controlled strictly within a margin of 2%. (5) CP. Unchanged. (6) Crawl-like arrangements (CLA). The exchange rate must remain within a narrow margin of 2% and higher than 1% (which is considered as the smallest fluctuation limit) relative to a statistically identified trend for six months or more (with the exception of a specified number of outliers or step adjustment) and the exchange rate arrangement cannot be considered as floating on the basis of crawling on the part of the central exchange rate. (7) Pegged exchange rate within HB. Unchanged.

(*Continued*)

Table 3.1: (*Continued*)

IMF Exchange Rate Arrangements Classification from November 1998 to January 2009 (micro adjustment in 2007)	IMF Exchange Rate Arrangements April 2009 till Today (the latest *de facto* classification)
(6) CB. The currency is adjusted periodically in small amounts at a fixed and predetermined rate or in response to changes in selective quantitative indicators (Shen and Liu, 2001).	**III. Other Managed Arrangements (OMA)**
III. Floating Exchange Rate Arrangements	(8) OMA. This residual term refers to any country's exchange rate arrangement which goes against any definitions included in the other nine. If a government frequently and irregularly intervenes on behalf of its exchange rate, its exchange rate regime falls under this classification.
(7) MF with no predetermined path for the exchange rate. Governments occasionally intervene in the exchange market and influence exchange rate fluctuation by open market operations and foreign exchange control, namely direct intervention; or they can have exchange rate adjustment and other economic policies and measures, namely indirect intervention.	**IV. Floating exchange rate arrangements**
(8) IF. The supply and demand relationship of the foreign exchange market determines the rate of home currency to a foreign currency. The exchange rate fluctuates freely to balance foreign exchange supply and demand and allow market clearing. That is to say, the *de jure* exchange rate adjusts internal and external shocks and the government should not have large amount of foreign reserves and intervene the foreign exchange market.	(9) Floating (F). Exchange rates are mostly determined by the market, unless there is adequate evidence to show that the current exchange rate stabilization is a non-governmental behavior, then exchange rate fluctuations must break the 2% of the SAs and CLAs (Xie *et al.*, 2010). Authorities can directly or indirectly intervene in the exchange rate market to mitigate exchange rate changes or prevent excessive exchange rate fluctuation, but the target of government intervention does not maintain a certain exchange rate level. In addition, indicators for governments to intervene exchange rates are obviously judgmental (such as balance of payments, international currency reserve and the market development balance). Certain exchange rate fluctuation would appear under floating exchange rate regimes, which are related to economic shocks.

(*Continued*)

Table 3.1: (*Continued*)

IMF Exchange Rate Arrangements Classification from November 1998 to January 2009 (micro adjustment in 2007)	IMF Exchange Rate Arrangements April 2009 till Today (the latest *de facto* classification)
	(10) FF. This requires more strict discipline regarding the exchange rate than the floating arrangement. Countries under this classification can only intervene when the market is out of order. And governments can only intervene at most three times in a six-month period, with each time not exceeding three business days. Moreover, monetary authorities must provide related information or data to prove they meet the conditions of FF; if not, they will be classified under the floating arrangement.

Data source: AREAER (IMF, 1999–2009).

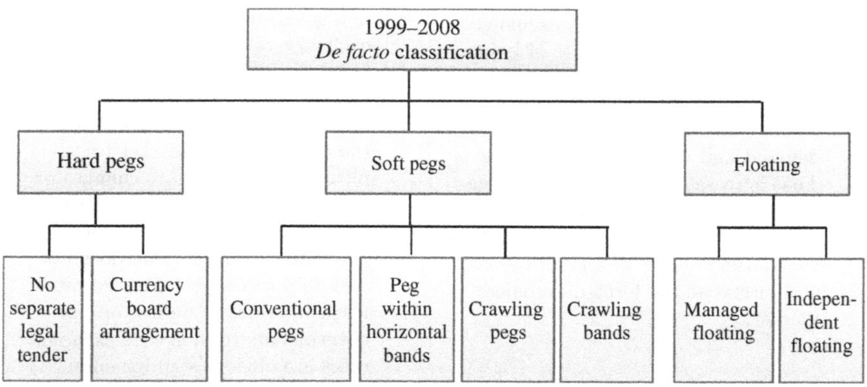

Figure 3.1: 1999–2008 IMF Exchange Rate Arrangement

In 2007, the IMF emphasized in the AREAER that its classification system was based on the real *de facto* arrangements of each member country. It deemed its classifications acceptable, though they differed from some announced arrangements of member countries. The classifications were based on exchange rate flexibility and various formal and informal promises made by countries regarding their exchange rate. Also in that year, the IMF made its first micro adjustment on the *de facto* classification, which had four aspects as follows:

(1) Adjustment to the classifications of exchange rates in a monetary union with NS. From 1999 to 2006, countries joining a monetary union were classified matter-of-factly as exchange rates with NS, based on the fact that such countries shared the same legal tender. In 2007, however, the IMF changed their classification criteria to include the exchange rate performance of linked currencies in a monetary union. In this way, exchange rate regimes such as the Eurozone, Africa's Franc zone and the East Caribbean Currency Union were classified into IF, conventional peg and CBAs (Ding and Sun, 2009). From 1999 to 2006, countries adopting IF exchange rate regimes dropped from 48 to 26, down 46%. However, after the classification adjustments in 2007, such countries have increased to 36. This adjustment is evidence that the IMF advocates a floating exchange rate regime and shows the guiding role of the IMF in international exchange rate regimes.
(2) Narrowing of the requirements for conventional pegs. Before the adjustment, the observation period of governments' restrictions on exchange rates within a very tight bad ($\pm 1\%$) was at least three months. After the adjustment, the observation period was extended to six months.
(3) Relaxation of the requirements for CPs. A CP originally meant that a government periodically adjusted a currency peg in small amounts at a fixed rate within $\pm 1\%$ to realize the gradual devaluation or appreciation of a single currency or a basket of currencies. In 2007, the requirement was relaxed and extended to *de facto* CPs. Thus, the currency authority can make exchange rate changes through intervention according to the above requirements for up to six months in a row, so long as it does not announce this exchange rate target and make any policy promises.
(4) Clarification about the direction of CPs. In its original definition, a CP's direction (devaluation or appreciation) was allowed to change. After 2007, however, such reversals in a peg's direction were reclassified as MF arrangements. (This includes the situation of setting a valid exchange rate as the standard of devaluation or appreciation, which may cause a reversal of direction in the *de jure* exchange rate.)

3.2.1.2 *The IMF's Latest Exchange Rate Arrangement Classification, 2009*

With changes in the international economic environment and financial order, the IMF's original *de facto* classification has been facing obvious challenges, especially in the following two aspects. First, under the old *de facto* classification, the exchange rate regimes included in other items of "MF with no predetermined path for the exchange rate" varied greatly. Classifying them together generally violates the basic principle of avoiding ambiguity between classifications. Second, the intervention measures of individual governments became more and more complicated, making it increasingly harder to acquire complete data on exchange rate interventions. A scarcity of data has left the IMF unable to precisely classify exchange rate arrangements (Wei *et al.*, 2011).

Therefore, in 2009 the IMF made extensive revisions to its original definitions when issuing the latest exchange rate arrangement classifications. These comprise three categories plus one residual item (ten sub-categories in all) including: Hard peg exchange rate regimes (including states with NS and CBAs); soft pegs (including conventional pegs, SAs, CPs, crawl-like pegs and pegged exchange rates within HBs); floating exchange rate regimes (including floating exchange rates and FF rates) and other items (other managed exchange rate arrangements). These are shown in Figure 3.2.

3.2.1.3 *Comparison of New and Old IMF* De facto *Classifications*

(I) Specific Revisions in the Classifications

After it greatly revised and adjusted the exchange rate arrangement classifications in 2009, the IMF continued using the 2009 *de facto* classification in its 2010 annual report. By comparing the new IMF *de facto* classifications

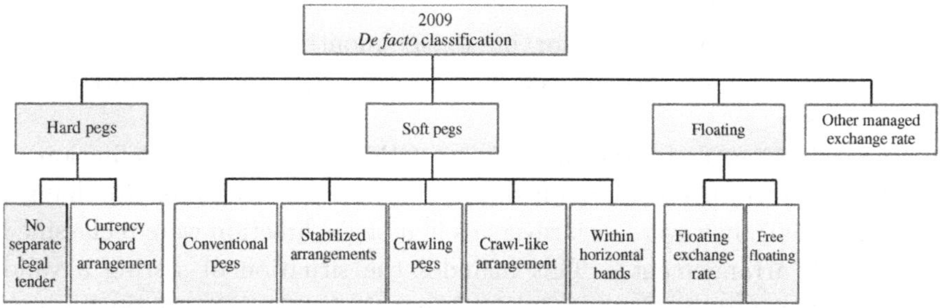

Figure 3.2: 2009 IMF Exchange Rate Arrangements

Table 3.2: Comparison between 1999–2008 Old *De facto* Classifications and 2009–2010 New *De facto* Classifications

	Old 1999–2008 *De facto* Classifications	New 2009–2010 *De facto* Classifications
Hard Pegs	Exchange rates with no NS	Exchange rates with NS
	CBA	CBA
Soft Pegs	Conventional peg arrangement (FP)	Conventional peg arrangement (FP)
		SA
	CP	CP
		CLA
	Pegged exchange rate within HB	Pegged exchange rate within HB
	CB	—
Others	—	OMA
F	MF rates with no predetermined path for the exchange rate	F
	IF	FF

Data source: AREAER (IMF, 1999–2010).

of 2009 to 2010 with the old classifications from 1999 to 2008, we found multiple changes. CPs were removed from the soft pegs category, while SAs and CLAs were added. MF rates and IF rates were replaced by floating and FF rates. In addition, other managed exchange rate arrangements were added. Please refer to Table 3.2 for specific changes.

After sorting out changes in the IMF's 2009 annual report, the author can offer several specific explanations regarding the changes:

(1) Conventional pegs include officially announced conventional pegs and *de facto* conventional pegs. The IMF separated the *de facto* conventional peg in 2009 and defined it as the SA, which refers to a government which does not clearly promise to maintain a stable exchange rate (with the provision that the spot market exchange rate should not exceed 2% for at least six months in a row). Noteworthy is that the RMB was classified under SA in 2009.
(2) CPs include both officially announced CPs and *de facto* CPs. The IMF separated the *de facto* CP in 2009 and defined it as a CLA.
(3) The CB was removed because it had seldom been adopted in the past decade.

(4) MF rates with no predetermined path for the exchange rate (meaning that the exchange rate is mainly determined by the market; the government can intervene on behalf of the exchange rate though, so long as it has no predetermined path or target) were broken down and reclassified under SA, crawl-like, floating and other managed exchange rates. This is because policies are flexible and the management of floating rates across countries has become increasingly heterogeneous. This adjustment captures this diversity by making the classification more specific.
(5) FF rates are clearly identified. In a six-month period, a government cannot intervene on behalf of the exchange rate more than three times, with each intervention not to exceed three business days and market imbalances caused by such intervention not to exceed one to two days. If the exchange rate is determined by the market but fails to conform to the strict definition of "FF", then it will fall under "floating".
(6) A category for other items was added (i.e., other managed exchange rates). This refers to a government which frequently and irregularly intervenes on behalf of its exchange rate, defying any consistent classification.

The above changes show that the new revised classifications do not reflect fundamental changes in the global exchange rate system. Instead, they adopt clearer means of judging information on exchange rates. This helps maintain the continuity and stability of the global exchange rate system, while also making it more transparent and thus more conducive to the IMF's responsibilities in bilateral and multilateral monitoring (Wei *et al.*, 2011).

(II) The Decision-making Process Under the New *De facto* Classification

Compared with the old *de facto* classifications, the new classifications adopt a certain decision-making process as to how exchange rate regimes should be classified, speeding up classifications and saving resources.

(The specific decision-making process is shown in Figure 3.3.) First, the IMF analyzes the exchange rate regimes announced by each member country to judge whether the *de facto* exchange rate arrangement performance of the past six months (at minimum) match the announced regime type. If so, then a country's *de facto* exchange rate regime is recorded as the one it has announced (Wei *et al.*, 2011). What requires attention is that the *de facto* exchange rate regimes announced by the IMF in its 2009 report

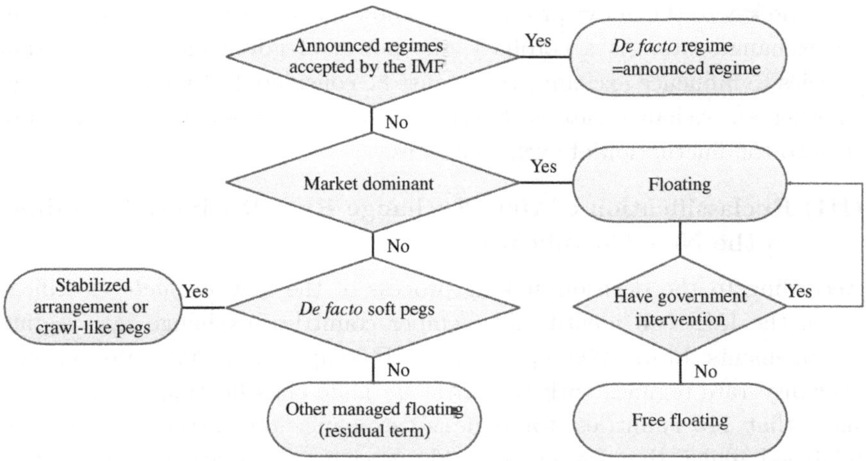

Figure 3.3: Decision-making Process in the 2009 Exchange Rate Arrangement Classifications

Data source: AREAER (IMF, 2009).

as hard pegs (including countries with NS or a CBA), conventional pegs, CPs and pegged exchange rates within HBs are the *de jure* exchange rate regimes of countries.

As for countries whose government policies and monetary performance conflict with the exchange rate regime that they have announced, the IMF uses the decision-making process shown in Figure 3.3 to judge their *de facto* exchange rate regimes. This process includes the following steps:

(1) Analyze whether the exchange rate arrangement is market-determined. If yes, the country is classified under a floating exchange rate regime. If no, the country falls under a non-floating exchange rate arrangement.
(2) Non-floating exchange rate regime arrangements are further divided into two sub-categories: SA and CLA. They are determined based on quantitative and qualitative factors. In most economic analysis, SAs are considered similar to a pegged exchange rate regime.
(3) A floating exchange rate regime is also further specified. To avoid the blurry boundary between MF and IF rates, a strict definition is applied in concert with a combination of quantitative and qualitative factors.
(4) After the above three steps, if a country's exchange rate does not fall under any classification, then it will automatically fall under the "other" items category (other MF rates).

The key to the above process lies in how much market forces determine an exchange rate. As a corollary, the power of government intervention policies to influence exchange rates must be considered. Therefore, to judge whether an exchange rate is determined by the market, one cannot only turn to the fluctuation of exchange rates.

(III) Reclassification of 2008 Exchange Rate Regimes According to the New Classifications

According to the decision-making process of the new *de facto* classifications, the IMF can identify all member countries' exchange rate regime arrangements. In its 2009 report, the IMF compared all 2008 international exchange rate regimes with the latest *de facto* classifications. The results show that 113 countries' (or regions') exchange rate arrangements were relabeled under the new system. The specific information is showed in Table 3.3.

As Table 3.3 shows, there were five changes:

(1) There were 68 countries adopting conventional pegs, among which 22 are now classified as SAs, one falls under "OMAs", one is a floating rate and the other 44 remain unchanged;

Table 3.3: Analysis of 2008 Exchange Rate Arrangements under the New Classification System

2008 Exchange Rate Arrangement under the New Classification System		Original 2008 Classifications	
Exchange Rate Arrangement Classifications	Number of Members	Exchange Rate Arrangement Classifications	Number of Members
SAs	24	Conventional pegs	22
		MF	2
CLA	2	CPs	2
OMA	13	Conventional pegs	1
		CPs	1
		CBs	2
		MF	9
F	38	Conventional pegs	1
		MF	33
		IF	4
FF	36	IF	36

Data source: AREAER (IMF, 2008–2010); calculated and sorted by the author.

(2) There were previously eight countries under a CP, among which two are now under a crawl-like peg, one falls under "OMAs", and the remaining five are unchanged;
(3) Two countries listed under CBs have been reclassified under "OMAs";
(4) Among 44 countries adopting a MF rate with no predetermined path, two are now classified under SAs, 33 are classified as floating rates, and nine as "OMAs";
(5) There were previously 40 countries adopting IF rates, among which 36 are now classified under FF rates (including 15 Euro zone countries), and four remain under a floating rate.

From the above analysis we can infer several things: The SAs of the new classifications are close to conventional pegs; CLA are close to CPs; floating rates fall into either IF and MF rates, with most countries classified as MF rates; and FF rate countries are mostly reclassified from the IF category. Notably, "OMAs" is a special category. Countries falling under this classification were previously considered to have a MF rate or a soft peg. Therefore, this category can be seen as a compromise between a floating exchange rate and a soft peg exchange rate regime. This matches the above conclusion and follows the IMF's report on exchange rate regimes in the 2009–2010 period (Xie *et al*, 2010).

While the above compares the 2008 classifications under both the old and new classification systems, it merely reflects the revision of the *de facto* classifications. It does not imply that the actual exchange rate arrangements, policies, or intentions of the countries concerned have changed.

3.2.2 *International Exchange Rate System Changes after the Financial Crisis*

After the 2008 financial crisis, the international exchange rate system has significantly changed, mainly in two respects: Changes caused by the IMF's exchange rate arrangement classifications and direct changes brought by the international financial crisis. Therefore, to analyze how the international exchange rate system has evolved out of the financial crisis, one needs to consider both factors. I thus compare the 2008 international exchange rate system based on the IMF's old *de facto* classification with the 2008–2010 international exchange rate systems (see Table 3.4). This allows me to correctly analyze changes in the international financial environment brought about from the financial crisis.

Table 3.4: Comparison of the 2008 Exchange Rate Arrangement (under the Old *De facto* Classification) and 2008–2010 Exchange Rate Changes (under the New *De facto* Classification)

Exchange Rate Arrangement	Old Classifications: At the End of April 2008	New Classifications: At the End of April 2008	New Classifications: At the End of April 2009	New Classifications: At the End of April 2010
NS	10	10	10	12
CBA	13	13	13	13
Conventional Peg Arrangement (FPA)	68	44	42	44
SA	0	24	13	24
CP	8	5	5	3
CLA	0	2	1	2
CB	2	0	0	0
Pegged Exchange Rate Within HB	3	3	4	2
OMA	0	13	21	21
MF	44	0	0	0
IF	40	0	0	0
F	0	38	46	38
FF	0	36	33	30

Data source: AREAER (IMF, 2008–2010); calculated and arranged by the author.
Note: From 2008 to 2009, the IMF's members included 185 member countries and the three regions of Hong Kong, the Netherlands Aruba, and Netherlands Antilles. In addition, Kosovo joined the IMF on June 29, 2009, so its data is not included in 2008 and 2009 reports.

3.2.2.1 *IMF Member Countries Situation Analysis*

From analysis of Table 3.4, we can see that the old classification divides international exchange rate regimes into eight sub-categories while the new classification divides them into ten. The two classification schemes have different requirements and there are large differences in the number of countries falling under each sub-category (complicating comparisons and statistical summaries). In order to facilitate a proper comparison, a two-dimensional category-classification can be adopted — one with three categories and the other with five. This is shown in Table 3.5.

(I) The Influence of Exchange Rate Arrangement Classification Changes on the International Exchange Rate System

As for changes in the international exchange rate system caused by the IMF's exchange rate regimes changes, here I compare and analyze the new and old classifications with 2008 data. The statistical requirements of both

Table 3.5: IMF Exchange Rate Regime System Classifications in Three and Five-Category Comparisons

Three Category	Old Classifications (2008)	New Classifications (2008)	Five-Category	New Classifications 2008–2010
Hard pegs	(1) NS (2) CBA	(1) NS (2) CBA	Hard pegs	(1) NS (2) CBA
Soft pegs	(3) Conventional pegs (4) CP (5) CB (6) Pegs within bands	(3) Conventional pegs (4) SA (5) Pegs within bands (6) CB (7) Crawl-like (8) OMAs	Soft pegs	(3) Conventional pegs (4) SA (5) Pegs within bands (6) CP (7) Crawl-like
			Others	(8) OMAs
F	(7) MF (8) IF	(9) F (10) FF	F	(9) F
			FF	(10) FF

Table 3.6: Comparison between Countries Adopting the Three-Category Exchange Rate Regimes under the New and Old Classification Standards

Exchange Rate Arrangement		Hard Pegs	Soft Pegs	F
Old Classification Standard	2008	23	81	84
New Classification Standard	2008	23	91	74
New Classification Standard	2009	23	86	79
New Classification Standard	2010	25	96	68

classifications are different: The old scheme has eight categories while the new one has ten categories. To keep uniform requirements and produce a consistent analysis, three categories are used: Hard pegs, soft pegs and floating. Among them, hard pegs include both countries with NS and those with a CBA (2008, 2009); soft pegs include conventional pegs, CPs, CBs, pegs within bands (2008), conventional pegs, SAs, pegs within bands, crawl-like rates and OMAs (2009); floating includes MF rates, IF rates (2008), floating rates and FF rates (2009).

As shown in Table 3.6, Figures 3.4 and 3.5, the 2008 exchange rate regime is different under the new and old classifications: Under the new scheme, ten countries are listed under soft pegs, the number of countries under floating arrangements is reduced by ten, and the number under hard pegs remains unchanged. This is because the new classification has a

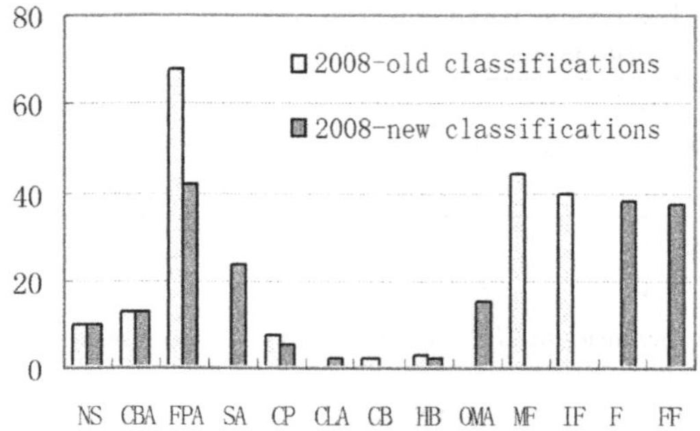

Figure 3.4: Comparison between the 2008 Exchange Rate Regime under the New and Old Classifications

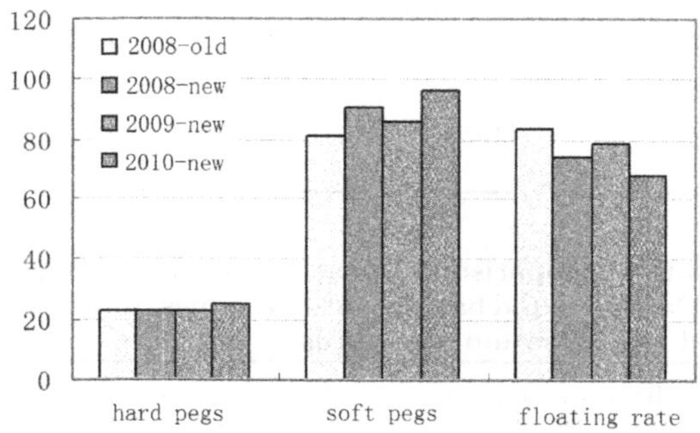

Figure 3.5: Three-Category Comparison between Exchange Rate Arrangements under the New and Old Classifications

clearer and stricter definition for a floating rate, moving countries previously labeled as such to the category of soft pegs. The advantage of the new classification is that it is useful for comparison between the new and old classifications standards. However, the classification is not specific enough to reflect the influences of economic and financial factors on the international exchange rate system.

(II) The Influence of Economic and Financial Factors on the International Exchange Rate System

As for changes in the international exchange rate system caused by economic and financial factors, I compare the 2008 to 2010 exchange rate system classifications with the new *de facto* classification. The statistical requirements are the same as with the new *de facto* classification methods, but a more specific five-category classification is adopted here: Hard pegs, soft pegs, OMAs, floating exchange rates and FF rates. Herein hard pegs include countries with NS and countries with CBAs; soft pegs include conventional pegs, SAs, pegs within bands, CPs and CLAs; OMAs remains a residual category; and floating and FF sub-categories are classified separately.

As shown in Table 3.6 and Figure 3.5, from 2008 to 2010, hard peg countries increased from 23 to 25 in 2010; soft peg countries decreased from 91 to 86 and then rebounded to 96; floating rate countries increased from 74 to 79 and then reduced to 68. The global financial crisis still lingered in 2009; the world economy stated to recover in 2010. This means that the international exchange rate system was volatile with increasing (if temporary) flexibility. Countries all intensified economic intervention and financial regulation, which led to decreased flexibility in international exchange rates in 2010.

The disadvantage of the three-category classification is that it is not specific enough. Therefore, the five-category one will hereafter be used to compare and analyze the 2008–2010 exchange rate system classifications under the new *de facto* classification. Hard pegs include countries with NS and countries with a CBA; soft pegs include conventional pegs, SAs, pegs within bands, CPs and crawl-like rates; OMAs remains a residual category; floating and FF rates are classified into separate categories (Table 3.7).

Comparing Figures 3.6 and 3.7 (covering 2008–2010) shows the following: Countries adopting hard pegs increased from 23 to 25; countries with soft pegs decreased from 78 to 65 and then rebounded to 75; countries with other managed exchange rates increased from 13 to 21; floating rate countries fluctuated from 38 to 46 and then back again to 38; and FF rate countries decreased from 36 to 33, and then finally to 30.

Since the financial crisis broke out, the international financial system has changed considerably. The above data reflects such changes. Since the financial tsunami hit the globe in the second half of 2008, the exchange rates of the world's major currencies have fluctuated greatly. Many developing countries have adopted soft pegs to keep stable rates in line with certain

Table 3.7: Comparison between Countries Adopting Five-category Exchange Rate Arrangements under the New Classification Standard

Exchange Rate Arrangement		Hard Pegs	Soft Pegs	Other Managed Exchange Rate	F	FF
New classification	2008	23	78	13	38	36
New classification	2009	23	65	21	46	33
New classification	2010	25	75	21	38	30

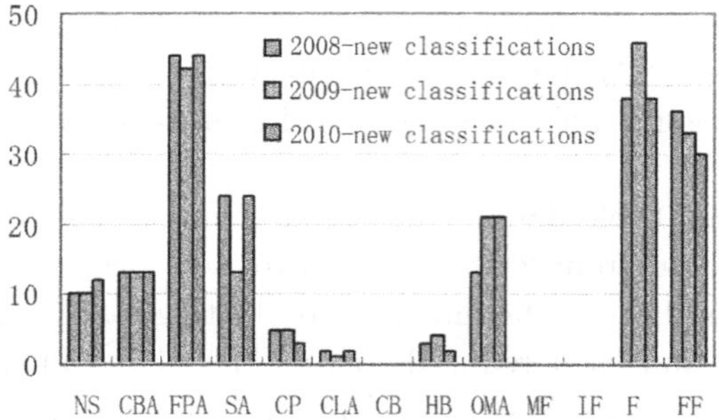

Figure 3.6: Comparison of 2008–2010 Exchange Rate Arrangements under the New Classifications

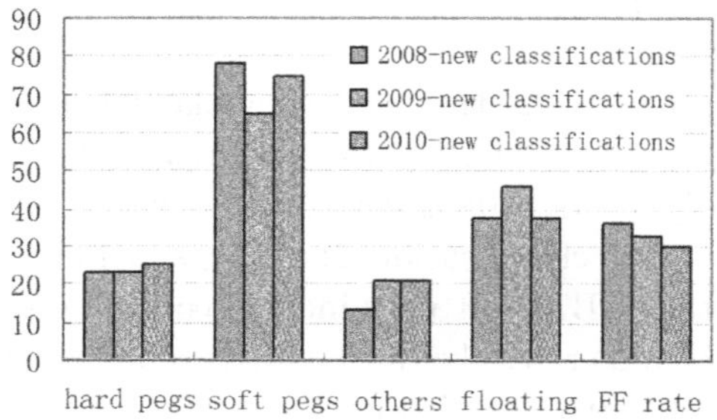

Figure 3.7: Comparison of Five-Category 2008–2010 Classifications under the New Classifications

major currencies. Thus, their exchange rates have fluctuated as well, prompting other countries to adopt managed exchange rate arrangements. The financial crisis gradually eased in the second half of 2009, and the global economy started to recover. However, governments did not relax their crisis-oriented economic interventions and financial regulations. This has left the number of OMAs unchanged and brought further decreases in the number of FF rate countries. However, the number of countries with a soft peg or floating rate has returned to pre-crisis levels.

3.2.2.2 *Comparison of Exchange Rate Regime Change Trends by Type of Economy*

Since the 2008 financial crisis broke out, the international exchange rate regime has changed greatly as a whole. But changes in developed economies and developing economies are obviously different. To compare the influence of economic and financial factors on different types of countries in the international exchange rate system, here the new classification standard is combined with the five-category system and AREAER data from 2008–2010.

(1) Developed Economies

As Table 3.8 and Figure 3.8 show, most of the 32 developed economies in the data set adopted a FF exchange rate regime. Among hard peg areas, Hong Kong has adopted a peg-to-dollar currency board regime. Among soft peg areas, Denmark has adopted a conventional peg arrangement while Slovakia first adopted a pegged exchange rate within HBs in 2008 and then changed to a FF rate after it joined the Eurozone on January 1, 2009. In 2009, the exchange rate regimes of developed economies did not greatly change, (excluding Slovakia's joining the Eurozone). Only Iceland changed from a FF to floating rate, due to a debt crisis and subsequent intensifying exchange rate intervention.

In 2010, the number of floating exchange rate regimes kept increasing while FF ones decreased. In 2008, only Singapore adopted a floating

Table 3.8: Changes in Exchange Rate Arrangement under the New Classification Standard and Five-Category System, 2008–2010

	Hard Pegs	Soft Pegs	Others	F	FF
Developed Economies					
2008	1	2	0	1	28
2009	1	2	0	2	28
2010	1	1	1	4	25
Emerging and Developing Economies					
2008	22	76	13	37	8
2009	22	63	21	44	5
2010	24	74	20	34	5

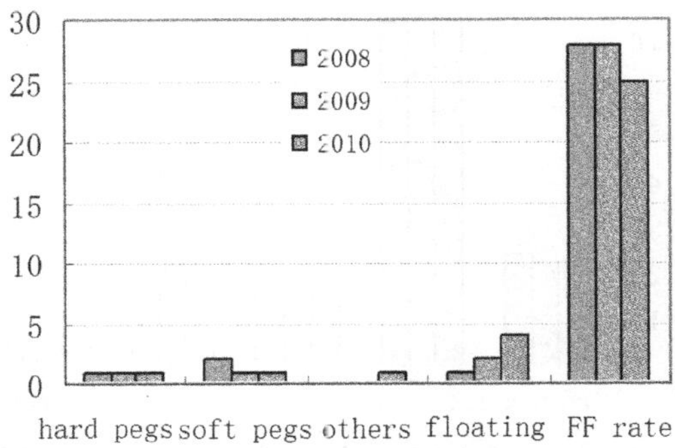

Figure 3.8: Comparison of the Number of Developed Economies under Different Exchange Rate Regimes, 2008–2010

exchange rate regime; Iceland joined Singapore in 2009. In 2010, Singapore changed to "OMA" and Israel, South Korea and Switzerland all changed from FF to floating rates. Importantly, Singapore, Israel, South Korea and Switzerland are countries with relatively small aggregate economies. They adopted certain policies in the financial crisis to achieve their specific currency policy targets.

Although during the financial crisis the exchange rate regimes of a few developed countries were impacted, these countries and regions have relatively small aggregate economies. Therefore, in general, exchange rate regimes in developed countries have not been seriously impacted by the financial crisis and are relatively stable.

(2) Emerging and Developing Economies

After analyzing Table 3.8 and Figure 3.9, we can see that most emerging and developing economies have adopted middle-of-the-road exchange rate regimes. Among hard pegs, Kosovo adopted a regime with NS after it joined the IMF in 2010. Likewise, Zimbabwe changed from the "OMA" category to "NS". Members adopting hard pegs increased from 22 to 24 over two years. Soft peg members decreased from 76 to 63 initially, but ultimately increased by 11 to 74 in 2010. Members of floating exchange rate regimes increased by seven in 2009 and decreased by ten in 2010 to 34. Members of FF regimes decreased from eight to five in 2009 and remained unchanged in 2010. Members of other exchange rate arrangements increased from 13 to 21 in 2009 and decreased to 20 in 2010. Most of the above changes occurred in soft peg, floating and FF regimes, but without clear regularity. Still, we can see that emerging and developing countries were influenced greatly by

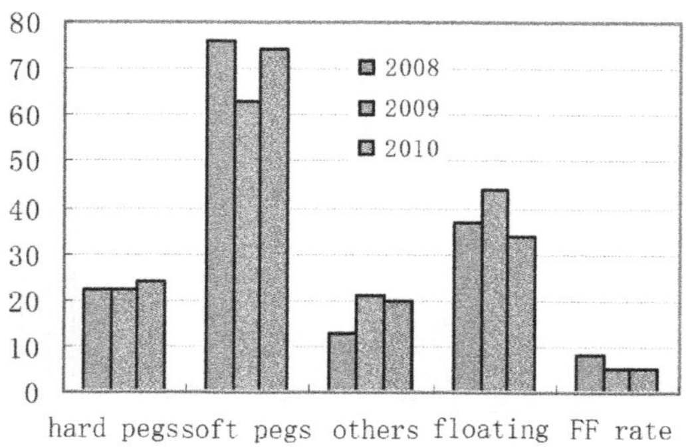

Figure 3.9: Comparison of the Number of Developing and Emerging Market Economies under Different Exchange Rate Regimes, 2008–2010

the financial crisis and their exchange rate regimes were easily impacted by the world financial environment (Wei and Wang, 2011).

3.2.3 *Concluding Remarks*

The IMF's exchange rate arrangement classifications serve an important guiding role in the evolution of the international exchange rate system. Changes in the 2009 international exchange rate system, on the one hand, were influenced by the IMF's exchange rate classification changes. On the other hand, the financial crisis (among other factors) played a role as well. This chapter first briefly reviewed the history of the IMF's exchange rate arrangement classifications and then focused on the new *de facto* classifications issued by the IMF in 2009.

By comparing and analyzing the original 2008 international exchange rate system under the old *de facto* classification and then tracing changes between 2008 and 2010 among countries under this system and the new *de facto* classifications, we can surmise the influence of both the 2009 exchange rate arrangement classifications and the financial crisis on changes in exchange rate regimes. The results show that the new exchange rate arrangement classification has stricter definitions for floating exchange rate regimes, leading countries which previously had floating regimes (under the old classification) to be reclassified as soft pegs (according to the new classification). In addition, the financial crisis temporarily increased the flexibility of the international exchange rate system in 2009, while each government's financial regulations and economic interventions greatly decreased its flexibility in 2010. By comparing developed, emerging and developing countries, we found that, after the financial crisis, emerging and developing economies experienced greater change in their exchange rate regimes than did developed countries. This reveals the vulnerability and potential instability of exchange rate regimes in emerging and developing countries, relative to developed countries.

3.3 Analysis of Factors Influencing Exchange Rate Arrangement

3.3.1 *Overview of Factors Influencing Exchange Rate Arrangements*

Research on factors influencing exchange rate arrangements has always been an important part of exchange rate theory. In terms of theories in this area, some representative ones include the optimal currency area theory, political economy theory, fear of floating theory and currency crisis theory. Research on exchange rate arrangements usually concentrates on one or several aspects of these theories and case studies have found explanatory value in all of the four theories.

(1) Optimal Currency Area Theory

This theory holds that it is infeasible to discuss the advantages and disadvantages of exchange rate regimes in a general way. One should discuss the rationality and applicability of exchange rate regimes based on the specific characteristics of different countries. The theory holds that economic size, level of economic development, degree of openness in a country's capital market, inflation differentials, production and product diversification, fragility to trade shock, level of foreign reserves, degree of openness to trade, and the geographical concentration of trade are all important factors that influence the choice of exchange rate arrangement for each country.

(2) Political Economy Theory

This theory emphasizes the impact of a government's inclination toward inflation and a country's political stability on the choice of exchange rate arrangement. It holds that countries' lack of political stability weakens political support for fixed exchange rate regimes. At the same time, a state's lack of ability to take the difficult measures needed to safeguard a fixed exchange rate regime ultimately incline it to choose a floating exchange rate regime. Such a choice of exchange rate regime has the benefit that, under a floating regime, rate changes may not strongly impact the public. This lowers the political cost of exchange rate depreciation, as compared to a fixed exchange rate regime.

(3) Fear of Floating Theory

This theory emphasizes the influence of currency substitution and currency balance sheet mismatches on a country's choice of exchange rate arrangement. It reasons that these lead some countries to nominally adopt a floating exchange rate regime, while actually maintaining a peg to the currency in which their main asset or foreign reserves are denominated. The theory holds that countries which have not written off their foreign debt position face greater exchange rate risks and are therefore more inclined to adopt a fixed pegged exchange rate regime. It suggests that asset currency substitution can be reflected by dollarization. Countries with a higher degree of currency substitution (e.g., dollarization) are inclined to choose fixed pegged exchange rate regimes.

(4) Currency Crisis Theory

The theory holds that the worsening of macro fundamentals — especially financial deficit monetization — in relation to a pegged exchange rate regime target is the root cause of monetary crises. Researchers espousing this theory show that the Impossible Trinity exists in an open economy. When this Impossible Trinity escalates, international speculative capital will strike pegged exchange rate regimes, cause a monetary and financial crisis, and even force governments to float their pegged exchange rate regimes.

Indicators of factors influencing exchange rate arrangements included in the above four theories are shown in Table 3.9.

Table 3.9: Indicators of Factors Influencing Exchange Rate Regimes

Exchange Rate Arrangement Choice Theory	Economic Indicator	Indicator Calculation Methods
Optimal Currency Area Theory	1. Economic development level	Dollar-dominated per capita gross domestic product (GDP) converted by exchange rates
	2. Foreign reserve	
	3. Trade dependency (trade openness)	Ratio of exports + imports to GDP
Political Economy Theory	4. Government preference	Historical average actual GDP growth rate
	5. Historical average inflation rate	CPI
Fear of Floating Theory	6. Degree of financial deepening	M2/GDP
	7. Debt currency substitution (foreign debt ratio)	Total foreign debt/nominal GDP
	8. Degree of currency mismatch	Foreign debts of domestic commercial bands/M2
Currency Crisis Theory	9. Balance of financial revenue and expenditure	The ratio of imbalance in fiscal revenue, and expenditure, and GDP
	10. Actual capital openness	The percent of the absolute value sum of securities investment inflows and outflows in GDP

The choice of exchange rate arrangement is an important yet complicated problem. It is not only influenced by domestic economic and political factors, but also by the international economic and financial environment. In standard research on the topic, evidence suggests that major factors impacting this choice include a mix of economic and political factors. Important economic factors include economic structural characteristics, potential sources of economic shock, price confirmation, exchange rate trade volatility, and economic fundamentals including financial vulnerability. Political factors include policy coordination, government reputation, public expectation and strategic ability. After summarizing the IMF's exchange rate arrangement choice and case study documents on said influential factors, I conclude as follows:

(1) There is no exchange rate that suits all countries in all periods. Exchange rate regimes of various forms have their advantages and disadvantages. No single exchange rate regime is perfect.
(2) Changes in the economic environment determine changes in the exchange rate regime. The advantages and disadvantages of different exchange rate regimes, as well as their adaptability and contradictions with the economic environment, determine changes in exchange rate regimes. In the current international exchange rate system, exchange rate regime choices change frequently, with the basic trend towards more flexible regimes.
(3) Compared with developed countries, in the current international monetary system, developing countries face a special economic and financial environment which places their choice of exchange rate arrangement in a dilemma. One exchange rate regime cannot be applicable permanently. Developing countries should make active adjustments and changes, following changes in economic fundamentals and the overall economic environment, and base such changes on their level of development (Zhao, 2009).

The following section analyzes the economic data of each country classified under the 2008 exchange rate arrangement classifications and compares this with 2010 data. However, cross-section data is not enough to filter out the factors influencing choice of exchange rate. Instead, the goal of this case analysis is to combine the above theories and factor indicators to isolate major differences in countries making certain rate regime choices. Namely, the goal is to discern what economic factors reflect each type of exchange rate regime. Then, combining the above theories and factor indicators, the analysis provides a reasonable explanation that supplements the overall research into factors affecting the choice exchange rate arrangements.

3.3.2 *Overview of Analytical Perspective*

This section will have descriptive statistics and qualitative analysis on the economic characteristics of 188 economies in the IMF's 2009 AREAER, based on the IMF's latest *de facto* exchange rate arrangement classification standards issued in that year (pertaining to world exchange rate regimes in 2008). The section will apply the above-mentioned five-category framework to divide the IMF's ten sub-categories of exchange rate regimes into FF, F, OMA, soft pegs and hard pegs. Then, it will select 118 economic indicators (using 2008 data) from the world development indicators (published by the World Bank in 2010) to construct a two-dimensional table with the five categories of exchange rate regimes. This will allow direct comparison of related economic factors among similar exchange rate regimes.

3.3.2.1 *Dimension 1: Country and Region*

In 2009, the IMF's ARER regimes included 188 economies, among which included 32 developed economies and 156 emerging and developing economies (countries and regions).

3.3.2.2 *Dimension 2: Exchange Rate Regime*

In 2009, the IMF made large adjustments to its exchange rate arrangement classifications, reclassifying member countries' exchange rate regimes into three categories plus one residual category, with ten sub-categories in all. According to the requirements of the present research, the ten sub-categories have been condensed into five categories. They are listed according to their flexibility as follows:

(1) Hard Pegs (23 countries and regions)

This includes exchange rates without separate legal tender and CBAs. Countries and regions covered are: Bosnia and the Republic of Montenegro, Bulgaria, Ecuador, Salvador, Estonia, Grenada, the Republic of Lithuania, Panama, Hong Kong China, and others.

Among the 23 countries and regions in this group, Hong Kong, China is a developed economy, while the others are all emerging and developing economies.

(2) Soft Pegs (65 countries and regions)

This includes conventional pegged arrangements, SAs, CPs, CLAs and pegged exchange rates within HBs. Countries and regions covered are: Angola, Azerbaijan, Bangladesh, the Republic of Belarus, Belize, Bolivia, Botswana, Cape Verde, China, Cote d'Ivoire, Ethiopia, Guyana, Honduras, Jordan, Kazakhstan, Latvia, Lebanon, Lesotho, Macedonia, Mozambique, Venezuela, Denmark, and others.

Among the 65 countries and regions in this group, Denmark is a developed economy, while all others are emerging and developing economies.

(3) OMAs (21 countries and regions)

Countries and regions covered are: Costa Rica, Croatia, Dominica, Egypt, Georgia, Namibia, Russia, Ukraine, Vietnam, etc.

The 21 countries and regions in this group are all emerging and developing economies.

(4) F (46 countries and regions)

Countries and regions covered are: Albania, Argentina, Armenia, Brazil, Columbia, Gambia, Guatemala, India, Indonesia, Kenya, Mexico, Moldova, Pakistan, Paraguay, Peru, the Philippines, Romania, South Africa, Sri Lanka, Sudan, Thailand, Tunisia, Turkey, Uganda, Uruguay, Zambia and others.

Among the 46 countries and regions in this group, 44 are emerging and developing economies and the other two — Iceland and Singapore — are developed economies.

(5) FF (33 countries and regions)

Countries and regions covered are: Australia, Austria, Belgium, Canada, Chili, Czech, Finland, France, Germany, Greece, Ireland, Israel, Italy, Japan, Luxembourg, Mauritius, New Zealand, Norway, Poland, Portugal, Slovakia, Slovenia, Sweden, Switzerland, Britain, the US, etc.

Among them, Poland, Chili, Congo, Mauritius and Somali are emerging and developing economies while the other 28 are developed economies.

3.3.2.3 *Dimension 3: World Development Indicator*

Because most of the exchange rate arrangements for each country in the IMF's 2009 annual report are due by the end of the previous year (e.g., December 31, 2008), this paper chooses 2008 world development indicators published by the World Bank in 2010. The data includes the following

12 categories of economic indicators and 118 sub-categories of indicators, all of which are related to exchange rates:

(1) Balance of international payments (8 indicators)
(2) Foreign debts composition and risks (12 indicators)
(3) Financial situation (9 indicators)
(4) Government finance (9 indicators)
(5) Foreign trade (8 indicators)
(6) Commodity trade index (5 indicators)
(7) Currency indicators (8 indicators)
(8) National economic accounting (20 indicators)
(9) Economic overview (8 indicators)
(10) Stock market (3 indicators)
(11) Foreign trade structure (19 indicators)
(12) Tariff barrier (9 indicators)

3.3.3 *Overview of Empirical Research*

As was stated in Section 3.3.1, the goal of this empirical research is to identify which economic indicators (among the above 118 indicators) can best distinguish each exchange rate regime (according to the previously defined five categories). In order to screen for such indicators, this sections applies a discriminant analysis method.

Discriminant analysis determines a discriminant function based on the characteristics of a variable's value, as well as the category to which it belongs. It is designed to classify items under unknown categories based on discriminant functions. Once we define the terms of classification and the values of all relevant variables, we need to screen the variables for more information and build a discriminant function to calculate the minimum rate of error.

According to different rules, discriminant analysis methods can be divided into distance discrimination, Fisher discrimination and Bayes discrimination. Distance discrimination and Fisher discrimination have no strict requirements on data distribution, while Bayes discrimination requires that data must follow a multi-dimensional normal distribution. This study uses Fisher discrimination.

Fisher discrimination is also called canonical discrimination. Its basic idea is to determine linear discriminant functions based on the principle of the largest distance between categories and the smallest distance inside categories. This logic is used to decide the category of an object. After being divided by discriminant functions, objects of the same category are closely distributed while objects of different categories have farther distances. The difference between the two is thus made obvious.

3.3.4 *Analysis of Economic Factors Influencing Exchange Rate Arrangements*

3.3.4.1 *Related Economic Factors Analysis of Five Categories of Exchange Rate Arrangements*

This section applies exchange rate arrangement data from the IMF's 2009 annual report and the World Bank's 2010 world economic development indicator data (both reflecting 2008 data) to build a cross-section data table. It then analyzes this table to determine the related economic factors of exchange rate regimes. Due to some missing economic data, this study borrows a method of bands data analysis to estimate the complete data needed for discriminant analysis.

Research shows that applying all 118 indicators directly into Fisher discrimination can lead to the optimal discrimination effect — namely the analysis can easily distinguish the five categories of exchange rate regimes from the provided indicators. But indicators acquired in this way are not representative in terms of their economic significance, have low correlations with the main factors influencing exchange rate regimes (as stated in Section 3.3.1), and therefore cannot be explained from economic theory. Moreover, these indicators do not capture large differences in the economic distributions among the five categories of exchange rate regimes. They are only an optimal display in mathematical, not practical terms.

Therefore, to better balance the results of our discrimination analysis with a theoretical explanation, the report adopts three steps for its data analysis:

(1) Screen 118 indicators by combining mainstream exchange rate regime determination theories and factor indicators that influence exchange rate regimes (as described in Section 3.3.1).
(2) Use the indicators screened in Step 1 to study the data distribution of the five categories of exchange rate regimes and remove any indicators with a smaller distribution difference.
(3) Conduct discriminant analysis with the indicators screened in Step 2. Conduct discriminant analysis on the indicator data of the five categories of exchange rate regimes and use the following five indicators to build discriminant functions, as displayed in Table 3.10.

Table 3.10: Indicators Returned from the Discriminant Analysis of the Five Categories of Exchange Rate Regimes

No.	Indicators
1	GDP per capita (current USD)
2	Inflation, GDP deflator (annual %)
3	Bank liquid reserves to bank assets ratio (%)
4	Money and quasi money (M2) as % of GDP
5	Money and quasi money (M2) to total reserves ratio

As an important macroeconomic indicator, GDP per capita can be used to measure the economic development of a country. Reflecting GDP price changes, a GDP deflator is used as a broad indicator of inflation. The ratio of bank liquid reserves to bank assets reflects the liquidity of the banking system and is an indicator representing financial depth and efficiency. Countries with high banking system liquidity are unlikely to experience banking and financial crises, even when they suffer a difficult macroeconomic environment. The percent of M2 in GDP is usually used as an indicator to measure an economy's degree of financial depth. M2/GDP actually measures the percent of trading, with currency being the medium among all economic trading. In general, it is a primary indicator measuring the financialization of a country. Usually, the higher the ratio is, the greater monetized an economy is. The ratio of M2 to total reserves is one of the indicators that reflects financial vulnerability. If the ratio is low, it means financial institutions are relatively vulnerable.

Among the five indicators, two reflect macroeconomic fundamentals: GDP per capita and the GDP deflator. Three reflect financial health: The ratio of bank liquid reserves to bank assets, the percent of M2 in GDP and the ratio of M2 to international reserves.

Discrimination results show that the accumulated contribution rate of function #1 and function #2 reaches 99.2% (Table 3.11). Therefore the report will mainly analyze these two functions.

Standardized typical discriminant function coefficients for the five categories of exchange rate regimes are shown in Table 3.12.

As for the standardized discriminant function coefficient, a bigger absolute value for a given coefficient means it has higher ability to distinguish its corresponding variable. In Table 3.12, the indicators most correlated to function #1 are GDP per capita and the ratio of M2 to international reserve. The indicators most correlated to function #2 are GDP per capita, the GDP deflator and the percent of M2 in GDP.

Table 3.11: Discriminant Function Eigenvalue of Five Categories of Exchange Rate Regimes

	Eigenvalue	% of Variance	Accumulated (%)	Positive Correlation
Function #1	173.402	84.0	84.0	0.997
Function #2	31.378	15.2	99.2	0.984
Function #3	1.725	0.8	100.0	0.796
Function #4	0.016	0	100.0	0.127

Note: The analysis applies the above four typical discriminant functions.

Table 3.12: Standardized Typical Discriminant Function Coefficients for the Five Categories of Exchange Rate Regimes

Indicators	Function #1	Function #2	Function #3	Function #4
GDP per capita (current USD)	−26.229	7.198	−1.357	−3.652
Money and quasi money (M2) to total reserves ratio	23.443	−3.474	1.524	4.678
Inflation, GDP deflator (annual %)	0.734	7.005	−3.332	−0.330
Bank liquid reserves to bank assets ratio (%)	0.859	−3.452	3.814	0.253
Money and quasi money (M2) as % of GDP	2.463	−6.715	−0.397	−0.475

Canonical discriminant function diagrams can directly reflect a function's classification results. From Figure 3.10, we can see that functions #1 and #2 can best distinguish the five categories of exchange rate regimes: #1 represents FF regimes; #2, #3 and #4 represent floating regimes, other MF regimes and soft pegs respectively; and #5 represents hard pegs. Figure 3.10 shows that FF and hard peg regimes have an obvious divergent trend, while floating, other MF, and soft peg regimes are relatively concentrated.

Regarding the direction of function #1, FF regimes have obvious differences with the other four categories, while floating, other MF, soft peg, and hard peg regimes have no large differences. As stated before, function #1 has a strong correlation with GDP per capita and the ratio of M2 to international reserves. Therefore, in terms of their level of economic development and financial vulnerability, countries with FF regimes distance themselves from the other four types.

Regarding the direction of function #2, hard pegs have obvious differences with the other four categories, while FF, F, other MF and soft

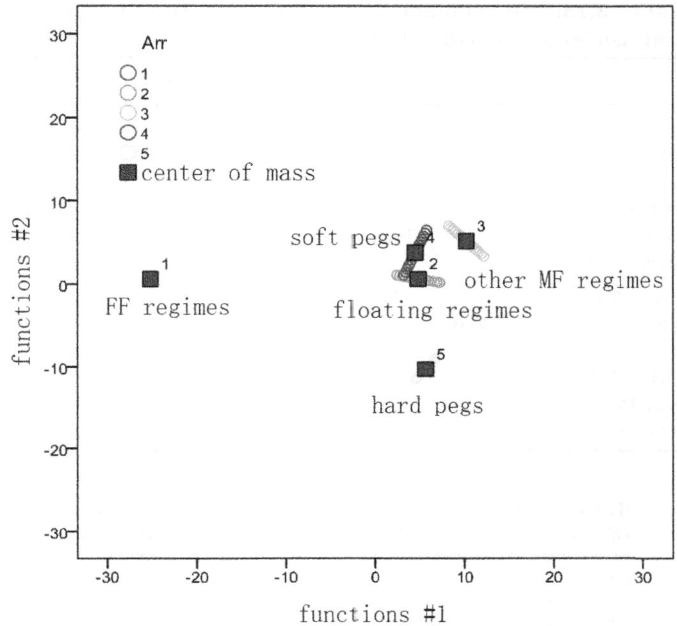

Figure 3.10: Canonical Discriminant Function Diagram of the Five Categories of Exchange Rate Regimes

peg regimes are almost the same. Since function #2 is closely correlated with GDP per capita, the GDP deflator and the percent of M2 in GDP, and GDP per capita plays such an important role in function #1, we can see that countries with hard pegs have obvious distances with the other four types in terms of inflation and financial development.

The classification results (Table 3.13) are accurate in 96.3% cases in the initial test, 95.0% of cases in the cross test, with the error rate less than 5%. Thus the discrimination results are very good.

We can see from the distribution of exchange rate regimes that 28 out of the 33 countries with FF are developed economies, while there are only four developed economies among the 155 other countries (in the other four categories of exchange rate regime). The remaining 151 are all emerging and developing economies. Therefore, in analysis of indicators, such natural attribution of the data distribution should be taken into consideration.

The indicator results of the discriminant analysis are factors related to exchange rate arrangement classification. However, developed economies, emerging, and developing economies have myriad and obvious differences. To weaken the impact of systemic differences caused by natural attribution

Table 3.13: Discrimination Classification Results for Five Categories of Exchange Rate Regimes

	FF	F	Other MF	Soft Pegs	Hard Pegs
Initial Test (%)					
FF	100.0				
F		100.0			
Other MF			100.0		
Soft Pegs		18.8		81.3	
Hard Pegs					100.0
Cross Test (%)					
FF	100.0				
F		100.0			
Other MF			100.0		
Soft Pegs		25.0		75.0	
Hard Pegs					100.0

Table 3.14: Indicators from Discriminant Analysis of the Four Categories of Exchange Rate Regimes

No.	Indicators
1	GDP (current USD)
2	Inflation, consumer prices (annual %)
3	External debt stocks (% of GNI)
4	Foreign direct investment, net inflows (% of GDP)

in the indicator results, this book also conducts discriminant analysis on the other four categories of exchange rate regimes (besides FF) in order to draw more complete conclusions.

3.3.4.2 *Related Economic Factor Analysis of Four Categories of Exchange Rate Arrangements*

Technical paths of discriminant analysis on the four categories of exchange rate regimes are similar to that of the five categories of exchange rate regimes. They involve the following four indicators for building the discriminant function building (Table 3.14).

GDP represents the economic size of a country. CPI is an important indicator of the overall level of inflation. The percent of total foreign debts in GNI represents a country's foreign debt burden, which influences the country's reputation and vulnerability to financial shocks. The percent of net FDI inflows in GDP shows the degree of international capital flows in a country. These four indicators represent economic size, inflation level, debt level and international capital flow level, respectively.

Table 3.15: Discriminant Function Eigenvalue of the Four Categories of Exchange Rate Regimes

	Eigenvalue	% of Variance	Accumulated (%)	Positive Correlation
Function #1	43.280	92.1	92.1	0.989
Function #2	2.823	6.0	98.1	0.859
Function #3	0.912	1.9	100.0	0.691

Note: The analysis applies the above three typical discriminant functions.

Table 3.16: Standardized Typical Discriminant Function Coefficients for the Four Categories of Exchange Rate Regimes

Indicators	Function #1	Function #2	Function #3
External debt stocks (% of GNI)	10.096	0.010	−3.560
Foreign direct investment, net inflows (% of GDP)	−5.783	−0.640	3.682
GDP (current USD)	5.775	2.588	0.682
Inflation, consumer prices (annual %)	−10.059	−1.733	−0.244

Table 3.15 provides the discriminant function eigenvalue of the four categories of exchange rate regimes. From Table 3.15, we can see that the contribution rate of functions #1 and #2 reach 98.1%. Therefore, this report will mainly analyze the characteristics of these two functions.

Standardized typical discriminant function coefficients for the four categories exchange rate regimes are shown in Table 3.16.

In Table 3.16, the indicators most strongly correlated to function #1 are the percent of total foreign debt in GNI and CPI. The indicators most strongly correlated to function #2 are GDP and CPI.

From Figure 3.11, we can see that functions #1 and #2 have relatively good discrimination results across the four categories of exchange rate regimes: #1 represents floating regimes; #2, #3 and #4 represent other MF, soft peg and hard peg regimes.

Regarding the direction of function #1, four regimes have obvious differences. Function #1 is closely correlated to the percent of total foreign debt in GNI and CPI. Therefore, countries with one of these four regimes have different performance in terms of foreign debt and inflation levels.

Regarding the direction of function #2, floating regimes have some differences with the other three, while other MF and soft peg regimes have little difference. Function #2 is closely correlated with GDP and CPI. As CPI also plays an important role in function #1, this suggests that countries

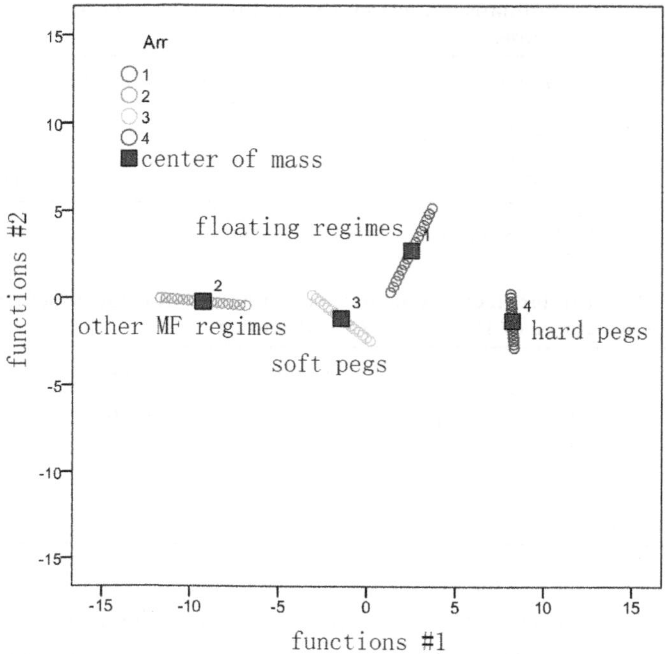

Figure 3.11: Canonical Discriminant Function Diagram of Four Categories of Exchange Rate Regimes

with floating regimes have obvious distances with the other three types in terms of economic size.

The classification results (Table 3.17) have correct classification on 100.0% cases in the initial test, 98.4% of cases in the cross test, and an error rate less than 2%. The discrimination results are thus very good.

3.3.4.3 *Comparison and Analysis of Two Discrimination Results (Five-Category and Four-Category results in Table 3.18)*

Through comparison of the two discrimination results we can see that both find indicators relating to the inflation level. The difference is that the five-category regime discrimination result also has indicators relating to finance, while the four-category regime discrimination has indicators relating to foreign debts and international capital flow levels.

In terms of the macro economy, most developed economies with high GDP per capita choose FF regimes. As is shown in Figure 3.12, countries adopting FF regimes have a scattering of different GDP per capita, but their

Table 3.17: Discrimination Classification Results of the Four Categories of Exchange Rate Regimes

	F	Other MF	Soft Pegs	Hard Pegs
Initial Test (%)				
F	100.0			
Other MF		100.0		
Soft Pegs			100.0	
Hard Pegs				100.0
Cross Test (%)				
F	93.8		6.3	
Other MF		100.0		
Soft Pegs			100.0	
Hard Pegs				100.0

Table 3.18: Comparison of the Two Discrimination Results

Five-Category Discrimination Results	Four-Category Discrimination Results
GDP per capita	GDP
GDP deflator (annual % change)	CPI (annual % change)
Ratio of bank liquid reserves to bank assets	Total foreign debt (% of GNI)
Currency and quasi-money (M2) (% of GDP)	FDI new inflow (% of GDP)
Ratio of currency and quasi-money (M2) to international reserves	

overall level of GDP per capita is obviously higher than that of countries in the other four categories. The latter countries have relatively the same level of GDP per capita.

In the remaining four regimes, except for FF, GDP is an important influencing factor, which means emerging and developing economies' economic size affects their choice of exchange rate arrangement. Figure 3.13 is a GDP box plot of the five regimes. From it we can see that the level of GDP of countries adopting a FF regime is far higher than that of countries adopting the other four regimes. Singular points marked in the diagram represent countries with GDPs over USD$1 trillion. The US, Japan and Germany, each with FF regimes, are all developed economies, while major emerging and developing economies have other regime types. For example, Brazil, India and Mexico have floating regimes. Russia has a regime classified as "other MF regime". China has a soft peg regime. Figure 3.14 is a GDP box plot of the four categories of exchange rate regimes. GDP levels of countries with floating and other MF regimes are noticeably higher than countries with soft or hard peg regimes. That means countries with larger economies

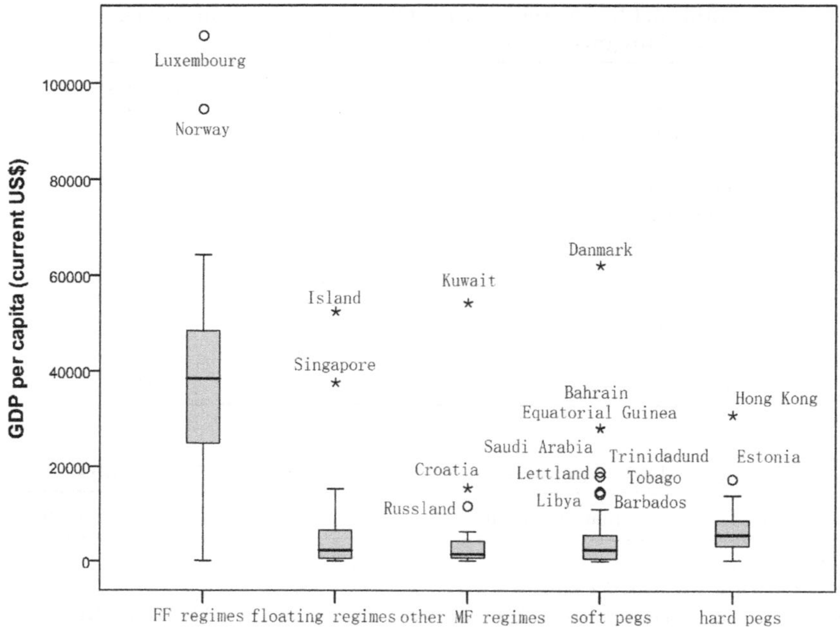

Figure 3.12: Box Plot of Five-Category Regimes versus GDP Per Capita

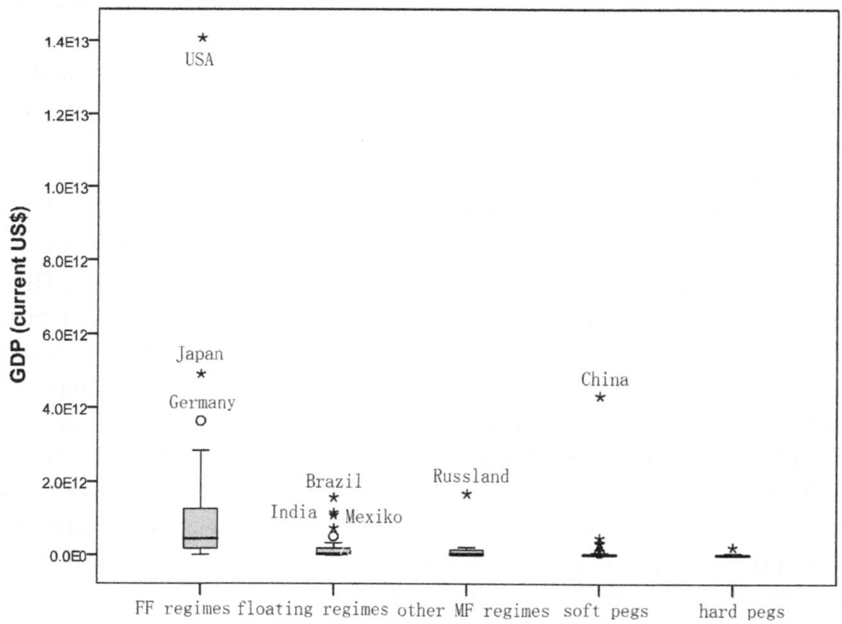

Figure 3.13: GDP Box Plot of the Five Categories

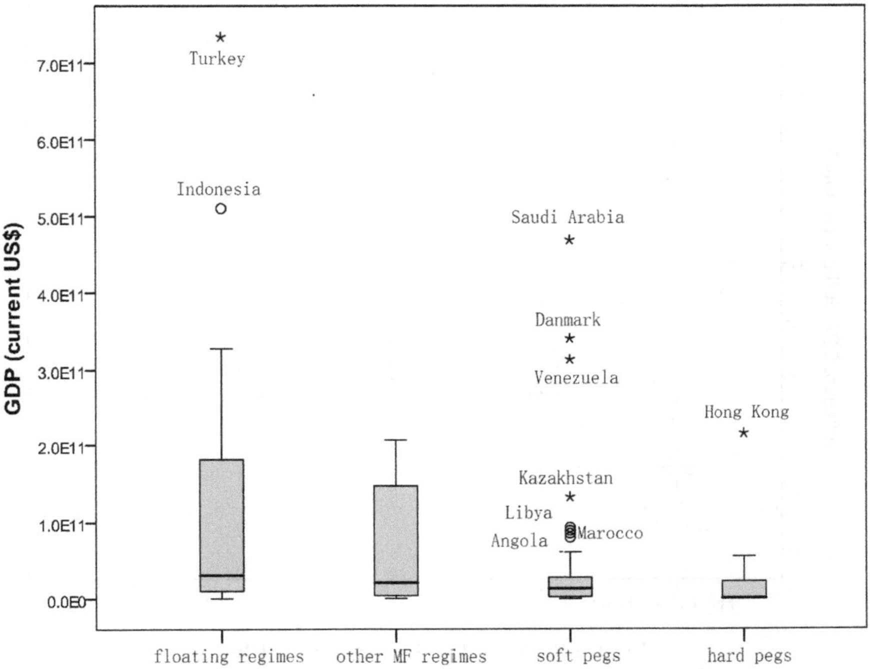

Figure 3.14: GDP Box Plot of the Four Categories of Regimes (individual data points removed)

are more inclined towards a floating currency regime while countries with smaller economies prefer peg regimes.

In terms of reflecting inflation, the GDP deflator and CPI appear in both five-category and four-category regimes discrimination analysis functions. Across the two index quadrant diagrams (Figures 3.15 and 3.16), five-category regimes have similar performance for inflation in the two indexes. Countries with FF regimes have obviously lower inflation levels than those of countries with the other four regimes. Further, in the remaining four regimes (excepting FF), countries with hard pegs have obviously lower inflation levels than countries with the other three regimes. Countries with floating, other MF and soft peg regimes also have similar inflation distribution. Therefore, in terms of inflation, since countries adopting FF regimes are basically developed economies, their performance is obviously better than that of countries with the other four regimes. Also, in emerging and developing economies with the four categories of regimes, the performance of countries with hard pegs is better than that of countries with the other three remaining regime types.

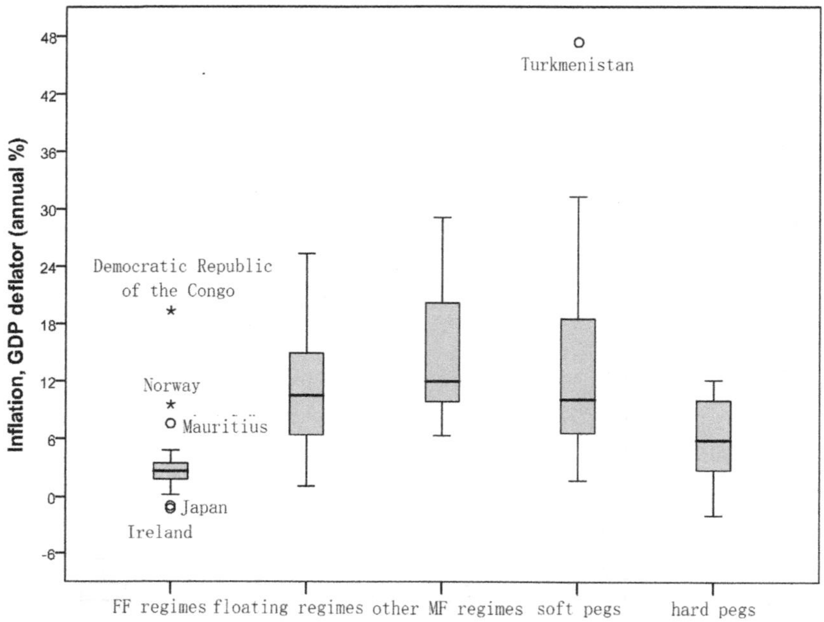

Figure 3.15: GDP Deflator Box Plot

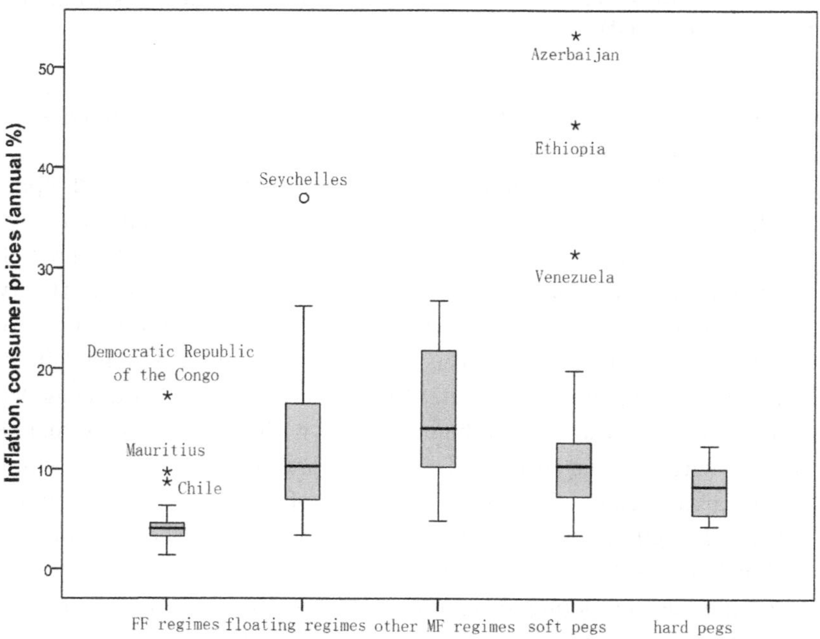

Figure 3.16: CPI Box Plot

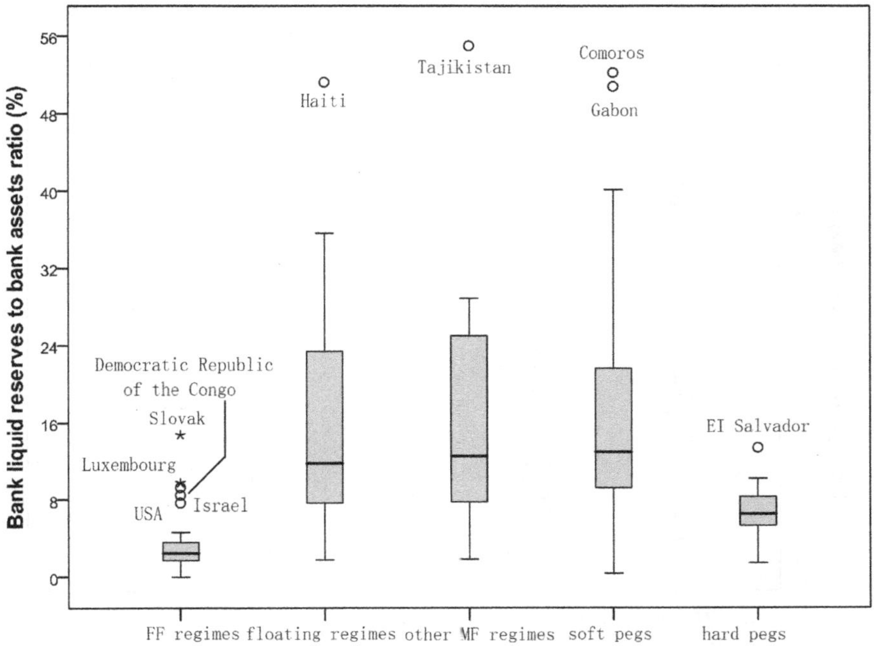

Figure 3.17: Box Plot of the Ratio of Bank Liquid Reserve to Bank Assets

From the perspective of finance, three indicators are used to discriminate between the five-category regimes. The ratio of bank liquid reserves to bank assets is used to measure the liquidity of the banking system. As is shown in Figure 3.17, the liquid reserve ratio of countries with FF regimes is the lowest and has small degree of dispersion. Countries with floating, other MF and soft peg regimes have similar ratios; countries with hard pegs likewise have low ratios. Therefore, in terms of the banking system, countries with FF and hard peg regimes have relatively poor liquidity and are at greater risk of experiencing a banking crisis.

The percent of money and quasi-money (M2) in GDP measures an economy's degree of financial depth. As is shown in Figure 3.18, the proportion of FF and hard peg regimes is higher than that for the other three regime types. Therefore, financial development in the former group is greater.

The ratio of money and quasi-money (M2) to international reserves is used to measure a country's vulnerability to balance of payment shocks. As is shown in Figure 3.19, the ratios of countries with FF regimes are much higher than countries with the other four regimes. Further, countries with hard pegs have higher ratios than other countries — except for those

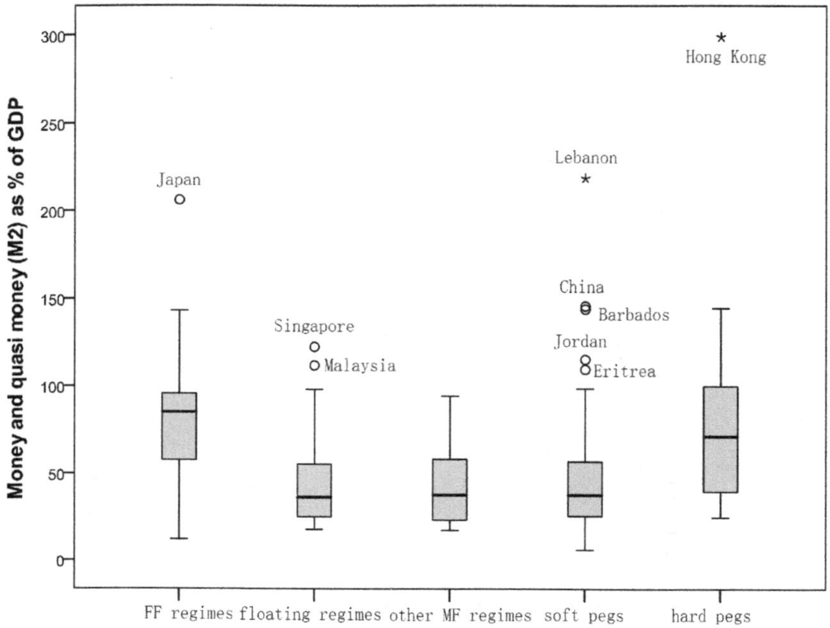

Figure 3.18: Percent of M2 in GDP Box Plot

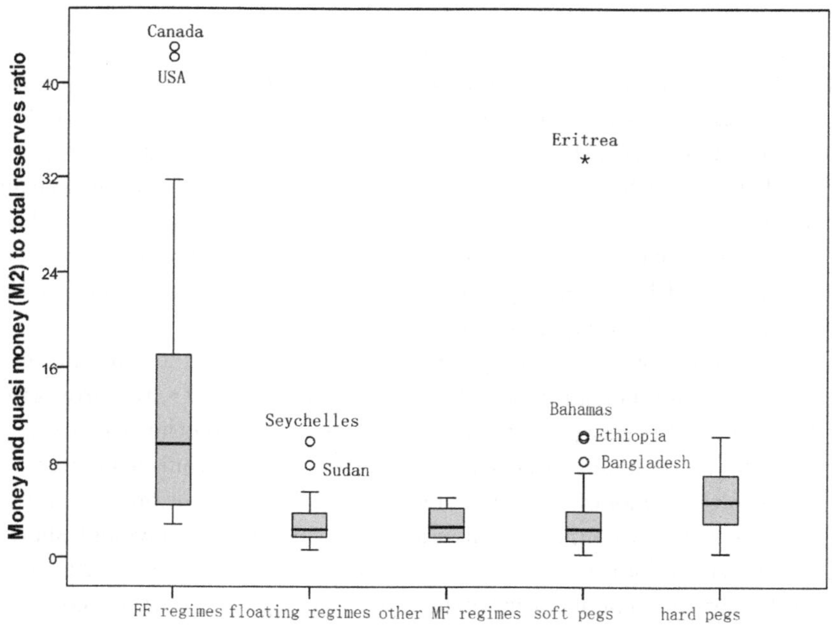

Figure 3.19: Ratio of M2 to International Reserves Box Plot

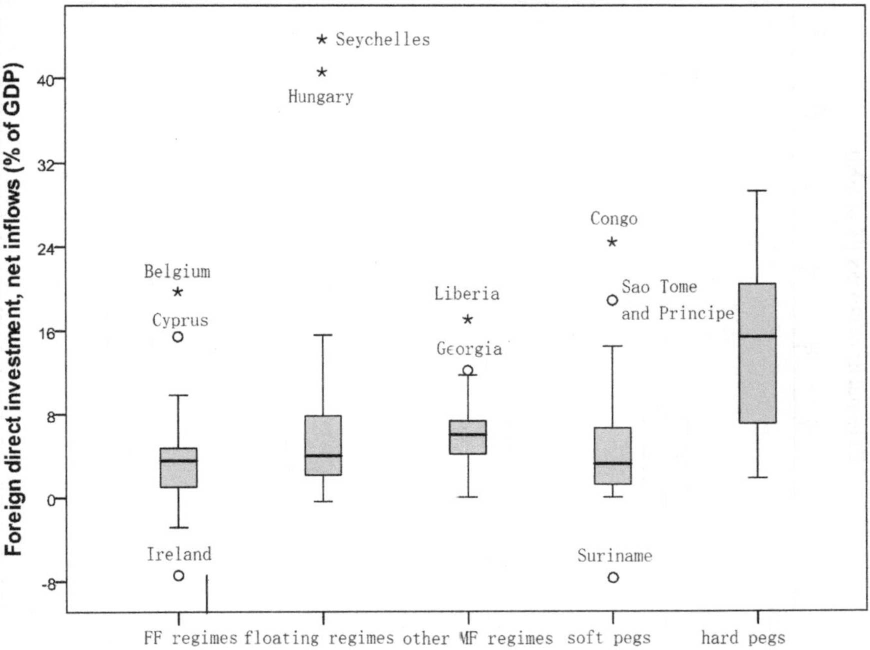

Figure 3.20: Percent of FDI Net Inflows in GDP Box Plot

with FF regimes. Therefore, the financial systems of countries with floating, other MF and soft peg regimes are more vulnerable, while countries with hard pegs have relatively better financial conditions and countries with FF regimes have the best financial system performance.

The two remaining indicators are total foreign debts (as a percent of GNI) and net FDI inflows (as a percent of GDP) in the four-category discrimination results. Regarding percent of foreign debt (Figure 3.20), countries with hard pegs have obviously higher ratios than countries with the other three regimes. In net FDI inflows (Figure 3.21), countries with hard pegs have higher ratios than countries with the other three regimes. Therefore, in terms of foreign debt performance and international capital flows, countries with hard pegs have higher ratios than countries with the other three regime types.

In conclusion, excepting for GDP, countries in the five-category regimes can be summarized with eight indicators. Among the five categories, FF and hard peg regimes show obvious differences from the other three regimes. Floating, other MF and soft peg regimes have shown some similarities.

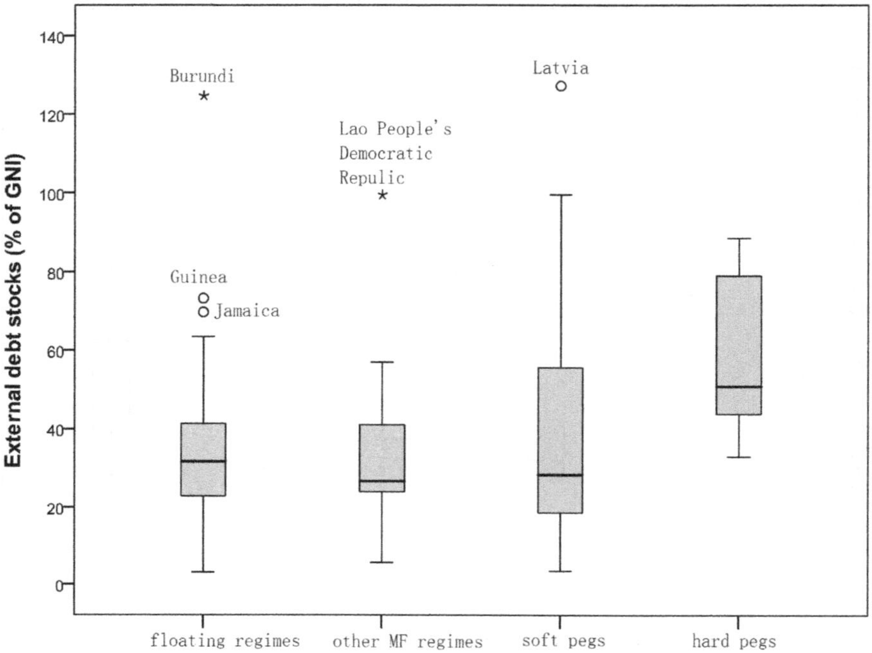

Figure 3.21: Percent of Foreign Debt in GNI Box Plot

3.3.4.4 *China's Exchange Rate Regime Classifications*

By putting China's economic data into the above functions, we can estimate the exchange rate regime to which China most likely belongs. China's relevant economic indicator data from 2008 to 2009 are displayed in Table 3.19.

In terms of the five-category exchange rate arrangement function, China's 2008 data classifies it as a hard peg regime. But China's 2008 exchange rate regime was actually labeled as a stabilized soft peg arrangement. This is reflected in China's 2009 data, which suggests it as a soft peg regime. In terms of the five-category exchange rate arrangement function, China's 2008 and 2009 data classify it as a hard peg regime.

Therefore, from the above results we can see that China's exchange rate regime from 2008 to 2009 belongs to the soft peg group in classification, but it is still more like a hard peg (using the overall discriminant function analysis results).

Among the five-category regime indicators, GDP per capita is a very important indicator. If we change China's 2008 GDP per capita, while holding all other indicators constant, and recalculate China's regime type,

Table 3.19: China's Economic Indicators

	Indicator	2008	2009
Five-category Regime Discrimination Result Indicators	GDP per capita (current USD)	3413.59	3744.36
	Ratio of money and quasi money (M2) to total reserves	3.48	3.64
	Inflation, GDP deflator (annual %)	7.80	−0.62
	Ratio of bank liquid reserves to bank assets (%)	24.84	21.37
	Money and quasi money (M2) as % of GDP	139.89	159.38
Five-category Regime Discrimination Result Indicators	External debt stocks (% of GNI)	8.29	8.68
	Foreign direct investment, net inflows (% of GDP)	3.27	1.57
	GDP (current USD)	4.52E+12	4.98E+12
	Inflation, consumer prices (annual %)	5.86	−0.70

we find that China will match a FF regime type when GDP per capita reaches USD$15,000.

In terms of the five-category exchange rate regime discrimination results indicator, China far exceeds the size of a common country in GDP and has no obvious difference in data level among the other three indicators, so no corresponding exchange rate regime forecast is made.

Analysis of China's situation shows that although China's GDP size has exceeded USD$1 trillion, ranking among the top in the world, it is GDP per capita still lags far behind developed economies, whose average GDP per capita climbs up to USD$40,000 (China's only exceeds USD$5,000). China has no outstanding performance in other important economic indicators. China is a major economy, but it is still far away from a dominant economic power. Therefore, China should adopt a reasonable exchange rate arrangement commensurate with its current economic level and avoid rapid and risky reforms, which could imperil further economic development.

3.3.4.5 *Comparison and Analysis between 2008 and 2010*

This section tracks and compares exchange rate regime changes across each economy in the IMF's 2011 AREAER. According to the latest *de facto* exchange rate arrangement classification standards published by the IMF in 2011 (mainly reflecting 2010 world exchange rate regimes), this section condenses the ten sub-categories of exchange rate regimes into five categories: FF, F, other MF, soft pegs and hard pegs. It then selects

Table 3.20: Exchange Rate Regime Classifications

	Hard Pegs	Soft Pegs	Others	F	FF
2008	23	65	21	46	33
2010	25	82	17	36	30
Changes	+2	+17	−4	−10	−3

118 economic indicators from the World Bank's 2012 world development indicators (2010 data) to build a two-dimensional table analyzing the five categories of regimes and their related economic factors. A similar analysis of 2010 data affirms the analysis summary of 2008 data.

By conducting statistical classification of countries' exchange rate regimes in the IMF's 2009–2010 exchange rate reports (reflecting conditions from 2008 to 2010), we can see the changes over two years (Table 3.20).

Table 3.20 shows that from 2008 to 2010, the number of countries within each of the five categories fluctuated. The number of countries in the floating regime category decreased, while those in the soft pegs category increased. The following section will discuss the changes in detail.

Hard pegs saw two net increases. Estonia belonged to the hard pegs group in 2008, but became a FF country in 2010. Such a change is quite rare. Estonia's reason was that it joined the Eurozone on January 1, 2011, which required it to change its exchange rate arrangement. Besides that case, three more countries have been reclassified under the category, while other hard peg countries remain unchanged.

Soft peg countries saw 17 net increases. Also, two soft peg countries in 2008 changed into other managed regimes in 2010.

The other managed regime group saw a net decrease of four. About 12 countries in this group changed in 2008: Ten became soft pegs in 2010, one became a floating regime, and one became a hard peg.

Floating regime countries saw a net decrease of ten. A total of 14 floating regime countries in 2008 changed groups in 2010: Eight became soft pegs and the remaining six became other managed regimes.

FF countries in 2008 decreased by four in 2010 — three became floating regimes and one became a hard peg regime. Including Estonia, the total number of countries with a FF regime decreased by three.

In general, countries which changed their exchange rate regimes basically transformed from loose regimes to tight ones. There are two major trends in the data. First, a total of ten countries with other managed regimes changed into soft peg regimes. Second, a total of 14 floating regime countries changed into other managed regimes and soft peg regimes. The greatest change was seen among countries with soft peg regimes, whose group increased by 17.

The above changes in rate regimes are related to the 2008 financial crisis and the subsequent European debt crisis (starting in 2009). Due to the two crises, the world economic system suffered a shock and many countries intensified intervention in the foreign exchange market. This had the effect of decreasing the flexibility of numerous exchange rate regimes.

From 2008 to 2010, although many countries changed their exchange rate regime classifications, these changes were mainly concentrated among floating, soft peg and other managed regimes. Countries with FF regimes — largely developed countries — changed little. This shows that the exchange rate regimes of developed countries were not seriously impacted by either the financial crisis or the European debt crisis, demonstrating that their regimes are mature and stable.

The following section uses the World Bank's 2010 world development indicators (issued in 2012) to identify the economic factors influencing exchange rate arrangements. To better balance discrimination analysis results with reasonable theoretical explanations, we apply the methods described in Sections 3.3.3 and 3.3.4 to screen economic indicators, ultimately identifying five indicators. Among these, GDP per capita and the GDP deflator reflect macroeconomic fundamentals; the ratio of bank liquid reserves to bank assets, the percent of M2 in GDP and the ratio of M2 to international reserves reflect financial conditions. Utilizing these screened indicators, the discrimination results show that the accumulated contribution ratio of function #1 and function #2 reaches 99.3% (see Table 3.21). Therefore, the following sections will mainly analyze the characteristics of these two functions.

Standardized typical discriminant function coefficients for the five categories of exchange rate regimes are shown in Table 3.22.

Table 3.21: Discriminant Function Eigenvalues of Five-Category Regimes

	Eigenvalue	Percent of Variance	Accumulated (%)	Positive Correlation
Function #1	173.303	84.1	84.1	0.997
Function #2	31.098	15.2	99.3	0.984
Function #3	1.382	0.7	100.0	0.792
Function #4	0.78	0	100.0	0.269

Note: The analysis applies the above four typical discriminant functions.

Table 3.22: Standardized Typical Discriminant Function Coefficients for the Four Categories of Exchange Rate Regimes

Indicators	Function #1	Function #2	Function #3	Function #4
GDP per capita (current USD)	−7.270	11.355	5.487	0.671
Money and quasi money (M2) to total reserves ratio	−10.245	−9.224	0.543	−1.122
Inflation, GDP deflator (annual %)	9.431	−12.808	−4.678	−0.278
Bank liquid reserves to bank assets ratio (%)	1.654	8.294	−2.515	1.170
Money and quasi money (M2) as % of GDP	6.569	3.213	2.024	0.766

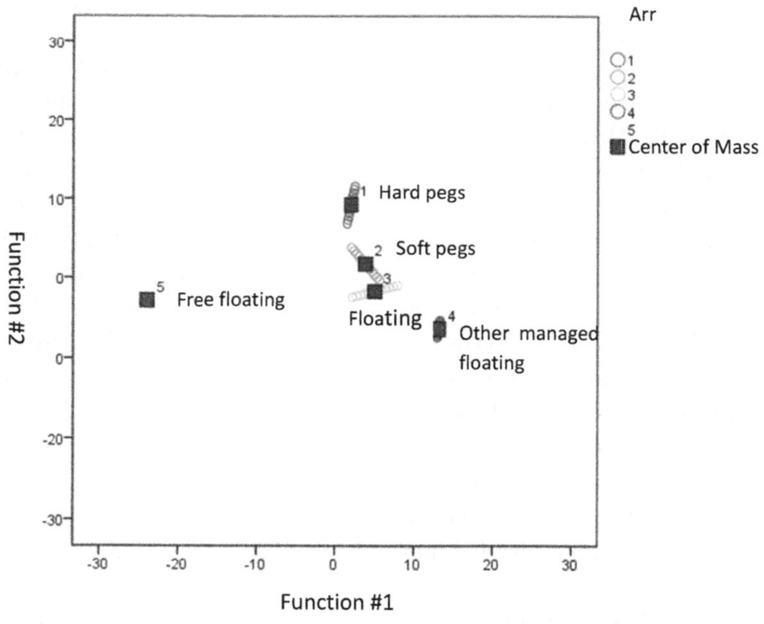

Figure 3.22: Canonical Discriminant Function Diagram for the Five Categories of Exchange Rate Regimes

The canonical discriminant function diagram directly reflects a function's classification results. From Figure 3.22, we can see that functions #1 and #2 can discriminate the five categories of exchange rate regimes. In Figure 3.22, points 1–5 represent the five regime types: Hard pegs, soft pegs, floating regimes, other MF regimes and FF regimes, respectively.

Table 3.23: Discrimination Classification Results of the Five Categories of Exchange Rate Regimes

	FF	F	Other MF	Soft Pegs	Hard Pegs
Initial test (%)					
FF	100.0				
F		100.0			
Other MF			100.0		
Soft Pegs				100.0	
Hard Pegs					100.0
Cross Test (%)					
FF	100.0				
F		91.7	8.3		
Other MF			100.0		
Soft Pegs				100.0	
Hard Pegs					100.0

The direction of function #1 shows that FF regimes have obvious differences with the other four categories. Also, those four categories — F, other MF, soft peg and hard peg regimes — appear to have no greater differences. The one exception is for hard peg regimes. Based on the direction of function #2, hard peg regimes show some differences with the other three in that cluster.

From the discriminant classification of the five categories of regimes (see Table 3.23), we can see that the discriminant function correctly classified 100% of the cases in the initial group and 98.3% of cases in the cross group, with an error rate within 2%. The discrimination results is very good.

By analyzing data from 2008 and 2010, we can see that FF regimes have obvious differences with the other four exchange rate regimes. Therefore, the following section will remove FF regimes from its analysis in order to discern more detailed relationships between the remaining regimes. This should allow more complete conclusions.

Similarly, the above method will be used to analyze indicator data on the four exchange rate regimes. Table 3.24 provides the discriminant function eigenvalues of the four categories of exchange rate regimes. From this we can see that the accumulated contribution rates of functions #1 and #2 reach 93.6%. Therefore, the following section will mainly analyze the characteristics of these two functions.

Standardized typical discriminant function coefficients for the four categories of exchange rate regimes are shown in Table 3.25.

Table 3.24: Discriminant Function Eigenvalues of the Four Categories Exchange Rate Regimes

	Eigenvalue	Percent of Variance	Accumulated (%)	Positive Correlation
Function #1	12.058	78.3	78.3	0.961
Function #2	2.354	15.3	93.6	0.838
Function #3	0.981	6.4	100.0	0.704

Note: The analysis applies the above three typical discriminant functions.

Table 3.25: Standardized Typical Discriminant Function Coefficients for the Four Categories of Exchange Rate Regimes

Indicators	Function #1	Function #2	Function #3
External debt stocks (% of GNI)	−3.885	2.091	−2.700
Foreign direct investment, net inflows (% of GDP)	1.850	−2.791	3.158
GDP (current USD)	0.219	0.916	1.815
Inflation, consumer prices (annual %)	1.964	−0.146	−1.806

Table 3.26: Discrimination Classification Results for the Four Categories of Exchange Rate Regimes

	Floating	Other MF	Soft Pegs	Hard Pegs
Initial Test (%)				
F	91.7	8.3		
Other MF		91.7		8.3
Soft Pegs			100	
Hard Pegs		16.7		83.3
Cross Test (%)				
F	83.3	16.7		
Other MF		83.3		16.7
Soft Pegs			100.0	
Hard Pegs		16.7		83.3

In Table 3.25, the indicator that is most related to function #1 is the percentage of foreign debt in GNI and the indicators most related to function #2 are the percentage of net FDI inflow in GDP and the percentage of foreign debt in GNI.

The classification results are shown in Table 3.26. We can see that the discriminant function correctly classifies 91.7% of cases in the initial group and 87.5% cases in the cross group. Although the discrimination accuracy is not as high as the former analyses, the overall error rate is still low and the results are acceptable.

3.3.5 *Analysis of Political Factors Influencing Exchange Rate Arrangements*

Exchange rate regimes have strong political dimensions. They are a policy choice made by governments to balance domestic and international political and economic interests. Therefore, political factors have important influences on the choice of exchange rate regime.

3.3.5.1 *Domestic Factors*

From the domestic perspective, "a country's political systems, including election system, election time, political type (degree of democracy), political stability, political transparency and central bank independence, have important impacts on the choice of exchange rate regimes" (Wang, 2005). This paper will analyze the impact of these major political factors, including political stability, interest groups, the degree of democracy, and electoral system on exchange rate arrangements.

(1) Political Stability

Zhuand Zhu (2012) point out that volatile political situations reduce investor confidence and cause large fluctuations in the exchange rate. On the one hand, political stability directly influences a country's exchange rate arrangements through trade partner countries and financial investors. On the other hand, political stability influences other domestic economic policies (such as monetary policies) and thus indirectly influences government's exchange rate arrangements. In countries with less political stability, the political authority is unwilling to implement monetary and financial policies at the cost of narrowing output and increasing unemployment (in order to consolidate its controlling position). Besides, floating exchange rates have the ability to control price imbalances with exchange rate changes, preventing the problem of monetary authorities implementing policies that narrow output. Therefore, in countries with less political stability, floating exchange rates are more welcomed (Guo, 2009).

For example, Malaysia implemented a dollar-pegged exchange rate regime from September 1998 to July 2005. The reasons for choosing a regime for as long as seven years are various, but a very important one is that after the Asian Financial Crisis, the choice of pegging to the US Dollar increased trust in the government and built market confidence — factors that maintain domestic economic and political stability.

(2) Interest Groups

Since Lucas (1976) criticized the macro research method, a large amount of macro research methods have begun to pay attention to the relationship between the micro and macro economy. To address macro problems, the newer methods consider rational forecasting and individual actor choices, as well as micro economy variables. This is also true for research on the choice of exchange rate regime. Relevant theories on interest groups hold that rational micro economy actors will not accept a given policy arrangement passively. Instead, they will form interest groups to conduct active political lobbying, seeking to influence the government's exchange rate arrangement in the hopes of benefiting themselves (Frieden, 1991; Hefeker, 1996; Broz and Frieden, 2001, 2006; Faia *et al.*, 2008; Liu and Jin, 2012).

Frieden (1991) built a set of theoretical analysis models to study how different interest groups form different preferences on exchange rate policies. Frieden (2001) thinks that, for export enterprises and foreign investment enterprises, exchange rate fluctuation brings risks to business. Thus, they prefer fixed exchange rate regimes. As for enterprises whose businesses are mainly concentrated in the domestic market, monetary policy independence is of greater benefit to them than exchange rate stability. They therefore prefer floating exchange rate regimes. Hefeker (1996) divided economic interest groups into those that produce tradable goods and those that produce non-tradable goods. He argued that the former prefer fixed exchange rate regimes while the latter floating rate regimes. Taking the forward exchange rate market into consideration, Ruland and Viaene (1993) build an economic model to explain interest group preferences and acquired different results than Hefeker (1996). They conclude that, if there were no forward exchange rate markets, related interest groups would all prefer fixed regimes. Conversely, if there are futures market, interest groups producing tradable goods will separate according to a country's new exchange rate exposure and their exchange rate regime preference will change in line with financial market risks.

(3) Degree of Democracy

Democracy is usually compared against oligarchy and autocracy. It represents rule of the people, which is to say that people possess the right to vote in elections, elect leaders, and choose government policies. In countries with a high degree of democracy, political actors seek to acquire a good reputation and secure reelection. Thus, governments will consider the different requirements of various interest groups, and policies will deviate along the lines of these interest groups. Conversely, in countries with a low degree of democracy, the governments' power is not directly related to peoples' policy preferences. Therefore policy-makers have more freedom to ignore peoples' interests. Kuang and Wang (2007) argue that policy-makers in democratic countries face grave pressures to formulate and implement policies which redistribute wealth. They need to utilize monetary policies to control the domestic economy to meet political and economic requirements, so they prefer a floating exchange rate regime accompanied by independent monetary policy.

(4) Political Parties and Electoral Systems

In Hibbs's (2001) analysis of monetary policy preferences among different political parties, he discovered that left-wing parties dislike inflation more than right-wing ones. Because fixed exchange rates can secure right-wing parties' promise of keeping inflation low, credible and low inflation brings benefits to voters of right-wing parties and voters themselves tend to prefer fixed exchange rate regimes (Simmons, 2000; Oatley and Gholamain, 1997). Left-wing parties think that inflation brings strong pressure on the government to control the domestic economy (often to adapt to the external economic environment), so they prefer floating exchange rate regimes (Simmons, 2000). Kuang and Wang (2007) introduce parties' as dummy variables (naming them left-wing or right-wing) into a model to analyze how political factors influence exchange rate regime choices in East Asia and Latin America emerging market countries. Their results show that the political ideology of a government is strongly correlated with a particular kind of rate regime. For example, Chili's exchange regime arrangement has consistently deviated towards a floating exchange rate regime when left-wing governments were in power.

Bernhard and Leblang (2009) show how the electoral systems of developing countries force politicians to choose exchange rate regimes in the post-Bretton Woods world. They believe that, under a floating exchange rate regime, politicians can manipulate monetary policies to make them favorable for their election (something impossible under fixed exchange rate regimes). Incumbent politicians hope to ensure their return to office through economic stimulus and thus prefer floating exchange rate regimes. However, in a system of proportional representation, political parties may prefer fixed exchange rate regimes to prevent widespread inter-party disputes over economic policies. Frieden (2001) thinks that the influence of election timing on exchange rate arrangements depends on whether the election time is an exogenous or an endogenous variable of political behavior. The context of regular and phased elections, election times are an exogenous variable and, because monetary policy can be used as an important tool to win elections, the ruling party chooses to maintain the independence of monetary policy and prefer a floating exchange rate. Otherwise, election time would be an endogenous variable and the ruling party has no need to maintain the independence of monetary policies to win elections. Therefore, they would prefer fixed exchange rate regimes.

Analysis of scholars at home and abroad who study the political factors influencing exchange rate arrangements cover various aspects of a country's politics and provide many important ideas for explaining choices of exchange rate. In general, different political situations directly or indirectly influence the government's preference of exchange rate regime (see Table 3.27) and there are important aspects one should consider when analyzing a country's exchange rate regime.

3.3.5.2 *International Factors*

The choice of exchange rate arrangements should entail not only domestic realities and policy targets but also the international political and economic context. On the one hand, implementation and target realization of exchange rate policies are impacted by international political relationships, which is especially obvious as globalization continues to gather momentum. On the other hand, exchange rate arrangements are an important part of the international economic system and an important means for countries striving to safeguard their international interests. Said countries are impacted by international domination, competition, cooperation and the general international political climate.

I. Governments' exchange rate arrangements must consider international political factors.

Ogawa (2002) sets the target of exchange rate arrangement choice as that of stabilizing competition and minimizing exogenous fluctuations in international trade balances brought by dollar–yen exchange rate fluctuations. Ogawa analyzed the strategy and coordination processes of each country among Asian emerging economies. These countries export to

Table 3.27: Influences of Domestic Political Factors on Exchange Rate Arrangement

Political Factor	Influences on Exchange Rate Arrangements	Relevant Studies
Political Stability	Volatile political situations reduce investor confidence and bring great fluctuations. Political stability influences the exchange rate arrangement through domestic policy choices and international trade.	Zhu and Zhu (2012)
	Countries with low political stability prefer floating exchange rate regimes.	Guo (2009)
Interest Groups	Export enterprises and foreign investment enterprises prefer fixed exchange rate regimes while enterprises whose businesses are mainly in the domestic market prefer floating exchange rate regimes.	Frieden (2001)
	Divides economic interest groups into ones that produce tradable goods and ones that produce non-tradable goods. The former prefer fixed regimes and the latter prefer floating regimes.	Hefeker (1996)
	If there is no forward exchange rate market, related interest groups would prefer fixed regimes. If there is a forward exchange market, their regime preferences change with financial market risk.	Ruland and Viaene (1993)
Degree of Democracy	Countries with a high degree of democracy prefer floating exchange rate regimes.	Kuang and Wang (2007)
Political Parties and Electoral Systems	Right-wing political parties prefer fixed exchange rate regimes while left-wing parties prefer floating exchange rate regimes.	Simmons (2000); Oatley and Gholamain (1997)
	Incumbent politicians prefer floating regimes. But in a system of proportional representation, political parties may prefer fixed regimes.	Bernhard and Leblang (2009)
	When the election time of ruling parties is an exogenous variable, they prefer floating regimes; when the time is an endogenous variable, they prefer fixed regimes.	Frieden (2001)

neighboring countries as well as to America, Japan and other countries. To avoid destabilizing risks brought by exchange rate changes, pegging to the Dollar or pegging to a basket of currencies are valid options (under Nash equilibrium). After the Asian financial crisis, almost all countries hit by the crisis gave up their pegged exchange rate regimes, except for Malaysia (which still retains theirs). This broke the original strategic balance and caused grave market pressure on Malaysia (Zhang, 2003).

The "fear of floating" theory (Calvo and Reinhart, 2002) analyzes the reasons developing countries give up the target of a stabilized interest rate and choose instead to target a stabilized exchange rate. This theory considers imbalances in the economy and trade between developed and developing countries, as well as the relatively low international reputation of developing countries.

II. Imbalanced positions in international politics and economics impact the international exchange rate regime system.

(1) Hegemonic Currency Theory

In the hegemonic stability theory, Kindleberger (1973) suggested that, when a single country or a political regime is a world dominating power (namely a hegemon), it is easy for the international political and economic system to remain stable. Implementing a relatively stable exchange rate regime system is one of a hegemonic country's five functions: It issues a hegemonic currency, opens markets, maintains long-term free flow of capital, manages exchange rates and builds a stable international monetary system. The theory holds that fixed exchange rate systems help a hegemonic country play its role and stabilize the international financial system. The theory can be used to partially explain changes in the international exchange rate system. For example, Britain's hegemonic position (from the Congress of Vienna to World War I) paralleled the Gold Standard, America's hegemonic position (1945–1971) pushed the establishment of the Bretton Woods system, and the instability of the Gold Standard between the two world wars was because no country was willing and capable to become a hegemony (Eichengreen, 1987). However, the theory cannot explain the differences and changes among countries' exchange rate regimes during the same period.

(2) Political Theory of International Currencies

This theory emphasizes the relationship between international politics and military power, rather than privileging only economic factors as impacting the choice of exchange rate arrangement. Strange (1971) studied the use of the Pound in the British colonies. He divides international currencies into categories and expands upon the reasons for choosing foreign currencies. Under some circumstances, it is a choice of their own accord due to the world dominating position of the issuing country, namely the Top Currency (equivalent to the hegemonic currency in hegemonic stability theory). Under some other circumstances, regions using such currencies have political dependence on the issuing country (including allied countries, protected countries and colonies). They are dominated politically by the metropolitan country, namely the Master Currency. When political power to dominate declines, master currencies will evolve into negotiated currencies. Under some other circumstances, the strong economic power of the issuing country makes its currency an international currency, namely a Neutral Currency. This theory distinguishes whether countries are adopting other countries' currencies voluntarily or otherwise. It is applicable to explaining changes in exchange rate systems when politically domination relationships break down, such as exchange rate changes after the Soviet Union disintegrated. However, it is not applicable in some other circumstances, for example, during the independence of Latin American countries (these do not conform to exchange rate changes as explained in the theory). In addition, the theory has a rough framework and is unable to be applied to correctly analyze real problems.

(3) "Core and Peripheral Theory" and Others

The "Impossible Trinity" explains malignant devaluation and inflation brought about by floating exchange rate regimes without explaining why such a vicious cycle mainly happens in developing countries instead of developed ones. In the "Impossible Trinity", the Dollar enjoys a privileged position as an international reserve currency accepted by each country. Therefore, unlike developed countries, America does not need to worry about its balance of payments. Its domestic monetary policy is not subject to exchange rate policy pressures. Without shaking the Dollar's dominating position as an international settlement currency and the unequal situation of the present international monetary standard, it is hard to change the inequality between the rate regimes of developed and developing countries. The core-peripheral theory put forward by Bordo and Rlandreau (2001) considers technological progress in financial and monetary industry, attributing the root of currency crises to the emergence of industrial countries which lack sufficient financial maturity. The financial market development of developing countries has been short, incomplete and peripheral. According to the "Original Sin Theory" (Hausmann *et al.*, 2000; Eichengreen, 1994), these countries will have to abandon floating exchange rate regimes in the end and directly use other countries' currencies to implement "dollarization". Compared with these countries, developed countries are in the core position and they can adopt flexible exchange rate regimes.

Table 3.28 summarizes some major theories and viewpoints on the influences of unequal political and economic relationships on exchange rate regimes.

Table 3.28: Summary of Theories on the Influences of Unequal Political and Economic Relationships on Exchange Rate Regimes

Theory	Content	Issues Explained	Issues Left Unexplained
Hegemonic Stability Theory	Countries with dominating power issue hegemonic currencies, implementing relatively stable exchange rate regime systems to maintain a stable international financial system.	Britain's hegemony → gold standard: America's hegemony → Bretton Woods system: No hegemony between two world wars → competitive devaluation of currencies.	Differences between and the changes of exchange rate regimes in the same period.
Political Theory of International Currency	Foreign currencies can be divided into the following, according to reasons for choosing them: Top Currency, Master Currency, Negotiated Currency and Neutral Currency	Whether a country is willing or forced to use international currencies: Changes in exchange rate regime after the Soviet Union's disintegration.	Latin American independence does not conform to exchange rate regime changes; lacks accurate analysis of details.
"Core and Peripheral Theory" and others	Developing countries and developed countries are unequal in international exchange rate regimes; developing countries have insufficient financial maturity and stay in a peripheral position.	Developing countries' original sin and dollarization; The Dollar's privileged position.	

III. International coordination, cooperation, and international organizations play a great role in the international exchange rate regime system.

(1) International Coordination

International coordination means that each country, out of their own interest, adopts relatively uniform policies and realizes a win–win scenario without mutual coordination. Global fixed exchange rate regimes can realize international monetary policy coordination (Frieden, 1993). When more countries join fixed exchange rate regimes, they gain from the benefits of stable international trade and investment. Such incentives become stronger when more countries follow suit, or become weaker in the opposite case. The Gold Standard system (dominated by Britain at the end of the 19th century) the Bretton Woods system and Euro integration all reflect the positive roles of this feedback incentive. The breakdown of the Gold Standard and the Bretton Woods systems, in contrast, reflect the negative role of this incentive.

(2) International Cooperation

International cooperation means each country cooperates to have mutual adjustment and support to choose related policies out of group interest (instead of purely their own). Frieden (1993) pointed out the need for international cooperation: If we regard international interest rate stability under fixed exchange rate regimes, individual countries may "take a free ride" to choose the devaluation of their home currency in order to increase their export competitiveness without impacting system stability. When such countries reach a significant enough number, the system will crash. Cooperation greatly improves the persistence of a fixed exchange rate regime, which helps improve international trade and investment levels, increasing domestic currency stability and decreasing international trade disputes (Frieden, 2001). Cooperation incentives are considered as joint benefits brought by maintaining currency stability, correlation of exchange rate policies and other policies. Overall, the incentive for international cooperation, the desire to acquire hegemony, and influences from the macroconomic environment combine to encourage cooperation (Willett, 1999; Simmons, 2000).

(3) International Organizations

The role of the IMF and other influential international organizations is an important political variable influencing the international monetary system. The IMF's major functions include making policies for exchange rates,

Table 3.29: Summary of International Political Cooperation Factors Influencing Exchange Rate Regimes

Influencing Factor	Influencing Mechanism	Case
International Coordination	Countries do not need to coordinate and adopt relatively uniform policies to realize win–win outcomes.	Establishment and breakdown of the Gold Standard system, Bretton Woods system, and Euro integration.
International Cooperation	Countries cooperate, adjust, support and choose win–win exchange rate policies out of group interests.	Avoid the free rider problem under fixed exchange rate regimes.
International Organization	The IMF's functions: Making policies for exchange rates, current item payment for member countries, and currency exchange rules; monitoring exchange rate regimes and maintaining the international exchange rate order.	IMF exchange rate policy suggestions have great influence on developing countries.

current item payment for member countries, and currency exchange rules. It also monitors exchange rate regimes and maintains the international exchange rate order. Opinions on exchange rates made by the IMF and other organizations are especially important for developing countries. Table 3.29 summarizes the above factors.

In summary, theories and research on the international political factors that influence exchange rate regimes have yet to mature. First, these theories are mostly qualitative, covering only judgments about the direction of rate regime change (theorizing why regimes are relaxed or tightened) without distinguishing degrees of change or specifying classifications (e.g., from among the various floating and pegged exchange rate regime types). Second, models and their related analyses tend to measure large areas — the entire world or whole international regions — and their results are broad judgments about international monetary regimes. They therefore lack specific description of the influences on each country. Third, theories' seek to explain long-term effects, but short-term fluctuations may fall outside this scope. Take the stability theory as an example. It divides the 500 years from the end of the 15th century to the middle and end of the 20th century into five periods, with the shortest period being 26 years of American hegemony from 1945 to 1971. Using such a rough model to explain changes in exchange rate regimes over only a few years is difficult.

Nevertheless, we can still gain some insight from these theories and their documentation. According to the comparison in Section 3.3.4.5, the exchange rate regimes of IMF member countries generally tightened from 2008 to 2010 and most of the changes happened in developing economies. In 2009, the world economy started to recover and the negative influences of the financial crisis on world politics and economies gradually declined (especially the America economy, which began to improve). But the European debt crisis — originating in Greece at the end of 2009 and gradually fermenting through 2010 — mired the world, and particularly Europe, in economic difficulties. During this period, the Euro weakened against the Dollar, giving the latter a dominating international position. From the perspective of international competition (and following several theories, such as hegemonic currency theory, political theory of international currencies, and core and peripheral theory), when an issuing country has a strong political influence and dominating power over other countries, the dominated countries are more inclined to use a relatively fixed exchange rate regime (if not the dominating country's currency outright). This partially explains the observed trend of exchange rate regime changes in this period.

3.3.5.3 *Conclusion*

From the analysis of this section, we can see that exchange rate arrangements are important policies that influence domestic and international balance. Given this broad importance, they are heavily influenced by a mix of domestic and international factors: domestic economic factors and international trade; the domestic political environment and the global political environment. Particularly complex are the political variables. Domestic factors involve a country's political stability, its interest groups, its degree of democracy, its political parties, and its electoral system. International factors can include the country's international competition and cooperation, as well as its relationship to international organizations.

Traditional economic theories cannot explain a country's choice of exchange rate arrangements (or its change in arrangements over time), which is why it is important to consider political factors as well. The political dimension can make up for some of the failures of economic theory, expanding analysis of exchange rate regime to include questions about society and human choice. Currently, academic research has reached a consensus that exchange rate arrangements are chosen by a dynamic, transformative process involving both economic factors and related political factors.

Domestically, political stability influences a country's exchange rate arrangements by affecting domestic policy choices and the country's international trade. Different groups have different requirements for exchange rate arrangements, and interest group have important influence in shaping government policy. Likewise, a country's degree of democracy, its political parties and its electoral system determine how much influence interest groups can exercise upon the exchange rate arrangement. Internationally, in pursuit of their own self-interest, countries need to have both long-term cooperation and competition. The IMF and other international organizations have important roles in rule making and stabilizing the global exchange rate system. They are important political powers influencing international monetary regimes.

Of course, just as economic factors cannot fully explain the choice of exchange rate arrangement, explanations resting on political factors likewise have limits. First, political factors are complicated, interconnected, and differ greatly between countries. Although we can regard the role of political factors as the results of mutual competition among different political powers, to precisely define political factors in regards to explaining exchange rate arrangements in a uniform, cross-country model is very difficult. Second, it is hard to quantify the influence of numerous political factors on exchange rate arrangements. So far few researchers studying exchange rate arrangements consider even qualitative political factors in their empirical research models. Even if such factors are taken into consideration, analyses are often defined based on specific countries and cases, which make them difficult to generalize. Lastly, a country's political factors may remain stable in the short term (and some even in the long term, such as political parties and electoral system), which makes it hard to explain short-term changes in exchange rate arrangements.

Therefore, the choice of exchange rate arrangement needs to combine both economic factors and political factors. We should not only consider the influence of political factors on the long-term trend of exchange rate arrangements, but also attach importance to the vital role of economic factors in explaining models and providing short-term analysis of changes. This section provided a framework for analyzing exchange rate regimes from the perspective of political factors. As a supplement to the economic perspective, it contributes to a larger research project considering the many factors influencing exchange rate regime choice and policy.

Bibliography

In English

Agénor P. and Masson P. (1999). Credibility, Reputation and the Mexican Peso Crisis. *Journal of Money, Credit and Banking*, 31(1): 82–83.

Aghion P., Bacchetta P., Ranciere R. and Rogoff K. (2006). Exchange Rate Volatility and Productivity Growth: The Role of Financial Development. NBER Working Paper, No. W12117.

Alesina A. and Wagner A. (2003). Choosing (and Reneging on) Exchange Rate Regimes. *Journal of the European Economic Association*, 4(4): 770–799.

Bernhard W. and Leblang D. (2009). Democratic Institutions and Exchange-rate Commitments. *International Organization*, 53(1): 71–97.

Bleary M. and Francisco M. (2005). Classifying Exchange Rate Regimes: A Statistical Analysis of Alternative Methods. CREDIT Research Paper No.07/05.

Blomberg S., Frieden J. and Stein E. (2001). Sustaining Fixed Rates: The Political Economy of Currency Pegs in Latin America.

Bordo M. D. and Rlandreau M. (2001). Core, Periphery, Exchange Rate Regimes, and Globalization. NBER Working Paper W8584.

Broz L. and Frieden J. A. (2006). *The Political Economy of Exchange Rates. Handbook of Political Science*, Oxford: Oxford University Press, 587–597.

Bubula A. and Otker-Robe I. (2002). Are Pegged and Intermediate Exchange Rate Regimes Crisis Prone? IMF Working Paper, No. 03/229.

Calvo G. and Reinhart C. (2002). Fear of Floating. *Quarterly Journal of Economics*, 117(2): 379–408.

Chang R. and Velasco A. (2000). Financial Fragility and the Exchange Rate Regime. *Journal of Economic Theory*, 92(1): 1–34.

Cibils and Bruce A. (2001). Exchange Rate Policy, Capital Controls, and Economic Stability in Argentina: A CGE Modeling Approach. The Doctoral Dissertation of the American University.

Coudert V. and Dubert C. (2004). Does Exchange Rate Regime Explain Differences in Economic Results for Asian Countries?. CEPII Working Paper No. 2003–05.

Detragiache E., Mody A. and Okada E. (2005). Exits from Heavily Managed Exchange Rate Regimes. IMF Working Paper No. 05/39.

Dooley M. (1995). A Survey of Academic Literature on Controls over International Capital Transactions. NBER Working paper. No. 5352.

Dubas J. M., Lee B. J. and Mark N. C. (2005). Effective Exchange Rate Classifications and Growth. NBER Working Paper, No. 11272.

Edwards S. (1996). The Determinants of the Choice between Fixed and Flexible Exchange-Rate Regimes. NBER Working Paper, No. 5756.

Eichengreen B. (1987). Hegemonic Stability Theories of the International Monetary System. CEPR Discussion Papers, DP193.

Eichengreen B. (1994). International Monetary Arrangements for the 21st Century. Washington, DC: Brookings Institution.

Faia E., Giuliodori M. and Ruta M. (2008). Political Pressures and Exchange Rate Stability in Emerging Market Economies! *Journal of Applied Economics*, 11(1): 1–32.

Frankel J. (1999). No Single Currency Regime is Right for All Countries or At All Times. NBER Working Paper, No. 7338.

Frankel J. A. (2003). Experience of and Lessons from Exchange Rate Regimes in Emerging Economies. KSG Working Papers, Series No. RWP03~011.

Frieden, J. A. (1991). Invested Interests: The Politics of National Economic Policies in a World of Global Finance. *International Organization*, 45(4): 425–451.

Frieden J. (1993). The Dynamics of International Monetary Systems: International and Domestic Factors in the Rise, Reign, and Demise of Classical Gold Standard. In Snyder J. and Jervis R., eds., *Coping with Complexity in the International System*, Boulder, CO: Westview, 345–379.

Frieden J. (2001). The Political Economy of International Monetary Relations. *Annual Review of Science*, 4: 317–343.

Genberg H. and Swoboda A. (2004). Exchange Rate Regimes: Does What Countries say Matter? Graduate Institute of International Studies, Geneva, Working Paper (May).

Ghosh A. R., Gulde A. M. and Wolf H. C. (2002). Exchange Rate Regimes: Classification and Consequences. In Ghosh A., Gulde A. and Wolf H., eds., *Exchange Rate Regimes, Choices and Consequences*. Cambridge: MIT Press.

Gilpin, R. (1987). The Political Economy of International Relations. Princeton: Princeton University Press.

Habermeier K. I. (2009). Revised System for the Classification of Exchange Rate Arrangements. IMF Working Paper, WP/09/211.

Hausmann R., Panizza U. and Stein E. (2000). Why Do Countries Float the Way They Float? Inter-American Development Bank Working Paper, No. 418.

Hefeker C. (1996). The Political Choice and Collapse of Fixed Exchange Rates. *Journal of Institutional and Theoretical Economics*, 152(2): 360–379.

Hibbs D. A. (2001). The Partisan Model of Macroeconomic Cycles: More Theory And Evidence For The United States. *Economics and Politics*, 6(1): 1–23.

IMF (1999–2009). *Annual Report on Exchange Arrangements and Exchange Restrictions*. Washington D.C.: IMF.

Johnston B. (1999). Exchange Rate Arrangements and Currency Convertibility: Developments and Issues. IMF Working Paper, 36.

Juhn G. and Mauro P. (2002). Long-Run Determinants of Exchange Rate Regimes: A Simple Sensitivity Analysis. IMF Working Paper, 02/104.

Kindleberger R. (1973). *The World in Depression: 1929–1939*. University of California Press.

Klein M. W. and Shambaugh J. C. (2008). The Dynamics of Exchange Rate Regimes: Fixes, Floats, and Flips. *Journal of International Economic*, 75(1): 70–92.

Krugman P. (1991). Target Zones and Exchange Rate Dynamics. *Quarterly Journal of Economics*, CVI: 669–682.

Krugman P. (1998). International Economics: Theory and Policy. *Oxford Review of Economic Policy*, 14(2): 7–17.

Levy-Yeyati E. and Sturzenegger F. (2003). A De facto Classification of Exchange Rate Regimes: A Methodological Note. *American Economic Review*, 93(4): 1173–1193.

Levy-Yeyati E. (2006). Financial Dollarisation: Evaluating the Consequences. *Economic Policy*, 21(45): 41–118.

Levy-Yeyati E. and Sturzenegger F. (2005). Classifying Exchange Rate Regimes: Deeds versus Words. *European Economic Review*, 49: 1603–1635.

Lucas R. (1976). Econometric Policy Evaluation: A Critique. In Brunner K. and Meltzer A. eds., *The Phillips Curve and Labor Markets. Carnegie-Rochester Conference Series on Public Policy 1*. New York: American Elsevier, 19–46.

Masson P. (2000). Exchange Rate Regime Transitions. IMF Working Paper, No. 134.

Masson P. (2001). Exchange Rate Regime Transitions. *Journal of Development Economics*, 64: 571–586.

Mundell R. (1961). A Theory of Optimum Currency Areas. *American Economic Review*, 51, 657–665.

Nilsson K. and Nilsson L. (2000). Exchange Rate Regimes and Export Performance of Developing Countries. *The World Economy*, 23(3): 331–347.

Oatley K. and Gholamain M. (1997). Emotions and Identification: Connections between Readers and Fiction. *Emotion and the Arts*, 263–298.

Obstfeld M. and Rogoff K. (1995). The Mirage of Fixed Exchange Rates. *Journal of Economic Perspectives*, 9(4): 81–85.

Ogawa E. and Takatoshi I. (2000). On the Desirability of a Regional Basket Currency Arrangement. NBER Working Paper, No. 8002.

Ogawa E. (2002). Economic Interdependence and International Coordination in East Asia.

Poirson H. (2001). How Do Countries Choose Their Exchange Rate Regime. IMF Working Paper No. 46, April 2001: 1–30.

Reinhart C. and Rogoff K. (2004). The Modern History of Exchange Rate Arrangements: A Reinterpretation. *Quarterly Journal of Economics*, 119: 1–48.

Rogoff K., Husain A., Mody A., Brooks R. and Oomes N. (2003). Evolution and Performance of Exchange Rate Regimes. IMF Working Paper WP/03/243.

Roubini N. and Wachtel P. (1998). Current Account Sustainability in Transition Economies. NBER Working Paper No. 6468.

Ruland L. J. and Viaene J.-M. (1993). The Political Choice of Exchange Rate Regime. *Economics and Politics* 5(3): 271–284.

Simmons B. A. (2000). International Law and State Behavior: Commitment and Compliance in International Monetary Affairs. *The American Political Science Review*, 94(4): 819–835.

Strange S. (1971). *Sterling and British Policy: A Political Study of International Currency in Decline*. London: Oxford University Press.

Svensson L. E. O. (2002). The Choice of Monetary-Policy/Exchange-Rate Regimes. Eco 553, Part 2, available at http://larseosvensson.se/files/und/553/5532o7.pdf.

Von Hagen J. and Zhou J. (2005). The Choice of Exchange-Rate Regime: An Empirical Analysis for Transition Economies. *Economics of Transition*, 13(4): 679–703.

Von Hagen J. and Zhou J. (2007). The Choice of Exchange-Rate Regime in Developing Countries: A Multinomial Panel Analysis. *Journal of International Money and Finance*, 26: 1071–1094.

Von Hagen J. and Zhou J. (2002). The Choice of Exchange Rate Regimes: An Empirical Analysis for Transition Economies. Center for European Integration Studies Working Paper.

Williamson J. (2000). Exchange Rate Regimes for Emerging Markets: Reviving the Intermediate Option. September.

Willett T. D. (1999). Development in the Political Economy of Policy Coordination, *Open Economics Review*, 10: 221–253.

Wittman D. (1989). Why Democracies Produce Efficient Results. *The Journal of Political Economy*, 97(6): 1395.

Wolf H. (2001). Exchange Rate Regime Choice and Consequences. NBER Working Paper, October.

World Bank (2010). *Development Research Group*. Washington, D.C.: World Development Indicators.

In Chinese

Chen S. M. (2007). Review on the Theory of Classification of Exchange Rate. *The Journal of World Economy*, 1: 89–96.

Cheng S. W. (2009). *On Economic Reform and Development of China*, 261–311. Beijing: China Remin University Press.

Deng L. L. (2004). *The Selection of Exchange Rate System and the Development Tendency*. Dalian: Dongbei University of Finance & Economics Press.

Ding Z. J. and Sun X. J. (2009). Transition of The System of International Exchange Rate over The Last decade. *Intertrade*, 12: 48–51.

Ding Z. J. (2004). The Evolution of Exchange Rate Regimes during 1999 to 2003. *Journal of Financial Research*, 5: 37–45.

Fang Z. (2002). Rethink on The Selection of Exchange Rate Regimes. *Studies of International Finance*, 10: 15–19.

Guo J. Q. (2001). The Trend of Exchange Rate Regimes and Our Choice. *Management World*, 3: 121–126.

Guo Y. Q. (2009). Analyzing the Choice of Exchange Rate Regimes — Selection of Macau Exchange Rate Regime. Jinan University.

Jiang F. (2001). The Choice of the Exchange Rate Regime. *Journal of Financial Research*, 5: 49–56.

Kuang M. and Wang H. (2007). Empirical Analysis on the Factors that Have Impacts on the Choice of the Exchange Rate Regime in Emerging Market Countries. *Studies of International Finance*, 10: 26–33.

Li J. P. and Yu S. (2005). The Selection of The Exchange Rate Regimes and Its Economic Performance: Review on Empirical Literatures. *Productivity Research*, 12: 253–254.

Liu C. and Tu H. (2009). The Choice of Monetary Policy Framework after Retreating from Fixed Exchange Rate Anchor. *China Money*, 2: 25–29.

Liu T. and Jin H. F. (2012). The Exchange Rate Political Economics: a Literature Review. *World Economic Papers*, 1: 106–120.

Liu X. H. and Fan C. L. (2007). The Selection of Exchange Rate Regime and the Development of Its Standards. *The Journal of World Economy*, 3: 86–96.

Lu B. M. (2009). Exchange-rate Targeting, Monetary Targeting and Inflation Targeting: Comparison and Application. *Studies of International Finance*, 1: 69–80.

Shi J. C. and Shen G. B. (2002). On the Institutional Change Theory and the Classification Standards of Institutional Change. *Economist*, 1: 41–46.

Sun B. (2004). Exchange Rate Regimes Study. *Economy and Management*, November.

Wang M. C. (2005). The Political Economic Analysis on Selection of Exchange Rate: A Literature Review. *Comparative Economic & Social Systems*, 3: 137–141.

Wei Z. and Wang S. H. (2011). On The Development of the System of International Exchange Rate during 1999 to 2010. *China Market*, 27: 55–56.

Wei Z., Wang S. S. and Wang H. W. (2011). The De Facto Classification of IMF and Its Frameworks. *Shanghai Finance*, 8: 84–89.

Xia B. and Liao Q. (2001). Money Supply have not Fitted to be Intermediate Target of Money Policy of China. *Economic Research Journal*, 8: 33–43.

Xie H. Y., Yang W. and Guo K. (2010). The Development of the System of International Exchange Rate after Financial Crisis. *Wuhan Finance Monthly*, 2: 19–22.

Yi G. and Tang X. (2001). A Theory Foundation of the Hypothesis of Comers Solution in Exchange Rate Regimes. *Journal of Financial Research*, 8: 5–17.

Yi G. (2000). The Selection of Exchange Rate Regimes. *Journal of Financial Research*, 9: 46–52.

Yuan Y. (2001). Property Right in Institutional Choice of Foreign Exchange Rate. *Nankai Economic Studies*, 2: 26–30.

Zhang Q. (2003). The Vanishing of Intermediate Exchange Rate Regime and Selections of Exchange Rate Regimes of 4 ASEAN Countries. *Asia & Africa Review*, 4: 27–30.

Zhang W. P. and Wang Y. M. (2007). Classification, Worldwide Pattern and History of Exchange Rate Regime. *Studies of International Finance*, 5: 54–60.

Zhang Z. H. (2002). New Development of Exchange Rate Regime: a Literature Review. *The Journal of World Economy*, 1: 13–22.

Zhou J. Z. (2004). The Choice of Exchange Rate Regimes in Developing Countries. *Journal of Finance and Economics*, 6: 30–43.

Zhu F. G. and Zhu Y. F. (2012). Fundamental Types of Exchange Rate Regimes and Analysis on Factors. *Hebei Finance*, 10: 9–12.
Shen G. B. and Liu Y. S. (2001). On the "Middle Hollow" Exchange Rate System Hypothesis. *On Economic Problems*, 11: 24–26.
Zhao W. (2009). Review on the Latest Theory of Exchange Rate Regimes Selection. *Consume Guide*, 07: 79.

Chapter 4

The Choice of Exchange Rate Arrangement — Case Study

On July 19, 2010, the People's Bank of China (PBOC) announced that it would resume reform of the RMB exchange rate system. It signed the "Settlement Agreement on the Clearing of RMB Businesses in Hong Kong" on July 19 of the same year with Hong Kong's RMB Clearing Bank; Bank of China (Hong Kong) limited (BOCHK). This accelerated the process of RMB internationalization. As of 2012, banks in Hong Kong have absorbed deposits of over RMB600 billion and 76 of them are authorized to engage in RMB business. Meanwhile, the scope of RMB usage outside of China has been increasing. In 2008, China and its eight neighboring countries (e.g., Vietnam) signed a bilateral local currency settlement agreement. Many other countries have enacted laws to admit settlements and payments for trade in RMB or have adopted the RMB as a currency in their foreign reserve portfolio. From 2009 to the end of 2012, China has signed bilateral currency swap agreements with 18 countries, including South Korea, adding up to a total value of RMB1600 billion. All these achievements mark the march towards RMB "internationalization".

Becoming freely convertible is the prerequisite for the internationalization of any currency. This means that we need to further enhance the convertibility of the capital account so as to move it toward the ultimate goal of full convertibility. RMB liberalization in trade, such as its role as a settlement currency in cross-border trade, will definitely give rise to multiple issues involving the capital account. For example, all foreign RMB-denominated investment in China (held by foreign banks and enterprises), as well as any RMB remittances originating from domestic enterprises' overseas accounts, will increase pressure on China to open its capital account. Liberalization would also lead to greater participation on the part of China's banking system in the global financial market, bringing with it the benefits of competition and international operating standards. These benefits will ultimately improve the efficiency of the domestic financial system, speeding up its reform and development and boosting overall economic growth. However, to maintain economic stability, we should also seek to avoid the potentially destructive impact of foreign capital on the still immature domestic financial system.

Due to the strong relationship between exchange rates, capital flows and financial development, it is necessary to prudently order their opening-up. Failing to properly sequence their liberalization — or worse, doing so blindly — could have undesirable financial effects. In particular, opening-up the capital account will expose formerly isolated domestic short-term interest rates to the influences of overseas short-term interest rate and exchange rate expectations. What is more, with an open capital account, a country which exerts control over its short-term interest rates and exchange rate simultaneously may experience large-scale capital flows. This sort of attempt to balance interest rates and exchange rates could thus imperil the stability of capital flows. It will thus be hard to realize both a stable exchange rate policy and an independent monetary policy at the same time. Further, without a sound financial system, misguided reform of the exchange rate system and the opening-up of the capital account will cause domestic financial disturbances — perhaps even leading to a financial crisis and economic turmoil. In the past, Chile undertook a reform of its exchange rate system and opened up its capital account in the 1980s. However, since the supporting financial basis was not solid enough, the country experienced a financial crisis. Later, only its second effort to reform its exchange rate system and open up the capital account from 1979 to 1999 proved steady and productive. For this reason, these several issues hold great significance in preventing financial turmoil and guaranteeing steady economic growth: How to achieve a proper arrangement in reforming the exchange rate system, how to open up the capital account, and how to pursue financial development.

This chapter will focus on countries which have already applied free floating exchange rate systems, including Japan, Chile, Poland and Singapore. I intend to use these four cases to discern beneficial and instructive lessons that may be applied to China's similar reform effort. To do this, I analyze each case, draw upon each country's experience in exchange rate reform, and study both the order of reforms undertaken and the reforms effects on each country's financial development. There are two parts in this chapter. The first part reviews the literature on the relationship between the reform of exchange rate systems, opening-up of the capital account and financial development. The second part will analyze the specific order of these three reforms in the four case studies (Japan, Chile, Poland and Singapore), sorting out each country's characteristic opening and regulatory measures. This second part concludes with analysis of the effects and lessons from each country's reform experience.

4.1 Review of the Literature

The history of academic research on exchange rate systems, the policy sequence for opening-up the capital account, and financial development is not very long. In the beginning, the literature was focused on discussing whether to open the capital account or the current account first. Representative ideas in favor of opening the capital account first include those of Lal (1987) and Bhandari (1989), who argued that opening the capital account first would make exchange rate information more transparent, reduce fluctuation in the exchange rate, reduce financial costs, and boost economic development. There are also many scholars in favor of opening the current account first. Edwards (1989a, 1989b) believed that, if the capital account were opened first, it might cause excessive fluctuations in the exchange rate or local currency appreciation, which would negatively affect domestic economic growth and thus overall decrease the wealth in a society. In a comprehensive literature review, Edwards (2007) summed up most scholars' opinions that the opening-up of the capital account should come second — after opening the current account — so as to prevent rising domestic financing costs resulting from unnecessary resource transfers (such as capital outflows).

Some scholars also hold that opening-up the capital account should be based on the sound development of the macro economy. After studying the experiences of Chile, Indonesia, South Korea and Thailand, Johnston *et al.* (1997) concluded that opening up the capital account should be integrated into reform of the economy's structure and the design of macroeconomic policies, and that the flow of securities capital should be coordinated with reform of the domestic financial sector. Nsouli and Rached (1998) further pointed out that if a large-scale imbalance existed in the inward and outward value of a currency, a prudent macroeconomic policy should be adopted as a priority. Influenced by the Asian Financial Crisis, Edwards (2007) added that, under most circumstances, a country should first tackle its major fiscal problems and achieve a basically stable macro economy in the early stage of the reform. It is now a general consensus that opening up the capital account should come after the realization of a stable macro economy (Nsouli *et al.*, 2002).

In the earlier research, discussion on opening up the capital account mainly centered on its relationship with the real economy, while the development of the financial system did not attract much attention. Later on, scholars began to study the role of financial system in the economic reform (Falvey and Kierzkowski, 1987; Edwards and Edwards, 1987). After the Asian Financial Crisis, people came to realize that the increased frequency of financial crises might have something to do with capital account liberalization (Edwards, 1986). Taking the development of the financial system into consideration, the implementation of opening the capital account requires certain preconditions, otherwise, just as an International Monetary Fund (IMF) official put it, "carrying out the opening of the capital account without a set of preconditions would be extremely risky" (IMF, 1998). These preconditions include prudent fiscal and monetary policy, the marketization of the exchange rate system, adequate foreign reserves, a sound financial system and a market-oriented incentive system (Ishii and Habermeier, 2002; Guitian and Saleh, 1996).

Regarding the relationship between capital account liberalization and financial development, the dominant opinion is to first develop domestic financial institutions and to mature a stable financial system. After this, the capital account can be opened. Donald and Rojas-Suarez (1993) and Edwards (2005) suggested that it was favorable to open the capital account in countries where financial development was going relatively well. For those countries where this was not the case, opening the capital account might have a detrimental impact. Therefore, opening-up the capital account should follow after domestic financial development. Johnston (1998) directly regarded the opening-up of financial accounts as an aspect of the liberalization of the financial sector. He pointed out that a country undergoing the opening-up of its financial accounts should strengthen the stability of its financial institutions so as to guarantee that the process proceeds smoothly, achieve the objectives of monetary policy, and sustain the stability of the macro economy in the new, liberalized environment. So the first priority is to establish an appropriate supervisory and regulatory framework. On the whole, the liberalization of the capital account ought to be put behind the establishment of a stable financial system with a sound financial supervision and regulatory framework (Eichengreen, 2001). Ishii *et al.* (2002) also proposed that opening up the capital account should be based on the evaluation of vulnerabilities in capital controls, the macro economy and the financial sector. These other factors should be included in timing the policy decision to open up the capital account.

Research on the policy sequence for opening up the capital account is the most significant, but also opens the most difficult questions. According to Eichengreen (2001), the basic standpoint of the IMF is that, since conditions in each country vary greatly, it is impossible to formulate a universal approach to decide the policy sequence for liberalization. Indeed, even the time needed to implement the liberalization of the capital account depends on each country's situation.

Among all empirical studies, a leading representative study is entitled "Capital Accounts and the Financial Sector", published by Ishii *et al.* (2002). It lists the experiences of nine countries in liberalizing their capital account. The study made several conclusions. First, there is no standard method for measuring the policy sequence for opening the capital account in coordination with other policies. Second, due to the complexity and innate interconnectedness of the variables involved, independent analysis of the effect of capital account liberalization compared with other policies is not feasible. Third, to determine the policy sequence for opening the capital account, it is necessary to carefully consider the specific conditions and demands of each country. Fourth, generally speaking, a gradual reform approach is needed, but this does not mean that there is a universally optimal order to the policies leading to liberalization. Fifth, if the macro economy in a country changes or becomes more volatile, the policy sequence for liberalization needs to be revised. Sixth, under specific conditions, some temporary measures for emergencies might be necessary to slow down the opening-up. Seventh, since the approach of one country cannot necessarily be successfully transplanted to another country's context, a prudent attitude is required.

With regard to the latest studies on the implementation sequence for opening the capital account, most scholars agree that restrictions on long-term capital flows should be lifted first, then restrictions on short-term capital flows, followed by controls over direct investment, and then finally restrictions on indirect investment (Eichengreen *et al.*, 1998). Nsouli *et al.* (2002) further claimed that capital flows should be explicitly divided into inward and outward flows. They argue that the restrictions on inward capital flows should be removed first, so that the country can make use of foreign capital and techniques to develop its domestic economy. As for the indirect investment, the opening of long-term capital flows should also come before that of short-term capital flows. Concerning different capital markets, since the bond market develops before the stock market, the former one can be opened first.

There are few empirical studies on the sequencing of specific policy changes within the capital account. Johnston *et al.* (1997) gave a detailed introduction on reform policies in Chile, Indonesia, South Korea and Thailand. This included each country's process of capital account liberalization, development of their domestic financial system, and reform of their exchange rate system. Johnston *et al.* (1997) judged that capital account liberalization should be deepened in step with the overall development of the macro economy and the exchange rate system. However, they provide no further recommendations on specific reform measures. Aramaki (2006) presented the Japanese case in detail — from the opening-up of the capital account to the reform of the exchange rate system and financial liberalization. Aramak recommended that, when financial markets are unstable, a country should slow down its reform steps and adopt prudent measures, evaluate the risks of each item on the reform agenda and pursue the least risky and most controllable changes first. Riskier and more complex items in the account can be opened later. Meanwhile, a control mechanism should be set up to protect the domestic economy from the potentially substantial influence of unexpected shocks.

There is other research specifically dedicated to the history of financial development, exchange rate reform and capital account liberalization in various countries. Some studies also consider the relationship between reform, economic growth and inflation. Nonetheless, studies on the relationship among exchange rate reform, financial development and capital account liberalization are very few. Even though some studies cover this topic, they often fail to research it in depth.

During the financial reform of a country, there is no common course of action. It is necessary to evaluate the specific conditions of that country and for said country to adjust their policy sequence or enact ad-hoc controls to postpone reforms when the macro economy experiences instability or other shocks appear (Habermeier, 2002). The current literature analyzes policy sequencing between the opening-up of the capital account and financial development, but lacks insight into many of the specifics of the reform process. It applies general measures, conclusions and commentary on the results of reform in various countries. Based on this existing literature, this chapter attempts to obtain the specific experiences of Japan, Chile, Poland and Singapore in regards to how they achieved and sequenced liberalization of their capital account.

4.2 Japan's Experience in Exchange Rate Reform

Before the 1970s, Japan had a fixed exchange rate system which entailed strict controls over the capital account and highly protective mechanisms for its financial market. The system included five notable aspects: (1) stringent control over capital inflows and outflows, (2) a relatively low level of financial market development, (3) separate operations between banking and non-banking financial intermediary activities (well-defined, legitimate channels for debt financing), (4) unified control over the interest rate of each market, (5) and bank loans offered exclusively to enterprises with low interest rates for preferential borrowers. After the war, with the rapid growth of Japan's economy, changes in the financing methods of giant domestic enterprises, as well as the direct financing (such as issuing large quantities of national bonds to cover the fiscal budget deficit), posed challenges for the traditional post-war financial system, with its indirect financing practices. However these challenges ultimately led to economic liberalization in Japan.

4.2.1 *The First Exchange Rate Reforms (1971–1980): From a Fixed to a Floating Exchange Rate System with Controls on Capital Accounts*

4.2.1.1 *Background to Reform*

The international environment in the 1970s was relatively turbulent. Oil crises occurred in 1973 and 1979, resulting in rising oil prices and pushing major economies into recession. In June 1974, the fall of West Germany's Hearst Bank due to its failure to deliver on its foreign exchange commitment led to turmoil across European financial markets, increasing the fluctuation of the international capital market.

In the early 1970s, America's economy had undergone an overheating stage because of the Vietnam War and, after a 1971 fiscal deficit, a trend of capital outflow emerged. In May 1971, after the Deutschemark (DM) adopted a floating system, large quantities of capital flowed into Japan, and it was expected that the Yen would also be subject to a float.

With regard to domestic economic growth, after the Second World War, Japan began its fast economic recovery plan with the support of America. Benefiting from a long-run fixed exchange rate system (with the Yen fixed at JPY360 per USD$1), the international competitiveness of Japan's export enterprises was much enhanced and the domestic economy experienced rapid growth. In 1955, Japan's economic strength had returned to its pre-war level and the value of exports in 1960 was over USD$4 billion. Meanwhile, through a series of policies such as "industrial rationalization", Japan achieved rapid economic growth. This thrust the country into the ranks of the industrialized world, bringing the share of heavy industry in Japan's economy to 64.2%.

However, from 1973 on, Japan's economy began to decline and the trend of Yen depreciation appeared. Later, with economic recovery and continued growth, the fiscal surplus increased and expectation pressured the Yen's appreciation. But since Japan's economy was in expansion, its domestic demand exceeded supply. Under the double effect of the Yen's appreciation and the country's net exports, the surplus of Japan's current account became increasingly lower.

In 1970, Japan's current account was already open and restrictions on foreign direct investment (FDI) and indirect investment by non-resident investors were partly removed. However, most of the capital account was controlled, gradually being relaxed afterwards. At that time, the ratio of indirect financing in Japan was as high as 80–90% while that in America and West Germany during the same period was only 30% and 65%, respectively (Fukao, 1990). Since the mid-1970s, the Japanese government loosened its control over the financial sector and embarked on the road to liberalization.

4.2.1.2 *Reform Measures*

Japan in this period, influenced by changes in the international environment, employed many capital control measures, most of which were devised to respond to external shocks. However, constant changes in policy also had an adverse impact on the domestic economy. Meanwhile, in the process of the exchange rate system reform, Japanese policy adopted two strategies. On the one hand, Japan relied on domestic enterprises with strong international competitiveness to invest overseas, in an attempt to buffer the impact of international capital inflows. On the other hand, through restraining the exchange of Yen and encouraging capital outflows, Japan sought to reduce the scale of net capital inflows.

With the rapid growth of Japan's economy and the turbulence of the international environment, large quantities of international capital flowed into Japan, subjecting the Yen to price fluctuations. Within merely 11 days after the "Nixon shock" on August 15, 1971, there was USD$4 billion flowing into Japan in the form of prepayments for exports, accounting for one third of Japan's then total reserves (Aramaki, 2006). This phenomenon indicated that, despite capital account controls, the opening-up of the current account had also given rise to large-scale capital flows. In response, on August 28, Japan announced its intention to implement a managed floating exchange rate system.

Japan took two policy approaches in the initial days of its new exchange rate regime. First, in order to prevent the excessive density of capital inflows and avoid increased economic risks (as well as maintain its enterprises' relatively strong international competitiveness), Japan accelerated the widening of the scope for foreign investment in its domestic economy. From 1971 to 1973, the Japanese government carried out two package plans for FDI enterprises (Wang, 2009). As of May 1976, excepting some industries (such as agriculture, forestry, fishery, mining and leather), Japan removed nearly all its FDI restrictions.

Second, Japan began to constrain capital inflows and encourage its outflows so as to reduce the net international capital inflows and diminish pressure on the Yen to appreciate. For capital inflow controls, the demand reserve amount for free Yen accounts was increased, and the maximum limit for Yen exchange was changed from a monthly average limit to a (more restrictive) daily limit. The set maximum amount for trade prepayments was decreased to USD$10,000 in February 1972, and then further cut down to USD$5,000 the following June. The purchase amount of stocks and bonds by non-resident investors was also set to not exceed their former selling amount (so as not to increase net capital inflows).

Seeking to encourage capital outflows, measures were taken such as improving the ratio of purchase volume of domestic securities by non-resident investors to selling volume. Japan abolished its central management of foreign exchange in 1972 and started to allow residents to hold foreign exchange assets. At the same time, areas for FDI were totally opened. To further encourage outward investment, in April 1970, Japan for the first time authorized trust investment companies to hold foreign securities. Then investment in foreign securities was gradually opened to certain domestic financial institutions, including life insurance companies, security institutions, and residents transacting through security brokers.

Based on its control over the capital account, Japan's central bank also began to strengthen its interventions in the foreign exchange market to stabilize the Yen. Nonetheless, after the Nixon Shock, the Yen continue to appreciate through the rest of 1971. To avoid deflation, the Japanese government implemented a proactive fiscal policy and loose monetary policy so that the expectation on Yen appreciation would decrease. Due to the J-curve effect, Japan's current account balance continued to increase. By the middle of 1972, under the rising pressure for Yen appreciation, Japan's central bank set the discount rate to the lowest level since war time. Meanwhile, Japan continued to employ a proactive fiscal policy to stimulate the economy. Consequently, the rate of increase in M2 reached 20% and it remained so until 1973, making it difficult to stabilize the Yen. Thus Japan launched the exchange rate reform in February 1973.

After the exchange rate system reform in 1973, along with the downturn of Japan's economy, the Yen's tendency to depreciate became evident. At this time, the capital control policy was diverted to encourage capital inflows and restrict outflows. The measures included lowering the reserve rate of Yen deposit accounts (from 50% to 10%), temporarily removing the restrictions on Yen exchange with the headquarters and branches of those major companies previously excluded from this right, increasing the limit for trade prepayments from USD$5,000 to USD$10,000 and then again up to $100,000, and gradually loosening control over resident's non-designated loans and the purchase limit of securities by non-resident investors (Wang, 2009). As for restricting capital outflows, the government's major action was to limit bond issuance by non-resident investors.

In June 1974, the West German Hearst Bank went bankrupt due to its failure to honor its foreign exchange commitments, causing turmoil in European financial markets. This made it difficult for Japan's authorized foreign exchange bank to gain US Dollars in the European market. Therefore, the Japanese government continued to strengthen its effort to bring in foreign capital, cancelled the reserve amount demand on Yen-denominated accounts, allowed the issuance of foreign bonds, eased control over trade prepayments, borrowed money from Saudi Arabia and other countries and put a limit on the amount of foreign currency exchanged for travelling abroad. These measures partly alleviated the stress of net capital outflows.

Through encouraging capital inflows and constraining outflows, Japan's economy began to revive, starting from the second half of 1974 with a surplus in the current account. Meanwhile, since the international environment was relatively stable, the measures taken by the Japanese administration to encourage capital inflows, such as putting limits on the

Yen exchange and spot exchange position, began to abate. The government further relaxed (in varying degrees) the restrictions on capital outflows affecting foreign loans of foreign exchange banks, residents' purchase of foreign securities and non-resident investors' issuance of securities. Along with the acceleration of foreign capital inflows, Japan encouraged capital outflows and gradually achieved a balance of international payments.

Influenced by the economic recovery, in 1977 the market expected the Yen to appreciate. International capital once again flooded into Japan, and the government accordingly resumed its control over foreign exchange and capital flows. The demanded reserve rate for non-residents' Yen accounts was raised to 50% and, in 1978, 100%. Meanwhile, the public sector ceased to issue short-term governmental bonds to non-resident investors.

With the outbreak of the second oil crisis in 1979, the Yen once again encountered pressure for depreciation. So the Japanese government adopted a set of measures to attract foreign capital, including reducing the demanded reserve of free Yen accounts from 100% to 50% and then 0%, relaxing the restrictions on non-resident investors' purchase of bonds, lowering the requirements for non-designated foreign loans and allowing residents to issue bonds overseas.

On balance, in order to avoid the impact of short-term capital flows caused by the sharp change in the international environment, the Japanese government made a complicated set of policy changes to their foreign exchange controls and capital account transactions in this period. But the resulting policy volatility also led to instability in the planning and production activities of enterprises and investors, thus worsening the domestic economic turmoil.

4.2.2 *The Second Reform of the Exchange Rate System (1980–2000): The Floating Exchange Rate System and the Opening-up of the Capital Account*

4.2.2.1 *Background to Reform*

From the early 1980s, Japan's economy began to revive and then sustained steady growth. In contrast, the economy in America experienced "stagflation". The American government employed a combination of proactive fiscal policy and tightened monetary policy to stimulate economic growth. However, Dollar appreciation enlarged America's trade deficit. From 1980 to 1984, America's trade deficit with Japan skyrocketed, making America the largest debtor country in the world (with Japan as the largest creditor country).

The economic growth rate and production rate in Japan had been far above that in America since 1980s. From 1980 to 1985, Japan's economic growth rate was 4.8% while that of America was 1.5%. The production rate in Japan was 3%, but only 0.4% in America. Against this backdrop, the US Dollar was rather weak against the Japanese Yen.

Just then, Japan's new regulation on foreign exchange began to take effect in December 1980. Compared with the former regulations, the new regulations changed the principle of foreign exchange control: "Forbidding foreign exchange transactions with exceptions in special cases" was replaced with "allowing free foreign exchange transactions with a few exceptions" (Aramaki, 2006). This signified that Japan had basically achieved its capital account liberalization. Its financial market enjoyed benign development both in scope and depth. With this sound prerequisite, the opening of Japan's financial market was mainly through the marketization of interest rates.

4.2.2.2 *Reform Measures*

On the whole, the Japanese Yen showed a tendency to appreciate in this period. In order to lower the Yen's appreciation expectation, an overly loose monetary policy was implemented. Additionally, the fast pace of financial liberalization resulted in severe inflation within Japan, giving rise to a serious economic crisis.

Expectations on Yen appreciation were strong in the early 1980's. On the one hand, America was mired in an economic slump; on the other, Japan's economy was experiencing rapid economic growth. International collaboration brought further pressure for appreciation. In September 1985, America, Japan, West Germany, Britain and France signed the "Plaza Agreement", which was the prologue to Yen appreciation. Within half a year, the exchange rate of Japanese Yen to USD$1 increased from JPY273 to JPY120 — an appreciation rate of over 100% (Ministry of Finance of Japan, 1990, etc.).

In the same year, the Japanese government released the announcement "The Status Quo and Prospect Regarding the Financial Liberalization and Yen's Internationalization", in which it claimed that Japan had entered a stage of full liberalization and internationalization in its economy and finance. However, the sharp depreciation of the US Dollar caused tremendous loss to Japanese investors, who gradually reduced their holdings of American assets in the middle of 1987. This further strengthened the Yen against the Dollar.

In an attempt to alleviate the impact of Yen appreciation, Japan's central bank began to employ a loose monetary policy. From 1986 to 1987, it lowered the interest rate five times successively and reduced the discount rate from 5% to 2.5% (the lowest level among major economies at that time). This loose monetary policy generated large capital surpluses, which flowed into the stock and real estate markets (for want of better investment opportunities) and caused securities and urban land prices to rise. Along with an increase of bank loans, an infamous economic bubble in Japan was forming.

In this period, the deposit rate in Japan was in constant liberalization. In 1979, Japan introduced certificates of deposit (CDs: Large-Denomination Negotiable Certificates of Time Deposit with an adjustable interest rate) and gradually carried out a liberalization policy for interest rates. Money market certificates (MMC's) were also introduced. The liberalization of term deposit rates was launched in 1985 and finished in 1993; the liberalization of demand deposit rate was finished in 1994. Interest rate liberalization worsened inflation problems in Japan. When the monetary authority raised interest rates to cool down the economy, it was a bubble already on the verge of bursting. In 1990, the stock bubble was broken and then, in 1991, the real estate market followed. Japan's economy fell into long-term recession.

The difficult economic environment led to an increase in non-performing loans and problems began to show up in the banking system. The Japanese government enacted a series of laws to undertake significant reform of its financial system. In 1997, the diverse operation of financial institutions saw improvements. Banks were allowed to engage in the trust and security business; securities companies broadened their business scope, beginning to conduct account settlement, which had long been monopolized by banks. In 1998, the regulations brought about by the financial system's reform gave further authority to financial institutions to undertake business in other sectors through setting up new branches. In 1999, banks were approved to obtain long-term financing through issuing bonds, which was previously exclusive to long-term credit banks and trust banks. As the reform moved on, the boundary between long-term and short-term financing was eliminated.

4.2.3 *Analysis of the Experiences and Effects of the Exchange Rate System Reform*

4.2.3.1 *Analysis of the Reform Experiences of the Exchange Rate System*

Scholars like Cheng and Shen (1992) reviewed the exchange rate system reforms and the opening-up of the capital account in Japan from 1949 to 1979, concluding that the decision process for determining which to reform enact first was very complicated and lengthy. Nonetheless, by combing through and charting Japan's process, we can discern some guiding rules in three major reform areas: Exchange rate system reform, opening up the capital account and financial development. In this section we analyze their sequence in an attempt to draw some conclusions that might support a proposal for our own reform in these areas.

From Table 4.1, we can see that Japan's current account had completed its opening-up when the country adopted a fixed exchange rate system. Liberalization of the capital account also had started in this period, but it took a long time (about 40 years). Compared with the capital account, marketization and opening-up of the financial system had a late take-off and lasted for a relatively long time. On the whole, the policy sequence among the current account, capital account and financial system was thus: First the current account underwent reforms, then the capital account, and finally the financial markets. But their order actually overlapped somewhat. For example, before the opening-up of financial accounts, the domestic financial market was soundly developed.

Table 4.1: The Exchange Rate System Reform and the Process of the Opening-up of the Capital Account and Financial Development in Japan

Time Period	Events
1945–1964	The stage of trade liberation
1945–1971	The fixed exchange rate system
1960	The start of borrowing foreign money
1960–1998	The opening-up of the capital account
1970	Trust investment overseas; non-resident investors' issuance of bonds in Yen
1970–1999	The financial liberalization
1971–1973	The managed floating exchange rate system
1973–1980	The floating exchange rate system with capital account controls
1980–2000	The floating exchange rate system with capital liberalization

Data sources: Ministry of Finance of Japan, research report of Kinzai Financial Study Institute, Aramaki (2006) and Takeda and Turner (1992).

Table 4.2: A Sketch of the Opening-up of Japan's Capital Account

Time Period	Events
1960	Implementing the act of foreign exchange and its transaction
April 1960	Beginning of payments of unrestricted foreign trade in Japanese Yen
November 1960	Approving foreign exchange borrowing
1961	Approving individuals' issuance of company bonds and stocks in US Dollars
1964	Allowing non-resident investors to open unrestricted Yen investment accounts
June 1967	Beginning the first liberalization of foreign capital
July 1967	Loosening control over the foreign investment share of Japanese stocks
February 1968	Introducing restrictions on Yen exchange
March 1969	Beginning the second liberalization of foreign capital
1969–1972	Beginning the liberalization process of overseas investment
1970–1975	Beginning the liberalization of overseas security investment in trust institutions, individuals and security company successively
September 1970	Beginning the third liberalization of foreign capital including banks and security companies
December 1970	Permitting non-residents to issue Yen-denominated bonds within Japan
1971	Beginning the fourth liberalization of foreign capital
May 1972	Cancelling the foreign exchange centralization scheme
May 1973	Beginning the fifth liberalization of foreign capital began; basically achieving full liberalization of FDI
1979	Revising the act of foreign exchange and its transactions; adding supervisory measures on fluctuations
1984	Removing the demanding principle in foreign exchange transaction; removing restrictions on Yen exchange
1998	Revising the foreign exchange act; completing liberalization of the capital account.

Data sources: The Ministry of Finance of Japan, research report of Kinzai Financial Study Institute, Aramaki (2006) and Takeda and Turner (1992).

From Table 4.2, we can conclude that the majority of measures related to opening-up of the capital account in Japan were taken during 1965 to 1975 — the same period in which Japan transitioned from a fixed to a floating exchange rate system. However, after implementation of the floating exchange rate system, Japan continued to push forward its opening-up of the capital account and development of its financial markets. This was to ensure that the monetary authority could take effective measures to control the impact of unexpected shocks arising from fluctuations in the exchange rate.

From Table 4.3, we see that Japan's financial development was relatively steady. The liberalization of interest rates only began after

Table 4.3: The Opening Process of Japan's Financial Markets

Time Period	Events
1970	Permitting non-residents to issue bonds in Yen
1972	Beginning interbank sale of US Dollars
1975	Placing restrictions on deficit-financing bonds
1976	Officially supporting the development of the repurchase market
1977	Permitting non-resident to issue discount national bonds in Japan in European Yen
1978	Add more variety of national bonds in the short-term interbank market
1979	Introducing six measures, including CDs and the liberalization of interest rates
1984	Permitting non-residents to issue bonds in European Yen and permitting the free transaction of European Yen
1985	Introducing money market deposit certificates
1986	Establishing the Tokyo off-shore market
1987	Introducing commercial notes
1992	Formulating the financial reform act; allowing mixed operation in bank branches
1993	Completing the liberalization of term deposit rates
1994	Completing the liberalization of demand deposit rates
1999	Allowing banks to engage in mixed operation with other financial institutions

Data sources: Ministry of Finance of Japan, research report of Kinzai Financial Study Institute, Aramaki (2006) and Takeda and Turner (1992).

implementation of the floating exchange rate system. Before the liberalization of interest rates, Japan mainly relied on introducing various monetary market vehicles to promote the development of its monetary market. With the improvement of its transaction turnover, the liberalization of interest rates was carried out. For this process, Japan first liberalized the term deposit rate and then the demand deposit rate — all while the liberalization of saving account rates was not in place until 2000, showing that the government still had some controls over the financial market. Additionally, the liberalization of term deposits also began with large-amount deposits first and then small-amount deposits later.

Figure 4.1 depicts the balance of Japan's current account, which, since 1977, was kept in surplus. This was beneficial to the opening-up of Japan's capital account as well as to its financial markets. Figure 4.2 lists the development process of Japan's current account, capital account, and financial market in respect to different stages of exchange rate system. We come to the following conclusions through analysis of this development.

(1) After employing the free floating exchange rate system, Japan retained its control over the capital account for some time, but then

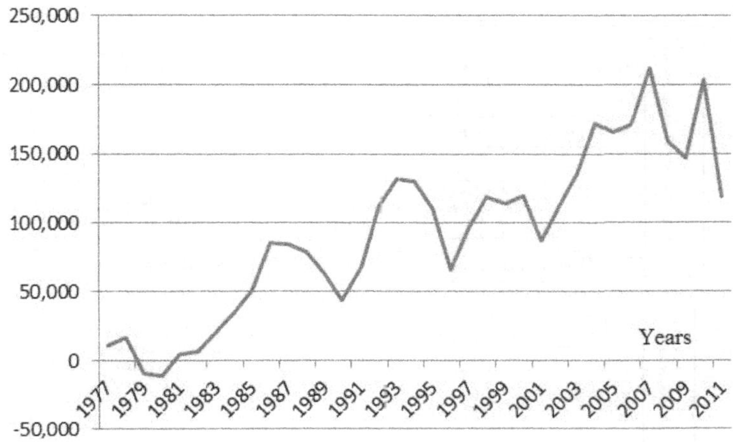

Figure 4.1: Japan's Current Account (USD million)
Data source: International Monetary Fund.

gradually opened it until at last achieving full liberalization. In this process, it first broadened the Yen's exchange rate trading band, while simultaneously keeping control over the capital account. During the free floating exchange rate system's existence, Japan was relatively effective in achieving a stable and gradual transition to an open capital account.

(2) The basic order for the opening-up of the capital account was the following: First the current account was opened, then the capital account, and finally the financial markets. However, each stage of opening could and did overlap. In this way, the overall growth of the country could remain stable, avoiding the buildup of imbalances. During the opening-up of its capital account, Japan chose to encourage capital inflows first and then later capital outflows. Notably, the reason that the Yen was utilized in foreign trade settlements from the beginning mainly lies in Japan's possession of an advanced manufacturing industry, granting it certain pricing power in international markets.

(3) In the process of opening inflows in the capital account, Japan started with FDI and then gradually allowed foreign capital to invest in various industries. The opening-up of Japan's industry was divided into five stages so as to diminish the risks of a rushed process. As for inward indirect investment, Japan first allowed domestic institutions to borrow money overseas, then their permitted their issuance of foreign bonds, and finally sanctioned stock issuance in foreign markets. Each step's financing method entailed greater risks and such gradual risk exposure was conducive to a

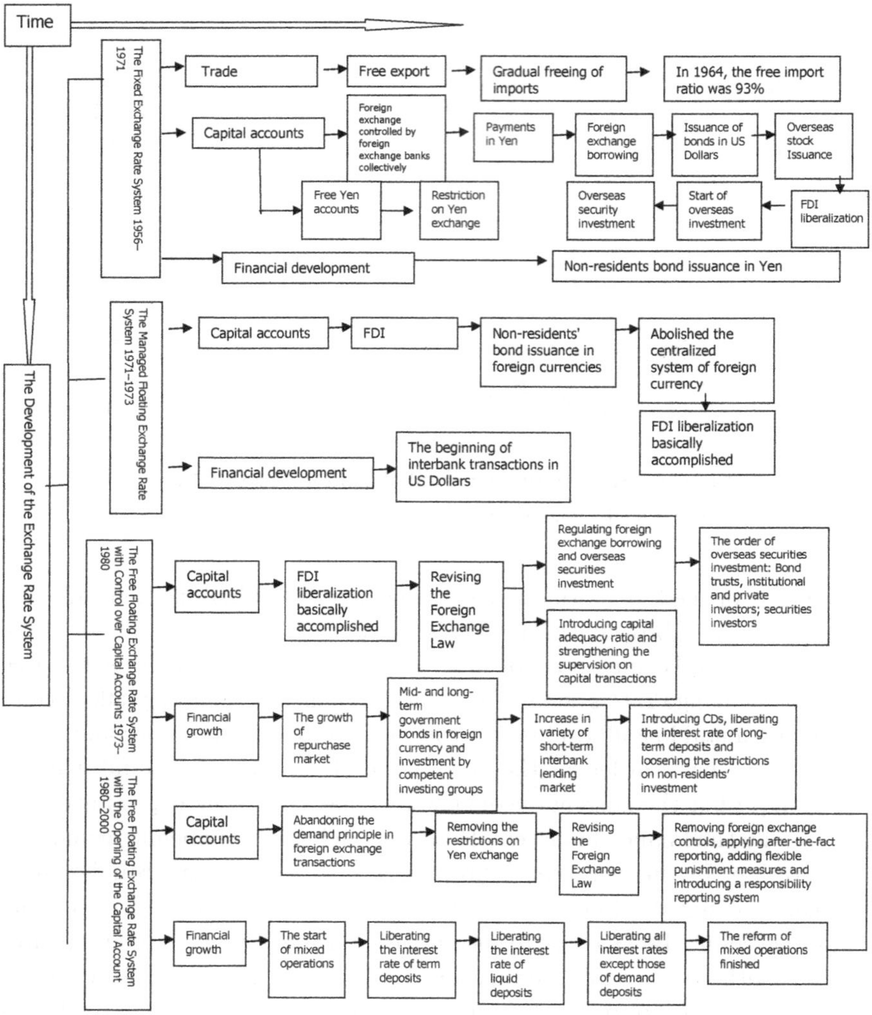

Figure 4.2: Sketch of the Process of Japan's Exchange Rate System Reform (Opening-up of the Capital Account and Its Financial Development)

steady advance of the liberalization process. In general, Japan first attracted FDI, then allowed domestic enterprises to engage in foreign borrowing and overseas issuance of bonds and stocks. Ultimately Japan achieved the liberalization of FDI in step with its capital account liberalization.

(4) Capital outflow liberalization followed capital inflow liberalization. Specifically, Japan first opened overseas direct investment (for the safety of

the overseas investment capital) and then allowed capital outflow for indirect investment. This means that non-resident investors were first allowed to issue bonds in Japan, followed by domestic enterprises being allowed to engage in overseas indirect investment. Authorization of participants in overseas direct investment proceeded from least to most risk-prone: First, bond trust institutions, then general financial institutions and individual investors, and finally securities companies.

(5) The opening-up of Japan's domestic industries lasted for a short period of time, mainly because Japan's sound industrial structure and the strong competitiveness of its enterprises were little affected by its opening-up. However, Japan did not open all its industries at the same time. Instead, the process was carried out step by step by evaluating the international competiveness of each industry. The least competitive industries were left to promote their own growth and make improvements in their competiveness. It is a scientific, reliable and prudent path to gradually realize the opening-up of domestic industries through evaluation and promotion. We should draw upon this experience.

(6) In the evolution of its exchange rate system, Japan adopted various measures to diminish the impact of shocks arising from violent fluctuations in the international environment. Among these measures, unrestricted Yen accounts and restrictions on Yen exchange were frequently employed, indicating that these two control measures are of some effectiveness. Other measures included imposing restrictions on specific activities like transnational investment, borrowing and trade prepayments as well as foreign exchange for purposes of tourism.

(7) In the process of opening-up the capital account, a significant step was the establishment of unrestricted Yen accounts. This innovation not only enlarged the scope of the Yen in Japan's foreign trade, but also marked an initial experiment in attracting short-term foreign capital. Another step was authorizing foreign exchange banks to manage foreign exchange. The authorized foreign exchange banks played an important role in tracking foreign transactions and inspecting their legitimacy. In addition, they also took measures to control the impact of short-term capital flows.

(8) In the process of its financial development and opening-up, Japan had finished developing various financial tools before implementing the liberalization of its capital account and financial sector. It then improved market liquidity and completed its infrastructure, until at last it carried out the marketization of interest rates and the opening-up. To promote the marketization of interest rates, Japan gradually developed its repurchase market

and interbank lending market. It first adopted some experimental measures, summed up the lessons from them and then enacted laws, which were used to regulate the path for its financial development. In the liberalization of interest rates, Japan first accomplished the liberalization of term deposit rates, then the demand deposit rates, and finally saving accounts rates. The liberalization of large amount deposits came before that of small amount deposits. The order of this arrangement was also determined according to their relative risk, with the lowest risk liberalizations occurring first.

4.2.3.2 *Analysis of the Effect of the Exchange Rate System Reform*

The evolving process of Japan's exchange rate system can be divided into three stages: The fixed exchange rate system before 1971, the managed floating exchange rate system from 1971,[1] and finally the floating exchange rate system from 1990 onwards. Figure 4.3 shows that, after each of the three changes in the exchange rate system, Japan's current account balance on the whole increased, signaling that the exchange rate system reform had

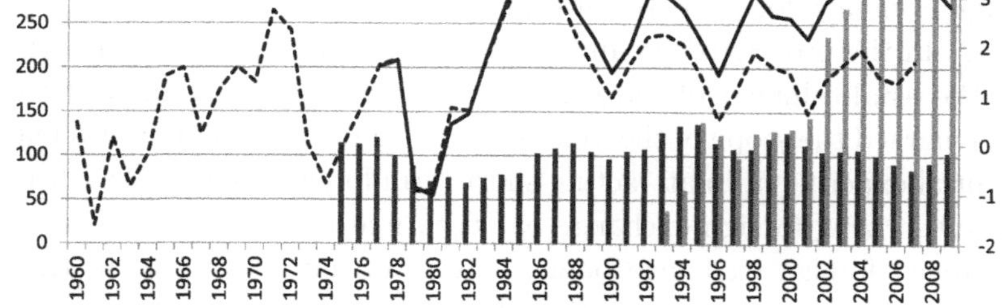

Figure 4.3: The Effect of the Exchange Rate System Reform on Japan's Foreign Trade

Note: The level line represents lack of date and the deep colored columns represent dates during the exchange rate system reform.

Data source: The World Bank.

[1]Here "managed" means that the capital account was not yet totally opened; further liberalization of the capital account was achieved only in 1980.

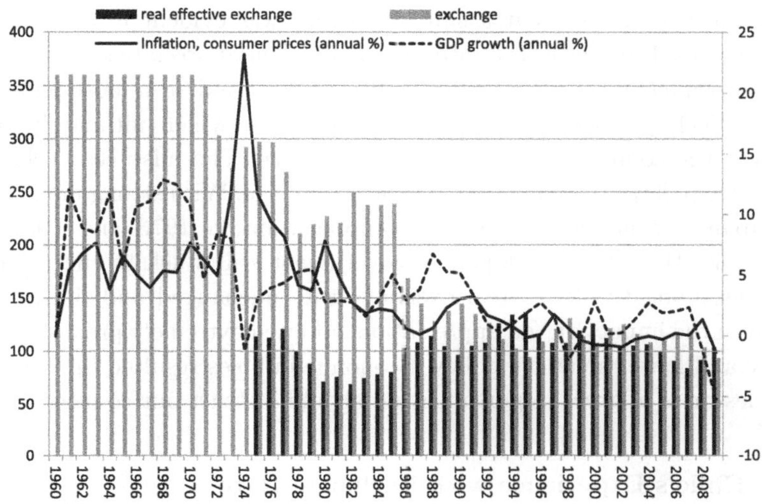

Figure 4.4: The Effect of Exchange Rate System Reform on Japan's Domestic Economy

Note: The level line represents lack of data; the deep-colored columns represent periods during exchange rate system reform.

Data source: The World Bank.

a positive impact on its foreign trade. After employing the floating exchange rate system, Japan's foreign reserves began to experience rapid growth from 1993 onwards (amounting to over USDS400 billion by 2009).

From Figure 4.4, we see that after the three exchange rate system reforms, the economy's growth rate first went up a bit and then slumped greatly, indicating that the result of these reforms was not satisfactory. Around 1972, Japan employed a proactive fiscal policy and a loose monetary policy, giving rise to severe inflation and asset bubbles. The following exchange rate system led to Yen appreciation, the decline of its international competitiveness, and bursting of the asset bubbles. For this reason, Japan entered an economic downturn after the exchange rate system reforms in both 1973 and 1980. And after the third reform, the Yen continued to appreciate. In an attempt to gain some competitiveness in the global market, Japan employed a loose monetary policy, resulting in an overheated economy. Due to America's stock market crash in 1987, Japan did not tighten its monetary policy but continued to offer large scale loans to the real estate market and construction industry. By 1989, bubbles had formed in Japan's economy. When Japan's central bank began to lower the interest rate in 1990, these bubbles burst and Japan once again confronted recession.

From this we see that a similar pattern was evident in all exchange rate reforms. First, after the rate reform, the Yen appreciated. In response, the government adopted a proactive fiscal policy and/or a loose monetary policy. Such policies created economic bubbles, which ultimately burst and left the country in an economic down turn. The mistakes in Japan's monetary policy are mainly to blame for this cycle. With strong momentum in Japan's economic growth, Yen appreciation in 1973 and 1987 was inevitable. However, the Japanese government still stuck to the principle of maintaining the Yen's real exchange rate unchanged and, in order to diminish the impact of Yen appreciation, adopted extremely proactive fiscal policy and loose monetary policy. Economic bubbles resulted in each case. This lesson is of great importance and should instruct our country.

4.3 Chile's Experience with Exchange Rate System Reform

The exchange rate system reform is an important part of Chile's new liberal economic reforms. Since the 1960s, Chile has implemented various exchange rate regimes: A pegged exchange rate system, a crawling peg system with the exchange rate fluctuating within a band, a crawling floating system and a free floating exchange rate system. During these transitions, the Chilean government has accumulated bountiful experiences in the preparation, timing and policy coordination of reform, setting a good example for other emerging markets in how to conduct marketization of an exchange rate system.

4.3.1 *The First Exchange Rate System Reform (1965–1979): From a Pegged Exchange Rate System to a Crawling Peg System*

4.3.1.1 *Background to the Reform*

Before 1974, Chile pursued inward-oriented economic development using industrial substitution (seeking to replace imported goods with locally produced ones). Nationalizing its domestic enterprises encouraged the government to increase restrictions on trade-related capital flows and enterprises. As a result, Chile's domestic economy fell into stagnation. At the same time, the sharp decline in international copper prices slashed government revenue (on which Chile greatly depended). In 1973, Chile's gross domestic product (GDP) fell by 5.6% year-on-year and the share of fiscal deficit in GDP was as high as 24.7%. What is more, its inflation rate reached an appalling level of 605% (Wang, 2004).

Meanwhile, Chile applied an interventionist policy toward its financial system, suppressing its financial markets and robbing them of all vitality. In the early 1970s, Chile's financial system constituted 20 state-owned commercial banks, one foreign-funded bank and several non-bank financial organizations.

4.3.1.2 *Reform Measures*

During this period, Chile began to reform its financial system, which included transitioning from a fixed exchange rate system into one with more fluctuation. In addition, the current account achieved full liberalization and the capital account also gradually opened up.

Starting in the 1960s, Chile began to apply a pegged exchange rate system. In the late 1960s, in order to cover its fiscal deficit and balance its international payments, it employed a crawling peg system, using the slight monthly depreciation of Peso (CLP) to boost its exports. In the mid-1970s, the Chilean government adjusted its exchange rate system by adopting the "tablita" exchange rate regime in February 1978 (De Gregorio and Andrea, 2004a), which decided and announced in advance the fluctuation range of the exchange rate. This was intended to lower the public's inflation expectations. In the beginning, the Chilean Peso was announced to depreciate by 2.5% monthly and, during the fourth quarter 1978, it would depreciate by 0.75% monthly. At the end of 1978, the government announced that the Peso would depreciate by 15% in 1979. Although the objective of this crawling peg system was to reduce inflation, from 1978 to June 1979, Chile's inflation rate remained at a relatively high level of 30% (Meller, 1996).

In this period, Chile gradually opened its current account and the capital account. By 1974, the Chilean government had achieved liberalization of the current account. From 1974–1976, it gradually opened its capital account for individuals, but still exerted control over capital account transactions for financial institutions. In 1976, the capital account for individuals and non-bank enterprises were all opened. In 1977, the Law of Foreign Exchange Control was revised, which allowed banks to attract foreign capital but also put limits on the terms of investments and positions. In 1980, the limit on positions was lifted and, in 1981, the average term of investment allowed by the government was set to five years.

4.3.2 *The Second Reform of the Exchange Rate System (1979–1999): From the Crawling Peg System to the Crawling Floating Exchange Rate System*

4.3.2.1 *Background to Reform*

Before 1972, the increasing strengthening of the government's market interventions hindered the optimal allocation of productive resources and discouraged private capital investment. The government had tried to maintain public expenditures and cover its fiscal deficits through an inflationary policy and by imposing many restrictions on foreign trade. As a result, Chile experienced the multifaceted plight of economic recession, large-scale fiscal deficit and serious inflation.

In order to dig out of this economic quagmire, Chile carried out its financial system reform in 1974 (De Gregorio *et al.*, 2000). It was a hasty reform: Within seven years Chile had basically completed its exchange rate system reform, opened up its financial account, liberalized interest rates, liberalized the capital account, and opened up the banking industry. Due to this fast speed, Chile's institutions were somewhat unprepared. Its international competitiveness and risk management capacity were still backward by international standards. Its financial market infrastructure, supervision, and regulatory framework all had considerable flaws. Aggressive financial reform resulted in a sharp expansion in credit and the subsequent closings of many financial organizations engaged in inappropriate operation. What is more, the Peso was highly appreciated.

4.3.2.2 *Reform Measures*

From 1974 to 1981, Chile underwent an aggressive reform of its financial system and the 1982 bank crisis ensued. Later, Chile called off the reform, bailed out the banking system and reassumed another, more prudent reform. In contrast to the first, this second attempt achieved remarkable achievements.

Under the tripartite burden of an economic recession, large fiscal deficit and serious inflation, Chile announced its intention to employ a fixed exchange rate system in June 1979. Intending to reduce inflation through exchange rate policy, it set the rate at CLP39 per Dollar (6% higher than that of the "tablita" system). However, this reform move did not solve the domestic inflation problem. Chile also removed restrictions on banks' positions on foreign accounts. The relaxing of control over banks' overseas debts brought in large quantities of foreign capital. Pressure on the

Peso to appreciate thus increased. The rising oil price also contributed to the worsening of Chile's current account. Ultimately, the 1982 bank crisis erupted and the fixed exchange rate came to an end. Chile's monetary authority resumed the crawling peg system to stabilize its economy, after which the Peso depreciated by 43%. The Peso was allowed to fluctuate within a narrow range (±2%) and, when the market was more prepared, the range was enlarged (to ±5%). In addition, the monetary authority made two interventions in the foreign exchange market: One was in 1984 (with the Peso depreciating by 23.7%) and the other was in 1985 (a depreciation of 9%). In both cases, the monetary authority was attempting to boost domestic economic growth.

Meanwhile, the Chilean government began a bailout of the financial market, temperately calling off its liberalization policies and instead strengthening its financial laws, regulations, and supervisory regime. In 1985, Chile undertook the rebuilding of its banking system and abandoned its former trade protectionism policy. It also suspended the liberalization of interest rates. In 1986, a new Bank Law was enacted and a framework for the supervisory regime of the banking system was established. This commenced the second financial system reform. By 1987, the rebuilding of the banking system was completed.

Chile's interest rate liberalization policy also underwent a gradual reform. In 1985, the Central Bank of Chile (CBC) announced that the instructive interest rate for 30-day deposits was to be substituted with public market operations. In 1987, indexation means were used to affect the domestic interest rate level. With domestic inflation and large inflows of foreign securities capital, the fluctuating range of interest rates was enlarged.

Starting from 1990, the monetary authority focused on the development of the financial market and financial vehicles. Future contracts were introduced in 1990; the investment scope of pension funds was expanded in 1993, as the electronic system for transactions and settlement was introduced. In the following year, the stock market brought in future transactions and the investment scope of pension fund was further enlarged from 1995 to 1996. Meanwhile, the money market and foreign exchange market continued to develop, as the central bank strengthened the operation of monetary policy by creating more transaction tools and extending contract terms in the money market. Except for those deals explicitly forbidden by the central bank, transactions in the foreign exchange market could be carried out freely. Since the exchange rate was not officially determined but open to fluctuation, the foreign exchange market became a legitimate, informal market.

Along with the rebuilding of its financial system, Chile gradually opened up capital inflows. In 1985, Chile authorized the inflow of FDI in the form of debt-for-equity swaps and allowed resident and non-resident investors to purchase domestic bonds with foreign currency. In 1987, "the foreign investment fund" was set up to facilitate domestic investment by foreign small and medium-sized investors. In 1990, the "America Deposit Receipts" (ADRs) were issued to attract foreign capital. Qualified pension funds were authorized to issue bonds overseas. At the same time, the Chilean government devised a set of measures to constrain short-term capital inflows. In June 1991, it stipulated that 20% of the value of all new foreign debts (excepting export credit) should be deposited in the CBC as unremunerated reserves (URRs). In 1992, this ratio was raised to 30% and, irrespective of debt's term structure, the URRs should be kept in the central bank for one year. The application scope of URRs was further expanded in 1994 and 1995. In the following few years, restrictions on the terms of foreign debt and ADRs, as well as their credit rating requirements, were all gradually loosened. In 2000, domestic funds were allowed to issue funds overseas and, in 2001, the liberalization of foreign debt issuance and ADRs was achieved.

Simultaneously, in order to ease the pressure of real exchange rate appreciation resulting from capital inflows, Chile proceeded prudently with the opening of its capital outflows. In 1991, residents were allowed to invest abroad any foreign exchange purchased in the informal foreign exchange market. In 1992, pension funds were authorized to employ a part of their assets in overseas investment. During 1993 to 1996, the remittance duration for foreign investors' profits was further extended and the permitted ratio of foreign assets in life insurance companies, banks and mutual funds was raised. Other restrictions on investment tools and investment destinations were also loosened. In 1996, foreign investment by mutual funds was liberalized. In 2001, there were no longer any restrictions on Chile's overseas direct investment (except that all transactions must be conducted in the formal exchange rate market). There still remained a few restrictions, however, on foreign investments made by pension funds.

Chile's financial system reform and economic restructuring had good effects. It stabilized foreign debt levels, improved domestic production capacity, and decreased the unemployment rate. Consequently, Chile raised the Peso's central rate by 2% and substituted the peg to the US Dollar with a peg to a basket of foreign currencies. What is more, the monetary authority was made responsible for determining the contents of the currency basket and the external inflation rate. The monetary authority was charged with basing their decision on future exchange rate expectations, rather than past and present observations (De Gregotio *et al.*, 2000). From 1990–1997, the Chilean Peso saw a yearly average appreciation of 5.4%. Since pressure on the Peso's trend movements was relatively insignificant, the monetary authority began to broaden its fluctuating range. For instance, in January 1992, the floating range was ±10% and in January 1997, it was increased to ±12.5%.

In the aftermath of the 1997 Asian Financial Crisis and the Russian debt crisis in 1998, Chile experienced multiple shocks, including domestic financing difficulty and decline in its import and export volumes. In order to maintain economic stability and domestic confidence, the CBC began to tighten the crawling range of the Peso's exchange rate between +2% and −3.5% and loosen its control over capital inflows. The requirements for URRs were also removed.

4.3.3 *The Third Reform of the Exchange Rate System (1999 onwards): From the Crawling Exchange Rate System to the Free Floating Exchange Rate System*

4.3.3.1 *Background to Reform*

From the second half of 1999, the impact of the Asian Financial Crisis and Russian debt crisis gradually abated. Asian economies began to revive and both the US and European Union economies returned to normal. Chilean exports subsequently began to increase.

In the meantime, the Chilean government launched a readjustment of its fiscal and financial system and continued to perfect its supervision of the financial system (especially the banking system). It also worked to reduce the tax burden on small and medium-sized enterprises and increased public investment, creating lots of employment opportunities. The favorable economic situation inside and outside the country propelled Chile towards economic recovery.

4.3.3.2 *Reform Measures*

In the period after the Asian Financial Crisis, Chile's economy began to recover within a sound economic environment at home and abroad. Its exchange rate system began to loosen with a wider range of fluctuation. Under steady economic environment, the free floating exchange rate system was applied.

As the domestic economy stabilized, the CBC began to relax its exchange rate policy. The floating range was changed to ±3.5% and, through daily adjustment, it was revised to ±5% by the end of the year. In determining the exchange rate, the foreign inflation rate was excluded from consideration and the central rate was decided in reference to future targets. These measures marked the first step of the monetary authority's attempt to apply a floating exchange rate system.

According to Table 4.4, we see that the Peso's fluctuation was within a reasonable range by international standards. At the end of 1999, as banks' debt in US Dollars was quite small, the foreign debt risks of enterprises were fully hedged in the foreign exchange market. Meanwhile, since the exchange rate began to float, the derivative products in the money market gradually achieved mature and stable development (Han, 2005). Domestically, Chile had been well prepared for the realization of the free floating of the exchange rate. At that moment, the Peso was under no pressure for either appreciation or depreciation. On September 2, 1999, with the canceling of the floating range, Chile began to employ a free floating exchange rate system.

After 1999, Chile further carried out its opening-up of the capital account. First of all, URRs were cancelled along with the stipulation that many kinds of capital inflows (in forms like foreign loans, investment, and

Table 4.4: The Exchange Rate Fluctuation of Various Currencies

	The fluctuating rate of each currency (against the US Dollar)		
	1990–1995	1996–2000	2001–2004
Argentine peso	1.71	0.45	15.67
Brazilian Real	25.25	6.68	16.63
Mexican Peso	8.9	8.08	8.02
Chilean Peso	7.44	4.99	9.25
Japanese Yen	10.67	11.79	9.43
Australian Dollar	8.14	9.94	11.41
New Zealand Dollar	6.67	10.12	12.06
Swiss Franc	5.93	9.58	18.55
Canadian Dollar	4.44	4.8	7.18
Swedish Krona	11.94	9.97	11.17
Euro	—	10.62	10.57

Data source: The CBC.

capital purchase) must remain in Chile for at least one year. Regulations on overseas bond issuance and foreign investment by institutional investors were also gradually loosened.

In 2001, Chile achieved the opening-up of its capital account. But this demanded that the foreign exchange transactions of the financial sector should be conducted on the foreign exchange market or should first gain the approval of the central bank. Therefore many kinds of capital flow had no restrictions. This included foreign loans and investments capital purchase, as well as the accompanying outflows of loan prepayments, investment earnings, dividends and other capital gains. Further, regulation stipulating that the purchase and sale of foreign currency must be conducted in the formal foreign exchange market and loan approval rules were all abolished.

4.3.4 *Analysis of the Experiences and Effects of the Exchange Rate System Reform*

4.3.4.1 *Analysis of the Experiences of the Exchange Rate System Reform*

Table 4.5 illustrates the relationship among Chile's exchange rate system reform, liberalization of its capital account and its financial development. During the period of its crawling peg system, Chile undertook financial liberalization. However, due to the reforms' fast pace, Chile's lack of a prudent financial supervisory regime, and ineffective means of hedging risk, capital flight and a bank crisis interrupted the reforms. In 1985, Chile resumed strengthening its supervision over the financial system

Table 4.5: The Process of Chile's Exchange Rate System Reform (Liberalization of the Capital Account and Financial Development)

Time Period	Events
1960–1965	The pegged exchange rate system
1965–1978	The crawling peg exchange rate system
1978–1982	The "tablita" exchange rate system
1982–1999	The crawling peg exchange rate system
1982–1990	The period of strengthening the supervision on financial markets
1985–2002	The opening stage of capital inflows
1990–2004	The rapid growth period of the financial market
1990–2004	The opening stage of capital outflow
1999–2004	The free floating exchange rate system

Data sources: Meller (1996), De Gregorio and Andrea (2004a, 2004b).

and encouraged capital inflows. It also widened the floating range of the exchange rate. In 1990, Chile began to approve capital outflows and promote the opening-up of its financial system. At the outset, it introduced URRs as a means of controlling short-term capital flows. During the initial stages of liberalizing the capital account and financial system (from 1990 to 1995), the levying scope of URRs was expanded. From 1996 on, however, Chile began to depend less on URRs and finally canceled them in 2000.

As Tables 4.6 and 4.7 show, the first capital account item liberalized by Chile was its FDI in 1985. Indeed, Chile's FDI reached the world's highest level in 2003 (*The Yearbook of the World Economy*, 2006). Chile also engaged in privatization of its banks and the strengthening of its

Table 4.6: Sketch of Chile's Opening-up of the Capital Account

Time Period	Events
1985	The introduction of FDI
1987	The enacting of the Foreign Investment Fund Law (promoting capital inflow)
1989	Reducing the tax on overseas remittance of investment earnings
1990	The issuance of ADRs; allowing the remittance of overseas capital earnings
1991	The application of URR; the beginning of overseas direct investment
1992	Allowing pension funds' overseas bond issuance; expanding the levying scope of URR; loosening restrictions on pension funds' overseas investment
1994	Loosening the restrictions on the overseas investment of insurance companies and mutual funds
1995	Expanding the levying scope of URRs
1996	The liberalization of mutual funds' investments
1997–1999	Loosening the restrictions on overseas investment
1998	The issuance of ADR and lowering the requirement for banks' overseas bond issuance
1999	Loosening the restrictions on insurance companies' overseas investment; lowering the requirements for non-bank institutions' overseas bond issuance
2000	The usage of local currency in the payment of foreign debts; the issuance of foreign funds; the cancelling of URRs
2001	The completion of the opening-up of the capital account; the liberalization of bond issuance and ADR; the completion of the liberalization of overseas investment
2002	Freeing the circulation of overseas capital in foreign markets
2004	Further loosening of the restrictions on pension funds' overseas investment

Data sources: Meller (1996), De Gregorio and Andrea (2004a, 2004b).

Table 4.7: Chile's Opening-up Process of its Financial Sector

Time Period	Events
1982	Start of the adjustment of bank's capital structure
1983	Debt restructuring
1984	Imposing limits on the bank's credit quotas
1985	Allowing pension funds to purchase certain stocks; CBC announced interest rate of 30-day deposit
1986	The revision of the general Bank Law and the Bank Supervision Law
1987	Stipulating the interest rate of 90-day index note
1989	The independence of the central bank
1990	The introduction of future contracts
1991	Lowering the requirements on reverse bank credit; increasing the permitted ratio of pension funds' investment in stocks
1992	Introducing the custody system for major securities; insurance companies' participation in interbank transactions; central bank's introduction of various bank notes
1993	The installation of an electronic operating system at the stock exchange; Central bank's introduction of mid-term notes
1994	The introduction of futures transactions
1995	Exerting supervision on pension funds' transactions
1996	Fixing the overnight lending rate; opening of saving accounts at the central bank by financial institutions
1998	Imposing the requirement of bank reserves
1999	Exerting supervision on currency matching and duration matching of financial institutions; introducing a variety of derivatives; the mutual financing between banks and other financial institutions

Data sources: Meller (1996), De Gregorio and Andrea (2004a, 2004b).

supervisory procedures. Five years after the implementation of capital inflows, Chile began to permit domestic capital outflows and authorized pension funds to invest in foreign financial markets (though still with some restrictions). In 1990, Chile began to introduce ADRs and, in the following year, overseas direct investment and pension funds' overseas bond issuance were introduced (again, both with some restrictions).

In 1994, after loosening restrictions on its pension funds' investment, Chile began to relax its control over the overseas investment of insurance companies and mutual funds. Later, in 1996, mutual funds' overseas investments were totally liberalized. Then, the opening scope of Chile's capital account was gradually widened. With the great progress made in indirect investments in 1997, Chile sped up its reform in overseas direct investment and achieved a total opening-up in 2001. In the same year, the issuance of ADR and foreign bonds also completed their liberalization. The opening-up of the capital account was then basically finished. However by

2004, overseas investments by pension funds had not yet achieved total liberalization.

In regard to its progress in financial markets, since 1982 the CBC has been exercising stringent supervision over banks. Although this supervision was loosened somewhat around 1999, it has remained relatively consistent. From 1999, the duration and currency matching of banks' assets and debts were brought under supervision and regulation. The scope of pension funds' investment in stocks was enlarged and its ratio increased, so as to vitalize the financial markets. Meanwhile, stock futures and option contracts were introduced in 1990 and 1994, respectively. Interest rate-linked derivatives were introduced in 1999. In the money market, Chile began to set the basic interest rate by announcing the instructive interest rate. First, the interest rate of 30-day notes issued by the central bank was set, later that of the 90-day index note, and finally the overnight lending rate. Along with changes in determining interest rates, the central bank also continually added a variety of new money market products. It then began to manage the domestic interest rate through open market operations, at last realizing the liberalization of interest rates.

From Figure 4.5 and previous information, we can conclude some basic characteristics of Chile's process of exchange rate system reform. It was during the period of a crawling peg exchange rate system that Chile underwent the opening-up of its capital account and advanced its financial development. With a wider fluctuating range, the opening-up of the capital account as well as financial markets commenced. Like other countries, Chile also began with capital inflows, targeting the major means of FDI in the forms of debt-for-equity swaps and the issuance of ADRs. Then reform of capital outflows began, first in the form of overseas direct investment.

After opening up the capital account, the Chilean government introduced the URR as a way to control capital flows. The securities investment market began to develop as a sort of capital outflow. It started with pension funds, followed by insurance companies and mutual funds. As the major investment institutions in Chile, pension funds were easier to control and therefore could be opened first. However, they could not be fully opened and needed some degree of control so as to prevent huge fluctuations. Later, Chile separately loosened the restrictions on the channels for capital outflow and inflow.

As for the development of Chile's financial markets, this began with increasing supervision over the banks, then the promotion of institutional investors' investment in the securities market (as well as extending

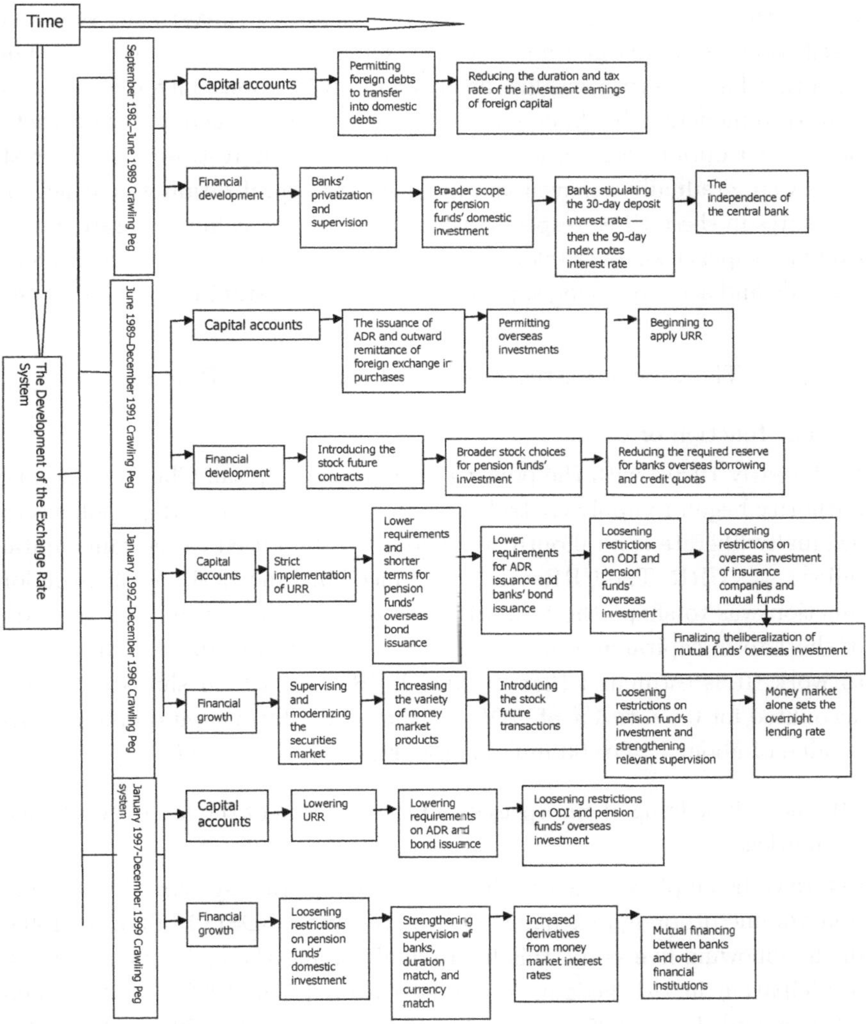

Figure 4.5: Sketch of the Process of Chile's Exchange Rate System Reform (Opening-up of the Capital Account and Its Financial Development)

supervision over them). Finally, the government increased the variety of money market products in step with its supervision. In addition, the central bank tried to stabilize the market through announcing the instructive rate. Other banking supervision mechanisms included lowering the requirement on bank reserves, duration matching and interest rate matching, and allowing banks to engage in mutual financing with other financial institutions.

As for the securities market, on the one hand the investment scope of institutions was enlarged and relevant supervision was put in place. On the other hand, derivatives like futures and options were introduced. With regard to monetary banking, supervision was strengthened and the variety of contract options was enriched. Alongside this, the restraints on interest rates were gradually removed and interest rate liberalization was achieved. Measures in these three respects overlapped, but the common strategy was exerting supervision over relevant institutions and transactions. A prudent attitude and accompanying supervision ensured the stability of the process.

4.3.4.1.1 The Characteristics of Chile's Liberalization Process

(1) The function of URRs

In the early 1990s, with the pouring in of foreign capital, Chile's monetary authority began to apply controls over capital inflows and adopt policies to gradually liberate capital outflows. The major tool used to restrain capital inflows was URR. The URRs were introduced in June 1991 and their major function was to shape the formation of capital inflows, reducing the share of short-term capital and increasing that of long-term capital. This proved to work. It is estimated that in 2006 UURs' impact on short-term debt accounted for 0.5% to 1% of GDP, slashing short-term capital inflows with a value of about USD$600 million (Bleakley and Kevin, 2005).

(2) The risk hedging of enterprises and the function of the foreign exchange market

Before Chile employed the crawling peg exchange rate system, the transaction volume of foreign exchange derivatives was USD$112 billion in 1998. In the following five years, this figure doubled and the ratio of enterprises' participation in risk hedging was raised from 1:5 in 1998 to 1:3 in 2003 (Cowan and Jose, 2005). By studying the data from 1995 to 2003, De Gregorio *et al.* found that before the crawling peg exchange rate system, enterprises had already realized the problem of currency mismatch. In 1998, enterprises' currency and risk exposure reached a height of 10% of their asset value, and thereafter steadily declined. This indicated that the risk management of the monetary authority over enterprises had born fruit.

Through studying the pattern of enterprises' currency exposure, Bleakley and Kevin (2005) discovered that, since the Peso depreciated in 1999 and the free floating exchange rate system was applied, the foreign exchange exposure of enterprises had begun to decline. This meant that the change of exchange rate system had made enterprises pay more attention to their own management of foreign exchange risk. Namely, better enterprise risk management diminished the impact of exchange rate system reform.

(3) Intervention in the foreign exchange market

Apart from a sound foundation at the micro level, when faced with violent fluctuations in the exchange rate, the Chilean government's macro operations also proved to be very potent in guaranteeing economic stability and reducing future exchange rate fluctuation. The measures taken include intervention in the foreign exchange market. The first intervention took place on August 16, 2001. At that time, Argentina was experiencing a crisis. The CBC announced that it was putting USD$2 billion in the spot foreign exchange market and issued a considerable amount of central bank notes in US Dollars (Esteban and Jorge, 2005). In this period, the Chilean Peso appreciated by 3.9% despite the fact that had it depreciated by 5% in September. The highest daily depreciation margin of that month was 2.8%. By October, the situation began to improve and the highest daily appreciation margin reached 1.8%.

In 2002, Brazil experienced an economic crisis. The Chilean Peso had depreciated by 7% against the US Dollar within a year. From October 10, 2002 to February 10, 2003, the CBC once again intervened in the foreign exchange market through issuing bonds in US Dollars: Two with a value of USD$500 million each in October and November, and two with a value USD$250 million each in December and January. This time, the central bank did not exert control over the spot foreign exchange market so as to guarantee the autonomy of the market as much as possible. In this period, the Chilean Peso appreciated by 2.1%. Its highest daily depreciation margin and appreciation margin was 1.3% and 2.3%, respectively.

4.3.4.2 *Analysis of the Effects of the Exchange Rate System Reform*

Due to a lack of data, this section will only list Chile's relevant economic indicators from the second exchange rate system reform (Figures 4.6–4.8). When comparing the effects of two exchange rate system reforms on foreign trade, after the second reform, foreign trade volumes fluctuated more violently. At first, trade volumes rose, but then declined sharply (mainly influenced by international capital flows and the rising price of oil). After the third reform, however, foreign trade sustained relatively stable growth.

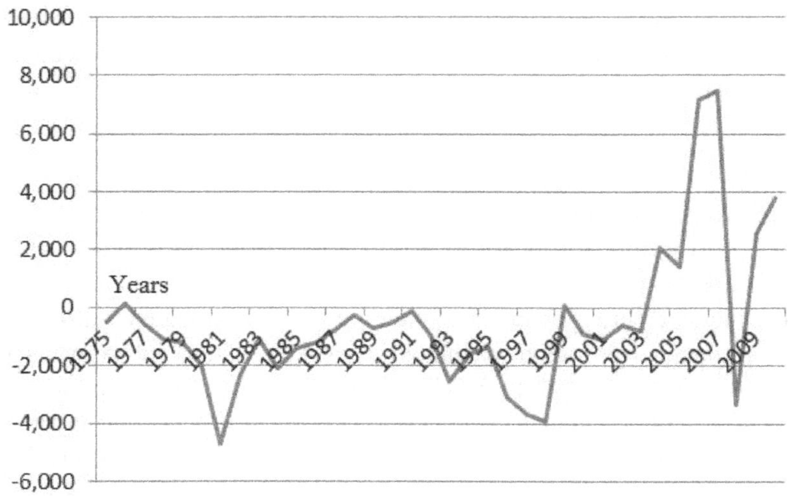

Figure 4.6: Chile's Current Account (USD million)

Data source: International Monetary Fund.

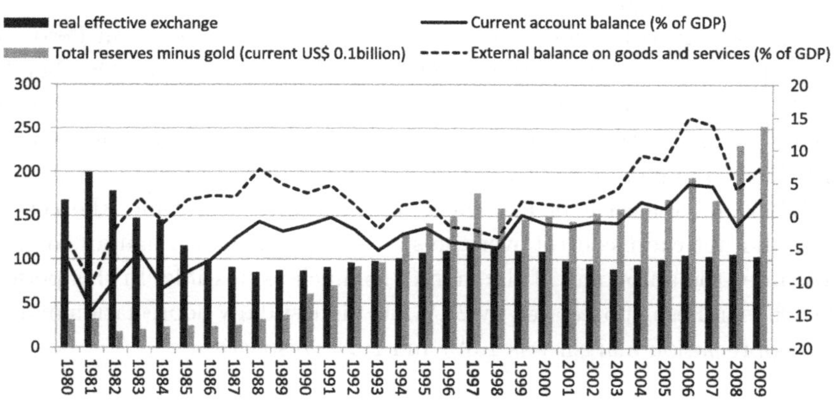

Figure 4.7: The Effect of Chile's Exchange Rate Reform on Its Foreign Trade

Data source: The World Bank.

In these two reforms, foreign exchange reserves managed to maintain quite stable levels.

In regard to domestic economic growth, after the second reform, Chile's economy still suffered a negative growth rate, but was in gradual recovery. After the third reform, the economic growth rate turned from negative to positive, displaying a benign tendency for growth. The inflation

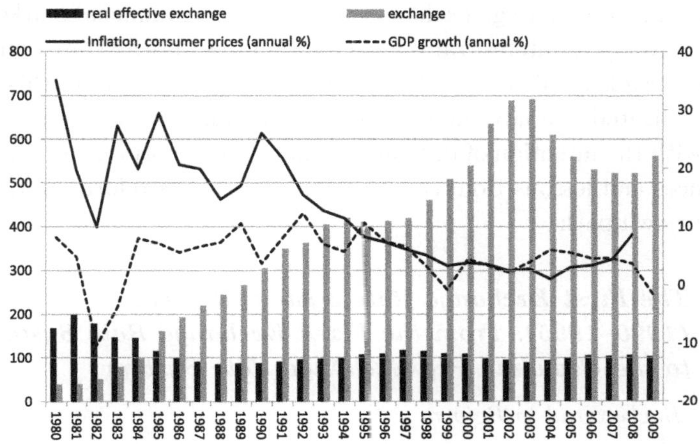

Figure 4.8: The Effect of Chile's Exchange Rate Reform on Its Domestic Economy

Data source: The World Bank.

rate only stayed at a low level during the third exchange rate system reform without significant fluctuations. This also indicated that domestic inflation experienced high fluctuations after the second reform, which was detrimental to domestic economic growth.

The cause of unsatisfactory results following the second exchange rate system reform might be the domestic volatility brought by financial liberalization and large capital inflows. The fluctuation in oil prices also affects Chile's foreign trade. On balance, Chile's exchange rate system reform was relatively ideal, which can mainly be attributed to Chile's prudent drawing of lessons from its banking crisis. It had always exerted stringent supervisions on the financial system and developed vigorously the foreign exchange derivative market, providing tools for enterprises to avoid risks and thus greatly reduce their external risk exposure during the exchange rate reform.

4.4 Poland's Experiences in Exchange Rate System Reform

Poland's exchange rate system reform and its relaxing of control over the capital account happened during its transition from a planned economy to a market economy (a case similar to China). When Poland carried out its exchange rate reforms, its macro economic conditions were similar to those of China: Before reform, Poland's exports were largely controlled by the government; its foreign exchange market and the financial markets were not well-developed; interest rates and credit quotas were all state-controlled. All these problems also existed in China's reform. Therefore, this section will be dedicated to analyzing the process of Poland's exchange rate system reform with the intention of drawing useful lessons for our own reform. The experiences and lessons from this transition country's reform journey may guide our own path.

4.4.1 *The First Exchange Rate System Reform (1990–1995): From the Fixed Exchange Rate System to the Crawling Peg Exchange Rate System*

4.4.1.1 *Background to Reform*

In 1989, Poland applied "shock therapy" to its economic transition. State assets were totally privatized in a short time. The sharp change from a planned economy to a market economy created great shocks in the overall economy. In the early days of the transition, Poland was confronted with a bottleneck, lacking both domestic savings and foreign exchange reserves. In order to strengthen the confidence of foreign investors, the Polish government encouraged more inflows of international private capital. Consequently, Poland had been actively opening its capital account from the outset of the reform, pushing forward marketization and attracting capital inflows.

4.4.1.2 *Reform Measures*

In this period, Poland's exchange rate system first switched from a currency pegged to the US Dollar to one pegged to a currency basket. Then, Poland moved to a crawling peg exchange rate system, with the Zloty (PLN) still tied to a currency basket. The main reason for the reform was that the Zloty's appreciation had caused imbalances in Poland's international payments.

On January 1, 1990, with joint funding from the IMF and a consortium of ten Western countries (contributing USD$715 million and USD$1 billion, respectively), Poland significantly depreciated its currency from PLN3100 per Dollar to PLN9500 per Dollar. Later, to stabilize the domestic economic environment, Poland began to apply a fixed exchange rate system pegged solely against the US Dollar (Wang, 2003; Ötker *et al.*, 2007). However, due to difference in inflation rates between Poland and America, the real exchange rate of the Zloty continued to rise. In May 1991, the

Polish government depreciated the Zloty against the Dollar by 16.8% and substituted the Zloty's peg to Dollars with a peg to a currency basket. In essence, the "peg to a currency basket" was still a pegged system, which could not truly solve the problem of the Zloty's real appreciation. Under this situation, the moderate fluctuation of the exchange rate was the key to tackling imbalances in international payments. So in October 1991, Poland gave up the "peg to a currency basket".

In October 1991, Poland introduced a crawling peg exchange rate system, depreciating the Zloty in several steps. The central exchange rate was announced monthly, each time with depreciation of 1.8%. The Zloty's depreciation, on the one hand, improved the international competitiveness of Polish commodities; on the other hand, it added pressure on domestic inflation. With the obvious improvement in the current account and large capital inflows, the central bank found it more and more costly and difficult to engage in hedging operations. As the Zloty once again faced appreciation pressures, the Polish government began to consider increasing the flexibility of the exchange rate level. In May 1995, the "crawling peg to a currency basket" exchange rate system was thus abolished.

To open up the current account and the capital account, Poland came up with a plan for stabilizing the exchange rate. The plan dictated free exchange in most current account transactions, to be followed by a total opening in 1994. The opening-up of the capital account began in the middle of 1991, marked by the enacting of the Securities Law and the Foreign Investment Law, which removed most restrictions on FDI and allowed non-residents to engage in stock investment in Poland. From 1992 to the early 1994, Poland lifted restrictions on foreign investors' investment in domestic treasure bills.

4.4.2 *The Second Exchange Rate System Reform (1995–2000): From the Crawling Peg Exchange Rate System to the Free Floating Exchange Rate System*

4.4.2.1 *Background to Reform*

In the fall of 1994, Poland applied to join the Organization for Economic Co-operation and Development (OECD), initiating a new round of legislation activities. In that same year, the Polish government negotiated with foreign creditors to lessen its foreign debt. Ultimately, Poland was exempted from 50% of its foreign currency debt. In 1995, the Polish government accepted the eighth article stipulated by the IMF, realizing the free exchange of its current account. Also, exporters were allowed to set up their own foreign exchange accounts without having to sell their foreign currency generated from export to the central bank. Along with the continual depreciation of the Zloty, these changes boosted Poland's exports and its current account began to record a surplus. Meanwhile, large quantities of international capital poured into Poland, pressuring the Zloty to appreciate and placing demands on the Polish government to reform the exchange rate regime.

4.4.2.2 *Reform Measures*

In accordance with OCED regulations, Poland gradually opened its capital account to OECD member countries and established a free floating exchange rate system.

In 1995, with the recovery of Poland's exports, its current account surplus, and the pouring in of foreign capital, the Zloty was under greater pressure to appreciate. Consequently, Poland began to apply a more flexible crawling band exchange rate system. The central exchange rate was announced monthly with a floating range of ±7% (the exchange rate for interbanks transactions was totally decided by the market).

In 1998, the Central Bank of Poland set up the Monetary Policy Committee (MPC). Along with the government, the MPC participated in devising exchange rate and interest rate policy, as well as establishing a monetary policy framework mainly aimed at curbing inflation. Meanwhile, the central bank announced that its exchange rate arrangement would gradually transition to a free floating regime within two years.

During the two-year transition period, Poland accelerated its opening-up of the capital account and financial liberalization. This resulted in large amounts of capital pouring into the country and the exchange rate fluctuating evermore violently. The government thus began to intervene in the foreign exchange market from time to time to maintain the exchange rate's stability. The Central Bank of Poland adopted some transitory measures to increase the flexibility of the exchange rate: It widened the floating band from ±7% to ±15% and ceased to intervene in the foreign exchange market (starting from July 1999). In this period, the MPC four times lowered the depreciation rate of the Zloty, bringing down the public's inflation expectations. In April 2000, after the two-year transition period, Poland established a totally free floating exchange rate system.

During the reform of the exchange rate system, Poland carried out the opening-up of the capital account in three stages. First, in January

1995, the first revision of the foreign exchange law began to take effect. It allowed the sale of Polish securities in international markets and permitted residents to invest overseas through FDI, real estate and financial tools with maturities greater than one year. This not only eased the imbalance between restrictions on capital inflows and outflows, but also gradually reduced the restrictions on the transaction volume of various activities. The restrictions on commercial credit activities with terms over one year (both for inflows and outflows) also began to loosen.

In the beginning of 1999, the second revision of the foreign exchange law took effect, abolishing formal restrictions on exchange. Other items of capital flow (such as futures operations) also gained some development. But bonds with a maturity less than one year and deposits with terms under three months were still restricted, encouraging inflows and constraining outflows.

In the fall of 2002, the third revision of the foreign exchange law took effect, which achieved the standards of both the European Union and the OECD. What needs to be stressed, however, was that Poland had not yet achieved total opening-up of the capital account. There still were some restrictions on short-term capital flows with non-European and non-OCED member countries (Ötker-Robe *et al.*, 2007).

In regards to the development of financial markets, Poland already had some variety among its domestic financial institutions in this period. Foreign banks began to participate in some major financial institutional reforms, which was conducive to the stability of the overall financial system and the improvement of the service quality (The Investigation Group of the State Administration of Foreign Exchange, 2003). However, commercial banks had taken up too large a share in the financial system. From Table 4.8,

Table 4.8: The Structure of Poland's Financial System in 1999

Type of institution	Assets (Million Zloty)	Percentage of Total Assets	Number of Institutions
Commercial banks	3,490,22	86.5	77
Insurance companies	28,935	7.2	56
Cooperative banks	15,410	3.8	781
Brokerage banks	3,604	0.9	48
Investment funds	3,215	0.8	15
Pension funds	2,256	0.6	21
Credit union	883	0.2	158
In total	4,03,325	100	1,156

Data source: The National Bank of Poland.

we see that commercial banks' assets had accounted for as high as 86.5% of the total. On the whole, financial intermediaries were underdeveloped. Compared with the assets of the banking system (making up 60% of GDP), private savings only accounted for 22%. Besides, stock transaction volumes in Poland in 1999 only accounted for up to 20% of that year's GDP.

Moreover, financial institutions were highly concentrated. Due to the relaxing of financial supervision in the early 1990s, by March 2000 Poland already had 77 commercial banks, but the total assets of the largest 11 banks accounted for three quarters of all bank assets. The three largest life insurance companies possessed 80% of the total assets in the life insurance industry (the ratio was 75% in the non-life insurance business). The three largest pension funds took up 67%. Financial services were also underdeveloped. There were only 5.8 branches on an average for every 100,000 residents (the EU members' average was 48).

Except for central bank notes, Poland's money market enjoyed good liquidity and competitiveness with continued growth during its transition. But it was mainly focused on short-term transactions. The three major transactions in the money market were unsecured loans (interbank money market), secured loans (repurchase transactions), and the exchange of central bank notes. The differences between Poland's Warsaw Interbank Offered Rate (WIBOR) and its Warsaw Interbank Bid Rate (WIBID) was relatively small (0.6%), indicating that the interbank money market was highly efficient and competitive.

4.4.3 *Analysis of the Experiences and Effects of Poland's Exchange Rate System Reform*

4.4.3.1 *Analysis of the Experiences of Poland's Exchange Rate System Reform*

Examining Table 4.9 and Figure 4.9, we find that Poland did not adopt many opening measures during the fixed exchange rate regime period. At that time it only began to attract FDI and allow residents to purchase and sell foreign exchange for tourism purposes. When it applied the crawling exchange rate system later, it began with the opening of capital inflow items. The order of capital inflow reform was relatively clear: First FDI, then domestic governmental bonds and finally domestic stocks. Their risks rose one by one, and the latter two continued to be implemented under the crawling exchange rate regime. With the widening floating range of the exchange rate, FDI and security transactions began to be

Table 4.9: The Process of Poland's Exchange Rate System Reform and Its Opening-up of the Capital Account

Time Period	Events
1989–1991	The fixed exchange rate system
January 1990	Permitting currency exchanging for going abroad
1991	Encouraging FDI inflow
1991–1995	The crawling exchange rate system
1993	Permitting non-residents to purchase government bonds
1994	Permitting non-residents to purchase stocks
1995–2000	The band crawling exchange rate system
1995	Liberalization of private capital flows; opening the current account
1996	Opening commercial credit; permitting non-residents to issue and transact stocks; opening-up of domestic industries, residents' purchasing stock in OECD member countries and offering guarantees
1999	Opening all securities transaction to (non)residents, except mortgage bonds
2000	Opening the international capital market for transactions
2000–2004	The free floating exchange rate system
2002	Opening all remaining accounts to OECD member countries

Data sources: Ötker-Robe *et al.* (2007), Wang (2003) and IMF (2001), etc.

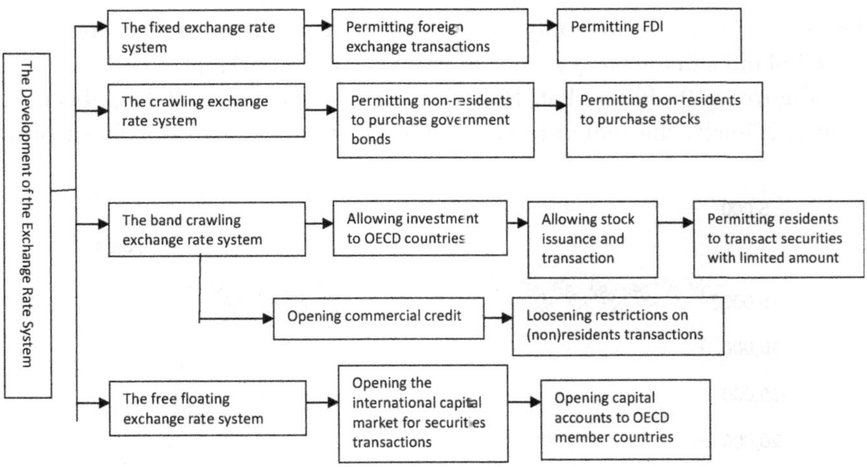

Figure 4.9: Sketch of the Process of Poland's Exchange Rate System Reform (Opening-up of the Capital Account and Financial Development)

Data sources: Ötker-Robe *et al.* (2007), Wang (2003) and IMF (2001), etc.

further opened. Among all current account and private capital items, the first to be liberalized were those with relatively small risk. Later, a breakthrough was made by opening domestic industry to the outside.

Regarding capital account outflows, Poland's major measures included allowing residents to purchase securities in the international market and beginning to open up commercial credit. These items were first opened to OECD member countries and then to other countries. The opening-up of security investments was gradually deepened and, by 1999, it was basically complete (excepting mortgage bonds). Poland achieved its opening-up of the capital account to OEDC member countries in 2002.

Poland's opening-up of the capital account was also conducted under the crawling exchange rate regime: first by targeting direct investment and then by targeting indirect investment. For direct investment, Poland first allowed capital inflows, then outflows; first bond investments, then the stock investments (in accordance with their relative risks). Notably, from the former analysis we see that during the decade of exchange rate system reform, Poland's financial system did not deeply develop. Though the equity share of foreign capital was quite large, it was relatively easy for the government to manage because it was highly concentrated in the financial system. It was only after realizing a free floating exchange rate that Poland's financial system gradually began to develop.

Figure 4.10 shows that Poland's current account had long been in deficit. Namely, the sum of the capital account and reserves was in surplus.

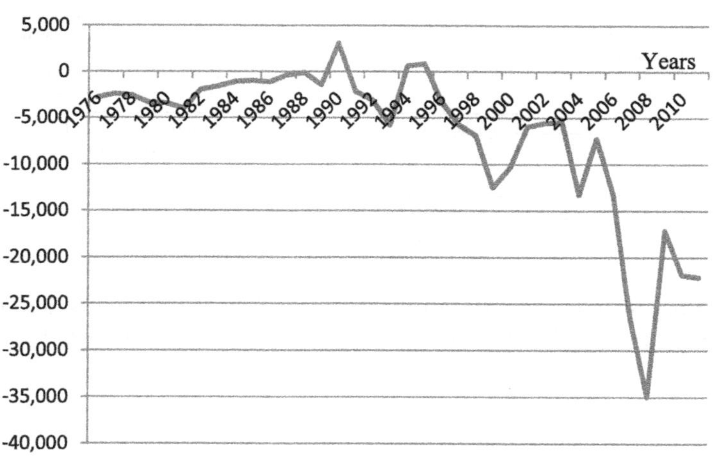

Figure 4.10: Poland's Current Account (USD million)

Data source: International Monetary Fund.

This indicates that, after the opening-up, capital account inflows were larger than outflows. The attractive effect of the liberalized capital account on investment capital is relatively obvious.

4.4.3.2 *Other Control Measures Used during the Opening-up of Poland's Capital Account*

(1) The treatment of non-performing assets

In 1992, Poland set up an institution especially dedicated to the treatment of non-performing assets. When adding registered capital to an enterprise, it demanded the enterprise to pay 70% of its debt and compelled it into asset restructuring (The Investigation Group of the State Administration of Foreign Exchange, 2003). This approach bore a high initial price. Enterprises went bankrupt, workers were laid off, and the unemployment rate reached 18% at its height. However, through these difficulties, three positive outcomes resulted. First, the bankrupt enterprises gradually adapted to the market economy. Second, the bad debts of banks decreased significantly from 35% in 1990 to 20% in 2003. Third, banks' capacity to make profits and defend risks was improved. According to statistics from the central bank, though the ratio of non-performing asset was still high at 20%, banks managed to set up enough provision for bad debts to maintain their profits.

(2) The opening of banks

Poland encouraged foreign banks to enter its market but required them to participate in the restructuring of domestic banks, as well as provide aid to any Polish bank in difficulty. Meanwhile, the foreign-funded banks were not encouraged to enter Poland in the form of an independent legal person. By the end of 2003, foreign banks inside Poland had basically become local independent legal persons through restructuring with local banks. At that time, the assets of foreign banks had accounted for 60% to 80% of Poland's total bank asset, which aroused social concerns that foreign banks monopolized Poland's banking industry. However, officials of the central bank were not worried. They mainly strove to prevent the monopoly of a single bank in the country.

(3) The monitoring of capital flows

The Central Bank of Poland put emphasis on strengthening the monitoring of cross-border capital flows during the opening-up of the capital account. It introduced two monitoring systems. One system monitored international payments. It collected all transaction information on banks' foreign exchange cash transactions (as well as related data), assembled this data, and reported a balance sheet of international payments. Especially after the opening-up of cross-border investment portfolios: both inward and outward — the Central Bank of Poland reinforced the importance and standards of statistics on investment portfolios.

The other system monitored short-term capital flows (SMOK). It mainly collected transaction information on foreign exchange swaps and futures between Poland's banks and non-residents. The system's purpose was to measure the scale as well as the motive behind transactions, discerning between swaps with real foundations (for instance, to hedge the risks of investment in Poland's national bonds) from other, more speculative transactions.

4.4.3.3 *Analysis of the Effects of the Exchange Rate System Reform*

Due to a lack of complete data before 1991, this section will leave out the analysis of former indicators.

After the first exchange rate system reform, Poland's exports did not improve. Under the pegged exchange rate regime, the cash account and the commodity and service account had a positive balance in 1990, but then levels sharply dropped by 4% and 7%, respectively. Despite these violent fluctuations, they returned to positive again in 1995. After the crawling peg exchange rate system was established in 1995, the cash account and the commodity and service account both slumped by 7%. After the second exchange rate system reform, however, foreign trade began to recover. Poland's foreign reserves were relatively stable during the two reforms. However, after the second reform, it experienced a higher and longer-term increase in reserves, amounting to USD$70 billion in 2009.

During its two exchange rate system reforms, Poland's GDP sustained growth of over 4%. After a shift to a crawling peg system in 1995, the GDP growth rate began to fall. Though it recovered a little later, its rate of fluctuation was still larger than that under the crawling peg exchange rate system. The Zloty's real exchange rate was significantly depreciated before 1991, but became comparatively stable under the crawling peg regime and barely changed under the free floating exchange rate regime. The nominal exchange rate was stable in the long run, but the real effective exchange rate was appreciating (Figures 4.11 and 4.12).

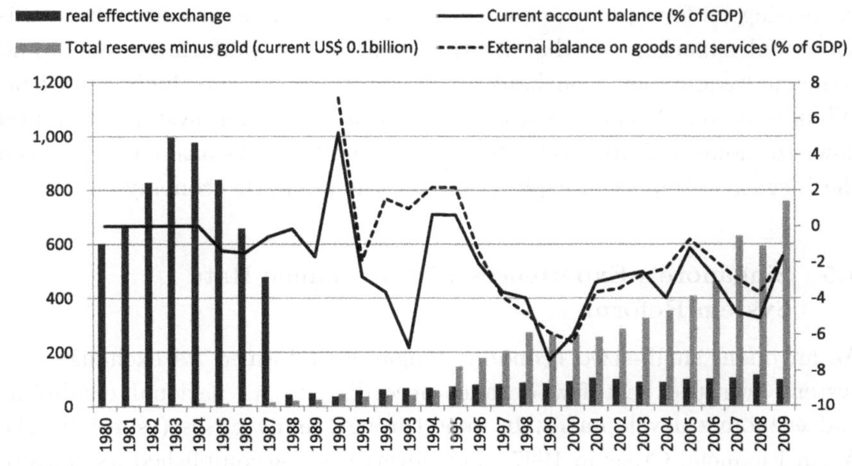

Figure 4.11: The Effect of Poland's Exchange Rate System Reform on Its Foreign Trade

Data source: The World Bank.

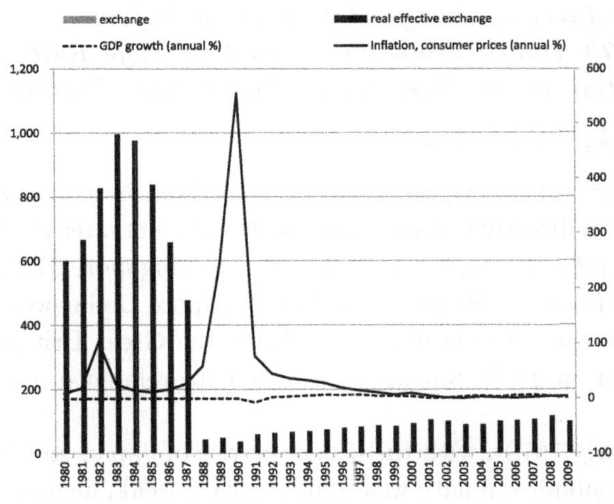

Figure 4.12: The Effect of Poland's Exchange Rate System Reform on the Domestic Economy

Data source: The World Bank.

On the whole, Poland's second exchange rate system reform had better results than the first. This was mainly because commodity prices in Poland were higher than those of its trade partners. Also the pegged exchange rate system could lead to a continuous appreciation of the Zloty, thus decreasing its foreign trade competitiveness. What we can draw from this successful experience is that its treatment of non-performing assets and stringent requirements on banks' risk management were highly prudent. What is more, Poland's establishment of a precaution system of capital flows to monitor short-term international capital flows ultimately reduced the (negative) impact of capital flows on the domestic economy.

4.5 Singapore's Experiences with Exchange Rate System Reform

As an open, small-sized economy, Singapore reformed its exchange rate system over the past few decades according to its national conditions and economic development. It went through many crises (especially the Asian Financial Crisis in 1997), but nevertheless accomplished its goals of achieving stable commodity prices, economic growth and a stable exchange rate for the Singapore Dollar.

4.5.1 *The First Exchange Rate System Reform (1973–1980): From the Fixed Exchange Rate System to the Floating Exchange Rate System*

4.5.1.1 *Background to Reform*

Formerly a British colony, Singapore remained on the pound sterling standard system (indirectly connected to the US Dollar) after its independence in 1956. In 1967, Singapore issued the new Singapore Dollar (SGD) to replace the Malaysian Ringgit. But the Singapore Dollar was still fixed to the pound sterling standard system. When the Great Britain Pound was made to float in 1972, Singapore changed its reference currency to the US Dollar.

In the early 1970s, with the economic rise of Japan and West Europe, America's economic strength was comparatively weak, increasing its foreign trade deficit. With large quantities of Dollars flowing out of the country, the "Dollar surplus" prevented the US from maintaining a fixed exchange rate for the Dollar. Meanwhile, influenced by the Vietnam War, America's fiscal deficit was swelling and over-issuance of currency gave rise to severe inflation. In 1973, the fixed exchange rate system (which pegged the currency to gold) was abandoned by all countries, causing the total collapse of the Bretton Woods system. International finance fell into chaos.

4.5.1.2 *Reform Measures*

Due to the US Dollar's depreciation in 1973, large quantities of international capital poured into Singapore's financial market. Singapore's fixed exchange rate, combined with such inflows, threatened to raise the domestic inflation rate. To prevent this, Singapore abandoned its long-running fixed exchange rate regime and in June of the same year announced that the Singapore Dollar would no longer be pegged to the US Dollar but instead be tied to a floating exchange rate system.

On June 1, 1978, Singapore removed all its foreign exchange control measures, providing extremely preferential conditions for Singapore's foreign exchange market. Though foreign exchange controls were removed, the Finance Administration of Singapore still imposed necessary restrictions on those banks that could otherwise freely manipulate the Singapore Dollar. Besides, in a small-sized county like Singapore, purely market-determined foreign exchange policies would bring chaos to the domestic economy. Consequently, the Finance Administration of Singapore has always adopted a prudent attitude toward the Singapore Dollar's internationalization.

To develop its financial market and attract foreign banks, the Singaporean government authorized such banks in 1991 to engage in all the businesses of local banks. However, in September of that year, the government issued a restrictive license to the newly entered foreign banks, putting limits on the scope of their business so as to protect local banks. In 1973, in an attempt to make Singapore an off-shore financial center, the Singaporean government called off this issuance of restrictive licenses and substituted it with an off-shore bank license. This new license stipulated that foreign banks could only conduct business in the off-shore market.

4.5.2 *The Second Exchange Rate System Reform (1981 onwards): From the Floating Exchange Rate System to the Managed Floating Exchange Rate System*

4.5.2.1 *Background to the Reform*

Upon entering the 1980s, Singapore began its so-called "second industrial revolution" with domestic economic restructuring and vigorous development of industries like petroleum refinement, electronic devices, shipbuilding and engineering design. Singapore transitioned from a labor-intensive economy to a capital and technology-intensive economy, ascending to become one of the newly industrialized Asian nations. Meanwhile, Singapore continued to refine its traditionally strong industry, namely the financial services industry. By relying on these two engines of economic growth — manufacturing and services — Singapore entered a golden age of rapid economic growth, becoming a world renowned oil refining, shipping and financial center.

Singapore was seriously affected by the Asian Financial Crisis in 1997, experiencing an economic downturn and not recovering until 2002. Meanwhile, the manufacturing industry in Singapore also met challenges from low-cost manufacturing countries like China. In response, Singapore sped up the development of its domestic financial and service industries. It successfully converted itself into a global financial services center, maintaining domestic economic development.

At the same time, the exchange rate policy of Singapore in 1981 became the center of its monetary policy, whose objective was to maintain the stable purchasing power of the Singapore Dollar. Singapore (alongside other small-sized, open economies) faces a periodic threat from large-scale international capital flows that can devastate its domestic economy. Consequently, the Singaporean government did not support the internationalization of its currency. It ultimately abandoned its free floating exchange rate system and established instead a managed floating exchange rate system (for the purpose of intervening when the currency fluctuates).

4.5.2.2 *Reform Measures*

Based on its own national conditions, Singapore's financial administration developed the managed floating exchange rate system that best suited its small-sized and open economy: A supervised and adjustable exchange rate system.

The basic framework of the regime includes several features:

(1) The currency basket

The basis for setting the Singapore Dollar's rate is a trade-linked basket of currencies consisting of currencies from its major trade partners. Each currency is weighted based on its importance.

(2) The floating range

Singapore's financial administration sets a secret floating range for the tradea-linked weighted exchange rate. Within this range the rate is allowed to fluctuate. When the rate falls outside the prescribed range, the foreign exchange administration intervenes through the sale of foreign currency and shepherds the rate back into the range.

(3) The crawling floating range

The Singaporean government does not set a completely fixed range for the rate, but instead regularly evaluates and adjusts the range. This keeps the range consistent with current economic conditions and avoids the rate deviating too much from the basic valuation.

(4) The foreign exchange rate objective

This is the principle that the exchange rate should not deviate from current economic conditions. When the economy is healthy, a strong Singapore Dollar policy is adopted to prevent economic overheating. When the economy is unhealthy, a weak policy is adopted to reduce deflation risks.

In regard to its banking system, Singapore gradually removed the restrictions on foreign banks so as to bridge the unequal treatment towards foreign and local banking. The equity share of domestic banks rose from 20% in 1990 to 40% in 1995. In the same period, Singapore began to open its domestic banking market and businesses. In the first stage, the retail banking business was opened. Through preferentially introducing banks that meet the standards to gain a comprehensive bank license, the administrative authority reinforced competition in the banking sector and improved the overall competitiveness of local banks. In 2001, Singapore undertook the second stage, allowing foreign banks to apply for a license to become comprehensive banks and contribute more directly to Singapore's local banking market. Two major changes were made at this stage. First, foreign banks were allowed to freely enter the domestic banking wholesale market. Second, all banks became subject to examinations and tests in an attempt to improve their competitiveness and create a more free banking environment.

As for the foreign exchange market, upon entering the 1980s, Singapore applied policies that changed its regulatory style from that of stringent central supervision to decentralized self-supervision. Singapore's financial administration began to relax its supervision over the foreign exchange market, reduced the brokerage commissions of foreign exchange transactions, and encouraged banks to engage in block transactions of foreign exchange. These changes contributed significantly to the vitality and expansion of the foreign exchange market. The daily transaction value of the foreign exchange market exceeded USD$10 billion at the end of 1984 and was as high as USD$24 billion in 1986, making Singapore one of the major international foreign exchange markets (Investigation Report of Singapore's Foreign Exchange Market, 2009). In 1998, Singapore's financial administration followed market trends and accelerated the development of its foreign exchange derivatives market. It lifted all controls on banks' provision of derivatives to residents, only retaining restrictions on derivative transactions between banks and non-residents (which were further reduced to only a few by 2004).

In order to promote the better management of funds and invigorate investment banks, Cabinet Councilor Li Guangyao released a series of liberating measures in 1994. The account holders of Central Provident Fund[2] (CPF) were allowed to engage in overseas investment, mainly in three stages. The first stage began on January 1, 1995. The CPF was allowed to invest in foreign bonds and stocks that traded on the Singapore Securities Exchange. The second stage began on January 1, 1997. The investment scope of unit trusts supported by the CPF was enlarged to the listed stocks in the wider Asian capital market and the share of foreign exchange investment was increased from 20% to 40%. The third stage began on January 1, 1999. The investment of unit trust and funds was allowed beyond Asia, including America, Germany, and Japan. Also the maximum investment in foreign currency was raised to 50% of the fund's total capital. All these measures deepened and broadened Singapore's capital market.

4.5.3 *Analysis of the Experiences and Effects of the Exchange Rate System Reform*

4.5.3.1 *The Analysis of the Experiences of the Exchange Rate System Reform*

In 1975, Singapore began to reform the exchange rate system under which the rate was pegged to a currency basket. In 1978, the Singapore Dollar achieved its free exchange status. Starting in 1981, Singapore's exchange rate system became the center of its monetary policy. Different from other

[2]The CPF is a fully accumulative compulsory saving plan. The private accounts of holders under age 55 was divided into three parts: The general account, the Medicare account and the special account. Deposits in general accounts can be used in expenditures like housing, insurance, approved investment, and education; deposits of Medicare accounts are used for hospitalizing fees and approved Medicare expenditures; special accounts are prepared for retirement and emergencies. When a holder is over 55 years old, the private accounts change to constitute the retired account and a Medicare account. If the required minimum amount of deposits in the CPF account is reached, part of the deposit can be withdrawn.

Table 4.10: The Process of Singapore's Exchange Rate System Reform (The Opening-up of the Capital Account and Financial Development)

Time Period	Events
1965–1973	The fixed exchange rate system
1968	The establishment of the Asian US Dollar market
1970	Enacting of the Foreign Exchange Control Law
1971–1973	Bringing in foreign banks and exerting control
1973	Establishing off-shore banks
1973–1980	The floating exchange rate system
1973–1991	The period of supervision over the finance sector
1980–2004	The managed exchange rate system
1990	Financial supervision transferred to autonomous supervision
1985–1997	The foreign exchange market achieves considerable scale
1991–2001	Liberalization of the finance sector
1998–2004	Acceleration of the development of the foreign exchange derivatives market

countries, Singapore had already achieved the opening-up of its capital account long ago. Despite the fact that the Singapore Dollar could be freely exchanged, Singapore still exerted stringent supervisions on non-resident financial institutions, which could be interpreted as a form of indirect exchange rate control.

Table 4.10 shows that under the fixed exchange rate regime, Singapore began to loosen its control, attract foreign banks, and set up the Asian US Dollar market. To ensure that the Financial Administration could effectively stabilize the financial market, Singapore founded a development bank and a savings bank. An investigation of Singapore's foreign exchange market deemed that this was a comparatively effective means of control (SFEMC, 2009).

Under the floating exchange rate regime, Singapore's major reform was to allow the free exchange of the Singapore Dollar. But, due to stringent domestic supervision, this did not have significant influence on the currency's exchange rate.

The establishment of the managed floating exchange rate system was prompted out of a dual need for both economic development and an international environment favorable to financial liberalization. With the gradual improvement of the domestic financial market, Singapore began to loosen financial controls. Given its prudent attitude towards the insurance industry, it first expanded the business scope for banks, then opened the fund management and investment bank businesses, followed by opening the foreign exchange market and bond market. Since Singapore's banks took

Table 4.11: The Opening Process of Singapore's Finance Sector

Time Period	Events
1968	The establishment of development banks and the Asian US Dollar market
1970	Revision of the Foreign Exchange Control Law and rapid growth of the foreign exchange market; revision of the Bank Law and the establishment of MAS
1971	Bringing in foreign banks
1972	Establishing the postal savings banks
1973	Restricting foreign banks and establishing off-shore banks
1978	Establishing the gold exchange; canceling foreign exchange controls
1980	Singapore's stock exchange entering the World Federation of Exchanges; financial policies changing from stringent supervision to self-constrain
1983	The restructuring of gold exchange
1984	Closing the insurance industry to foreign insurance companies
1985	Promoting the development of the foreign exchange market once again
1986	Strengthening supervision over the securities market
1987	Putting into operation the restructured national bonds market
1990	Closing the insurance industry to foreign-funded insurance companies
1995	Opening unsecured loans and auto loans
1996	Loosening restrictions on the business of off-shore banks and increasing the equity share of foreign capital in domestic banks
1998	Promoting the development of the foreign exchange market
1998–2001	Opening the bond market
1999	Opening the retail banking business
2001	Opening the wholesale banking business
2002	Opening the securities exchange to the outside
2004	The liberalization of non-residents' transactions in derivatives

up a large proportion of the financial sector, the further opening of banking was carried out at the end, with the retail business opened first and later the wholesale business. During the opening, as the banking industry was in a dominant market position with strong anti-risk capability, it was opened first and followed by investment funds and the investment banking industry (Table 4.11). In terms of development level, the degree of openness in the investment funds and investment banks industry was actually higher (and the rate of reform faster) than that of the banking industry. In the banking industry, there had been a long-term distinction between residents and non-residents. So we could conclude that though the pillar of the financial industry was opened first, it still has not realized total opening, even under the floating exchange rate regime.

Using Figure 4.13, we can see that Singapore, based on its own features, first achieved liberalization of its capital account and then

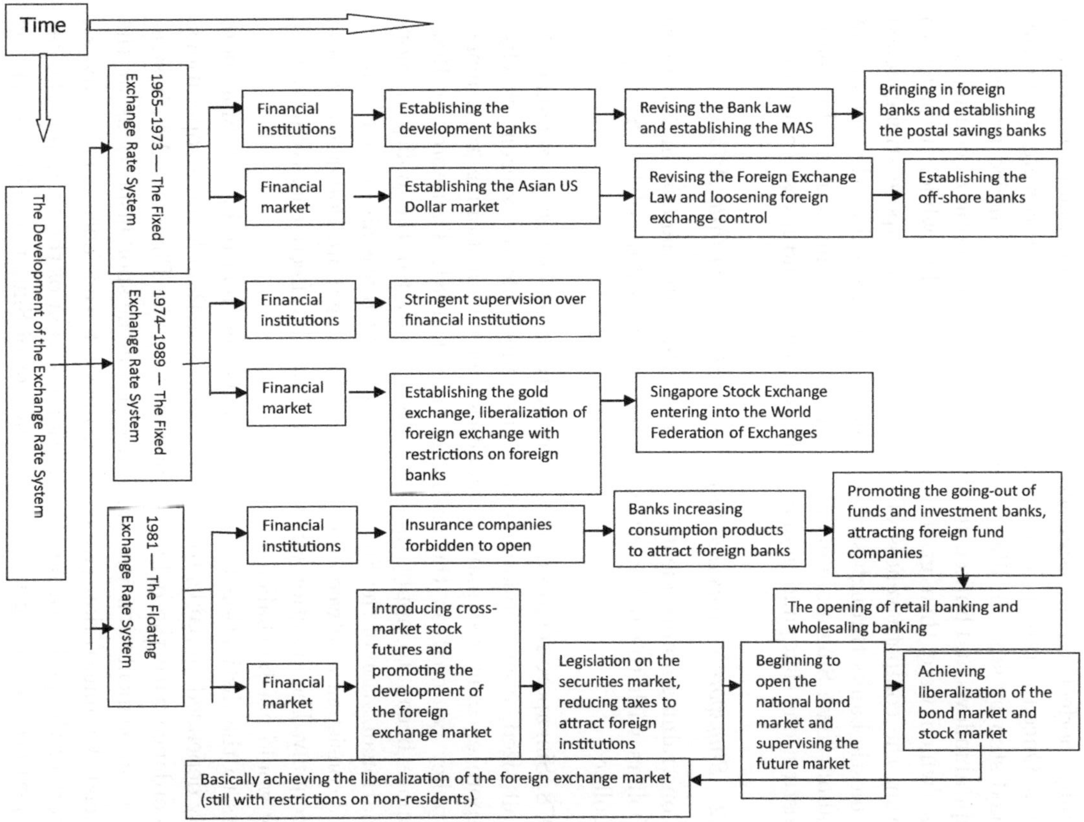

Figure 4.13: Sketch of Singapore's Process of Exchange Rate System Reform (the Opening-up of the Capital Account and Financial Development)

exerted stringent supervision over the capital transactions of residents and non-residents to guarantee the stability of its domestic economy. During its financial development, it established foreign banks and off-shore markets by attracting foreign capital, imposing restrictions on foreign banks, and gradually perfecting its transaction rules and supervision of financial markets. Once the post-reform market was stable, controls were summarily loosened step by step. In liberalizing, Singapore also removed restrictions on capital inflows and limited the business scope and quotas of non-resident banks (which were then gradually broadened). Meanwhile, in order to maintain the competitiveness of domestic banks, Singapore strengthened its domestic banks through strategic mergers. In regard to the opening of capital outflows, Singapore mainly targeted overseas investments by financial institutions (like fund management companies and investment banks).

4.5.3.2 *Singapore's Measures to protect its Currency from Attack*

(1) Constraining non-residents' speculation through financing in Singapore Dollars with the policy of non-internationalization of the Singapore Dollar

In 1978, Singapore removed all the restrictions on currency exchange. As a small sized, open economy (and thus vulnerable to external shocks), Singapore encountered many difficulties when transitioning to a monetary policy centered on the exchange rate in 1981. Therefore, in 1983, Singapore began to apply (and was long stuck to) the policy of non-internationalization of the Singapore Dollar, which was aimed at maintaining the consistency between the growth of the Singapore Dollar market and the economy. The intention was to ensure that the effectiveness of monetary policy would not be challenged.

As to the distinction between residents and non-residents, Singapore mainly depended on banks to apply this policy in their business operations, in accordance with the definition provided by the Financial Administration. Its implementation was examined in on-the-spot inspections by the Financial Administration (which took place at least once every 3 years). The core of the policy of non-internationalization of the Singapore Dollar was to strictly constrain the relative amount of Singapore Dollars held by non-residents. This measure blocked non-residents' from gaining Singapore Dollars, making it difficult for potential speculators to sell them and explicitly signaling that Singapore would not allow speculation on its own currency.

In regard to the market access of the Singapore Dollar business, its financial administration also put limits on foreign banks' branches in Singapore. Specifically, branches could only absorb foreign currency deposits from non-residents and provide international remittance service for them. They were forbidden to absorb deposits in Singapore Dollars.

In addition, there are other reasons that the Singapore Dollar was not attacked. (a) The Singaporean government had large foreign reserves, which accounted for 80% of the GDP in the 1980s. (b) The fiscal and monetary policy of Singapore had always been prudent, never allowing an excessive imbalance of macroeconomic factors. Indeed, the government had long enjoyed a good reputation in this regard. (c) Finally, as a small-sized, open economy, Singapore succeeded in sustaining its macroeconomic stability and avoiding any violent economic adjustment.

(2) Giving banks a key, limited supervisory role with stringent, detailed regulations and stern enforcement as part of an indirect compliance policy

Singapore's financial administration held that banks were the main channels for capital inflows and outflows, as well as the "information center" of foreign exchange transactions. Thus, banks should know their clients' backgrounds the best. After the liberalization of currency exchange, a large amount of compliance supervision directly fell on the shoulders of banks, which therefore became the "financial intermediaries" that exerted the supervision. They were not only important objects of supervision but also the first-line enforcers of supervision policies. Singapore commercial banks were obliged to assume compliance management duties in anti-money laundering, discerning between residents and non-residents, supervising transactions, reporting and submitting information, and implementation of the non-internationalization policy. To give meaningful powers to banks in their compliance supervision role, Singapore's financial administration held that:

(a) It should make banks realize that their compliance management was not only designed to meet the requirements of external supervision but also a means to prevent credit risks. Compliance could enhance clients' confidence towards the banks and bring "added value" to the banking industry.
(b) It must make banks fully grasp and understand the policy intention of the supervisory department.

(c) It should improve banking regulatory technology. The daily report forms and statements are all in electronic form.
(d) Singapore not only uses anti-money laundering reports to trace suspicious transactions, but also stipulates in stringent detail regulations to constrain the conduct of banks. For instance, the non-internationalization policy imposes a limit on the quantity of banks' financing for non-residents. In order to ensure that these regulations are effective at scale in control and supervision, the law explicitly stipulates that the bank should not split Singapore Dollar financing into several small transactions in an attempt to avoid supervision, otherwise it will be severely punished (Le, 2000).

(3) The main measures for exchange rate adjustments

Singapore applied a managed floating exchange rate regime that pegged the Singapore Dollar to a currency basket (the weight of each currency and the floating range was not publicly announced). From 2002 on, a notice has been released every half year to announce the exchange rate trend of the Singapore Dollar. The Financial Administration believed that this would not make it more difficult to regulate the market, because the market could not predict the timing and approach of the interventions. The main measures for adjusting the currency rate are:

(a) Intervening in the market with a combination of indirect participation by banks and the direct participation of the Financial Administration. The Financial Administration sometimes adopts direct intervention, sending out explicit intervention signals. It also sometimes selects some of the 11 banks qualified with the sale of governmental bonds (three local banks and eight foreign-funded banks) to conduct covert, proxy intervention on its behalf. Under some serious conditions, the Financial Administration could make local banks its first choice (in cases where the foreign banks might leak sensitive information). Through the currency basket, at present the Financial Administration only applies spot transactions between Singapore Dollars and US Dollars to intervene in the foreign exchange market (since it has full liquidity between the two currencies). Besides, when compared with Singapore's foreign reserves, the market scale for SGD to USD transactions is relatively small (in 2003, the daily transaction value of Singapore's foreign exchange market was USD$119.4 billion, among which the share of SDG to USD transactions was only 10%). Therefore, the interference power of the Financial Administration of Singapore is quite strong. In regards to maintaining liquidity, the Financial Administration either directly deals with banks or employs the tools of repurchasing and swapping. There are two major instruments in Singapore's open market operations: One is the direct sale and purchase of national bonds and the second are short-term monetary market vehicles, including the repurchase and reverse-repurchase of national bonds, foreign exchange swaps and direct borrowing from commercial banks.

(b) Through a combination of methods, Singapore reduces the market's capability to speculate against the Singapore Dollar. Singapore uses the exchange rate as a tool of its monetary policy, but its Financial Administration holds that relying on the exchange rate alone would not solve all problems and it must have other measures available. Therefore, in light of an already liberalized exchange environment, Singapore mainly employs the policy of non-internationalization of the Singapore Dollar to limit financing in its currency and constrain non-residents' use of its currency in short selling (Investigation Group of the Department of International Payments, 2005).

4.5.3.3 *Analysis of the Effects of the Exchange Rate System Reform*

Under the fixed exchange rate regime, the GDP of Singapore remained at a high growth rate. When Singapore began to apply the floating exchange rate system in 1973, its GDP growth rate declined at first (from 14% to less than 4%), but soon recovered to over 6%. The cash account under the floating exchange rate regime was negative (the 1974 deficit was equal to nearly 20% of GDP in that year), but the data on commodity and service accounts are not included in those statistics.

After the application of the supervised and adjustable exchange rate system, Singapore's GDP growth rate fluctuated more violently (even in falling into periods of negative growth, such as in 1989). But in the long run, Singapore's economy experienced rapid growth at an average rate of over 6%. The cash account began to turn from negative to positive. Though there was some turbulence, the economy kept growing at a high speed, remaining above 10% after 1994. According to data from 2000, the commodity and service accounts had long been in surplus, accounting for over 20% of GDP. The nominal exchange rate was greatly devalued shortly after the exchange rate system reform in 1973, but was soon restored to stability. The real

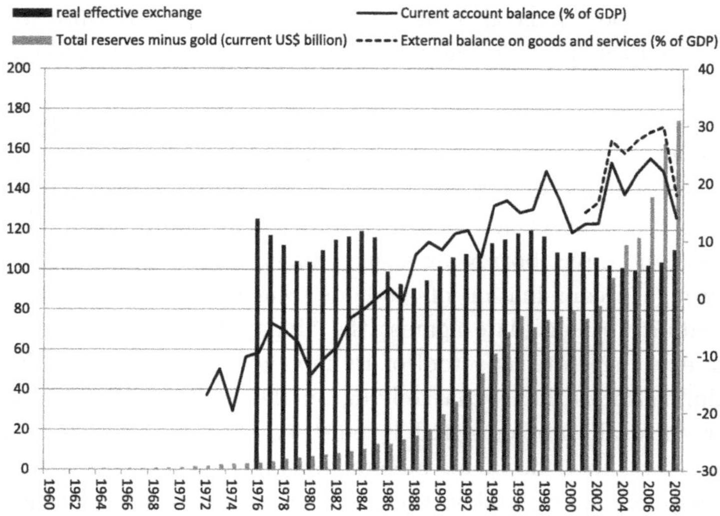

Figure 4.14: The Effect of Singapore's Exchange Rate System Reform on Foreign Trade

Notes: (1) The level line represents a lack of data.
(2) The line chart refers to the left axis, while the column chart refers to the right axis.
Data source: The World Bank.

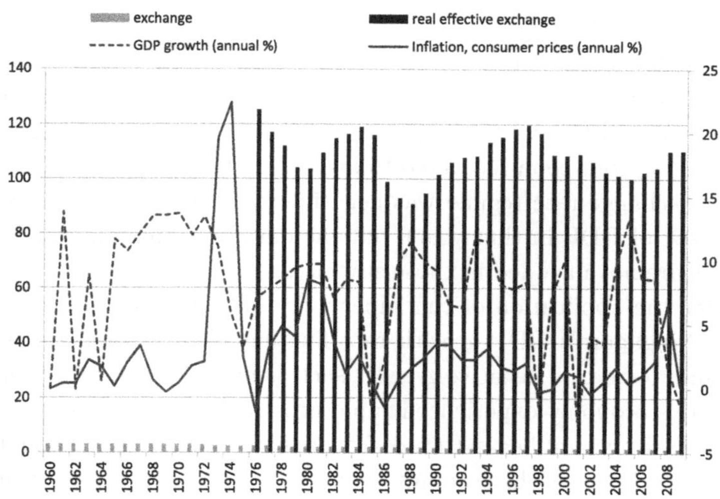

Figure 4.15: Singapore's GDP and Inflation during its Exchange Rate System Reform

Notes: (1) The level line represents a lack of data.
(2) The line chart refers to the left axis, while the column chart to the right axis.
Data source: The World Bank.

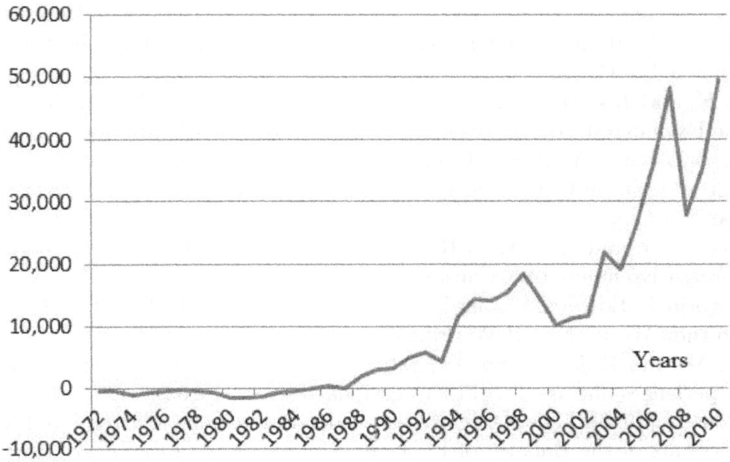

Figure 4.16: Singapore's Current Account (USD million)
Data source: International Monetary Fund.

exchange rate did not fluctuate severely, but entered a long-term cycle of adjustment. The inflation rate was stable, on the whole, and foreign reserves were consistently positive — indeed their total volume significantly increased, reaching over USD$170 billion in 2008 (Figures 4.14–4.16).

On the whole, after the second exchange rate system reform, Singapore's economy proceeded along steadily with an increased foreign trade surplus, rapid GDP growth, lower exchange rate fluctuation and a low inflation rate. This was mainly because Singapore, as a small-sized, open economy, would be greatly affected by fluctuations in its exchange rate. If it adopted a free floating exchange rate system, the domestic economy's growth would be put at risk. In contrast, the managed exchange rate regime could not only guarantee its international competitiveness in foreign trade but also contribute positively to domestic economic growth.

Bibliography

In English

Aramaki K. (2006). Sequencing of Capital Account Liberalization: Japan's Experiences and Their Implications to China. *Public Policy Review*, 2(1): 177–232.

Bhandari J. S. (1989). Trade Reform under Partial Currency Convertibility: Some Suggestive Results. *Staff Papers-International Monetary Fund*, 2: 494–513.

Bleakley H. and Kevin C. (2005). Corporate Dollar Debt and Depreciations: Much ado about Nothing?. Working Paper 05/532, Inter-American Development Bank.

Cowan K. and Jose D. G. (2005). International Borrowing, Capital Controls and the Exchange Rate: Lessons from Chile. NBER Working Paper 05/11382.

De Gregorio J. and Andrea T. R. (2004a). Overcoming Fear of Floating: Exchange Rate Policies in Chile. Central Bank of Chile Working Paper 04/302, Central Bank of Chile.

De Gregorio J. and Andrea T. R. (2004b). Flexible Exchange Rate Regime and Foreign Exchange Intervention. BIS Working Paper 04/ 24.

De Gregorio J., Edwards S., and Valdés R. O. (2000). Controls on Capital Inflows: Do they Work? NBER Working Paper 00/7645.

Donald M. and Rojas-Suarez J. (1993). Liberalization of the Capital Account: Experiences and Issues. IMF Occasional Paper 93/103.

Edwards S. (1986). The Order of Liberalization of the Current and Capital Accounts of the Balance of Payments. In *Economic Liberalization in Developing Countries*. NBER Working Paper 86/1507.

Edwards S. (1989a). On the Sequencing of Structural Reforms. NBER Working Paper 89/3138.

Edwards S. (1989b). *Real Exchange Rates, Devaluation, and Adjustment: Exchange Rate Policy in Developing Countries*. Cambridge, MA: MIT press.

Edwards S. (2005). Capital Controls, Sudden Stops and Current Account Reversals. NBER Working Paper 05/11170.

Edwards S. (2007). Capital Controls, Capital Flow Contractions, and Macroeconomic Vulnerability. *Journal of International Money and Finance*, 26(5): 814–840.

Edwards S. and Edwards A. C. (1987). *Monetarism and Liberalization: The Chilean Experiment*. Cambridge: Ballinger Publishing Co.

Eichengreen B. J. (2001). Capital Account Liberalization: What Do Cross Country Studies Tell Us? *The World Bank Economic Review*, 15(6): 341–365.

Eichengreen B. J., Michael M., Giovanni D., Enrica D., Gian M. M., and Andrew T. (1998). Capital Account Liberalization: Theoretical and Practical Aspects. IMF Occasional Paper 98/172.

Esteban J. and Jorge S. (2005). Is The FX Derivatives Market Effective and Efficient in Reducing Currency Risk? Central Bank of Chile Working Paper 05/325, Central Bank of Chile.

Falvey R. E. and Kierzkowski H. (1987). Product Quality, Intra-Industry Trade and Imperfect Competition. In Kierzkowski H., ed., *Protection and Competition in International Trade*, 143–161. New York: Basil Blackwell.

Fukao M. (1990). Liberalization of Japan's Foreign Exchange Controls and Structural Changes in the Balance of Payments. *Monetary and Economic Studies*, 8(2): 101–165.

Guitian M. and Saleh M. N. (1996). Currency Convertibility in the Middle East and North Africa. IMF Working Paper 96/05.

Habermeier H.-U. (2002). Basic Research in Materials Science and Economic Sustainable Growth. *The Journal of Materials Education*, 24: 87–98.

IMF (1998). An Irreversible Trend: Seminar Discusses the Orderly Path to Capital Account Liberalization. *IMF Survey*, 27: 81–84.

Ishii S. and Habermeier K. (2002). Capital Account Liberalization and Financial Sector Stability. IMF Working Paper 02/12.

Johnston R. B. (1998). Sequencing Capital Account Liberalization. *Finance and Development*, 35: 20–23.

Johnston R., Barry D., Salim M., and Echeverria C. (1997). Sequencing Capital Account Liberalization: Lessons from the Experiences in Chile, Indonesia, Korea, and Thailand. IMF Working Paper 97/157.

Lal D. (1987). The Political Economy of Economic Liberalization. *World Bank Economic Review*, 1(2): 273–299.

Le M. T. (2000). Reforming Vietnam Banking System: Learning from Singapore's Model. *Iseas Visiting Researchers Series* 00/05.

Meller P. (1996). *Un Siglo de Economía Política Chilena (1890–1990)*. Santiago de Chile: Editorial Andres Bello.

Ministry of Finance Banking Bureau. (1990). Annual Finance Report of the Banking Bureau. Various issues.

Nsouli S. M. and Rached M. (1998). Capital Account Liberalization in the Southern Mediterranean. *Finance and Development*, 35: 24–27.

Nsouli S. M., Funke N., and Rached M. (2002). *The Speed of Adjustment and the Sequencing of Economic Reforms: Issues and Guidelines for Policymakers.* Washington DC: International Monetary Fund.

Ötker-Robe I., Polański Z., Topf B., and Vávra D. (2007). Coping with Capital Inflows: Experiences of Selected European Countries. IMF Working Paper 07/190.

SFEMC (2009). Survey of Singapore FX. http://www.sfemc.org.

Takeda M. and Turner P. (1992). The liberalization of Japan's financial markets: Some major themes. BIS Economic Papers 92/34 BIS.

In Chinese

Cheng B. M. and Shen H. Y. (1992). Post-war Development of the Financial Markets in Japan and Implications for China. *Journal of Central University of Finance and Economics*, 1: 21–25.

Editorial Board of the Yearbook of World Economy (2006). *The Yearbook of World Economy.* Shanghai: Publisher of People's Republic of China Yearbook.

Han Y. (2005). *Chile's Financial Reform since the Pinochet Era.* Beijing: CASS Graduate School.

State Administration of Foreign Exchange (2003). Capital Account Openness and Reform of Exchange Rate Regime in Poland. *Foreign Exchange*, 6: 14–17.

State Administration of Foreign Exchange (2005). Characteristics of Exchange Rate Policy and Financial Regulation, and the Development of Financial

Derivative Market in Singapore. http://www.foxdoc.com/201308/277613.html.

Wang X. (2004). Chile: the Latin American vanguard of neoliberal reforms. *Latin American Studies*, 1: 29–45.

Wang Y. (2003). Reform of the Exchange Rate Regime in Poland. *Financial Information Reference*, 11: 52.

Wang Y. (2009). Liberalization of Foreign Exchange Controls: Japan's Experiences and Its Implications for China. *JCER Nikkei Asia Scholarship Research Report,* available at https://www.jcer.or.jp/eng/pdf/Wang.pdf.

Chapter 5

Evolution of the RMB Exchange Rate Regime

The exchange rate is the tie that links a country's economy and trade with other countries. The exchange rate regime is an important part of the national economic system and an appropriate exchange rate regime is an important guarantee of a country's economic growth. RMB exchange rate reform is an extremely complicated systematic project. As an important part of China's financial system reform, it is integral to improving the socialist market economy: not only to reshape the pattern of domestic and foreign interest groups, but also to confront the many uncertainties that will follow exchange rate regime reform. Therefore, it is difficult for the designers and decision-makers of the exchange rate regime to accurately predict the target of reform before it has begun. They will need to adjust their strategies in a timely manner during the reform.

Investigating and analyzing the history of the RMB exchange rate regime, and exploring the target of further RMB exchange rate regime reform, is of great importance for improving the socialist market economy and the internationalization of the RMB. Since the establishment of People's Republic of China, the RMB exchange rate regime has gone through a tortuous process of evolution — from a highly centralized planned management model in the early days of the new China to one that combines national plans with market operations, and then to one determined by supply and demand with government regulation. In the context of different economic systems in different times, reform of the RMB exchange rate regime has also experienced a tortuous and complicated evolutionary process which can be divided into the following six periods.

5.1 Economic Recovery Period (1949–1952)

5.1.1 *Background*

With gradual victory in the War of Liberation, and to meet the needs of social and economic development after liberation, China established the People's Bank of China (PBOC) on December 1, 1948 and issued a single currency, the Renminbi (RMB). In order to meet the needs of foreign trade, the PBOC, as China's central bank, first released RMB exchange rates in Tianjin on January 18, 1949, and the RMB–USD exchange rate was set at (old) RMB80 per USD$1. Back then, economic orders were not stable and, since price levels varied widely throughout the country, local governments were given the right to adjust PBOC exchange rates according to their local conditions. Later, with a unified financial and monetary system established and steadily improved, regional economic activities stepped on the right track. As differences between price levels became smaller, the PBOC announced nation-wide, unified RMB exchange rates. At that time, the new China was in its early years and suffered from a collapsed economy. Its primary mission for the first four years was to rapidly recover the national economy. Policy objectives during this period included accumulating foreign exchange reserves to support the country's economic recovery and development.

5.1.2 *Measures*

To maintain the unity and stability of monetary and financial systems during this period, and also to accumulate foreign exchange reserves to fully realize economic reconstruction, China adopted a centralized foreign exchange regime. Policy measures were taken to promote exports, reward overseas remittances, and ratify disbursements according to receipts. Exchange rates were determined based on price levels and were adjusted according to the value of the US Dollar. When price levels climbed up, the RMB was devalued. The reason for determining exchange rates according to price levels involved two factors. First, in the whole commercial system, private importers and exporters accounted for a dominant proportion of the market. According to statistics, in 1950, these agencies accounted for 98.7% of the total number of firms and commanded 85% of turnover in retail sales. But in 1952, the latter figure fell to 57.2% (Ye and Pan, 2001). The task of expanding exports depended on private importers and exporters, so they had to be given the likelihood to profit. Second, in the early days of the new China, our level of economic development was low with weak exports, so a large part of our exchange reserves came from overseas remittances. Such remittances, however, would shrink if their purchasing power were not guaranteed. Thus determining the exchange rates of RMB would certainly be consistent with the changes in domestic and international price levels.

5.1.3 *Effects*

This period saw little foreign economic and trade activity and relatively low import and export volumes. But still, the foreign trade was a significant improvement when compared with the old China. In the years 1950–1952, China's total imports and exports rose from RMB4.16 billion to RMB6.46 billion — a significantly larger increase in imports than exports. Imports and exports were close in 1950, and the trade deficits in 1951 and 1952 were around RMB100 million. Also, in the years 1950–1952, China's dependence on foreign trade was only about 10%–12%, reflecting a low degree of economic openness at that time (see the data in Table 5.1). In addition, in 1952, China's annual foreign exchange reserves were only USD$139 million, reflecting a severe shortage of foreign exchange.

Because of the large proportion of the private sector's share in foreign trade and volatile domestic price levels, the RMB exchange rates were mainly set and adjusted based on the relative price levels at home and abroad. In the period between 1949 and March 1950, there were 52 rate adjustments. The rate was only stabilized after the inflation rate lowered. Overall, the RMB exchange rates during this period were flexible, playing an important role in promoting the country's rapid economic recovery. However, there were still some problems. For one, price levels determining the exchange rate were based on purchasing power parity (PPP) theory, which usually applies to an environment where the market is fully open and fully effective. However our economy was not only in a recovery phase, but in the early stages of a planned economy where commodity prices were

Table 5.1: China's Foreign Trade and Dependence, 1950–1952 (unit: billion RMB)

Year	Total Trade Volume	Total Exports	Total Imports	Gross Domestic Product (GDP)	Foreign-Trade Dependence (%)
1950	4.16	2.02	2.14	42.6	9.77
1951	5.95	2.42	3.53	49.7	11.97
1952	6.46	2.71	3.75	58.9	10.97

Data source: *China Statistical Yearbook* (1983).

uniformly set by the state (not market-oriented). So using PPP theory to determine exchange rates was not well grounded. In fact, although the level of marketization had been increasing since the reform and opening up, still PPP theory does not apply to the RMB exchange rates, and China has been trying to find a suitable RMB exchange rate determination mechanism. A range of studies (Yi and Fan, 1997; Zhang, 2000; Wang *et al.*, 2004) have supported this view.

5.2 Socialist Planned Economy Period (1953–1972)

5.2.1 *Background*

In 1956, the socialist transformation of China's industry and commerce was completed. Following this, China entered the socialist planned economy period where the national economy was completely planned and prices were uniformly set by the state. During that time, the world followed the Bretton Woods system of fixed exchange rates with the US Dollar as the international reserve currency. China's guidelines for economic construction back then started with "focus on construction, and progress steadily", which later developed into "oppose both conservatism and rash advance, and progress steadily with comprehensive balance". This policy statement meant that the focus of this period was to ensure steady economic growth, implying that the exchange rate regime should seek stability.

5.2.2 *Measures*

During this period, as trading companies were operated by the state (which was responsible for all losses and profits), imports and exports did not need to be adjusted through exchange rate changes. In this context, the RMB exchange rates applied mainly to non-trade foreign currency settlement. Against the backdrop of a planned economy, the exchange rate regime was consistent with planned, fixed prices and the price management system. The exchange rate was in a basically stable state, maintaining the level of USD$1 to RMB2.46 from March 1955 to November 1971 (almost 16 years). The correlation between the RMB exchange rates and price levels weakened, and exchange rates were mainly used as an accounting tool for internal accounting and planning.

5.2.3 *Effects*

During the period from 1953 to 1972, China's scale of imports and exports was small and grew slowly. In 1953, its total value of imports and exports

Table 5.2: China's Dependence on Foreign Trade, 1953–1972 (unit: billion RMB)

Year	Total Trade Volume	Total Exports	Total Imports	GDP	Foreign-Trade Dependence (%)
1953	2.37	1.02	1.35	82.4	9.82
1954	2.44	1.15	1.29	85.9	9.86
1955	3.14	1.41	1.73	91	12.07
1956	3.21	1.65	1.56	102.8	10.57
1957	3.1	1.6	1.5	106.8	9.78
1958	3.87	1.98	1.89	130.7	9.85
1959	4.38	2.26	2.12	143.9	10.38
1960	3.81	1.86	1.95	145.7	8.82
1961	2.94	1.49	1.45	122	7.44
1962	2.66	1.49	1.17	114.93	7.04
1963	2.92	1.65	1.27	123.33	6.95
1964	3.47	1.92	1.55	145.4	6.71
1965	4.25	2.23	2.02	171.61	6.90
1966	4.62	2.37	2.25	186.8	6.80
1967	4.16	2.14	2.02	177.39	6.33
1968	4.05	2.1	1.95	172.31	6.30
1969	4.03	2.2	1.83	193.79	5.52
1970	4.59	2.26	2.33	225.27	5.01
1971	4.84	2.64	2.2	242.64	4.98
1972	6.3	3.44	2.86	251.81	5.83

Data source: *China Statistical Yearbook* (1981, 2000).

was USD$2.37 billion. By 1971, after almost 20 years of change, the total value of imports and exports had more than doubled, reaching USD$4.83 billion. China's closed economy and political factors hindered foreign trade and economic development, costing the country a decade (from 1959 to 1969) of progress on foreign trade. Chronic low productivity also led to a lack of competitiveness in the global arena, and an inability to develop the international market. Examining China's dependence on foreign trade, there were not many years that China's dependency index exceeded 10%. Especially since the 1960s, China's trade dependency index declined year by year, showing that during this period, China's foreign trade almost was trapped in a standstill (see more details in Table 5.2).

5.3 Western Countries' Floating Exchange Rates Period (1973–1978)

5.3.1 *Background*

In 1973, with the collapse of the Bretton Woods system, Western countries began to adopt a floating exchange rate system. This led to big swings in exchange rates, such that a single currency peg could not support the stable development of China's national economy. However, a basket peg is more flexible, and yet able to effectively avoid the negative impact of exchange rate fluctuations.

5.3.2 *Measures*

China began to open RMB-denominated trade and settlement to stabilize its exchange rates with its main trade partners. A floating exchange rate system with the RMB pegged to a basket of currencies was adopted. The basket included basically the currencies of countries and regions that were close trade partners with China. The types and weights of the currencies were determined by the state, which would adjust the exchange rates to float with the currencies and adapt to policy changes. During this period, the basic principles in adjusting the RMB exchange rates were to ensure stability of the RMB exchange rate, ensure mutual, beneficial, and equal trade as conducive to economic development, and to select representative and sound currencies to place in the basket.

5.3.3 *Effects*

During this period, the RMB exchange rate was basically in the middle to upper range among the exchange rates of other countries. However, despite China's claim that the RMB was pegged to a basket of currencies, the RMB exchange rate was basically set by the government, and in nearly seven years, the constitution and the weights of currencies in the basket were only adjusted a few times. Dependence on foreign trade in these six years is shown in the Table 5.3.

Table 5.3: China's Dependence on Foreign Trade, 1973–1978 (unit: billion RMB)

Year	Total Trade Volume	Total Exports	Total Imports	GDP	Foreign-Trade Dependence (%)
1973	11.08	5.88	5.21	272.09	8.09
1974	14.9	7.11	7.79	278.99	10.47
1975	15.61	7.69	7.93	299.77	9.69
1976	13.6	6.94	6.66	294.37	8.97
1977	14.67	7.52	7.15	320.19	8.51
1978	21.09	9.96	11.13	362.41	9.80

Data source: *China Statistical Yearbook* (1981, 2000).

Comparison of Tables 5.3 and 5.2 shows that from 1953 to 1995, the trade volume increased from USD$2.37 billion to USD$6.3 billion in 20 years (less than double). Yet in less than the seven years from 1972 to 1978, trade volume nearly tripled, indicating to some degree the promoting effect of foreign exchange policy on trade during this period. However, dependence on foreign trade in the two tables was still in the single digits. The contribution of China's imports and exports to the economy was still too small, and China's foreign exchange policy needed further adjustment to allow trade to better serve economic development.

In the above three periods, China was in a "secluded" state. Trade during these three periods, whether in terms of growth rate or absolute amount, was not satisfactory. During this long period of seclusion, the economy-promoting effect of foreign trade had not been fully exploited, and foreign exchange was taken mostly as an accounting tool.

5.4 Transition Economy Period (1979–1993)

5.4.1 *Background*

In November 1978, after the Third Plenum of the 11th Central Committee of the Communist Party of China, the economic system began to shift from a planned economy to a market one, and from closed to open, ushering in a transition period. Begun in the 1980s, with the fall of Communism and the collapse of the Soviet Union, some countries started shifting from a centrally planned economy to a market economy. Academic research gave increasing emphasis to the study of transition economies, especially those which faced high inflation, economic stagnation, high fiscal deficits and other macroeconomic difficulties under the "Washington Consensus" prescriptions. Thus people began to study the selection of exchange rate regimes and sequences of reform. The actual practice of China's economic transition (occurring before the rise of international interest in transition theory) formed China's unique model of economic transition and also created a unique RMB exchange rate regime.

5.4.2 *Measures*

China actually adopted a dual exchange rate system during this period — a system with two different exchange rates for the current account and the capital account respectively. The system aimed to use the exchange rate to influence and control trade, non-trade and capital flows, so as to achieve particular targets related to China's balance of payments. Many countries have adopted a dual exchange rate system in this particular stage of economic development. The form of the system may vary but most made a distinction between commercial rates and financial rates. The commercial rate gave the RMB a high valuation, and the state mandatorily stipulated that exporters should sell most or all of their foreign exchange earnings to the government at this rate, with strict control over importers' use of foreign exchange. The financial rate gave the RMB a lower value closer to the market rate, but lower than the commercial rate. The financial rate was mainly used in the capital account and the non-trade current account, aiming to promote exports, limit imports and increase foreign exchange earnings. (Such a system is usually based on a strict distinction between the current account and capital account). From the perspective of the evolution of the international exchange rate regime, the dual exchange rate system is only a transitional arrangement. The International Monetary Fund (IMF) regards implementing a dual exchange rate system as a temporary measure for member states to rectify their imbalances. When the balance of payments is improved, the two rates should be unified at the same level.

The RMB exchange rate regime during this period can be specifically divided into two phases. First, from 1981 to 1984, both official exchange rates and internal settlement prices were implemented. The former refers to a managed floating exchange rate system with a basket peg, and the latter applies to the settlement of foreign trade and profit accounting for foreign trade units (which was determined according to the exchange-based cost for export of products, fixed at RMB2.80 to USD$1). The objective of the exchange rate policy was to award exports and limit imports, so as to earn foreign exchange. Second, from 1985 to 1993, the internal settlement price was abolished and was replaced with a combination of official exchange rates and foreign exchange swap market rates. The objective of this second phase of the exchange rate policy was to maintain the balance of international payments.

5.4.3 *Effects*

China's total trade volume in 1978 was RMB35.5 billion (*China Statistical Yearbook*, 1996). It increased to RMB1.1271 trillion in 1993 — nearly 30 times in 15 years (an increase far greater than China's GDP growth of ten times). Our dependence on foreign trade steadily increased during

Table 5.4: China's Dependence on Foreign Trade, 1980–1993 (unit: billion RMB)

Year	Total Trade Volume	Total Exports	Total Imports	GDP	Foreign-Trade Dependence (%)
1980	57	27.12	29.88	451.78	12.62
1985	206.67	80.89	125.78	896.44	23.05
1986	258.04	108.21	149.83	1020.22	25.29
1987	308.42	147	161.42	1196.25	25.78
1988	382.18	176.67	205.51	1492.83	25.60
1989	415.59	195.6	219.99	1690.92	24.58
1990	556.01	298.58	257.43	1854.79	29.98
1991	722.58	382.71	339.87	2161.78	33.43
1992	911.96	467.63	444.33	2663.81	34.24
1993	1127.1	528.48	598.62	3463.44	32.54

Data source: *China Statistical Yearbook* (1996).

this period from less than 10% in 1978 to around 30% in the early 1990s. In both absolute and relative terms, after the reform and opening up, China's foreign trade has undergone enormous changes. Thus, we can see that foreign trade has become a powerful driving force in China's GDP growth. This is a huge difference from the days when foreign exchange was just used as a measurement tool inside the secluded state planning apparatus. Details are shown in Table 5.4.

However, when we rejoiced at the economic development brought by the reform and opening up, we also found some problems in the foreign exchange regime. As a product of transition from a planned economy to a market one, there are several major problems with the dual exchange rate system. On the one hand, although internal trade settlement prices solved the problem of high exchange costs, enhanced the initiative of foreign trade enterprises, and increased foreign exchange reserves, the enthusiasm of the non-tradable sector was weakened and disorder arose in the administration of foreign exchange. Therefore, the implementation of internal settlement prices was destined to be only an emergency measure, limited in its usefulness to the transition period. On the other hand, the establishment of a dual exchange rate system through the foreign exchange swap market enabled the flow of foreign exchange between exchange earners and users and enhanced efficiency in the use of foreign exchange. However, dual exchange rates also created a gap between official exchange rates and market rates, leading to excessive risks and fewer benefits for foreign investors. This tended to dampen the enthusiasm of foreign investors and also gave rise to a black market and corruption. In addition, the dual exchange rate system negatively affected our application for GATT contracting country status.

5.5 Socialist Market Economy Start-up Period (1994–July 2005)

5.5.1 *Background*

Since the mid-1990s, China's economic system has changed dramatically. After forming the now-familiar pattern of public ownership as the mainstay supplemented by diverse economic sectors, the role of the market in allocating resources expanded rapidly, and the planned economy gradually transitioned to a socialist market economy. This transition laid the foundation for the unification of RMB exchange rates. Property rights reform in the microeconomic field enabled enterprises to become self-managing and self-sustaining entities, which could independently bear a certain level of foreign exchange risks. In addition, reform measures in public finance, taxation, the financial sector, foreign trade, and the regulation of enterprises created a favorable environment for exchange rate unification.

As further efforts were made to open up China in the 1990s, investment and exports rapidly became the main engine for economic growth. Since the beginning of the 1980s, the foreign exchange management system was under a process of reform, restrictions on foreign trade were gradually liberalized, and the market played an increasingly important role in the allocation of foreign exchange resources. It is estimated that, by the end of 1993, except for the foreign exchange arranged by the state for imports and payment of foreign debt, about 80% of foreign exchange payments were adjusted by the market. China had gradually relaxed restrictions on regular foreign exchange payments, providing the basic conditions for unifying RMB exchange rates. Further, a series of drawbacks, such as rampant black market trading and financial disorder emerging from the dual exchange rate system spelt out the urgency for exchange rate reform.

5.5.2 *Measures*

On January 1, 1994, the official RMB exchange rates and foreign exchange swap market rates were unified. Foreign exchange was to be settled and sold through banks and an interbank foreign exchange market was established with a single, managed floating exchange rate system based on market supply and demand. However, due to China's low degree of marketization, the exchange rate of the RMB against the US Dollar floated only by around 0.3%. Thus the RMB exchange rate system was a de facto fixed exchange rate system pegged to the Dollar. In 1999, the IMF reflected this reality when they changed the classification of the RMB exchange rate regime from a "managed floating system" to a "fixed exchange rate system pegged to a single currency".

5.5.3 *Effects*

We will still review the dependence on foreign trade (as in the other sections). The details are shown in Table 5.5.

The "total imports" column in Table 5.5 shows that imports in 1998 declined slightly from 1997. This was as a result of the 1997 Asian Financial Crisis, which is here taken as a water shed by which to divide the period into two stages: Pre-crisis (1994–1997) and post-crisis (1997–2004).

The pre-crisis stage was one in which the single, managed floating exchange rate system based on market supply and demand was truly implemented. After the unification of the exchange rates, the RMB was drastically depreciated (from RMB5.80/USD to RMB8.70/USD). Then the exchange rate stabilized and was slightly appreciated, to RMB8.2982/USD by the end of 1996, with a total appreciation of approximately 5% in three years. These exchange rate movements reflected the characteristics of a managed floating system.

Table 5.5: China's Dependence on Foreign Trade, 1994–2004 (unit: billion RMB)

Year	Total Trade Volume	Total Exports	Total Imports	GDP	Foreign-Trade Dependence (%)
1994	2038.19	1042.18	996.01	4675.94	43.59
1995	2349.99	1245.18	1104.81	5847.81	40.19
1996	2413.38	1257.64	1155.74	6788.46	35.55
1997	2696.72	1516.07	1180.65	7446.26	36.22
1998	2684.97	1522.36	1162.61	7834.52	34.27
1999	2989.62	1615.98	1373.64	8206.75	36.43
2000	3927.32	2063.44	1863.88	8946.81	43.90
2001	4218.36	2202.44	2015.92	9731.48	43.35
2002	5137.82	2694.79	2443.03	10517.2	48.85
2003	7048.35	3628.79	3419.56	11739	60.04
2004	9553.91	4910.33	4643.58	13687.6	69.80

Data source: *China Statistical Yearbook* (2005).

However, the arrival of the crisis quickly disrupted the country's pace of marketization of exchange rates and had a profound impact on the post-crisis exchange rate system. During this crisis, the currencies of Thailand and Malaysia and other countries in Southeast Asia rapidly depreciated; Japan and South Korea also devalued their currencies. Depreciation of these currencies exerted enormous pressure on the RMB. Domestic capital was fleeing overseas for fear of declines in asset values caused by a (expected) devaluation of the RMB. To maintain stability, the central bank promptly used massive foreign exchange reserves to absorb the RMB dumped by speculators. The intervention succeeded in stabilizing the RMB. However, the relative appreciation of the RMB (caused by the devaluation of neighboring countries' currencies) posed great pressure on China's exports and caused a slight decline of imports in 1998, relative to 1997.

After the crisis, China maintained a highly stable fixed exchange rate system, with the nominal exchange rate of RMB against the Dollar stabilized at around RMB8.27. This fixed rate continued until July 2005. During that period, the nominal RMB managed floating exchange rate system had, without notice, transformed into a de facto fixed system pegged to the US Dollar.

Looking back at this period of history, the innovation of the 1994 foreign exchange system reform was the establishment of a market-based managed floating exchange rate regime, as well as the subsequent convertibility of the RMB under the current account since July 1, 1996. However, with the settlement and selling of foreign exchange through banks, foreign exchange was only marketized in a narrow sense. The foreign exchange market, the interbank foreign exchange market, and RMB exchange rates were not truly and totally market-oriented. This was manifested as follows. On the one hand, although there were basically no restrictions on the expenditure of foreign exchange under the current account during this period, the capital account was still under quite strict management. Foreign exchange trading relationship formed thereby could not adequately reflect supply and demand in the real foreign exchange market. On the other hand, for many years since 1994 (excepting 1997), the balance of payments maintained a twin surplus (i.e., an excess of exports under both the current account and the capital account). Foreign exchange was oversupplied, and to prevent the continued appreciation of the RMB, the central bank had to participate in foreign exchange market operations. By buying foreign exchange, the central bank achieved a managed float, demonstrating that the RMB exchange rate was not entirely market-driven.

5.6 Socialist Market Economy Development Period (July 2005–present)

5.6.1 *Background*

From 2001 to 2005, China was confronted with an extremely complicated economic situation both at home and abroad: The rapid growth in the balance of payments surplus; rapidly expanding foreign exchange reserves; excessive RMB funds outstanding for foreign exchange (and increasing pressure on the central bank to offset the increase of liquidity); growing trade friction brought about by the increasing export-oriented competitiveness forged through the undervaluation of the RMB (and China's growing share of global trade); and the influx of considerable hot money due to the appreciation of the RMB.

5.6.2 *Measures*

On July 21, 2005, China appreciated the exchange rate of the RMB against the US Dollar by 2%, and further adjusted the exchange rates from one pegged to the US Dollar to a managed floating exchange rate regime based on market supply and demand and pegged to a basket of currencies. This reform encompassed multiple exchange rate policies. First, according to the market conditions and the development of China's economic and financial situation, the PBOC would adjust the floating range of the exchange rate. It would also manage and regulate the RMB exchange rate, maintaining a normal float of the exchange rate to keep the RMB stable at a reasonable and balanced level. Finally, it would seek a balance of payments and maintain macroeconomic and financial market stability. On June 19, 2010, the central bank announced that it would further promote the reform of the RMB exchange rate regime. It would adjust exchange rates according to supply and demand (still with reference to a basket of currencies) and continue to implement dynamic management and regulation of the float of RMB exchange rates according to the published floating range.

5.6.3 *Effects*

First, we will still examine China's dependence on foreign trade in the above period. The details are shown in Table 5.6.

We can see from the table that both imports and exports in 2009 fell more than 10% from 2008, and that dependence on foreign trade dropped from 60% to 50%. This is because of the outbreak of the 2008 global

Table 5.6: China's Dependence on Foreign Trade, 2005–2012 (unit: billion Yuan)

Year	Total Trade Volume	Total Exports	Total Imports	GDP	Foreign-Trade Dependence (%)
2005	11692.2	6264.81	5427.37	18493.7	63.22
2006	14097.4	7759.72	6337.69	21631.4	65.17
2007	16686.4	9356.36	7330.01	26581	62.78
2008	17992.2	10039.5	7952.65	31404.5	57.29
2009	15064.8	8202.97	6861.84	34090.3	44.19
2010	20172.2	10702.3	9469.93	40151.3	50.24
2011	23640.2	12324.1	11316.1	47288.2	49.99
2012	24304.8	12878.4	11425.8	51932.2	46.80

Data source: *China Statistical Yearbook* (2012); Statistical Communiqué on the 2012 National Economic and Social Development.

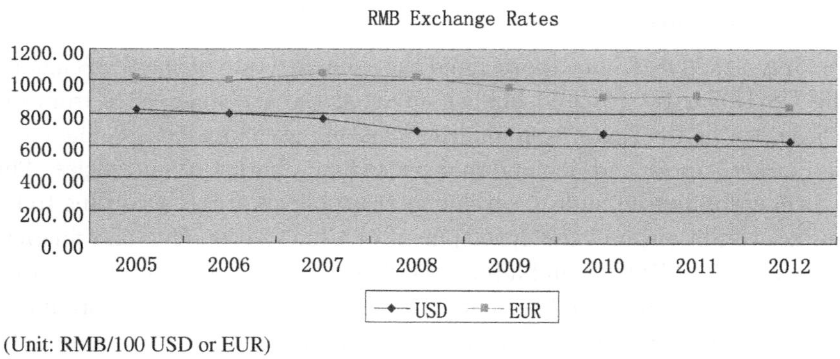

Figure 5.1: Change of RMB Exchange Rate during 2005–2012

financial crisis, which weakened the purchasing power of China's major trade partners (including the United States, Europe, and Japan) and led to a decline in China's exports. Also, exports from other countries shrunk, leading to a reduction in China's imports. We managed to maintain the stability of the exchange rates during this crisis (see Figure 5.1), basically fluctuating in the range of RMB6.82–6.84 (RMB/USD). By 2010, the impact of the financial crisis on China gradually waned with weakening external shocks and the central bank decided to restart the reform of the RMB exchange rate regime.

Overall, imports and exports grew steadily during this period, doubling between 2005 and 2012. Declining dependence on foreign trade during this period suggests that the economy-driving effect of external demand weakened. Sound and stable development of the economy ahead lies in stimulating domestic demand. Any future financial crisis is bound to be global and those countries that depend on foreign trade are destined for disaster.

The post-2010 reform of the RMB exchange rate regime is a return to the managed floating exchange rate system and a historic step. It is the most profound change since the exchange rate reform in 1994 (Yu, 2006). Looking at evidence from recent years, we can see that the reform of the exchange rate regime makes RMB exchange rates more flexible and market-oriented. The monetary authority is enhancing its initiative and control over the exchange rate and the targets of exchange rate policies are basically sound (Cheng, 2009). But it now seems that this exchange rate regime also has three significant shortcomings.

(1) Low transparency of the exchange rate regime (pegged to a basket of currencies)

On August 10, 2005, the central bank governor Zhou Xiaochuan first disclosed the principle of "a basket peg" and the major currencies in the basket: Currencies selected mainly from those of the major trading countries and regions under the current account on the balance of payments, with each currency being given an appropriate weight. There are basically four principles for the selection and weight setting. Currencies used in foreign commodities and service trade are the first choice and serve as the basis for the basket. Foreign debt currencies come as the second choice, followed by some foreign direct investment (FDI) currencies. Finally, included are some currencies for previous payments and transfers. A bigger weight is given to currencies used in foreign trade, as China's most important trade partners are the United States, Japan, Euro zone countries and South Korea. The currencies of these countries and regions are given a large weight in the basket. Russia, the United Kingdom, Canada, Singapore, Australia and Malaysia also have frequent trade with China, and currencies used in these areas also have a certain reference value. But the central bank has not revealed all the currencies, their weights, or the "target area" for exchange rate management (i.e., a "reasonable and balanced exchange rate level"). Therefore, the current system leaves great room to the central bank for discretion, making it difficult for the RMB exchange rate to be really based on supply and demand. Exchange rate management that relies on the decisions of the central bank will lead to deviation of said rate from market demand, either toward overestimation or underestimation, and is ultimately harmful to economic development (Cheng, 2009).

(2) A real managed floating system has not been achieved

In China's foreign trade, the US takes the largest portion, so although the exchange rate regime seems to be a basket peg (and no longer a USD-based peg), it is actually a "soft peg with the US Dollar as the main reference", and similar to the former fixed exchange rate system. The empirical research of some scholars (Han, 2006; Xu, *et al.* 2007; Wang, 2007; Zhou, 2009) shows that the majority of China's currency basket is composed of US Dollars, Japanese Yen and Euros. Further, it appears that the Dollar is dominant (with possibly over 90% of the total weight). Meanwhile, the determination mechanism of the RMB exchange rate, although changing over the time, is still stuck closely to the Dollar (Ogawa and Yoshimi, 2008; Peng, 2009; Zhu and Zhao, 2009).

Since China's capital account is not fully open, no matter what exchange rate regime the government announces, it will end up with a fixed exchange rate regime (Yi, 2000). Therefore, in order to adhere to the principles of initiative, controllability and gradualness in the RMB exchange rate reform, "management" seems to dominate over "floating." This may be an inevitable trade off, as the incentive to manage the exchange rate necessarily limits the extent to which it can float. For example, as the currency's floating range expands, its flexibility is immediately offset by intervention, rather than absorbed by the market. The market's "invisible hand" may be forced to succumb to the state's "visible hand" at any time. The exchange rate regime still has a strong government-led streak.

(3) A single trader in the foreign exchange market with the central bank as a major trader

On the one hand, although the 2005 reform of the exchange rate system greatly relaxed the eligibility for and control on bank-to-customer and interbank transactions, banks and customers could almost freely trade foreign exchange. But the main players in the foreign exchange market are still banks; non-bank financial institutions and other players are still quite few. For example, in late July 2007, two years after the reform of the exchange rate system, there were only two non-financial institutions in the interbank foreign exchange market. By the end of 2008, there were only 268 members of China's Foreign Exchange Trade System and the five largest commercial banks (Bank of China, China Construction Bank, Industrial and Commercial Bank of China, Agricultural Bank of China and Bank of Communications) accounted for more than 90% of all foreign exchange transactions. Indeed, the transactions between Bank of China and the central bank accounted for more than 60%, demonstrating the concentration of market players in the form of state-supported banks.

On the other hand, the current RMB exchange rate is basically adjusted through foreign exchange transactions by the central bank in the foreign exchange market. In the interbank foreign exchange market, when transactions between authorized banks for dealing in foreign exchange do not match, the central bank will make up for the insufficient position to ensure that the market clears. The central bank participates in such interbank foreign exchange market transactions for its policy considerations. Compared to letting the market decide the exchange rates, the central bank's adjustments (after considering various factors) control exchange rate fluctuations within a more appropriate interval. The central bank's interventions in the foreign exchange market have a strong negative impact on the exchange rate, counteracting forces that would allow rates to float and become more flexible. Maintaining effective operation of the market has, to some extent, come at the expense of a free floating exchange rate. Thus, there is less floating and rates are too rigid. This is a consequence of many non-market factors, such as the central bank's intervention.

Bibliography

In English

Ogawa E. and Yoshimi T. (2008). Widening deviation among East Asian currencies. RIETI Discussion Papers, 08-E-010.

In Chinese

Cheng S. W. (2009). *The Study of China Economic Reform and Development* (Vol. 3). Beijing: China Renmin University Press.

Han G. F. (2006). A Proposal for the Optimal Currency Basket Peg for the RMB. *The Journal of World Economy*, 4:8.

National Bureau of Statistics of China (1981). *China Statistical Yearbook*. Beijing: China Statistics Press.

National Bureau of Statistics of China (1983). *China Statistical Yearbook*. Beijing: China Statistics Press.

National Bureau of Statistics of China (1996). *China Statistical Yearbook*. Beijing: China Statistics Press.

National Bureau of Statistics of China (2000). *China Statistical Yearbook*. Beijing: China Statistics Press.

National Bureau of Statistics of China (2005). *China Statistical Yearbook*. Beijing: China Statistics Press.

National Bureau of Statistics of China (2012). *China Statistical Yearbook*. Beijing: China Statistics Press.

National Bureau of Statistics of China (2013). Statistical Communiqué of the People's Republic of China on the 2012 National Economic and Social Development. *China Population Today*, 2.

Peng Y. L. (2009). An Analysis of RMB Exchange Rate after "the Exchange Rate Reform". *Contemporary Finance & Economics*, 1: 64–68.

Wang H. (2007). Pegging Currency Basket and RMB Exchange Rate Reform. *Economic Review*, 1: 106–112.

Wang Z. Q., Qi P. J. and Sun G. (2004). The Boundary Test of RMB Exchange Rate Purchasing Power Parity. *Quantitative & Technical Economics*, 2: 116–124.

Xu J. G., Shao H. and Tang G. X. (2007). The RMB Exchange Rate Regime with Reference to A Basket of Currencies: Empirical Evidence. *Journal of Shanghai University of Finance and Economics*, 9(1): 66–72.

Ye S. C. and Pan L. G. (2001). *Chinese Ancient and Modern Financial History*. Shanghai: Fudan University Press.

Yi G. and Fan M. (1997). Determinants of the RMB Exchange Rate and Trend Analysis. *Economic Research Journal*, 10: 26–35.

Yi G. (2000). The Choice of Foreign Exchange Rate Regime. *Journal of Finance*, 9: 46–52.

Yu Y. D. (2006). A Historical Step in the Reform of the RMB Exchange Rate Regime. *World Economics and Politics*, 10: 7–13.

Zhang X. P. (2000). The Latest Evolvement of Purchasing Power Parity and its Application in the RMB Exchange Rate. *World Economy*, 23(9): 10–18.

Zhou J. Z. (2009). Reference Currency Basket of RMB: Composition, Stability and Commitment Level. *Studies of International Finance*, 3: 16–22.

Zhu R. M. and Zhao P. Y. (2009). The Empirical Analysis about the Reference Currencies Basket of RMB. *Economic Forum*, 8: 49–52.

Chapter 6

The Determination of a Central Rate for the RMB

To build the exchange rate target zone, a basket of central currencies should be adopted. This would allow the RMB to accurately reflect China's foreign trade and international balance of payments, fully embodying the RMB's international purchasing power. China's foreign trade, foreign capital and foreign debt structure should be taken into consideration when choosing currencies and weightings for the basket. In the initial stage of building an exchange rate target zone, it is not proper to strictly adopt the equilibrium exchange rate as the central rate. On the one hand, China has not yet formed a platform for the equilibrium exchange rate model to be fully accepted. On the other hand, China can use a weighted currency basket to maintain the relative stability of the RMB exchange rate, smoothing the transition to a flexible exchange rate target zone. In its adjustment stage, along with expansion of the target zone, the central rate can move slowly towards the equilibrium exchange rate, based on specific circumstances, and thus drive the whole target zone. In the final stage, the central rate should increasingly approach the equilibrium exchange rate. As reform is deepened, opening-up is extended, and the socialist market economy system is improved, the present rigid structure of China's foreign exchange market and the central bank's monopoly over said market will gradually change. Ultimately the central rate of the RMB exchange rate target zone should approach the equilibrium exchange rate. Only when enterprises and banks truly become market-driven entities can the RMB exchange rate be determined based on supply–demand relationships.

This chapter will discuss determining the RMB's central rate according to the relevant theories on the equilibrium exchange rate. First it will systematically review the determination theory of equilibrium exchange rates, settling on a theory of real effective exchange rate weighting factors. Then it calculates which factors are most influential on the exchange rate, as well the extent of the RMB's undervaluation. Based on this, the chapter adopts an international competitiveness model to determine currency weights in a basket, building an RMB real effective exchange rate index. With this index, and by utilizing an equilibrium exchange rate model, we calculate the RMB equilibrium exchange rate and identify this as the recommended reference of the RMB central rate.

6.1 Related Theories

6.1.1 *Exchange Rate Determination Theory from the Perspective of General Equilibrium*

Compared with a monetary model, general equilibrium model for real exchange rates boasts a firm microeconomics foundation. Exchange rates based on this model can indicate the relative commodity prices in different countries. Many researchers have carefully studied this property of the model. Stockman (1980) made early groundbreaking research, which was subsequently improved by followers, including Lucas (1982), Domowitz and Hakkio (1985), Svensson (1985a and 1985b), Hodrick and Srivastava (1986), Stulz (1987), Stockman and Dellas (1989), Dumas (1992), Engel (1992a and 1992b), Backus and Smith (1993), Bekaert (1994), Sercu, Van Hulle and Uppal (1995), and Apte, Sercu and Uppal (1996).

The model created by Apte, Sercu and Uppal (1996) represents the general structure of this type of model. This core model is as follows:

$$Max \quad E_t\left[\int_t^T U_1(c_1(s))ds\right] + \sum_{k=2}^{M} \theta_k E_t\left[\int_t^T U_k(c_k(s))ds\right]$$

In the formula, E stands for expectation, t for time, U for utility function, c for consumption and θ_k for the weighting of country k. As the planning party, central country 1 maximizes its own expected consumer welfare and its dependent countries from 2 to M. It is also subject to constraints in production and transport processing. In general, in an equilibrium model where consumer welfare is presumed to be maximized, the decisive factor for an exchange rate is the consumer preference.

6.1.2 *Theories of Exchange Rate Determination*

The research method which is currently most discussed in academic circles is that of determining the equilibrium exchange rate. Strictly speaking, theories of this kind are more like accounting equations than optimized general equilibrium models.

6.1.2.1 *Theory of Purchasing Power Parity*

The PPP model is short for the purchasing power parity model. This theory was originally proposed by British economist David Ricardo and later systematized by Swedish economist Gustav Cassel.

The comparison of monetary purchasing power between two countries is called purchasing power parity. It can also be divided into absolute purchasing power parity and relative purchasing power parity. Absolute purchasing power parity (Absolute PPP) determines the exchange rate at a certain point in time. We can calculate it through a static comparison between the price levels of two countries. Absolute PPP is actually an application of the law of one price.

$$e = \frac{EP^*}{P}$$

Here P^* stands for foreign commodity prices, while P for domestic commodity prices. E stands for the nominal exchange rate and e for the real exchange rate.

Relative PPP mainly dynamically demonstrates variation of the exchange rate across two points in time. Economists like Cassel firmly believe that, in a given period, the exchange rate will be adjusted according to the dynamic change in inflation rate differentials between two countries. Thus they postulate that comparing the change in one country's price level against that in another can be used to predict the likely percentage of the former country's currency depreciation (or appreciation), relative to the latter country.

However an exchange rate calculated with a PPP model may deviate greatly from the effective exchange rate. There are mainly four reasons for this. First, statistical standards are not uniform across countries. The PPP model is based on a price comparison of similar commodities across two countries. However, when compiling price indices, different countries set different weights for different commodities and services, making it difficult to compare commodities of exactly the same kind. When testing the predictive power of a PPP exchange rate model, these differences can distort the model's results. Second, transportation costs and trade barriers vary by country. Third, imperfect competition can skew PPP calculations. Purchasing power parity supposes that there is adequate competitiveness for commodities among countries (i.e., similar commodities can be sold at the same price in different countries). In fact, the international competitiveness of different commodities vary. For example, multinational corporations routinely conduct price discrimination across countries, distorting the international price in a non-market (non-competitive) way. The final problem relates to the difference between capital and commodity markets: the PPP model is built on the foundation of an international commodity arbitrage system, but it does not take into consideration the effect of international capital flows on exchange rates. The United States economist Rudiger Dornbusch (1976) once proposed a thought experiment. Suppose there is a world where capital markets are highly integrated and commodity market prices are slowly adjusted. In that world, the real exchange rate will cause a large deviation in purchasing power parity. That is to say, the commodity prices in different markets can be regarded as constant in the short term, but exchange rates are sensitive to information changes and economic policy changes. The PPP model cannot accurately forecast market rates. Exchange rates forecasted by the PPP model, in essence, only reflect the international competitiveness of a home market commodity.

6.1.2.2 *Fundamental Equilibrium Exchange Rates*

The theory of Fundamental Equilibrium Exchange Rates (FEER) was first proposed by Williamson in 1983 (Williamson, 1983) and later applied. FEER defines the equilibrium exchange rate as the effective exchange rate in line with macroeconomic equilibrium (internal equilibrium and external equilibrium combined). Internal equilibrium is regarded as the output level in line with full employment (specifically the employment level determined by the natural rate), a sustainable low inflation rate and the potential output level. External equilibrium is defined as the situation in which every country maintains internal equilibrium and a country's surplus or deficit is equal to the net capital flow, maintaining a stable international balance of payments. At such point, a country reaches its desired sustainable surplus (or deficit) growth rate.

When calculating FEER, it is important to balance the current account (CA) and the capital account (KA). The surplus of CA is the difference between savings (S) and investment (I), so the equilibrium condition can be stated as follows:

$$S - I = CA(q, Y) = -KA$$

In this formula, q stands for the nominal equilibrium exchange rate, Y for the gross output and CA for the function of these two variables. Based on this equilibrium condition, the equilibrium exchange rate can be worked out with an econometric model.

FEER is a method to calculate equilibrium, but not an application of exchange rate determination theory. As the effective exchange rate (which implies assumed reality) will gradually converge in calculation to meet the FEER, the closest exchange rate determination theory embodied by FEER is known as CA determination theory.

The main weakness of FEER is inefficient operability. As FEER involves a large number of parameters related to CA and KA (these parameter are calibrated in line with full employment and the sustainable net capital flow level), estimates produced under FEER are sensitive to model parameters. In addition, as a conception of the equilibrium exchange rate in a standard sense, FEER represents a normative economic analysis method of the equilibrium exchange rate. Some economic parameters which are proven to have influence on real exchange rate behavior are not included in FEER, so it is unclear whether the equilibrium real exchange rate calculated with FEER is empirically accurate. That is, it is unclear whether a FEER-based equilibrium real exchange rate truly reflects the mid-term influence of the determinants of a real exchange rate (Shi and Yu, 2005).

6.1.2.3 *Desired Equilibrium Exchange Rate*

The Desired Equilibrium Exchange Rate (DEER) does not in fact refer to a real exchange rate, but to the exchange rate level which appears when external and internal equilibrium meet the levels deemed desirable by a given monetary authority. Although DEER bears many resemblances with FEER, the difference between the two lies in the fact that FEER is a long-term determination theory, while DEER is a mid-term determination theory.

6.1.2.4 *Equilibrium Real Exchange Rate*

The Equilibrium Real Exchange Rate (ERER) theory was proposed by Sebastian Edwards in 1989 (Edwards, 1989). The equilibrium exchange rate is an exchange rate level which is constrained by both the inter-temporal balance and the supply–demand balance between tradable and non-tradable goods. The main determinants include interest rates, the price of import and export commodities, import and export duties, the price index, the output level and technological progress.

6.1.2.5 *Natural Real Exchange Rate*

The Natural Real Exchange Rate (NATREX) theory was proposed by Jerome L. Stein in 1994 (Stein, 1994). It disregards cyclical economic factors, speculative capital flows and international reserve changes, and instead determines the mid-term real exchange rate using real fundamental economic factors (targeted to achieve a sound balance of international payments). The theory mainly empirically explains when the mid- and long-term real exchange rate will change, based on fundamental factors such as frugality and productivity. The theory is subject to several equilibrium conditions: macroeconomic equilibrium, the ratio of optimal consumption to relative net wealth of external debt, the approach to long-term equilibrium between capital stock and external debt, and interest rate parity, etc.

FEER and NATREX build models based on the fundamental principles of internal and external macroeconomic equilibrium. They then extract endogenous and exogenous variables, determine which quantitative method to use, and finally produce estimates and draw conclusions. In contrast, both the Behavioral Equilibrium Exchange Rates (BEER) and Permanent Equilibrium Exchange Rate (PEER) theories omit the first two steps and instead directly utilize the quantitative method of integration to calculate historical data.

6.1.2.6 *Behavioral Equilibrium Exchange Rates*

The Behavioral Equilibrium Exchange Rates (BEER) theory was proposed by Peter B. Clark and Ronald MacDonald (1998) and then applied by them. In this theory, the equilibrium exchange rate can be stated as:

$$BEER = f(r - r^*, gdebt/gdebt^*, tot, tnt, nfa)$$

In the formula, r stands for the real interest rate while r^* for the expected interest rate; *gdebt* stands for domestic debt while $gdebt^*$ for external debt; *tot* stands for the terms of trade, *tnt* for the Balassa–Samuelson Hypothesis and *nfa* for net foreign assets. For its model strategy, BEER tries to explain actual behavior under related economic variables. In the BEER model, the related concept of equilibrium is given by a set of proper explanatory variables, while in the FEER model macroeconomic equilibrium is used to evaluate the concept of equilibrium relative to the effective exchange rate. As a result, BEER bears the characteristic that some variables of system behavior which connect the exchange rate to its determinants are directly implanted in the model. The main determinants of the exchange rate include: the difference between real interest rates (both home and abroad), the ratio of domestic and foreign government debt, the terms of trade, the Balassa–Samuelson Hypothesis and net external assets.

Note: The Balassa–Samuelson Hypothesis (BSH) refers to the phenomenon that the higher the economic growth rate in a country, the higher the real growth rate of wages, and the more rapidly the real exchange rate increases. When the production efficiency of the tradable goods sector (i.e., the manufacturing industry) increases rapidly, wage growth rates in these sectors will also increase. Wage levels tend to be equalized in every domestic industry, so wages in other industries will increase at roughly the same rate, although the production efficiency in the non-tradable sector (i.e., the service industry) increases slightly. This will lead to a rise in the relative price of non-tradable commodities against tradable ones. Suppose the price level of tradable commodities (calculated by foreign exchange) is constant and the exchange rate is also constant. In such a case, a change in relative prices will lead to a rise in the price of non-tradable commodities, causing a rise in the overall price level (the weighted average of tradable and non-tradable commodities). If a floating exchange rate is adopted to stabilize domestic commodity prices, the exchange rate will increase. In any case, the real exchange rate will decrease.

6.1.2.7 *Permanent Equilibrium Exchange Rate*

Based on an analysis of the equilibrium conditions and determining factors under BEER, the Permanent Equilibrium Exchange Rate (PEER) utilizes a cointegration equation to analyze the relationship between the equilibrium exchange rate and fundamental factors. Thus it can distinguish between short- and long-term factors that affect the exchange rate trend when calculating the overall determinants of the exchange rate.

6.1.2.8 *Exchange Rate Determinants from the Perspective of the Fictitious Economy*

The author (Cheng, 2010a) holds the view that along with ever-larger scale of the fictitious economy, capital flows have an appreciating effect on exchange rates. First, the global fictitious economy is huge in scale. The global total of shares (by market value), bond balances and counter-transaction balances produced by financial derivatives is almost ten times as large as the GDP of every country all over the world. The average daily trading volume in global currency markets is almost 50 times as large as that of the world. Second, the scale of international capital flows in recent years is increasing. Capital flows include three types: foreign direct investment (equity capital, reinvested earnings, and other capital), foreign portfolio investment (stocks, bonds, and financial derivatives), and other foreign investments (short-and-long term trade credit, loans, currency and deposits, trading equity and bonds, insurance and pensions). Capital flows can influence exchange rate. In theory, capital inflows will drive appreciation of a domestic currency. Lastly, after a currency is virtualized and made the fiat money, the exchange rate not only becomes a tool for countries to conduct international political competition, but even becomes a tool for some Western countries to conduct domestic political competition.

At the same time, it is problematic to use traditional PPP to determine the equilibrium exchange rate. PPP theory should strictly distinguish between domestic and international purchasing powers. This dual view of purchasing power theory should be adopted, because in the context of a nonconvertible RMB, differences do exist between domestic and international purchasing power. The domestic circulation of the RMB reveals its domestic purchasing power, while international purchasing power is revealed in RMB flows to international currency markets and currency conversions. As a result, both domestic and international purchasing power should be taken into consideration. The original PPP theory can be amended and the RMB exchange rate can be set at a rational level, as determined by a range of political and economic factors.

6.1.3 *Selection of Price Weight Coefficient When Calculating the Real Effective Exchange Rate*

The exchange rate is a key factor in determining the industrial competitiveness of a country. When export industries have strong competitiveness, the exchange rate will rise (for example, during the last ten years in China), but other factors can also lead to an exchange rate rise (for example, speculative capital inflows). In either case, along with a rise in the exchange rate, the competitiveness of related industries is bound to be eroded. The difference between various models and calculation methods lies in the price weighting of factors (especially against a basket of currencies), towards which observers pay attention. If observers are concerned about people's real living conditions, they can adopt a consumer price; if they are interested in the purchase cost of tradable commodities, they can adopt the prices of tradable commodities; if they care about production costs, they can choose PPI (Producer Price Index) or Unit Labor Cost (ULC).

Real effective exchange rate calculation methods based on ULC appeared in the 1990s, and since then have been often used by academics to observe imbalances, for example, within the Eurozone after the 2009 European debt crisis. However, because China has not yet released official data, this exchange rate calculation method is introduced here.

We can refer to Turner and Van't Dack's (1993) ideas to understand ULC from the perspective of cost segregation. Turner and Van't Dack thought that cost could be divided into the following categories: For imported commodities (such as raw materials), the purchase cost of imported, physical commodities was the main concern; in the commodity production process, labor, capital, taxes, and system costs were also taken into consideration. Usually what people care about is cost factors that can distinguish national competitiveness. Imported raw material can be traded freely without a global unified price, so it does not constitute a differentiating factor. Capital can flow internationally, so it too is not a clear differentiating factor. However, the cost of non-tradable labor, taxes and other institutional factors are often important determinants of competitive differences between countries. In order to evaluate the impact of labor costs on countries and industrial competitiveness, ULC often serves as a measure of competitiveness.

$$\text{Unit labor cost} = \frac{\text{single labor cost}}{\text{single labor output (labor productivity)}}$$

Based on different data and calculation methods, ULC can be divided into nominal unit labor costs and real unit labor costs.

The real effective exchange rate based on ULC is a calculation method wherein the nominal exchange rate is calculated based on the nominal ULC deflation.

$$REER_j = \prod_{i=1}^{N}\left(\frac{ULC_j}{ULC_i} * e_{ij}\right)^{w_i} = \prod_{i=1}^{N}\left(\frac{ULC_j}{ULC_i}\right)^{w_i} * \prod_{i=1}^{N}(e_{ij})^{w_i}$$

In this formula, e_{ij} stands for the nominal exchange rate while w_i stands for the weighting.

6.1.4 *The Academic Study of the RMB Exchange Rate*

6.1.4.1 *The Study of Factors Influencing the RMB Exchange Rate*

When studying which factors influence the RMB exchange rate, Chinese scholars take a sophisticated view. They base their empirical methods on traditional Western exchange rate determination theory, but also take China-specific factors into consideration. Typical studies in recent years are summarized in Table 6.1.

Notably, Jiang (2007) has come up with a basic model for a new theoretical framework for the RMB equilibrium exchange rate. This new model gives priority to the long-term RMB equilibrium exchange rate. In the long run, if technological progress is not a concern, the economic growth of a country can be achieved along with a continuous decrease in the nominal exchange rate (against global currencies), a continuous rise in the price level, and a continuous increase in currency supply. There can be multiple equilibrium exchange rates, which is termed the "theory of equilibrium exchange rate range". As a tool of expenditure-switching in an open economy, the exchange rate is also able to allocate (additional) national income sources between domestic markets and global markets.

Qin and He (2010) think that equilibrium exchange rate theory should analyze RMB valuation from both domestic and foreign equilibriums. External equilibrium refers to the current account balance (or balance of international payments), while internal equilibrium refers to full employment under stable commodity prices. Since China has no scientific and credible statistics for the unemployment rate, all studies that estimate the RMB equilibrium exchange rate under both domestic and foreign equilibriums do not seriously consider China's unemployment or its domestic equilibrium. The global financial crisis and economic recession had a massive impact on China's domestic employment — so to maintain a stable RMB exchange rate is one policy strategy for easing the impact. According to Qin and He, in order to maintain China's internal equilibrium and ease deteriorating employment conditions, it is reasonable to maintain a stable exchange rate of RMB against the Dollar and other currencies (or even to depreciate the RMB).

6.1.4.2 *Overseas and Domestic Calculation Results of the RMB's Degree of Undervaluation*

Existing literature shows that studies on the RMB equilibrium exchange rate involve FEER, DEER, BEER and PEER (see Table 6.2). Although some studies estimate the range of RMB undervaluation (or appreciation), these are just based on rough analysis and lack adequate empirical support (for example, Goldstein, 2007). Some studies based on FEER or DEER randomly give specific values for external equilibrium indicators and subjectively claim an undervaluation range for the RMB. For example, Williamson (2003)

Table 6.1: Chinese Studies of Determining Factors of the RMB Exchange Rate

Publishing Date & Data Period	Explanatory Variables (coefficient estimate and symbols; t stands for statistical significance of estimate value)	Data & Sources	Notes
Model 1 Published in 1995; yearly data from 1969 to 1993. Jing (1995)	Log of terms of trade (LOGTOT): −0.5964 (−0.995); Log of capital inflow and outflow (LOGCAP): 0.1347 (3.491): ratio of tariff to import (LOGRARIF): −0.1316 (−1.197); Exchange discount of black markets (PREMIUM): −0.025 (−2.456); Investment rate (LOGINVGNP): −0.6922 (−1.515); Industrial productivity (LOGPROD): −0.1134 (−0.677); Exchange rate movement lags (NORDEV-1): 0.0033 (2.948); Credit increase lags (CREDIT-1): −0.0040 (−0.986); Real equilibrium exchange rate lags (LOGREER): 0.7835 (7.939)	Data source: *China Statistical Yearbook (1994)*; International Financial Statistics (IMF); World Currency Yearbook, 1989; National Bureau of Statistics; State Administration of Foreign Exchange; IMF China Office.	—
Model 2 Published in 1999; yearly data from 1984 to 1999. Zhang (1999)	Trade balance stands for terms of trade (SURPLUS): −0.1325 (2.93); GDP for labor productivity (LGDPSA): 1.42 (5.02); Broad money supply (LM2SA): −1.48 (−7.34); Net foreign assets (LNFASA): 0.096 (1.85); One-year deposit rate of RMB (RSA): −0.04 (−3.97)	The explained variable is the REER of RMB released by IMF; no reports for independent variable data and data source.	Cointegration is utilized to examine if a cointegration relationship exists between REER and the explanatory variable.

(*Continued*)

Table 6.1: (*Continued*)

Publishing Date & Data Period	Explanatory Variables (coefficient estimate and symbols; t stands for statistical significance of estimate value)	Data & Sources	Notes
Model 3 Published in 2000; yearly data from 1978 to 1999. Zhang (2000)	Terms of trade: 2.45 (6.065); Import share of GDP stands for degree of openness (LOPEN): −0.432 (−3.96); Government expenditures as a share of GDP (LGOVEXP): 0.678 (5.582); (Improvement in terms of trade and increase in government expenditures make the REER appreciate, while widening of opening degree makes the REER depreciate).	Indirect labeling method is used to measure REER. Direct labeling method is used to measure nominal and real exchange rate in the same form (page 17).	Cointegration is utilized to filter and exclude explanatory variables such as labor productivity, investment rate, tariff level, and domestic credit growth rate.
Model 4 Published in 2001; yearly data from 1952 to 1997. Zhang (2001)	Trade formation stands for technological advancement (FINVEST): 0.374 (3.26); Government consumption for fiscal policies (GCON): −0.3225 (−2.38); Export growth for terms of trade (EXPORTG): 3.389 (5.914); Degree of trade dependence for business policy (OPEN): 0.878 (11.63); Virtual variable for disasters from 1961 to 1962 and dual exchange rate policies in 1981	Note 2 (page 86) shows most data comes from the IMF's International Financial Statistics; it discusses other data sources on the same page.	t is calculated by the writer based on the coefficient estimate of the report and the standard deviation.

Model 5 Published in 2002; yearly data from 1995 to 2001. Lin (2002)	Degree of trade dependence trade for opening degree (LOPEN): 0.856 (2.204); Terms of trade (LTOT): 0.822 (4.439); Broad money M2 growth rate (LMG): 0.917 (6.291)	Explanatory data source: *China Statistical Yearbook* and International Financial Statistics. It uses data provided by World Bank for the terms of trade after 1970, and then estimates China's data in other years based on global terms of trade (assuming the same standard for China).	LGM coefficient is reported as 9.17 in the estimating equation, while it is measured as 0.917 (page 67). So 9.17 may be a clerical error.
Model 6 Published in 2003; quarterly data from the first quarter in 1992 to the fourth quarter in 2004. Yang (2002)	Relative growth rate of GDP/employment (HBS): 0.08 (2.67); The ratio of total investment against total domestic absorption (ISHARE): −0.15 (3.75); Foreign direct investment (FDI): 0.18 (9.0); World export price (WORLDPI): −0.59 (7.375); Terms of trade demonstrated by the ratio of the export and import price index (TOT); Share of import–export value at a constant price of GDP for business policies including "tariff policy, export subsidy policy and other policies involved with system reform of foreign trade enterprises"(OPEN); Coefficient estimates of TOT and OPEN are not notable and not included in the estimation equation recommended by the author.	Explanatory data source: *China Statistical Yearbook* and National Bureau of Statistics. It is standard to use unit root to examine REER and fundamentals. Then the maximum-likelihood method is used to reject the null hypothesis where a cointegration vector does not exist; finally long-term parameters for the determining equation of the equilibrium exchange rate are estimated.	—

(Continued)

Table 6.1: (*Continued*)

Publishing Date & Data Period	Explanatory Variables (coefficient estimate and symbols; t stands for statistical significance of estimate value)	Data & Sources	Notes
Model 7 Published in 2002; yearly data from 1978 to 1994. Zhang (2005)	Terms of trade (LTOT): −7.185; Relative level of tariff stands for capital control system (LK): −0.703	—	The independent variable is the REER of tradable commodities
Model 8 Published in 2004; quarterly data from 1977 to 2002. Hu and Zeng (2004)	Import–export value as a share of GDP stands for "degree of trade restrictions and transaction control" (LOPEN): −0.6122 (−4.98); Terms of trade (LTOT): 2.4362 (6.07); Financial expenditure share of GDP for "government consumption data of non-tradable commodity (LGCGDP): 0.4689 (3.168); Assets such as foreign exchange reserves and gold substitute for foreign net assets, and stand for "capital flow control" (KCON): 0.0235 (1.28);	"Variables are from quarterly data from 1997 to 2002 (page 21)". GDP data, GDP deflator, import and export, domestic loan and government consumption are from IFS (International Financial Statistics). Data on tariff and investment is from *China Statistical Yearbook*. Data on terms of trade is from World Bank (note 2 on page 21).	Early estimates include measures of the productivity variable of GDP per capita. The result is significant but opposite to relationship between the theory and hypothesis.

Model 9 Published in 2004; yearly data from 1980 to 2000. Chu (2004)	Government financial expenditure share of GDP (LG): 0.4419 (5.31); Real federal fund rate of The United States (LR): 0.1014 (4.65); Terms of trade (LTOT): 2.2144 (8.44); Openness (LOPEN): −0.4987 (7.53); There are four estimate equations altogether. The author thinks the second equation in the second round estimate is best.	Definition of variable indicator is explained in detail, but there is no data source. It is standard to use unit root to examine REER and fundamentals and then to estimate long-term parameters for determining the equation of the equilibrium exchange rate.	GDP per capita is used to measure productivity variable. The result is significant but opposite to relationship between the theory and hypothesis.
Model 10 Published in 2005; quarterly data from the first quarter of 1991 to the third quarter of 2004. Shi and Yu (2005)	Terms of trade (tot): 0.408; Relative price of non-tradable commodities against tradable commodities stands for the relative increase of domestic productivity against that of foreign countries (tnt): 2.22 Net foreign asset (nfa): −0.1059; Degree of trade dependence simulates trade policies (trade): −0.776; There is no report estimating the significance of the coefficient, which shows "estimates of all coefficients are not obviously zero".	Data sources and figures are used to show related variables.	Essential exchange rate stands for "real exchange rate".

Table 6.2: Calculation of the RMB Exchange Rate's Degree of Undervaluation

Author	Year	Degree of REER Under-valuation (%)	Under-valuation by Degree of Dollar Exchange Rate (%)	Research Method
Anderson (2006)	2006	—	18–25	FEER
Bénassy-Quéré *et al.* (2004)	2001	16	41–44	BEER
Bénassy-Quéré *et al.* (2006)	2004	31–45	30–59	BEER
Big Mac Index	2007	—	138	PPP-S (a)
Bosworth (2004)	2004	—	67	PPP-E (a)
Cheung, Chinn & Fujii (2007)	2007	—	≈100	PPP-E (a)
Cline (2005)	2005	21	45	FEER
Cline (2007)	2007	11–18	34–39	FEER
Coudert & Couharde (2005)	2003	23–30	41–50	PPP-E (a)
	2002	—	18	BEER
	2002–03	23–30	44–54	FEER
Frankel (2006)	2000	—	56	PPP-E (a)
Funke & Rahn (2005)	2002	3–6	12–14	BEER
Goldstein (2004)	2004	15–30	—	FEER
Goldstein & Lardy (2006)	2004	20–35	—	FEER
Goldstein & Lardy (2007)	2007	35–60	—	FEER
Jeong & Mazier (2003)	2000	29	67	FEER
MacDonald & Dias (2007)	2007	8–42	—	BEER
Stolper & Fuentes (2007)	2007 (b)	—	7	BEER
	2007 (c)	—	15	FEER
Wang (2004)	2003	5	—	BEER
	—	0–5	—	FEER
	—	0 to –5	—	FEER
Wren-Lewis (2004)	2003	—	19–22	FEER
Average (Total)	All samples	20	40 (d)	—
Average A	2000–2004	17	42 (d)	—
Average B	2005–2007	27	38 (d)	—

Notes:
(a) PPP: purchasing power parity, –S: simple, –E: enhanced.
(b) GS-DEER model.
(c) Elasticities model.
(d) Excluding Big Mac.

mentions that Goldstein and Lardy claimed that the RMB should be appreciated by 15% to 25% while Bergsten claimed 20% to 25%.

Cline and Williamson (2008) analyze 17 global studies which used both the domestic and foreign equilibrium frameworks to research the RMB equilibrium exchange rate. They find that their results differed sharply from one another. The degree of RMB undervaluation across studies see huge differences in magnitude — from 0 to 55%. It should be noted that researches claiming RMB undervaluation all analyzed data from previous years. Thus, even if such claims could stand for that time, the undervaluation should disappear as the RMB has appreciated by 20% in the past few years.

6.2 Construction of RMB Real Effective Exchange Rate Index

6.2.1 *Status of Research at Home and Abroad*

6.2.1.1 *Literature Review*

Studies both home and abroad on currency basket-linked exchange rates mainly focus on two aspects. First, they consider the construction of a basket-linked exchange rate index, including the criteria for selecting basket currencies, weighting calculations for the basket currencies, selection of the price discount index of the real effective basket exchange rate, and so on. Second, they analyze trend correlations of basket-linked exchange rates and macroeconomic variables, including the relationship between a basket-linked exchange rate trend and a country's currency, economic development, inflation levels, and the relationship between a basket-linked exchange rate and major monetary exchange rate trends. Turnovsky (1982) utilizes a general equilibrium model for a small open economy to calculate weights for different kinds of basket currencies. based on model parameters and impulse response. The calculation method is very complicated, so it is not widely used in practice to compile a basket exchange rate index. McGuirk (1987) utilizes data from finished goods and consumption to make a convex combination of bilateral import and export weights in a currency basket, determining the currency competitiveness weights of each country. San *et al.* (2005) propose a way to amend data on entrepot trade and intra-regional trade and then use this data to calculate the RMB exchange rate index, finding that the weights of currencies in the basket of each Asian country had increased. Maxwell (2004) compares several compiling methods for Ghana's REER and concludes that the real effective exchange rate calculated using the GDP deflator index as a price discount index is better than the results using an effective basket exchange rate index. Lipschitz and McDonald (1992) use ULC to conduct a price conversion on the German REER index and find that it can better forecast changes in trade share. Bartolini (1993) finds that, in 1987–1993, the Irish basket exchange rate index had some relevance to its expected currency devaluation. Marsh and Tokaric (1996) study the relationship between the basket exchange rate index and the trade volume, finding that the short-term correlation is insignificant, while a change in the real basket exchange rate would impact trade volume in the long run. Kristian (2004) utilizes three methods to compile a Swedish REER index and uses a VAR model to analyze the influence of three kinds of indices on real GDP, investment and net exports, verifying that a REER index based on CPI can better describe the international competitiveness of a country.

Chinese scholars have conducted much research on the composition of a currency basket for the RMB exchange rate index. Zhang (2005) introduces a productivity index when calculating basket currency weight by using an advanced HBS (Harold–Barraza–Samuelson) model and, on this basis, compiling a RMB REER index utilizing various price adjustment indices. Wang and Ren (2003) discuss the difference between the NEER and REER on the foundation of ULC. Wan (2004) designs an RMB REER index and studies the influence of its trend and China's macroeconomic variables. Zhou (2007) compares different methods of compiling exchange rate indices and scientifically analyzes the feasibility of each method in theory and practice. Ba *et al.* (2007) study calculation methods for key international economic institutions on REER, proposing a way to compile an RMB REER index. Ding and Zhou (2009) introduce data on the competitiveness of multilateral markets and then compile an RMB exchange rate index using a chained index method.

Current studies on compiling a RMB basket exchange rate mainly use basket exchange rate compiling methods from foreign-related economic institutions, but do not consider key steps such as the disposal of trade data, the selection of basket currencies and the disposal of price conversion. Especially in trade data processing, when compiling the RMB exchange rate index, most domestic studies do not take into consideration the influence of entrepot trade on trade weightings in each country; neither do they consider the differences in trade data between countries. These problems cause deviations in basket currency weighting for each country.

6.2.1.2 *Various Compiling Methods for Exchange Rate Indices in Related Institutions and Countries*

(1) BIS's Compiling of the Exchange Rate Index

The Bank for International Settlements (BIS) calculates an effective exchange rate index for 58 countries and regions, including individual exchange rate indices for the 16 countries in Eurozone and that of the Eurozone as a whole. In addition, it also calculates exchange rate indices for many developed and emerging countries such as Algeria, Argentina, Austria, Brazil, Canada, China, India, Japan and Korea.

The BIS utilizes dual weighting methods to calculate the basket exchange rate index for developed countries or regions. It calculates both the weight for trade volume of finished goods and the weight for domestic finished goods output. Of this, import weight is determined by bilateral import share while export weight considers the competition of domestic suppliers vs. foreign exporters in each market. The sum of import trade weightings, which considers the average number of export weights for third markets, is called the overall trade weighting. The BIS conducts bilateral trade weighting in most emerging countries. That is to say, the BIS calculates weightings based on the share of trade volume of trade partners against domestic trade volume, while neglecting the competitiveness of local suppliers against other export countries in third markets. The basket currency weightings of the BIS are updated every three years. At the same time, when calculating the effective exchange rate index in each country or region, the BIS utilizes the consumer price index (CPI) as the price conversion index.

In the Chinese currency basket of the effective exchange rate, as compiled by the BIS, the US Dollar accounts for the highest proportion (21%), followed by the Euro (18.4%), then the Yen (16.8%) and the Won (8.2%). In addition, the currency basket also includes the Hong Kong Dollar, British Pound, Singapore Dollar, Canadian Dollar, Russian Ruble, Thai Baht, Australian Dollar, Malaysian Ringgit, Indian Rupee, Mexican Peso and Indonesian Rupiah.

(2) IMF's Compiling of the Exchange Rate Index

The International Monetary Foundation (IMF) began to compile multilateral exchange rate indices in as early as the 1970s and made an in-depth study of calculation methods for competitiveness weighting. In 1983, the IMF started the Information Network System (INS) to calculate the real and nominal exchange rates of IMF member countries.

When calculating currency weights, the IMF utilizes trade and consumption data of related finished goods to make a convex combination of bilateral import and export weightings in order to find the overall competitiveness weighting. This calculation method associates cost changes (both at home and abroad) with changes in the competitiveness of a country. The calculation process is similar to that of the BIS's, but there is at least one major difference. The BIS averages import and export weighting to calculate the final weight, while the IMF makes a more complicated convex combination of import and export weightings.

When calculating REER, the IMF uses the ULC of its old member states as a price conversion index and a consumer price index as conversion index.

(3) United States Federal Reserve's (Fed) Compiling of the Dollar Exchange Rate Index

The US Dollar basket exchange rate is one of the most important data items published by the Fed. Before 1998, the Fed's G10 exchange rate index compiled was based on the currencies of ten countries, including Belgium, Canada, France, Federal Republic of Germany, Italy, Japan, Netherlands, Sweden, Switzerland and Britain. The Fed uses the multilateral trade share of each country from 1972 to 1976 as a settled weighting from which to compile the G10 Dollar basket exchange rate index. Since the United States has increasingly more intense trade contact with countries and regions beyond these ten initial countries (and since the founding of the Eurozone), the G10 exchange rate index cannot fully reflect the international competitiveness of the Dollar. As a result, in December 1998, rather than continue using the G10 exchange rate index, the Fed adopted three new Dollar basket exchange rate indices: the Major Currency Index, the Broad Index and the Other Important Trading Partner Index. Among these, the Broad Index includes the most kinds of basket currencies while those of the other two are subsets of the Broad Index.

In 1997, the Fed included the currencies of 35 countries and regions (which exported more than 0.5% crude oil or imported arms from the US) in the Broad Index basket. In 1999, the Euro took the place of the ten European currencies, so the basket of broad currencies was reduced to 26 kinds of currencies. The Major Index includes currencies which could be freely traded and are widely accepted in international financial markets. These currencies included the Euro, Australia Dollar, Canadian Dollar, Japanese Yen, Swedish Krona, Swiss Franc and British Pound. Other currencies in the Broad basket (which were excluded from the Major currencies basket) are utilized to compile currency exchange rate indices for other important partner countries. These currencies refer to 19 countries or regions, such as Argentina, Brazil, Chile, Colombia, Mexico, Venezuela, Mainland China, Hong Kong (China), India, Indonesia, Korea, Malaysia,

Philippines, Singapore, Taiwan (China), Thailand, Israel, Saudi Arabia, and Russia.

When calculating weighting, the Fed uses a multinational competitiveness model to determine the weights of various currencies in its Major basket. It converts the weightings of other currencies in the Broad basket and the Other Important Trading Partner basket based on the currency's individual weighting in the Major basket. Weightings are updated annually. When calculating the effective exchange rate index, the Fed also utilizes CPI as a price conversion index.

(4) European Central Bank's (ECB) Compiling of the Euro Exchange Rate Index

Based on the trade relationship of a country with Europe, the ECB constructs two different baskets of currencies: a basket of core currencies and a basket of broad currencies. The core basket includes currencies of 12 countries or regions which are industrialized or being industrialized, such as the US, Japan, Switzerland, British, Sweden, Denmark, Norway, Canada, Australia, Korea, Singapore and Hong Kong, China. The broad basket includes a wider range of currencies from 38 important trading countries or regions.

When calculating weightings, the Euro exchange rate basket considers the trade weightings of a third party and adjusts the weighting every five years (with the weight of the first quarter in 1999 as a base). When compiling the REER of the core basket, to make a price conversion, the ECB utilizes five methods: CPI, Producer Price Index (PPI), manufacturing unit labor cost, GDP deflator and unit labor cost of the whole economy. For the broad basket exchange rate, the ECB only uses CPI to make a price conversion, because relevant data from some countries is missing or suffers a time lag.

(5) Bank of Japan's (BOJ) Compiling of the Yen Exchange Rate Index

The main purpose of the Yen exchange rate index is to measure the international competitiveness of Japanese products, so the BOJ mainly selects the currencies of its important export trading partners. Based on Japan's foreign trade situation in 2000, the BOJ selected currencies of countries or regions whose imports from Japan accounted for no less than 1% of Japan's total exports. These currencies included the US Dollar, Euro, New Taiwan Dollar, Korean Won, Chinese RMB, Hong Kong Dollar, Singapore Dollar,

British Pound, Malaysian Ringgit, Thai Baht, Philippine Peso, Australian Dollar, Indonesian Rupiah, Canadian Dollar and Mexican Peso.

In terms of weight calculations, the BOJ uses the export share of Japan against other countries or regions as its currency weighting, adjusting the weight every five years. When compiling the effective exchange rate, the BOJ uses CPI as price conversion index.

6.2.2 *Selection of Basket Currencies and Weight Calculation Methods*

6.2.2.1 *Selection of Basket Currencies*

The selection of basket currencies has much to do with the uses of exchange rate compilation. If the exchange rate is used to measure the overall competitiveness of a country, then the currencies of several important export trading partners should be selected. If it is used to reflect pressure from external inflation, then currencies of important import trading partners should be selected. In addition to the trade situation, it is necessary to select the final basket of currencies based on a country's own foreign debt structure, source currency, FDI, international immobility and the payment capacity of the currency.

6.2.2.2 *Calculation Methods for Weighting Basket Currencies*

There are many ways to determine weightings in a currency basket. The most common one is to use each currency's trade scale. According to different compiling purposes, we can choose either unilateral export trade weighting or bilateral trade weighting. We can also consider the competitiveness of domestic and foreign products in a third market, which is a way to determine the multinational trade competitiveness weighting. At the same time, some literature proposes determining weights using a general equilibrium model of a small open economy. However, this method is not widely used in practice because it involves too many statistics and is complicated. The three most widely used calculation methods are specified as follows.

(1) Export Trade Weighting

Export trade has a great influence on the economy of a country, so many countries only use export trade share to determine basket currency weights.

The formula is:

$$W_i = \frac{x^i}{\sum_{k=1}^{n} x^i}$$

In this formula, n stands for the number of currencies in a basket, x^i stands for the export volume of the host country to country or region i in the basket. The weight can be calculated just based on the export volume of the host country to other countries or regions.

(2) Bilateral Trade Weighting

Bilateral trade weight is calculated in a similar way as export trade weighting. The formula for bilateral trade weighting is as follows:

$$W_i = \frac{x^i + m^i}{\sum_{k=1}^{n} (x^i + m^i)}$$

In the formula, n stands for the number of currencies in a basket, x^i stands for the export volume of the host country to country i in the basket, and m^i for the import volume of the host country to country i. Bilateral trade weights are more comprehensive than unilateral export weights because the former not only considers export trade of the host country but also takes into account imports of the host country from other countries.

(3) Multinational Competitive Trade Weighting

Multinational competitive trade weighting takes competition in a third market into consideration. Thus the calculation is more complicated than those mentioned above. Weighting is first divided into export weight and import weight. Then the final weight W_i is the weighted array of import weight W_i^m and export weight W_i^x:

$$W_i = \left(\frac{m_c}{x_c + m_c}\right) W_i^m + \left(\frac{x_c}{x_c + m_c}\right) W_i^x$$

In the formula, m_c stands for the overall import volume of the host country, while x_c stands for the overall export volume of the host country.

W_i^m, the import weight of country i, can be calculated easily:

$$W_i^m = m^i / m$$

In the formula, m^i stands for the import volume of the host country from country i, while W_i^m stands for the proportion of import volume accounting for total import volume.

The calculation of W_i^x, the export weight of country i, is complicated:

$$W_i^x = W_i^{bx} + W_i^{tx}$$

$$W_i^{bx} = \left(\frac{x^i}{x_c}\right)\left(\frac{y_i}{y_i + \sum_{h\neq c} x_h^i}\right)$$

$$W_i^{tx} = \sum_{k\neq j}\left(\frac{x_c^k}{x_c}\right)\left(\frac{x_i^k}{y_k + \sum_{h\neq c} x_h^k}\right)$$

In the above formulas, y_i stands for sales of domestic products within country i and x_h^i stands for the exports of country k to country i. W_i^{bx} stands for bilateral export competitiveness, namely exports of the host country to country i. W_i^{bx} faces the problem of domestic supply y_i of country i and export competitiveness of other countries to country i. W_i^{tx} stands for export competitiveness weightings of a third party market, which means exports from the host country to the third party market k are affected by the competitiveness of exports from country i.

6.2.3 *The Current Status of China's Foreign Trade and Selection of Basket Currencies*

6.2.3.1 *The Current Status of China's Imports and Exports to Countries and Regions*

According to statistics from the National Bureau of Statistics, China's overall export volume in 2011 almost reached USD$18.983 trillion. Its exports to countries and regions in the world are displayed in Figure 6.1. In 2011, China's export volume to the United States totaled more than USD$324.4 billion — more than 17% of China's overall export volume, making the US the biggest export market for China. Countries and regions on the list of top ten export volumes include Hong Kong, China, Japan, Korea, Germany, Netherlands, India, British, Russia and Singapore. The export volume of China to those ten countries and regions accounts for 60% of overall export volume.

China's imports from other countries and regions in 2011 are displayed in Figure 6.2. From the figure, we find that China's imports from Japan reached their highest level at USD$194.5 billion, accounting for more than 13% of the overall import volume. The top ten countries from which China imported included Korea, the United States, Germany, Australia, Malaysia, Brazil, Saudi Arabia, Russia and Thailand. Import volumes

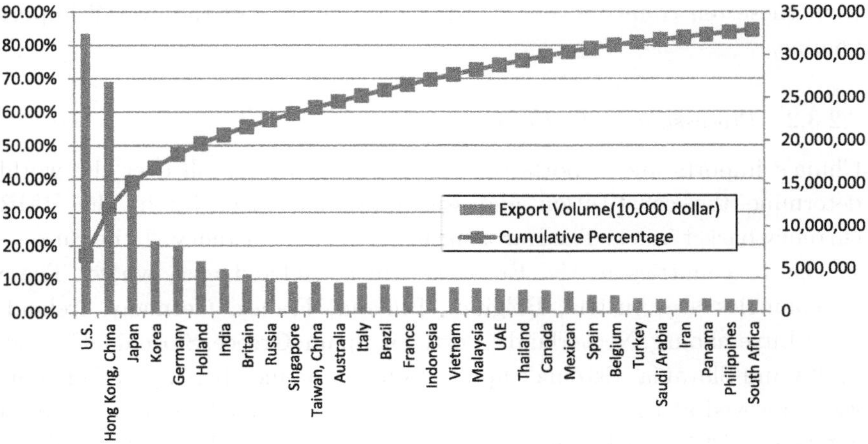

Figure 6.1: China's Export Volume to Main Countries and Regions

Data source: CEIC Database

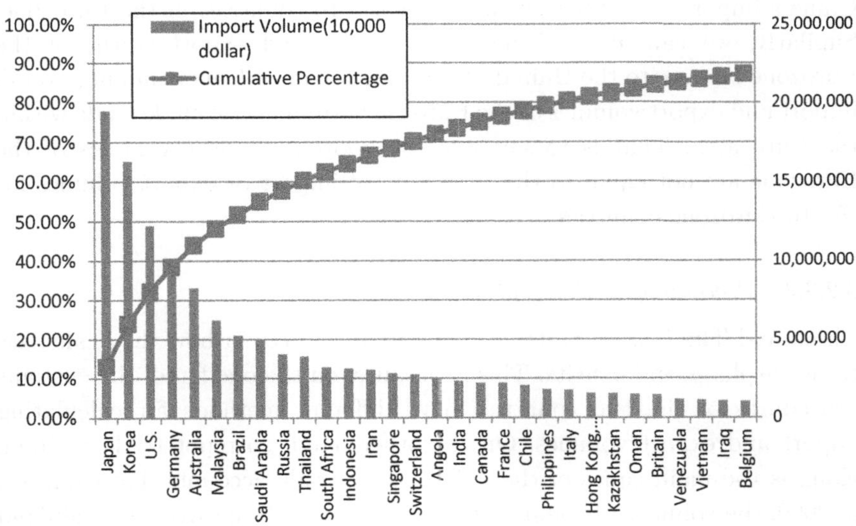

Figure 6.2: China's Import Volume from Major Countries and Regions

Data source: CEIC Database

from these ten countries accounted more than 60% of the overall import volume.

6.2.3.2 *Processing of the Eurozone*

China's imports and exports to countries and regions all over the world determine the constitution and weightings of currencies in the RMB currency basket index. The Eurozone uses a unified currency — the Euro — so the 16 countries in the Eurozone are considered as a whole. These 16 countries are Austria, Belgium, Finland, France, Germany, Ireland, Italy, Luxembourg, Netherlands, Portugal, Spain, Greece, Slovenia, Cyprus, Malta and Slovakia. Estonia's application for the membership of Eurozone was approved at the end of 2008, but it formally joined the Euro area on January 1, 2011, so Estonia is excluded when we deal with data of the Euro area.

Take China's exports to the Eurozone as an example. We can calculate the overall trade status of China relative to the Eurozone if we add up China's import and export volumes for the 16 countries in the Eurozone. Similarly, we can also calculate the import and export status of the Eurozone relative to the United States and Japan. When examining overall import and export volumes of the Eurozone, we should exclude trade within the Euro area. That is to say, overall export or import volumes of the Eurozone are not equal to the total sum of import or export volumes for the 16 Eurozone countries.

6.2.3.3 *Processing of Entrepot Trade*

China and The United States have large differences in how they calculate trade surpluses and deficits. This is because, on the one hand, the customs procedures of the two countries have different methods for calculating import and export volumes. On the other hand, entrepot trade in Hong Kong is the main cause of the difference in trade accounts. For example, in 2009, the volumes of commodity transited from Hong Kong to mainland China reached their highest share in the overall entrepot volume, accounting for more than 50%. In the same year, the volumes of commodities transited from China to Hong Kong also reached the highest share, accounting for more than 60% of the overall entrepot volume.

There exist significant differences regarding entrepot trade in Hong Kong in the customs statistics of each country, which is one of the major reasons for the differences in each country's balance of trade accounts. In terms of balance of trade, exports from China to the US, in theory, are equal to US imports from China. However, due to various reasons, there are huge differences in the statistics of these two countries — especially in export statistics from China to the US. To a large extent, the difference is caused by entrepot trade in Hong Kong.

Entrepot trade volume in Hong Kong reveals limitations in the customs statistics both in China and the United States. The US sees Chinese commodities transited via Hong Kong as imports from China and does not exclude entrepot earnings from Hong Kong. At the same time, part of the commodities exported from the US to Hong Kong is also transited to China and this part is not calculated either. China's export statistics to the US do not fully count commodities exported to the US via Hong Kong (Feng and Liu, 1999; Yang, 2008).

As a result, trade statistics between China and the United States need amendment. US exports to China and US imports from China, as calculated by the US, are defined as $USEX_{US-CN}$ and $USIM_{CN-US}$ respectively. Chinese exports to the US and Chinese imports from the US are calculated by China's definition as $CNEX_{CN-US}$ and $CNIM_{US-CN}$, respectively. In theory, $USEX_{US-CN}$ is equal to $CNIM_{US-CN}$ while $USIM_{CN-US}$ is equal to $CNEX_{CN-US}$. However, there are many unavoidable errors in calculating real statistics, so great deviations exist in the official statistics. Customs in Hong Kong uses the Hong Kong Dollar as its unit of measurement, so this book converts all entrepot trade statistics via Hong Kong using the rate of HKD1 as equal to USD$0.13. In this way we can find the trade volume TR_{CN-US} from the source area of China to the US via entrepot trade in Hong Kong. Likewise, we can find the trade volume TR_{US-CN} from the source area of the US to China via entrepot. All the trade volumes are priced in US Dollar. In addition, according to a report by Hong Kong customs (2009), we assume that the entrepot earning ratio of commodities from China R_{CN} is 27% and that of commodities from the United States R_{US} is 18%.

(1) Amend $USIM_{CN-US}$ by excluding the entrepot earnings of Hong Kong. First, based on entrepot earnings, we convert TR_{CN-US} into the export volume of Hong Kong, namely $TR_{CN-US}/(1+R_{CN})$. Suppose freight from Hong Kong to the United States is 10%, then CIF (cost, insurance and freight) of TR_{CN-US} recorded by the United States is $TR_{CN-US}\times(1+10\%)$.

So the amended $USIM_{CN-US}$ should be:

$$USIM_{CN-US'} = USIM_{CN-US} - [TR_{CN-US} \times (1 + 10\%) - (TR_{CN-US}/(1 + R_{CN}))(1 + 10\%)]$$

(2) Amend $USEX_{US-CN}$ by including trade to China via entrepot in Hong Kong. First, based on the entrepot earnings of US commodities, we convert TR_{US-CN} into the real import volume of Hong Kong, namely $TR_{US-CN}/(1+R_{US})$. Suppose freight from Hong Kong to the United States is still 10%, FOB (free on board) as recorded by the United States is $[TR_{US-CN}/(1 + R_{US})]/(1 + 10\%)$. This part is not calculated in the US's exports to China. So the amended $USEX_{US-CN}$ is:

$$USEX_{US-CN'} = USEX_{US-CN} + [TR_{US-CN}/(1 + R_{US})]/(1 + 10\%)$$

(3) Amend $CNEX_{CN-US}$ by adding in Hong Kong's entrepot trade (which is not calculated by China). Imports from mainland China calculated by Hong Kong customs are notated as $HKIM_{CN-HK}$, which include retained commodities and commodities for entrepot. Exports to Hong Kong as calculated by Chinese customs are notated as $CNIM_{CN-HK}$, which refer to retained commodities in Hong Kong and any commodities not counted from entrepot via Hong Kong. Suppose freight from mainland China to Hong Kong is 4%, then CIF of $CNIM_{CN-HK}$ is $CNIM_{CN-HK}(1 + 4\%)$. That is to say, exports to Hong Kong (as reported by China) do not include calculated trade transited to other countries. Commodities volume transited to the United States is converted into China's FOB, namely $[TR_{CN-US}/(1 + R_{CN})]/(1.04\%)$. So the amended $CNEX_{CN-US}$ is:

$$CNEX_{CN-US'} = CNEX_{CN-US} + [TR_{CN-US}/(1 + R_{CN})]/(1.04\%)$$

(4) Amend $CNIM_{US-CN}$ by excluding entrepot earning of Hong Kong. This is amended is similar to that of $USIM_{CN-US}$. The entrepot volume of US commodities to China via Hong Kong is small and the entrepot earnings have a small influence on China's accounting of import volumes from the US, so its influence can be neglected.

After amending entrepot trade, the gap in trade surplus and deficit between China and the United States is greatly narrowed. Similarly, we can use statistics from Hong Kong's entrepot trade to amend China's trade statistics with Japan and the Eurozone. As the import and export reports of Hong Kong only publish statistics of main entrepot trade countries, when amending the Eurozone statistics, we use the entrepot volume of commodities transited to Germany, the Netherlands and Italy as the total volume of commodities transited to the Eurozone. We also use commodities from Germany transited to China as that of the Eurozone's commodities transited to mainland China via Hong Kong. The entrepot trade volumes of other countries and regions transited via Hong Kong are so small that they need no amendment. What is more, although Singapore is also one of the world's most important entrepot trade ports, this book does not amend the entrepot trade of Singapore because exports from China to Singapore are far less than those from China to Hong Kong. Also, detailed data on entrepot trade in Singapore is unavailable.

6.2.3.4 *Processing of Import and Export Statistics for Each Country*

Entrepot trade is not the only factor that causes differences in import and export statistics between China and the US. Other differences still exist in the amended statistics. The fact that the exports of, for example, country A to country B are not equal to their import records is not a problem unique to Sino-US trade. Due to unavoidable factors such as statistical deviations, import and export statistics are often dissimilar in the customs records of each country. In order to ensure statistical consistency, the IMF's INS (Information Network System) defines a series of countries as "priority reporters".[1] For trade between two countries (both of which may or may not be of "priority reporters"), the average of bilateral imports and exports is adopted. For two countries, of which one is a member of the "priority reporters" and one is not, the trade volume of the country which is a "priority reporter" is adopted. This book uses the amended trade statistics of each country by adopting the INS processing method.

6.2.3.5 *Selections of Currencies for the Basket*

After processing the trade statistics of each country and fully considering the importance of various countries and regions in China's trade and international payment capacity, we finally determine two types of currency

---

[1]They include Australia, Austria, Belgium, Luxembourg, Denmark, France, Germany, Greece, Ireland, Italy, Japan, the Netherlands, New Zealand, Norway, Portugal, Spain, Sweden, Switzerland, Britain, the United States, Iceland, Israel, South Africa, Mainland China, Hong Kong (China), India, Korea, Singapore and Taiwan (China).

baskets. The first type only selects currencies of the four most important trading partners and regions for China (where the unilateral or bilateral trade volume is bigger than that of other countries and regions). These are the US Dollar, Euro, Japanese Yen and Korean Won. This basket we call the narrow currency basket. The second basket selects more trading partners. In addition to the four currencies in the narrow basket, the second basket includes eight more currencies such as the British Pound, Australian Dollar, Singapore Dollar and Indian Rupee. We label this basket the broad currency basket. Based on these two different baskets of currencies, we can build indices for each — one based on a narrow RMB exchange rate basket and another based on a broad basket. If a broader basket of currencies is considered, then the currencies of Brazil, Malaysia and Canada should be included.

6.2.4 *Calculating Weightings in the Currency Basket*

Based on the three calculation methods mentioned above, we calculate and compare the weightings of various currencies in 2012. The results are shown in Table 6.3.

When calculating the narrow basket of currency weights using the three methods, we find the same results: If currency weights are ranked in order from largest to smallest, the results are the US Dollar, Euro, Japanese Yen and Korean Won. When we use the unilateral export volume to calculate

Table 6.3: Comparison of Three Weighting Methods

	Narrow Basket of Currencies			Broad Basket of Currencies		
Calculating Method	Unilateral Export	Bilateral Trade	Multinational Competitiveness Trade	Unilateral Export	Bilateral Trade	Multinational Competitiveness Trade
US Dollar	43.12%	34.08%	32.58%	36.26%	28.52%	27.08%
Euro	31.04%	29.06%	29.10%	26.10%	24.32%	24.46%
Japanese Yen	17.35%	22.42%	24.00%	14.59%	18.76%	19.88%
Korean Won	8.49%	14.44%	14.32%	7.14%	12.09%	11.79%
Pound	—	—	—	4.90%	3.66%	3.42%
Singapore Dollar	—	—	—	3.71%	4.07%	2.73%
Rupee	—	—	—	3.87%	3.50%	4.12%
Australian Dollar	—	—	—	3.44%	5.08%	6.52%

weights, there is a large gap between the Dollar and the Won. However, when we take bilateral trade into consideration, the gap between the Dollar and the Won is narrowed. After we further consider competition in a third party market, the gap between each currency further narrows.

When calculating the broad basket of currency weights using the three methods, the ranking order (from largest to smallest) changes. No matter which method is used, weights of the four currencies (Dollar, Euro, Yen and Won) in the narrow basket are remarkably larger than those of the remaining four currencies. To some extent, this proves that it is scientific to include the former four currencies in the narrow basket of currencies. When we use the unilateral export volume to calculate weights, the resulting rank of weights (from largest to smallest) is the British Pound, Indian Rupee, Singapore Dollar, and Australian Dollar. However, when bilateral trade volume is used to calculate weights, the resulting order is the Australian Dollar, Singapore Dollar, British Pound, and Indian Rupee. Lastly, when the competition of a third party market is considered, the results change again: Australian Dollar, Indian Rupee, British Pound, and Singapore Dollar.

In order to clarify whether it is appropriate to calculate basket currency weights in 2012 based on trade statistics from 2011, we, according to global trade statistics from 2006 to 2011, calculate the multinational competitiveness trade weights of a broad basket of currencies by considering competition in a third party market. As shown in Figure 6.3, the US Dollar's weight in the broad basket decreases year by year, and the weight of the Japanese Yen is similar to that of the US Dollar. At the same time, the weight of the Euro in the RMB broad basket of exchange rate index from 2006 to 2010 increased remarkably, but decreased in 2011 because of the European debt crisis, before returning to previous levels in 2012. Although there is some change in weights, the weights of the four currencies (US Dollar, Euro, Japanese Yen and Korean Won) in the narrow basket are far larger than those of the other four currencies (British Pound, Singapore Dollar, Indian Rupee, Australian Dollar) in the broad basket. Weights for the British Pound, Singapore Dollar, Indian Rupee and Australian Dollar do not experience large changes in the four year period (2006–2010). However, the weighting of the Australian Dollar does experience a slight increase, due to increasing exports from Australia to China in recent years.

Although weights in the broad basket of currencies have changed in the following six years after exchange rate reform, the largest amount

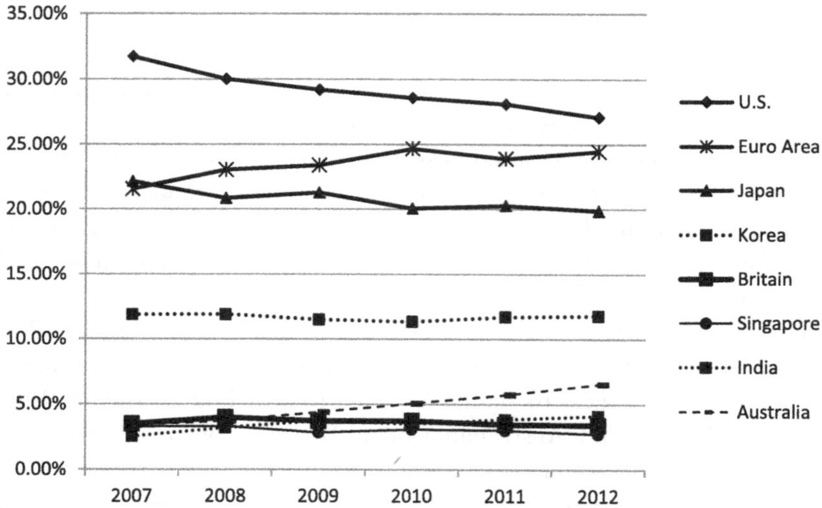

Figure 6.3: Change of Weights in the Broad Basket of Currencies

of variation is not more than five percentage points. In order to ensure the continuity of the basket, major international institutions adjust the exchange rate index on a three to five year cycle. As a result, in the following section we will utilize the weights calculated on the basis of trade in 2011 to compile the RMB exchange rate index.

6.2.5 *Construction of a Basket for the RMB Exchange Rate Index*

6.2.5.1 *RMB Nominal Effective Exchange Rate Index*

We have determined the weights of various currencies in both the narrow and broad baskets, using several methods. However, we think also considering the weights of multinational competitiveness trade in a third-party market better reflects the significance of various currencies to China. Therefore, we also utilize the weights of multinational competitiveness trade when building a basket for the RMB exchange rate index.

On July 21, 2005, the RMB exchange rate was no longer pegged to the Dollar, but instead referred to a basket of currencies. Immediately, the RMB's exchange rate against the Dollar appreciated by 2%. In order to ensure the continuity and stability of the exchange rate index, we choose data from January 2006 as the base period. Taking the exchange rate index of January 2006 as 100 points, we then use a chained index compiling method (widely used around the world) and calculate a weighted geometric average:

$$I_t = I_{t-1} \times \prod_{i=1}^{n} \left(\frac{e_{i,t}}{e_{i,t-1}} \right)^{w_{i,t-1}}$$

In this formula, e stands for the nominal exchange rate, w for currency weights, n for the number of currencies in a basket and I for the exchange rate index.

In order to keep statistical consistency when calculating the REER, in the following section we take the US Dollar as the base currency and utilize Dollar-related data published by the Fed to convert the nominal exchange rate of each country.[2] After synthesizing the RMB nominal exchange rate index of both narrow and broad baskets, we find that the fluctuation trend of the narrow basket's nominal exchange rate is consistent with that of the broad basket. Both trends experienced great fluctuations before the financial crisis, but the fluctuation trend of the narrow basket is obviously smaller than that of broad basket.

6.2.5.2 *RMB Real Effective Exchange Rate Index*

Calculating the REER index is more complicated than calculating the NEER index, because when calculating the former, we have to select the appropriate price conversion deflator (besides determining both the base period and the weighted currency basket). Generally speaking, widely used price conversion deflators include the GDP deflator, CPI, PPI and ULC. Since we are compiling the monthly exchange rate index and ULC of each country (which has a time lag) and since the GDP deflator is calculated differently for each country, we instead select CPI or PPI as the price deflator. There is a strong correlation between CPI and PPI, so this book adopts the IMF's method to compile the exchange rate index of major developed countries. We select the monthly CPI of each country as our price deflator index and still utilize the chained index to build the RMB REER index. The formula is:

$$EI_t = EI_{t-1} \times \prod_{i=1}^{n} \left(\frac{e_{i,t} \cdot P_{0,t}/P_{i,t}}{e_{i,t-1} \cdot P_{0,t-1}/P_{i,t-1}} \right)^{w_{i,t-1}}$$

[2]Data source: https://www.federalreserve.gov/datadownload.

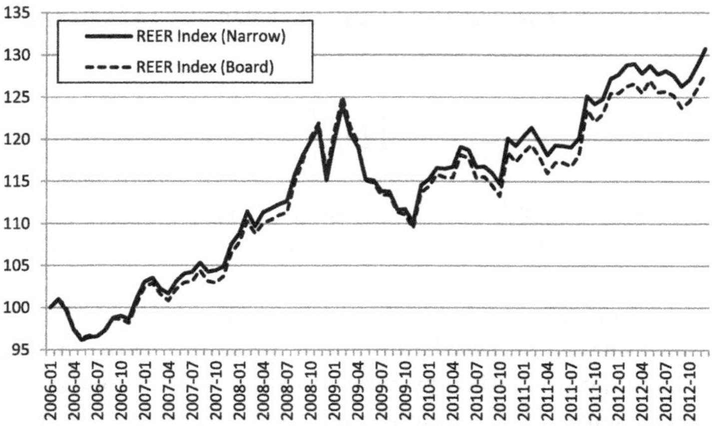

Figure 6.4: RMB REER Index

In this formula, $P_{0,t}$ stands for the price index of the country in the period t, while $P_{i,t}$ stands for the price index of country i in the period t.

We converted the CPI of 9 countries and regions including China into index form with the CPI of January, 2006 as the base period. In addition, for Australia (which only released quarter CPI data), we adopted interpolation to process its data and convert the quarterly data into monthly.

We calculated the RMB REER index for the narrow and broad baskets, respectively. From the result shown in Figure 6.4, we see that the REER index's fluctuation trend is basically consistent with that of the NEER. At the same time, the fluctuation trend of the broad index is smaller than that of the narrow exchange rate index.

If we compare the basket of the RMB exchange rate index compiled in this paper with that of BIS's, we find that the trends of the two indices are nearly the same, but the former index has, on the whole, experienced a greater increase since 2006.

6.3 Calculating the RMB Equilibrium Exchange Rate Index

6.3.1 *ERER Model*

The Equilibrium Real Exchange Rates (ERER) theory was proposed by Sebastian Edwards in 1989 (Edwards, 1989). The equilibrium exchange rate is a kind of exchange rate level which should satisfy the inter-temporal balance of government and the supply-demand balance between tradable and non-tradable goods. The main determinants in the model include: interest rates, import and export commodity prices, import and export tariffs, the price index, the level of outputs, and technological progress, etc.

The ERER model is a simulation of a small country or dependent country — one which is too small to affect its own terms of trade. The signature characteristic of the ERER model is that it takes features of transition economies (i.e., economies of developing countries) into consideration, so it applies to the problem of measuring the equilibrium exchange rate and evaluating the real exchange rate of developing countries. Based on the long-term ERER model, Edwards built a structural dynamics equation for changes in the real exchange rate:

$$\log(e_t) = \theta[\log(e_t^*) - \log(e_{t-1})] - \lambda[Z_t - Z_t^*] + \varphi[\log(E_t) - \log(E_{t-1})] + [PMPT_t - PMPT_{t-1}]$$

In the above equation, e_t stands for the real exchange rate, e_t^* for the ERER, Z_t for the index of macroeconomic policy, Z_t^* for the index of macroeconomic policy on long-term equilibrium level, E for the nominal exchange rate, and $PMPR$ for the differences among foreign exchange rates of parallel markets. In the equation, the first item stands for the automatic adjustment mechanism of the exchange rate, which means the real exchange rate gradually adjusts to the equilibrium exchange rate. The second item stands for the adjustment mechanism of policy, which means macroeconomic variables such as monetary policy and fiscal policy will gradually adjust to a sustainable level. The third item stands for the lag adjustment mechanism and the fourth one stands for the adjustment mechanism, which gradually narrows the differences between exchange rates of coexisting, but different markets of foreign currency. As the equilibrium exchange rate (e_t^*) is the function of the basic economic factors (including terms of trade, capital flow, tariff level, labor productivity and government consumption), we can also express the function as follows:

$$\begin{aligned}\log(e_t) = {} & \beta_1 \log(TOT)_t + \beta_2 \log(NGCGDP)_t + \beta_3 \log(TARIFES) \\ & + \beta_4 \log(TECHPRO)_t + \beta_5 \log(KAPELO)_t + \beta_6 \log(OTHER)_t \\ & - \theta \log(e_{t-1}) - \lambda[Z_t - Z_t^*] + \varphi[\log(E_t) - \log(E_{t-1})] \\ & + [PMPT_t - PMPT_{t-1}] + \mu\end{aligned}$$

In the function, TOT stands for terms of trade, $NGCGDP$ for the ratio of non-tradable commodities consumed by the government against GDP, $TARIFES$ for tariff level, $TECHPRO$ for technological progress, $KAPELO$ for capital flow and $OTHER$ for other basic factors.

6.3.2 Selections for the Fundamental Indicators

Based on Edwards' model — and combining characteristics of China's economic system — we have selected the following variables and elements that affect China's real exchange rate.

Economic openness (OPEN): (export volume + import volume)/GDP, namely the share of import-export volume to GDP. Imports and exports are the two important factors affecting the exchange rate. Factors such as trade barriers, tariffs, regulation and export rebates can indirectly affect China's exchange rate level by affecting imports and exports. Openness can embody these influential factors in a comprehensive way. Generally speaking, the higher the level of economic openness, the greater the impact it has on the current account, which can lead to deficits in the current account and subsequently cause currency depreciation and a decrease in the real exchange rate.

Broad money supply (M2): An increase in money supply leads to a rise in prices. If the nominal exchange rate is set firm, the appreciation of the real exchange rate will reduce the competitiveness of export commodities and worsen the current account balance. This will then beg depreciation of the real exchange rate in order to maintain the sustainability of the external balance.

Terms of trade (TOT): Export commodity value/import commodity value. The increase of the ratio of TOT means improvement of TOT. If not, it means the deterioration of TOT. In the long run, if TOT improves, the current account balance will also improve, begging appreciation of the equilibrium exchange rate to maintain the sustainability of the current account balance. Otherwise, TOT will deteriorate, begging depreciation of the equilibrium exchange rate.

The ratio of government expenditures to GDP (GOVG): Government expenditures account for a large part of domestic expenditures and are mainly used in non-tradable commodity consumption (commodities and labor services consumed at home). Thus an increase in government expenditures will stimulate a relative increase in the supply of non-tradable commodities, which will cause a rise in their relative price and in the real exchange rate. Statistics on government expenditures in non-tradable commodities is unavailable, so it will be replaced by total government expenditure. That is to say, the government expenditures level is equal to the ratio of total government expenditure to GDP.

Net foreign assets (NFA): They mainly includes foreign exchange reserves and gold. If NFA increases, the current account balance will improve, which begs appreciation of the equilibrium exchange rate to maintain the sustainability of the external balance. Otherwise NFA decreases, which begs depreciation of the equilibrium exchange rate.

Technological progress (TECH): Total factor productivity (TFP), calculated based on a production function.

Debt servicing ratio (DEBT): Principal and interest of external loan servicing/foreign exchange earnings.

Domestic excessive credit supply (EXC): The growth rate of credit/ growth rate of GDP.

The ratio of the financial deficit to high-powered money (DEH): financial deficit/M2.

According to related studies (both at home and abroad), we conclude that the fundamental factors affecting the real exchange rate in the ERER (and their direction) are as follows:

(1) Labor productivity (+) and total factor productivity (+)
(2) Terms of trade (+) and trade openness (−)
(3) Net foreign assets (+) and debt servicing rate (+)
(4) Money supply (−)
(5) Government expenditures on non-tradable commodities (+)
(6) Domestic investment rate (+) and foreign direct investment (+)
(7) Relative price of non-tradable commodities (+)

6.3.3 *Statistical Process and Model Construction*

Some indices of the fundamental index (such as total factor productivity and the debt servicing ratio) are annual indices. If they are included in the model, the sample size is too small to properly construct the model. As a result, when we construct the final model, we only take the following factors into consideration: OPEN, M2, TOT, GOVG, NFA and EXC. We select the broad RMB REER index compiled previously as the real exchange rate. In order to ensure the model's stability, we adopt statistics from after the 2005 exchange rate reform. The sample range is from the first quarter in 2006 to the fourth quarter in 2012. After basic statistics from the Wind financial database[3] are processed, they become the fundamental statistics that we need.

After logging the data of all variables used in the unit root test, we find that the raw data fails the unit root test, but the first difference data passes the test. Thus all data becomes integrated at the 5% significance level. The results of the unit root test are shown in Table 6.4.

Table 6.4: Unit Root Test of Variables

Null hypothesis: D(OPEN) with unit root
exogenesis: constant
Length of lag phase: 0 (based on SIC principle, the longest lag phase is 5)

		t Statistic	Probability*
ADF test	—	−4.401337	0.0022
Test statistics:	1%	−3.737853	—
	5%	−2.991878	—
	10%	−2.635542	—

Null hypothesis: D(M2) with unit root
exogenesis: constant
Length of lag phase: 0 (based on SIC principle, the longest lag phase is 5)

		t Statistic	Probability*
ADF test	—	−3.068551	0.0427
Test statistics:	1%	−3.737853	—
	5%	−2.991878	—
	10%	−2.635542	—

Null hypothesis: D(TOT) with unit root
exogenesis: constant
Length of lag phase: 0 (based on SIC principle, the longest lag phase is 5)

		t Statistic	Probability*
ADF test	—	−5.549678	0.0001
Test statistics:	1%	−3.737853	—
	5%	−2.991878	—
	10%	−2.635542	—

(*Continued*)

[3]For information about the database, please visit http://www.wind.com.cn/En/Default.aspx.

Table 6.4: (*Continued*)

Null hypothesis: D(GOVG) with unit root
exogenesis: constant
Length of lag phase: 0 (based on SIC principle, the longest lag phase is 5)

		t Statistic	Probability*
ADF test	—	−14.12276	0.0000
Test statistics:	1%	−3.788030	—
	5%	−3.012363	—
	10%	−2.646119	—

Null hypothesis: D(NFA) with unit root
exogenesis: constant
Length of lag phase: 0 (based on SIC principle, the longest lag phase is 5)

		t Statistic	Probability*
ADF test	—	−3.156095	0.0357
Test statistics:	1%	−3.737853	—
	5%	−2.991878	—
	10%	−2.635542	—

Null hypothesis: D(EXC) with unit root
exogenesis: constant
Length of lag phase: 0 (based on SIC principle, the longest lag phase is 5)

		t Statistic	Probability*
ADF test	—	−3.865817	0.0075
Test statistics:	1%	−3.737853	—
	5%	−2.991878	—
	10%	−2.635542	—

Null hypothesis: D(INDEX) with unit root
exogenesis: constant
Length of lag phase: 0 (based on SIC principle, the longest lag phase is 5)

		t Statistic	Probability*
ADF test	—	−4.930701	0.0006
Test statistics:	1%	−3.737853	—
	5%	−2.991878	—
	10%	−2.635542	—

*: Significance level for all the tests is at 5%.

We construct the ECM model with the Engle–Granger (EG) two-step method. The Real equilibrium exchange rate is the function of each fundamental index:

$$\text{lERER} = \text{f}(\text{OPEN}, \text{M2}, \text{TOT}, \text{GOVG}, \text{NFA}, \text{EXC})$$

6.3.4 *Model Results*

6.3.4.1 *Long-term Equilibrium Equation*

First, we construct a multiple regression model by regarding the ERER index as the dependent variable and other fundamental statistics as independent variables. The result is shown in Table 6.5. Although the results of the model fitting are good and can pass the F test, the coefficients of some independent variables are not notable. These independent variables include EXC, GOVG and TOT. If we eliminate these variables and rerun the regression analysis, the new result is shown in Table 6.6. The remaining three independent variables can pass significance testing and the result of the overall model fitting is acceptable. We thus have the following regression function:

$$\begin{aligned}\text{LNREER\_LN\_SA} = {} & -0.2473 * \text{LNM2} + 0.1155 * \text{LNNFA} \\ & - 0.4886 * \text{LNOPEN} + 3.1729\end{aligned}$$

Table 6.5: Result of the Multiple Regression Model

	Coefficients	Standard Error	*t* Statistic	Probability
Constants	2.923846	0.345787	8.455625	0.0000
LNEXC	−0.004392	0.025244	−0.174003	0.8637
LNGOVG	−0.026478	0.063274	−0.418461	0.6803
LNM2	−0.248637	0.062967	−3.948686	0.0009
LNNFA	0.139706	0.038883	3.593000	0.0019
LNOPEN	−0.471242	0.110631	−4.259597	0.0004
LNTOT	0.117785	0.125968	0.935039	0.3615
R-square	0.955920	—	—	—
Adjusted R-square	0.942000	—	—	—
Standard Deviation of Regression	0.025362	—	—	—
Residual Sum of Squares	0.012221	—	—	—
F statistic	68.67292	—	—	—
Probability (F statistic)	0.000000	—	—	—

Table 6.6: Result of the Multiple Regression Model after Eliminating Variables

	Coefficients	Standard Error	t Statistic	Probability
Constants	3.172872	0.104544	30.34966	0.0000
LNM2	−0.247344	0.048599	−5.089518	0.0000
LNNFA	0.115476	0.026457	4.364684	0.0002
LNOPEN	−0.488610	0.097513	−5.010729	0.0001
R-square	0.952968	—	—	—
Adjusted R-square	0.946555	—	—	—
Standard Deviation of Regression	0.024346	—	—	—
Residual Sum of Squares	0.013039	—	—	—
F statistic	148.5904	—	—	—
Probability (F statistic)	0.000000	—	—	—

Table 6.7: The Stationary Test of Residual Terms

		t Statistic	Probability*
ADF test	—	−3.167378	0.0343
Test statistic:	1%	−3.724070	—
	5%	−2.986225	—
	10%	−2.632604	—

*: Significance level is at 5%.

This regression function is a long-term equilibrium one. It reflects the long-term equilibrium relationship between the RMB equilibrium exchange rate and these basic economic variables. The estimated results show that NFA has a positive influence on the RMB REER while OPENNESS and M2 have a negative influence. The result is in line with that of classical theory.

6.3.4.2 *Short-term Dynamical Equation*

We define the residual as ECM and conduct a stationary test with it. The result is shown in Table 6.7. The t statistic tested by ADF is −3.167378. Falling under the significance level of 5%, it is against the original hypothesis — namely that the residual sequence is stable. So the long-term equilibrium relationship is tenable.

So, we can build a short-term dynamical equation. With the first difference of the REER index as the dependent variable and the first

Table 6.8: The Short-term Dynamic Equation

	Coefficients	Standard Error	t Statistic	Probability
Constants	0.015035	0.007579	1.983640	0.0612
ECM(−1)	−0.678848	0.208598	−3.254328	0.0040
DLNM2	−0.147553	0.049663	−2.971115	0.0076
DLNNFA	−0.146361	0.117347	−1.247252	0.2267
DLNOPEN	−0.346921	0.072464	−4.787474	0.0001
R-square	0.631350	—	—	—
Adjusted R-square	0.557621	—	—	—
Standard Deviation of Regression	0.019126	—	—	—
Residual Sum of Squares	0.007316	—	—	—
F Statistic	8.563017	—	—	—
Probability (F Statistic)	0.000339	—	—	—

lagged terms of the residual term EMC and other fundamental variables as independent variables, we can build a multiple regression equation. The fit result of this model is shown in Table 6.8.

The error correction model combines both short- and long-term variable parameters, describing the adjustment mechanism of the negative influence that the long-term equilibrium relationship between variables has on short-term changes. The results show that the modulus of elasticity of the first lagged error correction term is −0.678848, reflecting that the model has a dynamic self-correction mechanism. The absolute value of the coefficients reflects the strength of self-correction function of the model.

6.3.4.3 *The Long-term Equilibrium of Fundamental Factors*

We can calculate the long-term trend of the RMB equilibrium exchange rate index based on the relationship between the RMB REER and each variable in the long-term equilibrium equation. However, the equation fails to solve the problem of whether each factor itself is in equilibrium. So we have to process each variable to know its long-term trend, for the purpose of calculating the long-term equilibrium exchange rate. This book adopts the Hodrick–Prescott filter (HP filter) method to smooth each variable and then calculates the long-term trend value of the RMB equilibrium exchange rate according to that of each variable. After applying the HP filter, the long-term trend of each variable is shown as follows (Figure 6.5):

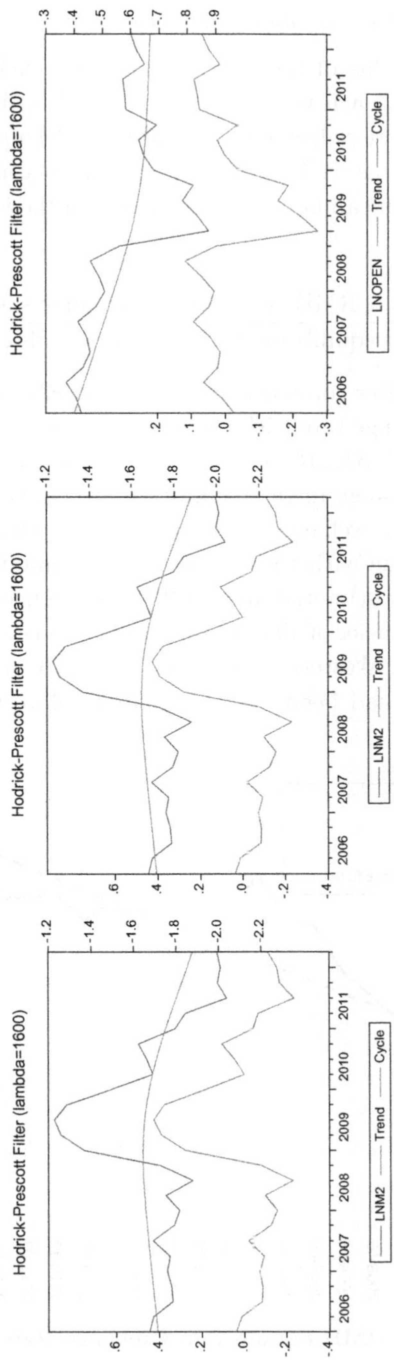

Figure 6.5: HP Filtering of Fundamental Factors

6.3.4.4 *RMB Equilibrium Exchange Rate Index*

The long-term trend value of the RMB equilibrium exchange rate can be calculated according to each variable. The comparison between the RMB equilibrium exchange rate reflected by the ECM model and the REER index processed by HP filter, as well as the REER, is shown in Figure 6.6. The degree of overestimation can be calculated based on the following equation:

$$\text{Overestimation} = \frac{\text{RMB REER} - \text{RMB equilibrium exchange rate index}}{\text{RMB equilibrium exchange rate index}} \times 100\%$$

From Figure 6.6, after comparing the RMB REER and the RMB long-term equilibrium exchange rate with the filtered equilibrium exchange rate, we find that the RMB REER always fluctuates around the equilibrium exchange rate and a change in the equilibrium exchange rate always leads to a change in the real exchange rate, proving that changes in the RMB exchange rate are in line with those of macroeconomic factors. The RMB exchange rate was overestimated around 2009. Influenced by the financial crisis of that year, currencies of all major economies were depreciated. Under the pressure of US-led Western countries, the RMB appreciated against the Dollar. The RMB had been underestimated before the crisis and has

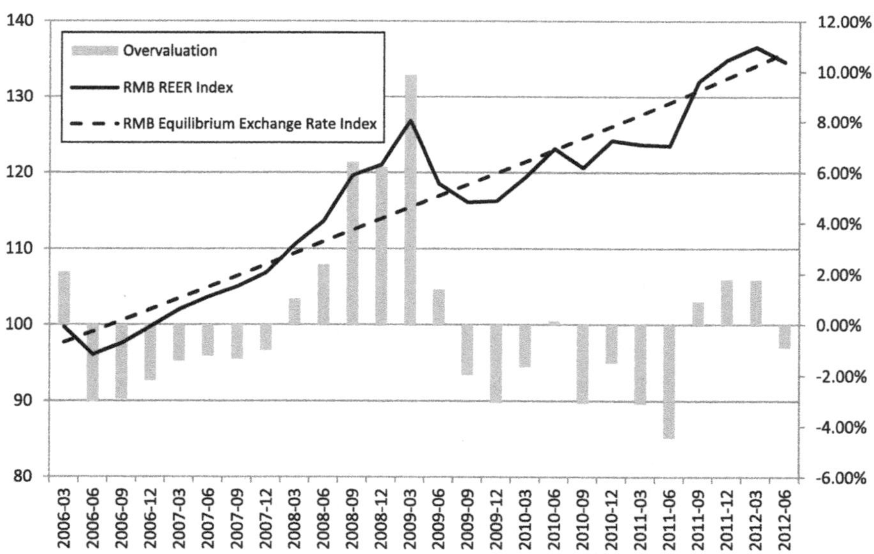

Figure 6.6: RMB Equilibrium Exchange Rate Index

remained so afterwards, but the underestimation was not so great. During the period from the first quarter in 2006 to the fourth quarter in 2012, the RMB REER was overestimated by 4.4% (which took place in the second quarter in 2011). In fact, the RMB has been appreciating consistently over time. After it experienced a fast appreciation around 2009, it could hardly be substantially undervalued.

6.4 Conversion of the RMB Equilibrium Exchange Rate to the Central Exchange Rate

6.4.1 *Conversion of the Multilateral Equilibrium Exchange Rate to Unilateral Equilibrium*

What we found in the above section is the equilibrium exchange rate index, which could serve as the reference standard (the central rate of RMB against a basket of currencies) to determine the central rate. However, in the real management of an exchange rate, it is always necessary to determine the unilateral central rate, such as the central rate of the RMB against the Dollar. This requires us to calculate the unilateral equilibrium exchange rate. In the following section, we will take the equilibrium of the RMB against the Dollar as an example.

According to the method used previously for calculating the equilibrium exchange rate index, we construct the long-term equilibrium equation of the RMB against the Dollar. After filtering out fundamental variables, we find the fit result shown in Table 6.9. Compared with the fit result of the REER index calculated previously (and in addition to the three

Table 6.9: The Result for the Long-term Equilibrium Equation of the RMB against the US Dollar

	Coefficients	Standard Error	t Statistic	Probability
Constants	3.260025	0.053014	61.49317	0.0000
LNM2	0.114616	0.028271	4.054173	0.0006
LNNFA	−0.145623	0.013417	−10.85403	0.0000
LNOPEN	0.143022	0.049453	2.892051	0.0087
LNEXC	−0.026810	0.009131	−2.936229	0.0079
R-square	0.979041	—	—	—
Adjusted R-square	0.975049	—	—	—
Standard Deviation of Regression	0.012325	—	—	—
Residual Sum of Squares	0.003190	—	—	—
F Statistic	245.2439	—	—	—
Probability (F statistic)	0.000000	—	—	—

variables: M2, NFA, and OPEN), EXC also appears in this equation. The regression coefficients of M2 and OPEN are negative while those of NFA and EXC are positive, which is in line with economic significance (Because of the exchange rate from domestic currency valuation, the sign symbols of the regression coefficients are opposite to those before). All the coefficients in the model pass the significance test. R-square in the equation can reach 0.979, and the fit equation can also pass the F test. So, the long-term equilibrium equation of the RMB against the Dollar is:

$$\begin{aligned} \text{LNUSD} &= 3.26 + 0.1146\ \text{LNM2} - 0.1456\ \text{LNNFA} \\ &\quad + 0.143\ \text{LNOPEN} - 0.0268\ \text{LNEXC} \end{aligned}$$

Similarly, we can find the long-term trend of each variable after processing them with the HP filter. Then we can calculate the long-term equilibrium exchange rate of the RMB against the Dollar. M2, NFA and OPEN have already been decomposed with HP filter, and the decomposition results of EXC are shown in Figure 6.7.

The unilateral equilibrium exchange rate of the RMB against the Dollar can be calculated based on the trend terms of each fundamental variable. The comparison between the equilibrium exchange rate and the real exchange rate is shown in Figure 6.8. Similar to the multilateral exchange rate, under the pressure of US-led Western countries, the exchange rate of the RMB against the Dollar was appreciated dramatically during 2008–2009, leading to overvaluation. At other times, the rate was undervalued to some extent, but the magnitude of undervaluation was relatively low,

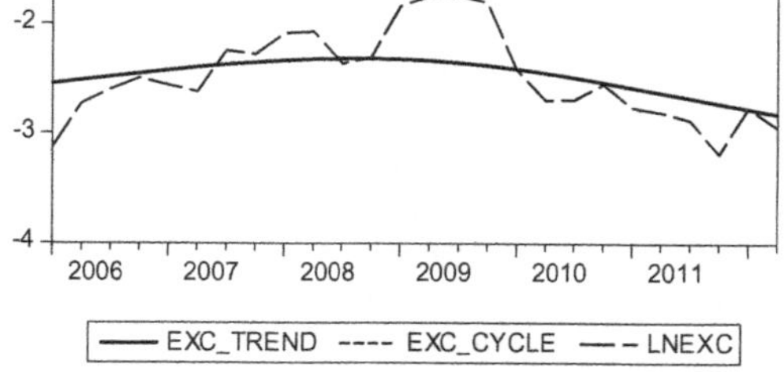

Figure 6.7: HP Filtering of EXC Factor

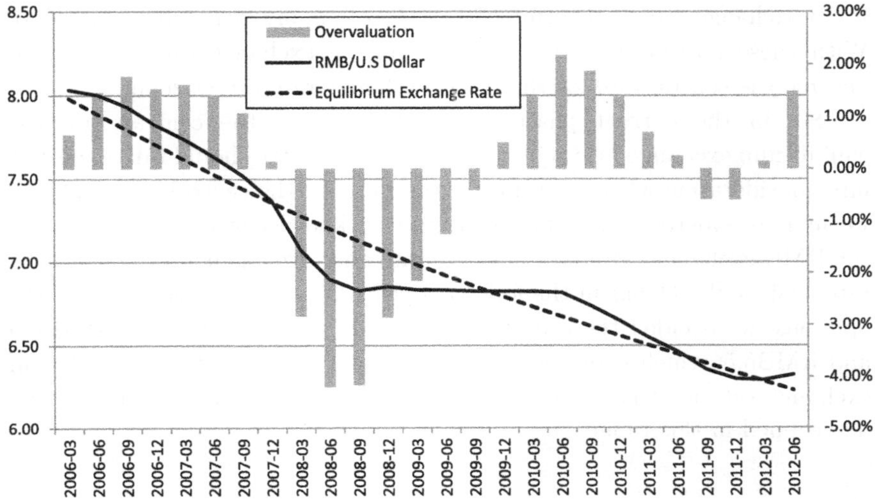

Figure 6.8: The Equilibrium Exchange Rate of the RMB against the Dollar

with the highest magnitude reaching only 2.16%. In 2012, the equilibrium exchange rate of the RMB against the Dollar was about RMB6.2–6.3 to USD$1.

6.4.2 *The Relationship between the Unilateral Equilibrium Exchange Rate and the Central Rate*

The author holds the view that in the initial stage of constructing the exchange rate target zone, it is not proper to strictly adopt the equilibrium exchange rate as the central rate. There are several reasons for this. First, China is not yet ready to form a foundation for the RMB equilibrium exchange rate model to be accepted. Second, the stability of the RMB exchange rate is primary. China can use an exchange rate referenced to a basket of currencies to achieve a smooth, stable transition towards a flexible exchange rate target zone. In the adjustment stage, when extending the target zone, the central rate can slowly change to the equilibrium exchange rate, based on the situation at hand, while ultimately driving the whole target zone towards its objective. In the integration stage of the exchange rate target zone, the central rate should approach the equilibrium exchange rate (Cheng, 2010b). As reform is deepened, opening is extended, and the socialist market economy is improved, the lack of diversified market entities and the central bank's monopoly in markets is bound to gradually change. Only when enterprises and banks become market entities can the

RMB exchange rate be determined based on a supply–demand relationship. With these reforms in place, the equilibrium exchange rate is likely to become the central rate for the RMB exchange rate target zone.

So, in the current phase, when determining the central rate the equilibrium exchange rate is just a reference value. We should take expertise into consideration when determining the range of the central rate. In 2010, we invited experts and administrators with knowledge and experience in the RMB exchange rate to discuss the rate and give a general range for the rate against the Dollar in the following year (2011). After assembling their opinions, we decided the central rate should be a value between RMB6.0 and RMB6.5, which is in line with the calculated result of the equilibrium exchange rate for that year. The specific value of the central rate can be determined in this range.

Bibliography

In English

Anderson J. (2006). *The Complete RMB Handbook*, 4th ed. Hong Kong: UBS.

Apte P., Sercu P., and Uppal R. (1996). The Equilibrium Approach to Exchange Rates: Theory and Tests. NBER Working Paper No. 5748.

Backus D. K. and Smith G. W. (1993). Consumption and real exchange rates in dynamic economies with non-traded goods. *Journal of International Economics*, 35(3–4): 297–316.

Bartolini L. (1993). Devaluation and Competitiveness in a Small Open Economy: Ireland 1987–1993. IMF Working Paper No. 93/82.

Bekaert G. (1994). Exchange Rate Volatility and Deviations from Unbiasedness in a Cash-in Advance Model. *Journal of International Economics*, 36(1–2): 29–52.

Bénassy-Quéré A., Amina L., and Valérie M. (2006). World Consistent Equilibrium Exchange Rates. Paris: CEPII Working Paper No. 2006-20.

Bénassy-Quéré A., Pascale D., Amina L., and Valérie M. (2004). Burden Sharing and Exchange Rate Misalignments Within the Group of Twenty. In Bergsten C. F. and Williamson J., eds., *Dollar Adjustment: How Far? Against What?*, 69–94. Washington D.C.: Peterson Institute for International Economics.

Bosworth B. (2004). Valuing the Renminbi. Paper Presented to the Tokyo Club Research Meeting.

Cheung Y., Menzie D. C., and Eiji F. (2007). The Overvaluation of Renminbi Undervaluation. NBER Working Paper No. 12850.

Clark P. and MacDonald R. (1998). Exchange Rates and Economic Fundamentals — A Methodological Comparison of BEERs and FEERs. IMF Working Papers 98/67, Washington D.C.: International Monetary Fund.

Cline W. R. and Williamson J. (2008). Estimate of the Equilibrium Exchange Rate of the Renminbi: Is There a Consensus and If Not, Why Not?.

In Goldstein M. and Lardy N. R., eds., *Debating China's Exchange Rate Policy*, 131–168. Washington D.C.: Peterson Institute for International Economics.

Cline W. R. and Williamson J. (2009). Estimates of Fundamental Equilibrium Exchange Rates. Policy Brief 09-10, Washington: Peterson Institute for International Economics.

Coudert V. and Cécile C. (2005). Real Equilibrium Exchange Rates in China. CEPII Working Paper No. 2005-01.

Domowitz I. and Hakkio C. (1985). Conditional Variance and the Risk Premium in the Foreign Exchange Market. *Journal of International Economics*, 19(1–2): 47–66.

Dornbusch R. (1976). Expectations and Exchange Rate Dynamics. *Journal of Political Economy*, 84(6): 1161–1176.

Dumas B. (1992). Dynamic Equilibrium and the Real Exchange Rate in a Spatially Separated World. *The Review of Financial Studies*, 5(2): 153–180.

Edwards S. (1988). Exchange Rate Misalignment in Developing Countries. Washington D.C.: The World Bank.

Edwards S. (1989). Real Exchange Rates in the Developing Countries: Concepts and Measurement. Working Paper No. 2950. NBER.

Engel C. M. (1992a). On the Foreign Exchange Risk Premium in a General Equilibrium Model. *Journal of International Economics*, 32(3–4): 305–319.

Engel C. M. (1992b). The Risk Premium and the Liquidity Premium in Foreign Exchange Markets. *International Economic Review*, 33(4): 871–879.

Frankel J. (2006). On the Yuan: The Choice between Adjustment under a Fixed Exchange Rate and Adjustment under a Flexible Rate. *CESifo Economic Studies*, 2006.

Funke M. and Jőrg R. (2005). Just How Undervalued is the Chinese Renminbi?. *The World Economy*, 28(4): 465–489.

Goldstein M. (2004). Adjusting China's Exchange Rate Policies. Paper Presented to the IMF Seminar on China's Foreign Exchange System at Dalian, China, May.

Goldstein M. and Nicholas L. (2006). China's Exchange Rate Policy Dilemma. *American Economic Review*, 2006, 96(2): 422–426.

Goldstein M. and Nicholas L. (2007). China's Exchange Rate Policy: An Overview of Some Key Issues. Paper Prepared for the Conference on China's Exchange Rate Policy, Peterson Institute for International Economics, Washington, October 19.

Hodrick R. J. and Srivastava S. (1986). The Covariation of Risk Premiums and Expected Future Exchange Rates. *Journal of International Money and Finance*, 1986, 5(Supplement): S5-21.

Jeong S. and Jacques M. (2003). Exchange Rate Regimes and Equilibrium Exchange Rates in East Asia. *Revue économique*, 54(5): 1161–1182.

Kristian N. (2004). Do Fundamentals Explain the Behavior of the Swedish Real Effective Exchange Rate? *Scandinavian Journal of Economics*, 106(4): 603–622.

Lipschitz L. and McDonald D. (1992). Real Exchange Rates and Competitiveness. *Empirica*, 19(1): 37–69.

Lucas R. (1982). Interest Rates and Currency Prices in a Two-Country World. *Journal of Monetary Economics*, 10(3): 335–359.

MacDonald R. and Preethike D. (2007). BEER Estimates and Target Current Account Imbalances. Paper Presented to a Workshop at the Peterson Institute for International Economics sponsored by Bruegel, KIEP, and the Peterson Institute for International Economics, February.

Marsh I. W. and Tokarick S. P. (1996). An Assessment of Three Measures of Competitiveness. *Review of World Economics*, 132(4): 700–722.

Maxwell O. (2004). Measuring the Real Effective Exchange Rate (REER) in Ghana. Credit Research Paper of Centre for Research in Economic Development and International Trade, University of Nottingham.

McGuirk A. K. (1987). Measuring Price Competitiveness for Industrial Country Trade in Manufactures. IMF Working Paper No. 87/34.

San S. F., Klau M., Ma G. and McCauley R. (2005). Effective Exchange Rates in Asia with Entrepot and Growing Intra-Regional Trade. Paper presented at the joint BIS/SAFE Seminar on "Effective Exchange Rates: International Experience" in Beijing.

Sercu P., Van Hulle C., and Uppal R. (1995). The Exchange Rate in the Presence of Transaction Costs: Implications for Tests of Relative Purchasing Power Parity. *Journal of Finance*, 50(4): 1309–1319.

Stein J. L. (1994). The Natural Real Exchange Rate of the U.S. Dollar and Determinants of Capital Flows. In Williamson J., ed., *Estimating Equilibrium Exchange Rates*. Washington D.C.: Peterson Institute for International Economics.

Stockman A. and Dellas H. (1989). International Portfolio Nondiversification and Exchange Rate Variability. *Journal of International Economics*, 26(3–4): 261–290.

Stockman A. C. (1980). A Theory of Exchange Rate Determination. *Journal of Political Economy*, 88(4): 673–698.

Stolper T. and Fuentes M. (2007). GSDEER and Trade Elasticities. Paper Presented to a Workshop at the Peterson Institute for International Economics sponsored by Bruegel, KIEP, and the Peterson Institute for International Economics, February.

Stulz R. (1987). An Equilibrium Model of Exchange Rate Determination and Asset Pricing with Nontraded Goods and Imperfect Information. *Journal of Political Economy*, 95(5): 1024–1040.

Svensson L. E. O. (1985a). Currency prices, terms of Trade, and Interest Rates: A General Equilibrium Asset Pricing Cash-in-Advance Approach. *Journal of International Economics*, 18(1–2): 17–42.

Svensson L. E. O. (1985b). Money and Asset Prices in a Cash-in-Advance Economy. *Journal of Political Economy*, 1985, 93(5): 919–944.

Turner P. and Van't Dack J. (1993). Measuring International Price and Cost Competitiveness. BIS Economic Papers, No. 39, Basel.

Turnovsky S. J. (1982). A Determination of the Optimal Currency Basket. *Journal of International Economics*, 12(5): 333–354.

Wang T. (2004). Exchange Rate Dynamics. In Prasad E., ed., *China's Growth and Integration into the World Economy: Prospects and Challenges*. IMF Occasional Paper No. 232, Washington D.C.: International Monetary Fund.

Wren-Lewis S. (2004). The Needed Changes in Bilateral Exchange Rates. In Bergsten C. F. and Williamson J., eds., *Dollar Adjustment: How Far? Against What?*. Washington D.C.: Peterson Institute for International Economics.

Williamson J. (1983). *The Exchange Rate System*. Washington D.C.: Peterson Institute for International Economics.

Zhang Z. C. (2001). Real Exchange Rate Misalignment in China: An Empirical Investigation. *Journal of Comparative Economics*, 29(1): 80–94.

In Chinese

Ba S. S., Wu B., and Zhu Y. Q. (2007). Analysis on Estimation of RMB Real Exchange Rate and Its Impact on International Trade and Foreign Exchange Reserves after Exchange Rate System Reform. *Studies of International Finance*, 4: 56–62.

Cheng S. W. (2010a). The Next Step for Reform of RMB Exchange Rate System: Establishing Flexible Double Target Zone for RMB Exchange Rate (I). *Economic Affairs*, 1: 4–10.

Cheng S. W. (2010b). The Next Step for Reform of RMB Exchange Rate System: Establishing Flexible Double Target Zone for RMB Exchange Rate (II). *Economic Affairs*, 2: 4–14.

Chu Y. Y. (2004). Empirical Study on RMB Equilibrium Exchange Rate. *Studies of International Finance*, 5: 19–24.

Ding J. P. and Zhou J. F. (2009). Research on Properties of Currency Exchange Rate from Multi-Standard Perspective. *Journal of Financial Research*, 12: 45–58.

Hu Y. C. and Zeng C. (2004). The Realistic Choice and Regulation of Exchange Rate Regime in China. *Journal of Financial Research*, 12: 59–74.

Jiang B. K. (2007). New Exploration on the Theory and Policy Framework of Equilibrium Exchange Rate. *Southeast Academic Research*, 2: 96–102.

Jin Z. X. (1995). On Reform of Chinese Real Exchange Rate Management. *Economic Research Journal*, 3: 63–71.

Lin B. Q. (2002). Estimating RMB Equilibrium Real Exchange Rate and Measuring Real Exchange Rate Misalignment. *Economic Research Journal*, 12: 60–69.

Qin D. and He X. H. (2010). Measurement of RMB Exchange Rate Imbalance: Definition, Calculation Method and Empirical Analysis. *The Journal of World Economy*, (3): 3–24.

Shi J. H. and Yu H. F. (2005). Renminbi Equilibrium Exchange Rate and China's Exchange Rate Misalignment: 1991–2004. *Economic Research Journal*, 4: 34–45.

Wan Z. X. (2004). Research on RMB Exchange Rate Based on Trend of Real Effective Exchange Rate. *Quantitative & Technical Economics*, 2: 5–15.

Wang H. M. and Ren R. E. (2003). Research on Real Effective Exchange Rate based on International Competitiveness Index Using ULC. *Productivity Research*, 1: 94–96.

Williamson J. (2003). The RMB Exchange Rate and Global Monetary System. *Studies of International Finance*, 12: 53–56.

Yang C. J. (2002). *Study on the Long-term Trend of RMB Exchange Rate Adjustment*. Shanghai: Shanghai University of Finance & Economics Press.

Zhang B. (2005). RMB's Real Exchange Rate: Concept, Measurement and Decomposition. *China Economic Quarterly*, 2: 317–334.

Zhang H. J. (2005). Determination for the Structure and Weight of RMB Effective Exchange Rate Index in the Transition Period. *Journal of the University of Petroleum*, 21(3): 18–23.

Zhang X. P. (1999). The Theory and Model of RMB Equilibrium Exchange Rate. *Economic Research Journal*, 12: 70–77.

Zhang X. P. (2000). Balance and Imbalance: Reasonable Evaluation for 1978–1999 RMB Exchange Rate. *Journal of Finance*, 8: 13–24.

Zhou Z. G. (2007). Choice of Construction Method for RMB Real Exchange Rate Index. *Statistical Education*, 12: 14–15.

Chapter 7

The Opening Up of Capital Account

7.1 The Definition and Trend of Capital Account Opening

7.1.1 *The Definition of Capital Account Openness*

The capital account — the capital and financial account of a country's balance of international payments — records transfers of financial capital between one country and other countries. Before 1993, the balance of international payments was divided into two major accounts: the current account and the capital account. In 1993, the International Monetary Fund (IMF) updated the content of the capital account and redefined it as the capital and financial account in the fifth edition of the *Balance of Payments Manual* (IMF, 1993). However, the term "capital account" is still in general use. The capital account of the balance of international payments is divided into the capital account and the financial account. The capital account portion consists of capital transfers and the acquisition/disposal of non-produced and non-financial assets; the financial account portion covers all transactions associated with changes of ownership in the foreign financial assets and liabilities of an economy (mainly including direct investment, portfolio investment, other investment and reserve assets).

Opening the capital account refers to relaxing controls on the transactions under the capital account. Controls include prohibiting the free flow of capital, differentiated levying of tax and fees, and the pre-registered approval. The goal of opening up the capital account is to realize capital account liberalization (Shi, 2007). During the opening-up process, capital controls are relaxed in a gradual way, residents and non-residents are allowed to hold cross-border assets and engage in cross-border assets transactions, and free currency convertibility is realized.

It is worth mentioning that the concept of "capital account convertibility" is closely related but not equivalent to that of "capital account openness". Capital account convertibility refers to the removal of control, taxation and subsidies of international capital transactions (Quirk and Evans, 1995). According to Jiang and Zou (2002), it refers to "elimination of restrictions imposed on capital account transactions, such as restrictions on currency conversion, international payments and international transactions, to basically realize free capital flows." And as a process, capital account convertibility can also be called capital account liberalization (Jiang and Zhu, 2004). Capital account convertibility emphasizes the removal of restrictions on currency conversion under the capital account while capital account openness places an emphasis on the removal of restrictions on transactions. This difference indicates that the capital account is not always open in the process of capital account convertibility, while capital account convertibility is the prerequisite to capital account openness.

In the *Annual Report on Exchange Arrangements and Exchange Restrictions 2011* (IMF, 2011), or AREAER, the capital account is divided into 7 main categories and 40 sub-accounts. The seven main categories include: capital and money market instruments, derivatives and other instruments, credit operations, direct investment, liquidation of direct investment, real estate transactions and personal capital transactions. The yearly AREAER provides detailed information on changes in capital account restrictions of member countries and records the restrictions imposed on every sub-account under the capital account.

Although the IMF does not require member countries to remove capital controls and realize capital account convertibility, it encourages member countries to loosen capital controls and realize capital account liberalization progressively. On the one hand, capital account openness leads to economic growth and promotes financial depth; on the other hand, it makes the economy of a country more prone to being affected by the international economic factors, meaning that blind capital account openness could even result in a financial crisis. The level of capital account openness varies, which means that not every sub-account under the capital account is fully open. Based on their macroeconomic situation and financial development, many countries more or less impose restrictions on some accounts under the capital account to maintain national security and/or to keep their currency policy independent. Currently, there is not a single country that enjoys a fully open capital account. Countries with highly open capital accounts often impose restrictions to different degrees. For example, non-residents in America are forbidden to purchase stocks of restricted industries within the boundaries of America. The process of capital account openness will proceed step by step. Countries need to make a comprehensive analysis of the drawbacks and benefits before deciding when (and to what extent) to open the capital account.

7.1.2 *Measurement of Capital Account Openness*

Many researchers have measured the extent of capital account openness. Two major methods are recognized, which are the *de jure* measurement of capital account openness and *de facto* measurement of capital account openness. The *de jure* measurement, which includes the binary measurement, share measurement, Quinn measurement and the Organization for Economic Co-operation and Development (OECD)-Share measurement, is based on countries' *de jure* capital account openness and relies on the AREAER. The *de facto* measurement, which includes the measurement of the saving rate–investment rate, the measurement of interest rate parity and the measurement of *de facto* capital scale, is based on the countries' *de facto* capital account openness (Lou and Qian, 2011). The followings gives a brief introduction to these measurements.

7.1.2.1 *The* De Jure *Measurement of Capital Account Openness*

(1) The Binary Measurement

Before 1996, the AREAER provided information about whether countries have imposed capital account restrictions. The binary measurement provided rough descriptions of capital account openness in each country. The value of "0" indicates the presence of capital account restrictions, while the value of "1" indicates the opposite. This measurement provides a general description of each country's situation of capital account restrictions without distinguishing the degrees of capital account restrictions in each country. After 1997, the IMF no longer just simply divided the capital account of each country into restricted capital account and open capital account, but made detailed records of each member country's controls on capital flows.

(2) The Share Measurement

Grilli and Milesi-Ferretti (1995) put forward the share measurement to measure the level of capital account openness. The Share indicator records the proportion of years a country had an open capital account in the sample years. The value of "1" indicates restrictions are non-existent, while the value of "0" indicates complete restrictions. As with the binary measurement, the share measurement is too simple to record the degree of intensity of a country's capital account openness.

(3) The Quinn Measurement

Quinn (1997) divides the capital account into capital inflows and capital outflows, and subdivides the degree of intensity of each part's capital account controls. The value of "0" indicates capital transactions are completely forbidden, "0.5" indicates capital transactions are restricted in volume and with policy, the value of "1" indicates a heavy tax is levied on capital transactions, the value of "1.5" indicates a light tax is levied on capital transactions, and the value of "2" indicates capital transactions are unrestricted. Quinn indicator captures the intensity of capital controls in terms of inflows and outflows of capital account, with a value from 0 to 4. A Quinn value of greater than 2 indicates a relatively open capital account; a value less than 2 indicates a strongly controlled capital account.

(4) The OECD-Share Measurement

The OECD divided capital accounts into 11 sub-accounts, including direct investment, the liquidation of direct investment, the approved access of capital market securities, money market instruments, collective investment securities, real-estate investment, financial credit and loans, and special provisions formulated for commercial banks and other credit institutions or institutional investors. The OECD-Share method first requires data on the level of openness in every sub-account within the sample period. It then divides the sub-accounts into two categories: open accounts and none-open accounts. The average yearly percentage that open capital accounts have taken up in the total 11 capital accounts within the sample period is the OECD-Share index (a value from 0–1). A larger value indicates a higher level of openness.

The above-mentioned measurements of capital account openness are based on each country's capital controls, as enforced by their respective laws and regulations. Due to the insufficient enforcement of regulations and flaws in the management and institutions, the real situation is not what presented to us. For some countries, stronger capital controls are stipulated in law, but in fact there may be large capital flows. The opposite situation also can be observed in many other countries. Therefore, the *de facto* measurement of capital account openness can better reflect one country's level of capital account openness.

7.1.2.2 *The* De Facto *Measurements of Capital Account Openness*

The Measurement of the Saving Rate–Investment Rate

Feldstein and Horioka (1980) tried to describe the level capital account openness with the relationships between saving rate and investment rate in one country. If one country enjoys a high level of capital account openness, the increase in domestic investment will, to the large extent, be sourced from global capital. Thus, no evident relationship between savings and investment is observed in this country. If a country imposes strict controls on its capital account, the investment is mostly sourced from national savings. Thus, savings is highly related to investment.

The Measurement of Interest Rate Parity

This measurement judges the level of free capital flows and then the level of capital account openness in one country by assessing whether the relationship between domestic interest rates and international interest rates conforms to the theory of interest rate parity. According to the theory, under the conditions that there are differences in interest rates between countries, arbitrage activities will facilitate international capital flows to eliminate these differences. The larger the difference between domestic interest rates and international interest rates in a country, the lower its level of capital account openness and the higher its level of capital controls (and vice versa).

7.1.2.3 *The Measurement of* De facto *Capital Scale*

This measurement judges the level of capital flows and calculates the percentage of actual foreign direct investment (FDI), international securities investment, and other international investment taken up in gross domestic product (GDP). If the capital inflows and outflows take up a larger percentage of GDP in a country, this country enjoys a larger scale of capital inflows and outflows with a higher level of capital account openness (and vice versa).

7.1.3 *Capital Account Openness in Major Countries*

The IMF and OECD have made constant efforts in promoting the establishment and perfection of the global financial system since their establishment. Early when the IMF was established, it was stipulated in the Article VIII that "member countries are obliged to realize free currency convertibility under [the] current account", but specific requirements on capital account openness were not included. Member countries which accept Article VIII obligations are called Article VIII countries.

After the 1920s, most of the member countries have realized currency convertibility under their current account. It was then that the IMF began to focus on the monitoring of member countries' capital accounts and pushing forward the policy of gradual capital account openness. In September 1997, the interim committee of the IMF published the "Interim Committee's Letter on the Amendment of IMF Agreement to Realize Free Capital Flows" to include capital flows liberalization in the IMF's principles. This played an important role in the process of promoting global financial liberalization. At the same time, the OECD formulated "The General Rule of Capital Flows Liberalization" and "The General Rule of Intangible Transactions Liberalization" in order to remove trade barriers and promote capital flows. It imposed restrictions on capital account controls, such as controls in the money market, foreign exchange market, and non-residents' credit and deposit accounts. These explicit restrictions promote the deepening financial liberalization in developed economies.

As mentioned previously, capital account openness does not mean that controls imposed on every sub-account are eliminated, but it is a progressive process to fully realize openness. The 2012 AREAER provides information on every member country's capital account controls. We can tell from Table 7.1 that the country with full open capital account does not exist. Among the 192 member countries included in the statistics, 75% of them have imposed controls on portfolio transactions, direct investment, and real estate transactions. Special clauses have also been formulated for commercial banks, other credit institutions and institutional investors. And 50% of member countries have imposed controls on money market instruments, collective investment securities and financial credit.

Table 7.1 shows that among the major developed countries, the United Kingdom enjoys the highest level of capital account openness with some controls on direct investment and special provisions formulated for commercial banks and institutional investors. The United States has been acknowledged to be a country with full capital account openness. However, according to its own macroeconomic development situation and the capacity of its financial system to fight against risks, the US has formulated some restrictive provisions for some sub-accounts under the capital account. For example, it has imposed controls on capital market securities transactions, money market instruments, derivatives, direct investment, and real

Table 7.1: The Capital Account Controls in IMF Member Countries

Accounts	Number of Countries	Developed Countries					BRICS				
		US	Japan	UK	Germany	France	China	India	South Africa	Russia	Brazil
Controls on:											
Capital Market Securities	147	√	√	—	√	√	√	√	√	√	√
Currency Market Instruments	124	√	√	—	√	√	√	√	√	√	√
Collective Investment Securities	123	√	√	—	√	√	√	√	√	√	√
Derivatives and Other Instruments	98	√	√	—	√		√	√	√	—	√
Commercial Credits	83	—	—	—	—	—	√	√	√	—	—
Financial Credits	112	—	√	—	√	—	√	√	√	—	√
Guarantees, Sureties and Financial Backup Facilities	77	√	—	—	—	—	√	√	√	—	
Direct Investment	150	√	√	√	√	√	√	√	√	√	√
Liquidation of Direct Investment	46	—	—	—	—	—	√	√	√	—	—
Real-estate Transactions	145	√	√	—	√	—	√	√	√	—	√
Individual Capitals	94	—	—	—	—	—	√	√	√	—	—
Provisions specific to:											
Commercial Banks and Other Credit Institutions	168	—	—	√	—	√	√	√	√	√	√
Institutional Investors	141	√	√	√	√	√	√	√	√	—	√

Data source: Annual Report on Exchange Arrangements and Exchange Restrictions (IMF, 2012).

estate transactions. Among Brazil, Russia, India, China and South Africa (BRICS), capital account controls are present on a relatively large scale. China, India and South Africa are countries facing low levels of capital account openness, with controls imposed on the sub-accounts under the capital account (as listed by the IMF). Russia, in contrast, enjoys relatively high level of capital account openness.

7.1.4 *The Acceleration of Global Capital Account Openness*

Although each country has imposed controls on its capital account to some extent, based on their respective national conditions, global financial liberalization is in continuous, long-term development and many countries are gradually seeking ways to open their capital account and financial account.

In fact, the opening up of developed countries' capital accounts started from the end of World War II. OECD member countries signed the "OECD Capital Flows Liberalization Agreement", consenting to start liberalizing their capital accounts together. Some countries removed the controls on their capital account in one move, such as Canada, Germany, the UK, Australia and New Zealand. Other countries realized capital account openness in a gradual process. Starting from 1964, Japan took 20 years to progressively realize capital account openness; Denmark started to loosen capital controls from the 1970s and realized capital account openness after 15 years of reform; Holland gradually revoked capital controls from 1977 to 1986. In terms of the sequence to remove controls, most of the OECD countries first removed controls on the transactions directly associated with normal business, with a view to avoiding negative effects from volatile short-term capital flows.

After the end of the 2008 US financial crisis and the European sovereign debt crisis from 2010 to the present, the trend of international capital flows has been in constant change and the international macroeconomic environment is becoming ever-more complicated. Each country, especially emerging market countries, have started to adjust the scope and measures of their capital controls in order to better respond to international financial risks.

In early 2011, there was an influx of international capital to emerging countries — mainly in the form of securities portfolio and bank capital. Many countries adjusted their capital controls to stem the risks brought by these inflows. In the latter half of 2011, the international economic environment was poor, with the large-scale capital flows back to developed countries and many emerging countries responsively adjusting their capital control policies. Specifically, gradually loosened controls on the inflow of capitals and money market instruments can be observed. For example, China started to allow qualified foreign financial institutions to invest in the domestic RMB-denominated securities market, to accelerate the internationalization of the RMB; India raised the ceiling for non-resident investment in government bonds to enhance non-resident investment in domestic securities market; Brazil reduced the tax rate and the levying scope on foreign capital inflows to promote capital inflows. Affected by the international financial crisis, each country's opening process for derivatives market slowed down. However, in terms of direct investment, controls were loosened on capital inflows and outflows. For example, South Africa started to allow direct investment unrelated to existing transactions; China allowed people to directly invest with RMB earned from overseas; Russia allowed international investors to directly invest in domestic strategic industries (nuclear energy, aeronautical technology, and military industry).

To sum up, in the short run, each country is formulating different policies concerning capital account controls based on the international economic environment, their own national conditions and the integrity of their financial system. In the long run, each country, especially the emerging countries, will gradually promote their capital account openness in line with the international drive for financial liberalization.

7.2 The Opening-up Process of the Capital Account in China

In recent years, with deepening financial reform, China has accelerated the opening up process of its capital account. From 2002 to 2012, China implemented more than 50 reform measures concerning the capital account. At the same time, the construction of the RMB off-shore markets in Hong Kong and Singapore have advanced step by step. The business of cross-border RMB trade settlement can be witnessed on a national scale. The RMB is allowed to rise or fall 1% each day around the daily official middle rate against the US Dollar — double its previous trading range of 0.5%. All of these are important measures for the RMB's process of internationalization. The gradual opening up of the capital account is the prerequisite to RMB internationalization. This section will briefly review the history, status quo and significance of capital account openness in China while summarizing various indicators to measure the degree of capital account openness. In addition, analysis on the paths of capital account openness in China in future will be made based on the "three-step strategy" developed by the People's Bank of China (PBOC).

7.2.1 *The History and Status Quo of Capital Account Opening Up in China*

During the opening up process of the capital account, capital controls will be loosened in a gradual way, residents and non-residents will be allowed to hold cross-border assets and engage in cross-border assets transactions, and free currency convertibility will be realized. Specifically, local residents in a country will deal in foreign stocks, bonds and other securities without any restrictions. They will have access to foreign real-estate, long-term equity and loans. Foreign residents in said country will likewise deal in stocks, bonds and other securities without any restrictions. They too will have access to real-estate, long-term equity and loans in-country.

The opening up process for the Chinese economy accompanies the opening up of the capital account. In December 1996, the president of the PBOC wrote to the IMF, announcing that China had accepted the obligations stipulated in the second, third and fourth items of Article VIII in the IMF agreement. That is, China had basically realized free RMB convertibility under the current account. However, the financial market in China is neither sound nor perfect, with weak capability to resist shocks brought by international capital flows. The marketization reform of interest rates and the reform of the exchange rate determination mechanism are not completed. Due to these factors, China still faces a low level of capital account openness.

7.2.1.1 *The History of the Opening Up of China's Capital Account*

China has furthered the opening up of capital account step by step since the dawn of its historic opening up and reform. In 1993, China set the goal to realize RMB convertibility in the long term through reform of the foreign exchange management mechanism. Based on the principle of "inflow first and outflow later; long-term first and short-term later; direct investment first and portfolio later; institutional investors first and individuals later", the RMB's capital account convertibility will be driven step by step, in a planned, prudent way.

The history of capital account openness can be traced back to the period of the opening up and reform. According to Lu, Wang and Qiu (2012), the opening up process of the capital account has undergone four phases.

In the 1980s, China massively supported the use of FDI through the implementation of relevant policies. In 1986, the State Council issued "The Provisions Concerning the Encouragement of FDI Inflows" that loosened restrictions on FDI inflows. China has poured great efforts into, and has witnessed a rapid increase in, FDI inflows over more than a decade — from USD$1.258 billion in 1984 to USD$33.8 billion in 1994. FDI has accounted for the biggest share of China's absorption of foreign investment. Since 1992, China has been the world's largest FDI recipient among developing countries for 20 successive years. To this day, FDI has been one of the major driving forces of economic development in China and the world. Both developed and developing countries regard FDI as a strategic resource worth competitively seeking.

In the mid and late 1990s, China started to value and stimulate Outbound Direct Investment (ODI) with measures supporting and encouraging the "going out" of Chinese enterprises initially formulated. According to the statistics of the United Nations Conference on Trade and Development (UNCTAD), during the early period of the "going out policy", ODI flows into China rapidly increased from USD$0.913 billion in 1991 to USD$5.498 billion in 2004. In 2012, ODI in China reached USD$84.22 billion, which will continue to rise accompanied by the stimulated overseas investment and Merger and Acquisition (M&A) activity of China's corporations.

At the beginning of the 21st century, China eased restrictions step by step on cross-border capital transactions. In 2003, it was further specified at the Third Plenary Session of the 16th Communist Party of China's (CPC) Central Committee that "the restrictions on the cross-border capital transactions should be relaxed selectively and step by step to realize capital account convertibility on the premise of effective resistance against risks." Over more than a decade, the China Securities Regulatory Commission (CSRC) has first implemented the Qualified Foreign Institutional Investor system (QFII) and then the Qualified Domestic Institutional Investor system (QDII). At the same time, the RMB off-shore market was established. In 2003, the PBOC and the Hong Kong Monetary Authority signed the "Mainland and Hong Kong Closer Economic Partnership Arrangement", allowing Hong Kong banks to operate RMB services for individuals. In 2005, the RMB settlement business in Hong Kong was expanded with the

RMB off-shore market in Hong Kong officially being born. Hong Kong has progressively become the major platform for cross-border RMB trade settlement and its role as the RMB's off-shore financial center has become entrenched. In February 2012, a wide range of enterprises dealing in foreign trade and other current account transactions were allowed to settle, price, receive, and pay in RMB. The cross-border trade settlement in RMB has proceeded at full speed. The total amount of RMB trade settlement handled by banks in Hong Kong reached RMB2.63 trillion throughout 2012, accounting for 89.4% of the accumulative settlement amount of actual overseas RMB receipts and payments. Thus, Hong Kong has become the primary platform for cross-border trade settlement in RMB.

The end of the financial crisis has witnessed expanded openness in China's capital account and acceleration of the RMB's internationalization. In October 2010, the decision was made to include the target of "progressively realize capital account convertibility" into the 12th five-year plan on the Fifth Plenary Session of the 17th CPC Central Committee. Events have moved relatively quickly to realize this target. Firstly, there has been a rapid development of cross-border trade settlement in RMB. In July 2009, the RMB clearing and settlement of cross-border trade transactions pilot program was officially launched in five cities, including Shanghai. In March 2012, a wide range of enterprises dealing in foreign trade and other current account transactions were eligible to settle, price, receive, and pay in RMB. Secondly, RMB settlement under the capital account was pushed forward. January 2011 saw the beginning of cross-border RMB settlement for ODI under the capital account. In October of that year, cross-border FDI with RMB commenced. Thirdly, policies were introduced to support the remittance of RMB back to the mainland. RMB deposits in Hong Kong reached RMB603 billion by 2012, and a feasible "remittance scheme" became necessary for the off-shore RMB (Ba, 2012). Channels for off-shore investment with RMB should be widened and on-shore institutions could issue off-shore RMB bonds to remit the off-shore RMB. The accumulative settlement amount of RMB-denominated ODI handled by banks in China reached RMB20.15 billion by 2011 and that of RMB-denominated FDI reached RMB90.72 billion. In January 2012, China allowed RMB Qualified Foreign Institutional Investors (RQFII) to invest in the on-shore bonds market with initial approved capital of RMB20 billion. Mainland institutional investors in Hong Kong have the priority to apply for this new program. Since that time, the remittance scheme under the capital account has been initially established, and the channels for off-shore RMB investment have been increasingly pluralized.

7.2.1.2 *The Status Quo of the Capital Account Openness in China*

With over 30 years of reform, great progress has been made in the opening up of the capital account and the level of RMB capital account convertibility has been obviously promoted in China. Foreign exchange management regime has transferred from "easy inflows and strict outflows" to "two-way balanced management" with administrative controls gradually declining and differential treatment gradually eliminated between domestically-funded enterprises and wholly foreign-owned enterprises, state-owned enterprises and private enterprises, institutions and individuals.

According to the classification in the AREAER 2011 by the IMF (by which the capital account is divided into 7 categories with 40 sub-accounts) and considering China's existing laws, regulations and policies, the PBOC's Financial Survey and Statistics Department has divided the previously mentioned 40 sub-capital accounts into four categories: convertible, basically convertible, partially convertible and non-convertible. At present, although a fully convertible capital account does not exist in China, the non-convertible capital accounts represent a relatively low percentage of total accounts. Please refer to Table 7.2 for the status quo of openness of the 40 sub-accounts.

To the end of 2011, the partially convertible and aforestated RMB sub-accounts represented 90% of total accounts, while non-convertible accounts amounted to only 10% (mainly referring to non-residents engaging in the domestic money market, the trust fund market and the trading of derivatives). There are 22 partially convertible accounts in the Table, totaling 55% and including bond market transactions, stock market transactions, real estate transactions and individual capital transactions. There are also 14 basically convertible accounts which mainly represent transactions of credit operations, direct investment, direct investment liquidation, etc. Currently, China has no fully convertible accounts.

As a whole, China is a country with a relatively high level of capital controls. In 2012, Zhou maintains that China has not realized, but does not refuse to realize, capital account convertibility. Meantime, many researchers maintain that RMB capital account convertibility enjoys a higher level in practical economic terms than the appraised results might suggest.

Firstly, there are several liberal economy zones that reside "within national territory but outside customs territory": Hong Kong, Macau and

Table 7.2: The Specification Sheet of Capital Account Convertibility in China

	Non Convertible	Partially Convertible	Basically Convertible	Fully Convertible	In Total
Transactions of Capital and Money Market Instruments	2	10	4	—	16
Transactions of Derivatives and Other Instruments	2	2	—	—	4
Transactions of Credit Operations	—	1	5	—	6
Direct Investment	—	1	1	—	2
Liquidation of Direct Investment	—	—	1	—	1
Real Estate Transactions	—	2	1	—	3
Personal Capital Transactions	—	6	2	—	8
Subtotal	4	22	14	—	40

Data source: "The Promotion of a More Mature Environment for Capital Account Openness" from the PBOC's Financial Survey and Statistics Department; AREAER (IMF, 2011). "Partially convertible" refers to the existence of strict restrictions on access and credit; "basically convertible" refers to existing but relatively loose restrictions, which can be removed for complete conversion with registration or approval.

Taiwan. Thanks to convenient geography, frequent personnel contacts, and economic and trade exchanges, mainland China can easily trade with enterprises and financial institutions in Hong Kong. Thus, RMB convertibility may enjoy a higher level than the assessed results.

Secondly, as put forward by Wang in 2008 and other researchers, the IMF's qualitative division of capital account transactions into "non-convertible", "partially convertible", "basically convertible" and "fully convertible" solely considers the amount of sub-accounts, but does not consider the scale of these sub-accounts in the international balance of payments. It is difficult to accurately judge the conditions of capital controls without taking scale difference of sub-accounts into consideration. For example, assuming that most of the sub-accounts with a low volume of trade have been liberalized, while few accounts with high volume of trade are still strictly controlled, it is inappropriate to say that China has an overall low level of capital controls.

Moreover, most current accounts have been largely liberalized. Flows of funds under the capital account can proceed in the disguise of transactions under the current account. International companies, in particular, have become the major channel for global trade, providing arbitrage channels for capital between countries. Hence, the real inflow and outflow level of capital accounts may be higher than the assessed results (Ma, 2012a).

7.2.2 *The Measure of Capital Account Openness in China*

De jure and *de facto* measurements were introduced in Section 7.1. They adopt different indicators to reflect the level of capital account openness in a country. The following will summarize the conclusions made by scholars from home and abroad on measurements of capital account openness and analyze the applicability of each measurement for China. Finally, from the perspective of actual capital flows, the capital account openness in China from 1992 to 2012 will be analyzed using the capital flows index, financial market index, and saving–investment correlation index.

7.2.2.1 *The* De Jure *Measurement of Capital Account Openness*

De jure capital account openness, also called legislation-based capital account openness, refers to the qualitative measurement of capital account openness based on the legislation and regulations in a country. It reflects the intensity of a government's control over the capital account. In this measurement, the frequently used indicators to reflect the degree of capital account openness are: the binary dummy variable indicator, Share indicator, Quinn indicator and OECD-Share indicator. The binary dummy variable indicator only roughly measures the restrictions imposed on the capital account, with a value of 0 or 1. It does not distinguish between degrees of restrictions and is thus seldom used in current academic research. The Share indicator and OECD-Share indicator can only reflect the level of capital account openness in a specific period of time. Same as the binary dummy variable indicator, for a single year, the Share indicator just measures whether the restrictions on a capital account (or its sub-account) exist but not distinguishes between the degrees of restrictions, and it does not apply to the conditions of partial capital account controls in China.

The Quinn indicator is often employed in research on capital account openness by foreign scholars. Arteta *et al.* (2001) hold that basically the openness of the capital account is conducive to the increase of per capita income and the deepening of financial reform — both of which promote economic growth. By grading the restrictions of each item under a country's capital account, the Quinn indicator can fairly reveal the status of capital controls of a country with perfect market economy system and controlling capital flows through indirect taxation. But this measurement is hard to apply to China for mainly two reasons. First, China has neither any fully convertible accounts nor many fully inconvertible accounts. Laws and regulations are the major means of imposing quantitative and regulatory restrictions on the capital flows. Second, taxation has never been used in China to restrain capital flows. Therefore, if we use the Quinn indicator to estimate the intensity of China's capital controls, the results from year to year would barely change. But this is obviously inconsistent with China's gradually relaxed capital control system. Thus, the Quinn indicator is not suitable for a country which mainly relies on direct administrative controls, like China (Jin, 2004).

Studies conducted by Chinese scholars discover that, although the aforementioned nominal measurement is crude, it can still show how China's capital account has tended to become increasingly open year by year. Lei and Zhao (2008) used the improved Klein–Olivei index,[1] suggesting a prudent and progressive liberalization of China's capital account. As China's capital account has grown increasingly open since 1996, it reached an average level of openness in 2006. The liberalization of capital account items has followed the principle of opening direct investment before indirect investment, and inflows before outflows. Jin (2004) measured the degree of nominal capital openness and analyzed the changes in China's capital control intensity, concluding that the capital account regime has gone through a "relaxed" (1994–1999), "tight" (1997–1998) and then "relaxed" (1999–2003) transition. Overall, the openness of the capital account has been promoted.

To sum up, traditional nominal measurements, such as the Share and Quinn indicators, are unsuitable for measuring China's capital account openness. Since these measures are based upon a country's legal restrictions on its capital account, they cease to be effective when the national law enforcement is inadequate or capital evades supervision and control by other legal means. Furthermore, even if the laws and regulations of a country are strictly enforced, measurements will be affected by differences in scale

[1]The improved Klein–Olivei index is a kind of Share index. The author distinguishes the levels of restriction on different sub-items. To be specific, the author divides the restrictions into four levels: 0 represents basically no control on a capital account transaction item, 1/3 little control, 2/3 extensive control, and 1 rigid control. As a result, a higher value suggests a more severe control on capital and a less opened capital account.

among different capital account items. For example, assume that we have opened most of the items with less transaction volume, while also rigidly controlling a small number of items with large transaction volumes. In this scenario, the earlier-mentioned measures will hardly suggest an overall relaxed capital control.

Hence, even the improved nominal measurement still cannot comprehensively show the degree of openness of China's capital account.

7.2.2.2 *The Measurement of the Degree of Actual Capital Account Openness*

The degree of actual capital account openness is based on the actual capital flows in a country, which can reflect its actual capital inflows and outflows. One of the most common approaches is to measure the scale of actual capital flows. A country's balance of international payments and the status outflows and inflows can roughly reflect the level of openness of its capital accounts. Meanwhile, as China's financial market has not been open completely, some financial market indexes (such as the AH stock market premium and A-B stock market premium) can also indirectly reflect how strong China's capital controls are.

In academic research, the following methods are mainly adopted to measure the degree of actual capital account openness: the interest rate parity method (Gros, 1987; Chinn and Frankel, 1995), Edwards' method on openness (Edwards and Khan, 1985), and the saving–investment correlation method (Feldstein and Horitoka, 1980). According to Yang and Shi (2007), there are deficiencies in these methods. First, the interest rate parity method suggests that, if yield differentials between homogeneous domestic and foreign financial assets have long diverged from interest rate parity, the interest rate parity method will indicate that this country has effective capital controls (namely, a low level of capital account openness). But capital controls are only one reason for the divergence of interest rate parity — political risks and taxes are other possible explanations.

Second, the Edwards method on openness, based on the interest rate parity, categorizes economic openness into three types, suggesting that the interest rate in semi-open countries is the weighted average of the rates in both fully opened countries and completely closed countries. The weight is the openness of this country, and the degree of openness reflects both the openness status of a country's capital account and the effectiveness of capital controls. However, this method assumes that one country's economic openness remains unchanged through a period of time. This contradicts the fact that, in developing countries, capital control policies are always subject to change.

Third, the saving–investment correlation method assumes that, on the premise of free capital flows, the correlation of investments and savings is, in theory, comparatively low. The investment–saving correlation coefficient can be adopted to study the degree of a country's capital openness. However, this method cannot be used to theoretically explain the margin of investment rate and saving rate. To sum up, as China's interest rate is not fully market-driven, there could be deviation in the estimation of interest rate parity. Therefore, the applicability of both the interest rate parity method and the Edwards method based on it, is debatable. Here we adopt saving–investment correlation method to measure the degree of China's capital account openness.

In the following paragraphs, we will first review several indexes of China's scale of actual capital flows, roughly illustrating the degree of domestic capital account openness since 1992. Second, based on the actual status of domestic capital controls, we will analyze the stock market premium index among A-shares, B-shares and H-shares, which indirectly reflect the effectiveness of capital controls. Third, we adopt the saving–investment correlation method to quantitatively illustrate the evolution of China's capital account openness.

(1) The Measurement Index of the Actual Scale of Capital Flows

The degree of capital flows,[2] financial depth[3] and financial openness[4] are regularly applied to measure a country's capital account openness. This study measures the degree of capital flows on the basis of the proportion of actual cross-border capital flows in nominal GDP. This measurement index is often used in many studies, like Xiong (2009). The proportion of broad money supply M2 taken from nominal GDP is used to measure China's level of financial depth. In 1993, King and Levine have used such measures to reflect a country's financial development. In addition, this study chooses the proportion of transnational direct investment (bi-directional) and stock investment in GDP to reflect the degree of China's financial openness. In

[2]The degree of capital flows = (capital inflow + capital outflow)/GDP.

[3]Finance deepening degree = M2/GDP.

[4]Financial openness has two aspects: direct investment and portfolio investment. In this study, the amount of portfolio investment/GDP = (portfolio investment: creditor + portfolio investment: debtor)/GDP, direct investment/GDP = direct investment balance/GDP.

Table 7.3: Indexes Measuring the Degree of Domestic Capital Account Openness[5]

	GDP per Capita (Yuan)	Amount of Capital Flows/ GDP	M2/GDP	Amount of Portfolio Investment/ GDP	Balance of Direct Investment/ GDP	Outward Direct Investment/ GDP	Foreign Direct Investment/ GDP
1992	2311	12.13	—	0.36	1.43	0.80	2.23
1993	2998	12.19	—	1.10	3.60	0.69	4.29
1994	4044	15.61	—	0.93	5.46	0.34	5.80
1995	5046	12.78	—	0.37	4.47	0.26	4.74
1996	5846	11.43	—	0.56	4.27	0.24	4.50
1992–1996	**4049**	**12.83**	—	**0.66**	**3.85**	**0.47**	**4.31**
1997	6420	16.68	12.26	1.17	4.23	0.26	4.49
1998	6796	17.70	13.39	0.72	3.93	0.25	4.19
1999	7159	16.20	14.74	1.35	3.36	0.16	3.52
2000	7858	15.27	15.80	1.65	3.14	0.08	3.22
2001	8622	12.48	16.32	2.86	2.84	0.52	3.36
2002	9398	15.42	17.00	1.03	3.22	0.17	3.39
2003	10542	26.15	17.99	1.40	3.00	0.00	3.00
2004	12336	35.43	17.75	2.56	3.09	0.10	3.19
1997–2004	**8641**	**19.42**	**15.66**	**1.59**	**3.35**	**0.19**	**3.54**
2005	14185	38.23	17.70	2.48	3.95	0.60	4.55
2006	16500	50.81	17.38	6.01	3.58	0.86	4.44
2007	20169	54.04	17.07	3.93	3.97	0.49	4.46
2005–2007	**16952**	**47.69**	**17.39**	**4.14**	**3.83**	**0.65**	**4.48**
2008	23708	42.43	16.79	3.07	2.52	1.25	3.77
2009	25608	29.93	19.26	3.78	1.71	0.86	2.57
2010	30015	34.39	20.11	1.73	3.12	0.97	4.10
2011	35198	36.00	19.81	1.15	3.17	0.66	3.83
2012	38449	33.17	20.80	1.41	2.29	0.75	3.03
2008–2012	**30595**	**35.18**	**19.36**	**2.23**	**2.56**	**0.90**	**3.46**

Data sources: State Administration of Foreign Exchange; National Bureau of Statistics. The data has been processed by the author.

order to reveal a more accurate bi-directional flow of portfolio investment, the portfolio investment is made up of absolute values of both debit and credit accounts.

Table 7.3 shows values of the aforementioned indexes between 1992 and 2012. We divide this period with three specific time nodes: the 1997

[5]For the calculation formula of each index, please see footnotes 3–5. During the compiling of this book, the final accounting figures of GDP in 2012 and Balance of Payment Presentation were not released yet.

Asian Financial Crisis, China's 2005 exchange rate reform, and the 2008 global financial crisis. We find that, since 1992, as the economy has developed, reformed and opened up, China's transnational capital flows have been obviously on the rise. When the Asian Financial Crisis took place, China's capital account was comparatively less opened and thus the crisis only exerted a limited impact on China's capital flows. However, with increasingly more domestic capital accounts opening up, the financial crisis in 2008 struck China heavily and capital flows dropped sharply.

The degree of financial deepening (M2/GDP) reflects the domestic financial development status of a country. This index has been constantly rising for the past 20 years, indicating that China's capital market has continuously deepened and its financial services industry plays an ever greater role in resource allocation.

Transnational direct investment and portfolio investment reflect the degree of domestic financial openness, in terms of the real economy and investment in securities, respectively. For the past 20 years, both FDI and ODI have been rising in China. However, since the financial crisis took place in 2008, FDI has decreased. On the one hand, this can be attributed to economic stagnation and decreased investment in major countries. On the other hand, according to Peng and Miao (2008), Yan (2012) and others, this follows foreign investment development cycle theory. In that view, this is an inevitable result of China's economic development and GDP per capita growth. China's outward investment will generally increase in the future, and its balance account of direct investment will, on the whole, shrink. In the past two decades, the amount of China's transnational portfolio investment has also been increasing and the 2008 financial crisis had quite a large impact on this type of investment as well.

(2) Financial Market Index

A study by Wang in 2008 showed that a useful way to measure the effectiveness of a country's capital control is by comparing domestic and foreign rates of return on an asset. The difference can reveal if the interest arbitrage between two places has not been fully exploited (and thus suggesting restrictions preventing arbitrage). Based on the interest parity theory and the price of RMB–USD Non-Deliverable Forward (NDF), Ma and McCauley (2008) calculated the implicit RMB interest rate in the Hong Kong market. Due to the constant and remarkable discrepancy between the RMB interest rate in the Hong Kong market and that in the mainland market (for the same period), they concluded that China's capital controls are still effective. Capital controls and liberalization are contrary to one another. Therefore, by examining the difference between domestic and foreign returns on an asset, this study aims to analyze the degree of openness in China's capital account.

As for the equity securities, there are three stock markets in mainland China: A shares, B shares and H shares.[6] Numerous domestic enterprises have gone public in these three markets simultaneously — for example the Industrial and Commercial Bank of China (SH.601398, HK.01398). Since domestic investors of H shares and overseas investors of A shares are under certain restrictions, the price premium (or discount) among A, B, and H shares cannot immediately be narrowed by arbitrage to smooth the price spread. AH share premiums and A-B share premiums are shown in Figures 7.1 and 7.2 respectively.

The Hang Seng China AH Share Premium Index measures premiums between the A shares and H shares by compiling data on more than

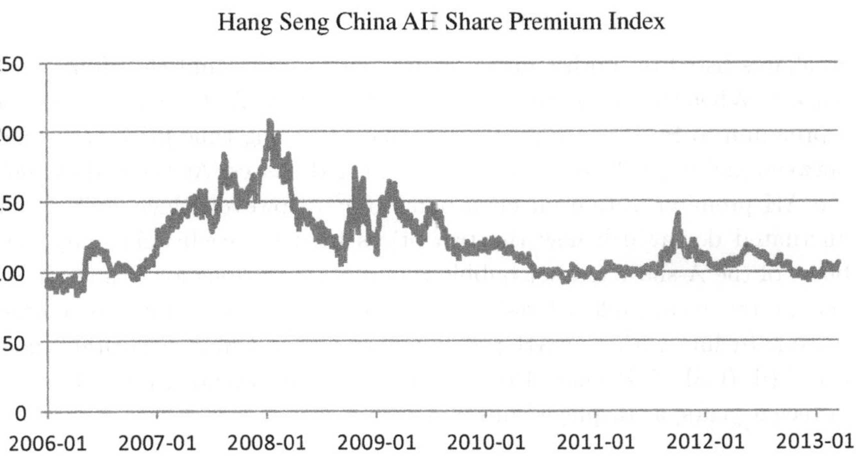

Figure 7.1: Hang Seng China AH Share Premium Index
Data source: Wind Database.

[6] "A shares" is the main-board market of Mainland China, whose stock is issued by domestic companies, for Chinese institutions, organizations and individuals (not including investors from Taiwan, Hong Kong and Macao) to purchase and trade. The RMB special share — "B shares" — carries a face value dominated in RMB. It is subscribed and traded in foreign currencies on domestic (the Shanghai and Shenzhen) Stock Exchanges. "H shares" refers to the shares of companies incorporated in mainland China that are listed on the Hong Kong Stock Exchange.

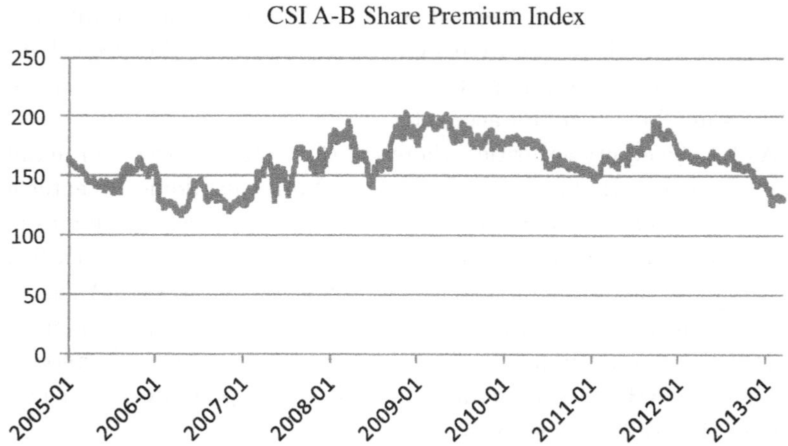

Figure 7.2: China Securities Index Co., Ltd. (CSI) A-B Share Premium Index

Data source: China Securities Index Co., Ltd.

80 shares listed on both China's main-board market and the Hong Kong market. When the index rises above 100, it indicates A shares are trading at a premium to H shares. Figure 7.1 displays the long-time price divergence between mainland A shares and Hong Kong H shares. At the end of 2007, the AH premium rate even hit around 100%. However, since 2008, it has fluctuated downward; now the two prices tend to reach uniformity. The burst of the A-share market bubble is one of the reasons for this tendency, and at the meanwhile China's relaxed restrictions on capital is another reason. In line with the AH premium index, the China Securities Index Co., Ltd. (CSI) A-B Share Premium Index has also tended toward decline in recent years, as displayed in Figure 7.2.

(3) National Savings Rate and National Investment Rate

According to Feldstein and Horioka' research method in 1980, when a country's capital account is highly opened, the global capital makes up most of the domestic investment increase while the saving–investment correlation is less evident; when strictly controlled, most of the investment comes from national savings, while the country's savings and investment are highly related. Based on *China Statistical Yearbook*, we have analyzed China's saving–investment behavior since 1992 and their correlation, as shown in Tables 7.4 and 7.5.

Table 7.4: China's National Savings Rate and Investment Rate, 1992–2009[7]

	Total Disposable Income	Final Consumption	Savings Rate (%)	Investment Rate (%)	GDP Growth	RMB to USD Exchange Rate
1992	26,716	15,952	40.29	36.60	14.20	5.51
1993	34,628	20,182	41.72	42.60	14.00	5.76
1994	46,785	26,796	42.73	40.50	13.10	8.62
1995	57,615	33,635	41.62	40.30	10.90	8.35
1996	67,028	40,004	40.32	38.80	10.00	8.31
1997	73,568	43,579	40.73	36.70	9.30	8.29
1998	77,322	46,406	39.93	36.20	7.80	8.28
1999	80,988	49,723	38.61	36.20	7.60	8.28
2000	98,523	61,516	37.56	35.30	8.40	8.28
2001	108,771	66,934	38.46	36.48	8.30	8.28
2002	120,170	71,817	40.24	37.82	9.10	8.28
2003	136,421	77,686	43.05	40.96	10.00	8.28
2004	161,349	87,553	45.74	43.02	10.10	8.28
2005	185,572	99,358	46.46	41.54	11.30	8.19
2006	218,142	113,104	48.15	41.74	12.70	7.97
2007	269,243	132,233	50.89	41.62	14.20	7.61
2008	319,027	153,423	51.91	43.78	9.60	6.95
2009	342,482	169,275	50.57	47.16	9.20	6.83

Data sources: *China Statistical Yearbook* (National Bureau of Statistics); Wind Database.

Table 7.5: Correlation Coefficient between Savings Rate and Investment Rate

Time Interval	Correlation Coefficient
Years 1992–2009	0.8503
Years 1992–1996	0.7106
Years 1997–2004	0.9583
Years 2005–2009	0.4866

Table 7.5 shows that, during the 18 years from 1991 to 2009, the correlation coefficient between the savings rate and investment rate was 0.85. This indicates a high correlation and thus severe capital account controls in China. Based on GDP growth and the middle rate of the RMB

[7]Limited by the contents of *China Statistical Yearbook*, we can only analyze the data before 2009.

against the US Dollar, the 18-year period was divided into three phases. Examining these phases suggests a transition in the saving–investment correlation first from low to high, then again to low.

The 1992–1996, the first phase, was the early stage of China's reform and opening up, featuring rapid economic growth and a high saving–investment correlation. Except for the policies to attract FDI and encourage Chinese enterprises to "go global", there was little investment under the capital account, indicating an overall closed status. When the Asian Financial Crisis broke out in 1997, China was less impacted than other Asian countries because of its restrictive capital account. Nevertheless, its economic growth slowed down following the crisis.

During 1997–2004 (the second phase), the saving–investment correlation coefficient reached its peak among the three phases of 0.89. This demonstrates that China's capital account was severely controlled and least open in this phase. The RMB was stable at RMB8.28 against the US Dollar. Although the Chinese government had set up an interbank foreign exchange market, put an end to the official exchange rate, and implemented "a single, managed, floating exchange rate system based on the market supply and demand", the exchange rate regime was still quite rigid.

The saving–investment correlation coefficient in 2005–2009 (the final phase) was 0.49 — much lower than the first two phases. Since reform of exchange rate system began in 2005, China moved into "a managed floating exchange rate regime based on market demand and supply with reference to a basket of currencies". With the deepening of reform and further opening up of its capital account, China established the RMB off-shore market and the RMB settlement for cross-border trade. This phase saw acceleration of RMB on a course towards internationalization.

As to the measurement of nominal capital account openness, we have summed up the research conclusions made by domestic and foreign scholars. Since the nominal measurement indicator does not apply to China's practical situation, we have not conducted an empirical analysis. As to the measurement of actual capital account openness, we have used three approaches: the index of the scale of actual capital flows, the financial market indexes, and the correlation of savings to investment. With these we examine the degree of China's capital account openness during 1992–2012, concluding that China's capital account has tended to be increasingly open up over the past 20 years. In light of the characteristics of China's capital account, our practical measurement index is more convincing than other, more theoretical approaches.

7.2.3 The Significance and Role of Capital Account Openness

7.2.3.1 Capital Account Openness Is a Means to Optimize Allocation and Spread Risks

Capital account openness optimizes the allocation of capital, thereby benefiting economic development. According to the theory of comparative advantage, a country with capital scarcity (relative to labor) has a higher rate of capital returns, while a country with capital surplus (relative to labor) has a lower rate of capital returns. Similarly, a country with advanced technology and/or efficient systems has a higher rate of capital returns than one with low technological standards or inefficient systems. When capital can be moved freely and can optimize its returns, private capital will be transferred from the country with a low rate of returns to the one with a higher rate of returns, generating great economic benefits and realizing the comparative advantage of both (or even all open) countries. Capital account openness has the added benefit of spreading capital risks worldwide.

In contrast, the essence of capital controls is government intervention in the market to distort profit-seeking behavior. The effectiveness of controls may also be very limited. In recent years, the efficiency of China's domestic capital controls has continually decreased. In 2006, the net error and omissions reported inflow USD$3.628 billion, followed by inflows of USD$13.290 billion in 2007. However, the net error and omissions in 2012 reached outflow USD$79.7 billion, accounting for 78.05% of reserve capital changes in that period. To a certain degree, this is evident that the efficiency of capital controls decreased — that significant portions of capital are avoiding the controls (the same could also be assumed for outflows).

7.2.3.2 Capital Account Openness Benefits Domestic Enterprises' Investments Abroad

Currently China is in a strategic position to reap the full benefits of capital account openness. The financial crisis inflicted heavy losses on Western financial institutions and enterprises, leaving the market valuations of some companies relatively low. We now have a great opportunity for Chinese enterprises and individuals to go global and expand into the world market. Opening up the capital account can exploit this position in two ways. First, an open capital account facilitates a faster pace of overseas investment by domestic enterprises. Second, the competitiveness of domestic firms can greatly benefit from the acquisition of cutting-edge products and technologies from overseas companies, as well as easy access to foreign markets and resources. China's gross national product (GNP) is, at present, lower than its GDP (the ratio is approximately 6:9), which is absolutely contrary to the statistics of other major countries in the world. It exemplifies that China's investment abroad is much lower than foreign investment in China. This does not match China's economic status as the second largest economy in the world. Thus, the strategic phase for China's enterprises to go abroad is coming (Sheng, 2012b).

7.2.3.3 *Capital Account Openness Benefits the Internationalization of the RMB*

Capital account openness facilitates the cross-border use of RMB and the establishment of the RMB off-shore center in Hong Kong, boosting the RMB's internationalization. Since 2009, when the pilot RMB settlement for cross-border trade was established, the volume of RMB settlement has been greatly expanded. In 2012, RMB settlement for cross-border trade had reached RMB2.94 trillion (an increase of 41.3% compared to RMB2.08 trillion in 2011). The demand for RMB as the currency of payment is constantly increasing.

Meanwhile, as the development of the RMB off-shore center in Hong Kong has deepened, Hong Kong has emerged as the center for the pricing and trading of overseas RMB capital investments (leading in the pricing of the China Offshore Yuan (CNH) exchange rate and RMB bonds). In 2012, RMB trade settlement handled in Hong Kong reached RMB2.63 trillion, accounting for 89.4% of the actual settlement overseas RMB receipt and payment. The balance held on deposits in Hong Kong was RMB603 billion and the balances of RMB loans was RMB79 billion.

7.2.3.4 *Capital Account Openness Benefits the Restructuring of the Domestic Economy*

Capital account openness is beneficial for adjusting the economy's industrial structure. One outstanding contradiction of China's economy is its high saving rate, low consumption rate, excessive foreign exchange and overcapacity. On one hand, as China's labor costs rise, the competitiveness of labor-intensive industries declines. Capital account openness will contribute to some transfer of low, value-added productivity from China to those countries and regions where labor has a greater comparative advantage.

This reallocation of resources will raise the overall level of value added by domestic industries and strengthen aggregate productivity. On the other hand, China is relatively short of individual investment channels, and larger saving funds cannot maintain or increase their value. In the pilot financial reform projects launched in Wenzhou and other regions, one key experiment is conducting FDI for individuals. The pilot capital project will expand foreign investment channels for Chinese families, helping them accumulate wealth and, therefore, ultimately improving the level of domestic consumption.

7.2.3.5 *Capital Account Openness "Forces" Domestic Financial Institutions to Reform*

The significance of capital account openness in financial institutions reform is to strengthen the reform through competition. Research from the IMF and Zhu (2004) summarized how certain conditions are needed for capital account openness to facilitate economic growth and welfare improvement. Such conditions include a stable macro economy, suitable exchange rate and institutions, effective financial supervision, adequate foreign exchange reserves, successful financial institution reforms, etc. The gradual opening of the capital account needs such conditions. Hence, the opening process is also one of strengthening and reforming institutions and therefore advances two key reforms: the marketization of both domestic interest rates and exchange rate institutions.

In April 2012, the PBOC released a research report titled *To Coordinate and Advance the Opening-up of Interest Rates, Exchange Rate Reform and the Capital Account*, in which it indicated that a range of reforms (the marketization of interest rates, reform of exchange rate determination mechanism, RMB internationalization and opening of the capital account) have no fixed sequence. They should be conducted gradually, in coordination, and be mutually facilitated: Interest rate marketization should be advanced, the exchange rate determination mechanism should be reformed, and an open capital account needs to be gradually and cautiously approved.

Take the development of the RMB off-shore market in Hong Kong as an example. As the RMB off-shore market in Hong Kong is constantly developing, more and more off-shore RMB needs backflow channels, which forces domestic supervisory authority to deregulate part of the capital account. The off-shore RMB market can therefore build a normal "backflow mechanism" with eased regulation, and the market can be made more mature (Ma, 2012b). At this point, RMB internationalization does not have to wait for the complete opening of the capital account. The pressure from this "forced" approach is very important.

During the process of opening the capital account, we shall firmly stick to the fundamental principal of "opening one account item when it is ready ", cautiously managing the opening of the capital account, enhancing the level of financial supervision, improving the management of financial institutions, and preventing large, negative impacts from rapid overseas capital flows.

7.2.4 *The "Three-Step" Strategy of Capital Account Openness in China*

In February 2012, the PBOC's Financial Survey and Statistics Department Research Group released a report titled *The Conditions for Accelerating Capital Account Openness are Fundamentally Ripe*, suggesting that the recent period is a strategic one for capital account openness in China. The research group proposed a "three-step" strategy for opening capital account (Sheng *et al.*, 2012a).

The sequencing for opening each item under capital account is a very important aspect in managing liberalization of the capital account. Its fundamental principle is to open one account item when it is ready. Following the opening procedure of the domestic capital account, the general opening sequence can be summarized as: inflows first, outflows second; long-term capital first, short-term capital second; direct investment first, indirect investment second; institutions first, individuals second. The basic strategy follows a risk–reward calculation, where the reforms with the greatest expected benefits and lowest risks are tackled first, and the most risky and bearing the least benefits are handled second. Likewise, incremental reforms should come first, with large, stock reforms following.

According to the vision promoted by the PBOC's research group, the short-term, mid-term and long-term deployment of opening the domestic capital account can be summarized across ten years, as follows.

(1) Short-term deployment (1–3 years): Ease the control of direct investment backed by real trade, and encourage enterprises to "go global"

Direct investment itself is comparatively stable, and not much affected by economic fluctuations. Thus, easing controls on direct investment bears the fewest risks. China's promotion of overseas direct investment is now entering a strategic period: Excessive capacity makes direct overseas investment very attractive; rich foreign exchange reserves are available to provide investment with sufficient foreign exchange funds; a bullish RMB exchange rate now provides cost advantages for direct overseas investment; the contraction of Western financial institutions and enterprises has made room for China's investment.

(2) Mid-term deployment (3–5 years): Ease the controls on commercial credit backed by real trade, and help with the RMB's internationalization

Commercial credit backed by real trade is closely connected with the current account. Such credit has strong stability and comparatively few risks. As Chinese companies progressively acquire dominant positions in international trade, investment, manufacturing and financial activities, controls on commercial credit should be generally eased. Easing commercial credit control supports the development of import and export trade, and also expands RMB backflow channels for RMB cross-border settlement and the Hong Kong off-shore market.

(3) Long-term deployment (5–10 years): Strengthen the building of the financial market and open up inflows first, followed by outflows; prudently and orderly open up the real estate, stock and bond markets; generally replace Quantity-based Controls with Pricing Management

Market real estate prices are prone to increases rather than declines, and require quite a long time to return to reasonable price levels. The domestic stock market pays more attention to financing than to investment, and the price discovery mechanism is yet to be improved. The bond market is relatively small, and interest rate marketization is still in the process of development. What is more, the separation between the interbank bond market and the exchange bond market has not yet been settled, and problems caused by bullish supervision are still prominent (the PBOC, National Reform and Development Commission [NDRC], CSRC and the interbank association supervise the issuance of financial bonds, enterprise bonds, company bonds, short-term financing bonds and medium term notes, respectively). The bond market is yet to be improved. In general, the real estate market is the most mature, followed by the stock market, with the bond market being the least mature of the three. During the opening-up process, the principle "to open up the primary market first and then the secondary market; to open non-residents' domestic trade first and then residents' overseas trade" should be followed with quantitative controls generally replacing price management. This will reduce risks caused by opening up.

The three-step strategy only involves part of the 40 sub-account transaction items in the capital account. Items like personal capital transactions, financial institution credit (not related to capital transactions), money market instruments, collective investment stocks, financing facilities (such as warranties) and derivatives could be open at an appropriate time. The transaction liberalization of foreign exchange (which is unrelated to capital transactions) should be put last. Opening items such as short-term external debt, which is strongly speculative, can be delayed for a long time.

If China's capital account openness can be managed in the light of the aforementioned "Three-Step" plan, then the level of domestic openness can cover the basic needs of rational capital transactions among countries, and capital account openness will be basically realized in ten years.

7.3 Strategic Analysis of China's Capital Account Openness

According to the study in Chapter 4 on the relationship between capital account opening, reform of exchange rate regime and development of the financial market, it was found that opening the capital account will render the domestic short-term exchange rate sensitive to predictions of the national monetary exchange rate and foreign short-term interest rate. Meanwhile, in opening the capital account, if a country regulates interest rates and exchange rates at the same time, it will lead to large-scale capital flows. Therefore, after the capital account is opened, it will be difficult to simultaneously achieve a stable exchange rate policy and independent monetary policy.

However, without a prudent financial system, irrational pursuit of exchange rate regime reform and capital account openness will cause financial shocks, perhaps a financial crisis, or even economic upheaval. Reviewing the past, we can see that Chile experienced exchange rate regime reform and opening of its capital account in 1980s, but due to unstable support from the financial system, Chile was hit by a financial crisis. Therefore, reform of the exchange rate regime, opening of the capital account and development of the financial market are mutually reinforcing and should proceed together.

Consequently, before studying the strategic analysis of China's capital account openness, this section will draw a conclusion about the experience of capital account opening, exchange rate regime reform and financial market development. It will emphasis the formulation of an opening strategy for China's capital account, in order to provide relevant information for monetary policymakers.

7.3.1 *Learning from International Experience of Exchange Rate Regime Reform*

A series of valuable international experiences can be drawn from reviewing the evolution of exchange rate regimes in such countries as Japan, Chile, Poland and Singapore.

(1) According to the experience of other countries, the evolution path of exchange rate regime reform is always as follows: (a) First, a country uses a pegged exchange rate regime (including "real and fixed" exchange rate regimes, an adjustable pegged exchange rate regime, crawling pegs, and/or exchange rate pegged to a currency basket). (b) Second, a country adopts a basket-band-crawl system (including a crawling band exchange rate regime and target zone system). (c) Ultimately, a country shifts to a floating exchange rate regime (including a managed floating and/or free floating regime). Reform of the exchange rate regime is not independent of (but rather closely related to) opening of both the capital account and the financial market. Additionally, a stable macro economy should be realized in the process of reform, so that macroeconomic imbalances do not accumulate.

(2) In the process of exchange rate reform, the exchange rate's fluctuation band should be enlarged gradually. Chile and Poland adopted the band floating exchange rate regime, and then broadened the fluctuation range — all while opening the capital account and financial market step by step. The aim of their monetary policy was to achieve a "flexible exchange rate regime + inflation target". Japan, however, gradually opened the capital account and developed the financial market only after adopting a floating exchange rate regime.

(3) Japan first liberalized inward capital flows, and then outbound flows. When liberalizing inward capital flows, they first liberalized inbound direct investment. This process should be a gradual one, fostering and developing domestic competitiveness step by step, with the ultimate goal

of liberalizing inbound direct investment. Regarding indirect investment, domestic institutions should be allowed to lend money from foreign borrowers, then issue bonds in foreign countries, and at last issue stocks. This order of opening gradually increases the risks from reform, helping to foster stability. With respect to capital outflows, ODI should be liberalized first. This will help ensure the security of capital directed toward outbound investment. Then indirect investment should be allowed. The order of participatory institutions in indirect investment could first be trust investment, then financial institutions and individuals, and finally securities companies last.

(4) Opening the capital account should, to a certain extent, be a flexible process. When liberalizing the capital account, adjustments can be made according to the domestic and external economic situation. For instance, when large-scale capital flows inward, the outbound capital account can be opened moderately. This can, on the one hand, ease the pressure brought by capital inflows, while, on the one hand, accelerate the pace of opening when risks are relatively small. When capital outflows reach a large scale, moderate regulation can be applied.

(5) A monitoring system for short-term capital flows should be established. Through collecting information about swap and forward exchange transactions between banks and non-residents, the scale and motivation of transaction can be discerned. By analyzing such information, one can determine which swap transactions are real and which are speculative (i.e., which might impact the exchange rate). Swap transactions are monetary tools — a means of making credit between residents and non-residents. While swap transactions in themselves are not risky, risks may be formed when they are combined with other investments. This calls for close attention.

(6) The foreign exchange market should be speedily developed. Vigorously developing the foreign exchange market, as well as improving the activity level and fluidity of transactions within it, will not only enhance the hedging of monetary risks, but also provide space for foreign exchange intervention. Such intervention can start with the spot market, but the ultimate goal should be indirect and efficient interventions through means of monetization — i.e., buying and selling securities.

(7) The variety of transaction items and the number of traders on the money market should be increased, with a view toward increasing market liquidity in preparation for the liberalization of interest rates. For example, Japan increased different kinds of treasury bonds, and Chile increased

central banks notes. In the process of liberalizing the interest rate, the long-term fixed-term deposit rate can be liberalized first. Then guidance information can be released about the current deposit rate. Ultimately the interest rate of current deposits should be liberalized as well. Considering the sizes of deposits, the interest rate of large-sum deposits should be liberalized before the interest rate of small-scale deposits.

(8) In the process of opening the financial market, the financial institutions that take a leading position in the domestic financial market should be valued. The pension fund in Chile, for example, played a crucial role. When opening up its financial market, Chile first and foremost opened part of the business of pension insurance funds, and then other businesses of other financial institutions with the intention of eventually open all the businesses in these institutions. However, not until 2004 was Chile's pension fund business completely opened. This opening model for major financial institutions can help increase their resilience to risks and safeguard the stability of domestic financial market.

(9) The monitoring awareness of banks ought to be increased. Banks should be made aware that compliance management is not only necessary for dealing with external regulation, but is also a means to prevent credit risks, increase the trust the clients put in a bank, and bring "extra value" to bank services. In the process of opening, the currency match and duration match of financial institutions should be monitored. Market fluctuations during reform can only be reduced after setting up a relatively sophisticated monitoring framework.

7.3.2 *Conclusion of Lessons in the Exchange Rate System Reform*

A number of countries have experienced some twists and turns (and in some cases, suffering) from serious consequences in their reform process. For instance, a financial crisis erupted when Chile was carrying out financial deregulation for the first time, and Japan witnessed an economic recession in the 1990s. Judging from foreign practices of exchange rate system reform, we may learn some lessons in their failures, providing reference for China's own reform of its exchange rate system, opening of its capital account, and steady development of its financial market.

(1) The reform of the exchange rate system should be treated with caution. In spite of the fact that Chile and Poland achieved faster development in their exchange rate system reform and capital account liberalization (only taking around ten years), it has taken a relatively

longer time for Japan to develop. In the phase of financial deregulation, Japan's off-shore financial market developed excessively fast. Moreover, the arbitrage opportunity between Japan's off-shore and domestic financial markets propelled frequent capital flows. Considering that today financial globalization is even more advanced, and capital flows move even more quickly, China should develop step by step and pursue a perfect market regulatory framework and exchange rate mechanism.

(2) The regulatory framework of the domestic financial system should be basically improved before opening up. In light of Chile's lessons, before opening China's capital account and financial market to the outside world, we should try our best to perfect the regulatory framework for the domestic financial system and to further mature the foreign exchange market. This will guarantee steadiness in the domestic financial market and the currency matching and risk management ability of foreign trade enterprises.

(3) In the process of exchange rate reform, price stability should take up a major position. When Chile and Poland were introducing their exchange rate reforms, price stability had always been the target of their exchange rate policies. Japan, in contrast, mainly focused on stabilizing the Yen's value and overlooked the stability of its domestic prices. After the Plaza Accord, in order to alleviate the impacts brought forth by higher Yen quotations, Japan implemented an easy monetary policy at home by drastically reducing interest rates. But this came at the cost of sacrificing stable domestic prices and reasonable asset prices. As a result, in the 1990s asset bubbles in stock and real estate markets burst, and Japan fell into ten years of economic recession. Therefore, China ought to learn a lesson: intervening in the exchange rate should by no means be at the cost of sacrificing domestic price stability.

(4) Management of short-term capital movements should be reinforced. When opening the short-term capital market, there is a risk of capital shocks. The monetary authority must possess ready tools for influencing short-term capital movements and mediating risk. In the process of opening, Japan introduced its free Yen account system and set limits on Yen exchange. Chile carried out its Unremunerated Reserve Requirement (URR) system. Other methods include management of transnational investment, loan contracting, trade and payment, tourism swaps, etc.

(5) The exchange rate must become market-based before capital flow limits are basically removed. Judging from Japan's experience in the 1980s, if there is a large difference between domestic and foreign interest rates,

it will create a one-way expectation for capital flows. The consequences of such a trend will be either transmitted inflation at home (with too much inflow of hot money), or a slowdown in the development of the domestic economy (due to excessive capital outflows).

7.3.3 *An Analysis of China's Opening Strategies for Capital Account*

According to summaries of experience in exchange rate reform, capital account opening, financial development and other aspects from four countries (such as Japan), we hold that China's capital account openness should be analyzed from both general and specific perspectives. Specifically, the general perspective is mainly aimed at analyzing the successful sequencing among exchange rate reform, capital account opening and financial development. The specific perspective analyzes the opening order of individual items within the capital account. Considered as a whole, the following two principles should be noted:

(1) An increase in the RMB exchange rate's flexibility is the basis of capital account openness. The enlarging of the RMB exchange rate's elastic range can eliminate expectations for unilateral appreciation or depreciation. And it facilitates the discovery of foreign exchange market price, alleviates shocks brought by one-way capital flows and mitigates the impact of speculation. Furthermore, higher volatility in the exchange rate can also curb the excessive flow of short-term capital. Therefore, China should reform the exchange rate system at an earlier stage, or during the process of capital account opening. For the time being, China is implementing a managed float exchange rate system and the fluctuation margin of the exchange rate could be further widened in the future. Firstly, a monetary policy target should be set. Take the inflation rate as an example. Before the capital account is completely opened and the financial market is not yet mature, a system of exchange rates within a crawling band can be introduced. Then the former system can achieve a gradual transition to a "flexible RMB exchange rate target-zone system" (Cheng, 2009). While the exchange rate target zone is being gradually expanded, the capital account should, accordingly, be gradually opened.

(2) Interest rate marketization should be synchronized with capital account opening. In the context of interest rate liberalization, flows of international capital can be regulated through interest rate fluctuations after capital account opening. If there are large inflows of international

capital, as a result, interest rate levels will be lowered and capital gains will be decreased, which will in turn lead to capital outflows. In this way, the market is able to regulate the flow of international capital independent of government intervention. Besides, interest rate liberalization improves the efficiency of resource allocation and the anti-risk capability of the financial system, guaranteeing that capital account openness can be carried out smoothly.

Currently, China's money market rates and bond market rates have already become market-oriented. The upper and lower limits of the RMB loan rate and lower limit of RMB deposit rate have been loosened. Only the upper limit of the deposit rate is yet to be relaxed. China should expand the scale and increase the number of products transacted in the financial market, increase alternative investment products, and improve the depth and scope of the financial market. Then the process of interest rate liberalization should be carried out in the following order: "Long-term and large deposits at first, then short-term and petty deposits, and demand deposit interest rates at the end".

Furthermore, interest rate liberalization should be synchronized or alternate with capital account opening, which can speed up development of the financial market, the opening process itself, and China's overall economic development. However, interest rate liberalization does not mean that the control over interest rate fluctuations has been completely removed. When the interest rate level fluctuates abnormally, it still needs intervention from the monetary authority.

Specifically, the liberalization of components belonging to the capital account can be implemented in the order of "long-term capital before short-time capital; capital inflows before capital outflows; direct investment before indirect investment; institutional investment before individual investment." The details are as follows.

(1) Open the capital inflows of direct investment, especially FDI, which China is basically able to open completely for the time being. However, opening is far from enough — the ultimate goal is to improve the management and international competitiveness of domestic enterprises through importing foreign capital and experience. After domestic enterprises' international competitiveness has improved and their anti-risk capability has been strengthened, it will be high time to encourage those enterprises to "go global". At this point, the long-term foreign capital outflows account

can be opened, lowering the probability of failed investments when domestic enterprises are confronting capital outflows.

(2) Open financial institutions' foreign capital account. To begin with, open the long-term inflow account belonging to the indirect capital account. Simultaneously, the domestic financial market should be developed to enhance the depth and scope of transactions in the market. Likewise the risk management capability of financial institutions should be improved to prevent shocks from large-scale inflows of international capital (and to protect financial institutions from thereby suffering serious losses). Similarly, when domestic financial institutions are able to independently handle impacts from capital inflows, the capital outflow account can be opened to those financial institutions with the strongest risk management capability. As to those financial institutions whose risk management capability is not strong enough to make overseas investments, they should be regularly examined. If they pass examinations, they can be allowed to make overseas long-term indirect investments.

(3) After financial institutions' long-term capital account has been liberalized, then institutions' short-term and indirect investments can be opened. At the moment, there are high requirements for the anti-risk capabilities of the domestic financial market and financial institutions. Therefore, in the opening process of the short-term capital account, close attention should be given to fluctuations in the financial market and the flow of short-term capital. Learning from Japan, Chile and other countries' experiences, we can establish a supervisory system for short-term capital flows to avoid any risks they might bring.

(4) After opening measures for institutional investment have been basically finished, individual indirect investment can be gradually opened, based on previous experience. Its opening principle should also follow the maxim of "capital inflows before capital outflows; long-term before short-term". It is important to note that, when opening indirect investment, the bond market should be opened before the stock market to reduce risks brought by capital flows.

On the whole, capital account opening is not an independent process and it has to be connected to reform of the exchange rate system and financial development. Otherwise, it may exert large, negative impacts on domestic economic development, price stability and the financial market's steady development. This could lead to an outcome where the losses from reform outweigh the gains. Reform of the three accounts can be implemented alternatively and simultaneously so as to shorten the whole course of capital account opening in China.

As for the opening sequence for items within the capital account, the process can basically operate from small to large items, according to their level of risk exposure. By doing so, steady economic and financial development in China can be ensured. Yet it is not necessary that opening all of those accounts should be carried out entirely in a certain order. Parallel opening might be introduced according to domestic and foreign growth trends in the economy and finance, as well as China's own characteristics. However, when it comes to industries concerning rigid national demand, such as real estate, they should be left under strict control. Those industries should be opened in the last phase of capital account opening. Further, constant attention should be fixed on them and the government should be willing to intervene them at any time, if necessary. Such industries could negatively influence the domestic demands of people's livelihood and even perhaps bring social unrest.

Bibliography

In English

Arteta C., Eichengreen B. and Wyplosz C. (2001). When Does Capital Account Liberalization Help More Than It Hurts?. NBER Working Paper No. 8414.

Chinn M. D. and Frankel J. A. (1995). Who Drives Real Interest Rates around the Pacific Rim: The USA or Japan?. *Journal of International Money and Finance*, 14(6): 801–821.

Edwards S. and Khan M. S. (1985). Interest Rate Determination in Developing Countries: A Conceptual Framework. NBER Working Paper No. 1531.

Feldstein M. and Horioka C. (1980). Domestic Saving and International Capital Flows. *The Economic Journal*, 90(358): 314–329.

Grilli V. and Milesi-Ferretti G. M. (1995). Economic Effects and Structural Determinants of Capital Controls. *IMF Staff Papers*, 42(3): 517–551.

Gros D. (1987). Protectionism in a Framework with Intra-Industry Trade: Tariffs, Quotas, Retaliation, and Welfare Losses. *IMF Staff Papers*, 34(1): 86–114.

IMF. (1993). *Balance of Payments Manual*, 5th edition. Washington D. C.: International Monetary Fund.

IMF. (2011). *Annual Report on Exchange Arrangements and Exchange Restrictions 2011*. Washington D.C.: IMF.

King R. G. and Levine R. (1993). Finance and Growth: Schumpeter Might Be Right. *The Quarterly Journal of Economics*, 108(3): 717–737.

Ma G. N. and McCauley R. (2008). Do China's Capital Controls Still Bind?. In Eichengreen B., Park Y. C. and Wyplosz C., eds., *China, Asia, and the New World Economy*, 312–340. Oxford: Oxford University Press.

Quinn D. (1997). The Correlates of Change in International Financial Regulation. *American Political Science Review*, 91(3): 531–551.

Quirk P. J. and Evans O. (Eds.). (1995). Capital Account Convertibility: Review of Experience and Implications for IMF Policies. IMF Occasional Paper No. 131.

In Chinese

Ba S. S. (2012). The Construction of Hong Kong RMB Offshore Market. *Economic Review*, 7: 14–17.

Cheng S. W. (2009). *Economic Reform and Development in China.* Beijing: China Renmin University Press.

Jin L. (2004). Research on the Capital Control in China. *Journal of Finance*, (12): 9–23.

Jiang B. K. and Zou Y. M. (2002). Research on the Convertibility of RMB Capital Account. *Shanghai Finance*, 10: 4–7.

Jiang B. K. and Zhu Y. G. (2004). Study on the Openness of the Capital Account: An Analytical Framework Based on Internal and External Equilibrium. *Studies of International Finance*, 4: 12–19.

Lei D. and Zhao Y. (2008). Estimating the Opening Level of Capital Account in China. *Economic Theory and Business Management*, 5: 5–15.

Lu F., Wang H. and Qiu M. Y. (2012). The Priority of Financial Reform — from the Perspective of RMB Convertibility. *China Market*, 33: 32–40.

Lou L. L. and Qian M. (2011). The Measurement Method of Capital Account Liberalization: Comparison and Synthesis. *Studies of International Finance*, 8: 41–49.

Ma J. (2012a). The Internationalization of RMB and Its Capital Control. *CFO World*, 2: 44–45.

Ma J. (2012b). RMB Offshore Market and Its Capital Account Opening. *Financial Development Review*, 4: 1–41.

Sheng S. C. (2012a). China Is Basically to Accelerate the Opening of the Capital Account. *China Finance*, 5: 14–17.

Sheng S. C. (2012b). Path of RMB Capital Account Convertibility. Speech at the Lujiazui Forum in Shanghai.

Peng L. H. and Miao C. (2008). The Development Stage of the International Direct Investment in China. *Contemporary Economic Research*, 5: 27–31.

Shi J. H. (2007). The Opening of Capital Account in China: Significance, Development and Comments. *International Economic Review*, 6: 59–64.

Wang X. (2008). The Effectiveness of China's Capital Control. *Studies of International Finance*, 8: 66–71.

Xiong F. (2009). The Quality of Institution and Capital Account Liberalization: An Empirical Test Based in China. *Journal of Financial Development Research*, 8: 8–12.

Yan S. Q. (2012). Analyzing Some Fallacies about the Statement and Application of the Investment Development Cycle Theory in Some Literature. *Asia-Pacific Economic Review*, 5: 76–79.

Yang H. Z. and Shi H. (2007). A Review of Empirical Studies on the Effectiveness of Capital Control. *Management Review*, 19(10): 10–16.
Zhou X. C. (2012). Issues on the Formulation and Implementation of Financial Industry Standards. *China Finance*, 1: 9–14.
Zhu Y. G. (2004). The Dynamic Conditions on Capital Account Opening. *The Study of Finance and Economics*, 10: 41–50.

Appendix One: 7 Categories and 40 Sub-categories under the IMF Capital Account

I. Capital and Monetary Market Instruments
- 1. Securities Trading Instruments in the Capital Market
  - (1) Trading of stock or other securities with shareholding property
    - Non-residents purchase within borders
    - Non-residents sell or issue within borders
    - Residents purchase overseas
    - Residents sale or issue overseas
  - (2) Bond and Other Debt Securities
    - Non-residents purchase within borders
    - Non-residents sale or issue within borders
    - Residents purchase within borders
    - Residents sale or issue overseas
- 2. Monetary Market Instruments
  - Non-residents purchase within borders
  - Non-residents sale or issue within borders
  - Residents purchase overseas
  - Residents sale or issue overseas
- 3. Collective Investment Securities
  - Non-residents purchase within borders
  - Non-residents sell or issue within borders
  - Residents purchase overseas
  - Residents sale or issue overseas

II. Controls over Derivative Instruments and Other Instruments
- Non-residents purchase within borders
- Non-residents sell or issue within borders
- Residents purchase overseas
- Residents sale or issue overseas

(Continued)

(*Continued*)

III.	Controls over Credit Operations
	1. Commercial Credit
	Residents offer for non-residents
	Non-residents offer for residents
	2. Financial Credit
	Residents offer for non-residents
	Non-residents offer for residents
	3. Guarantee, Assurance and Standby Facility Convenience
	Residents offer for non-residents
	Non-residents offer for residents
IV.	Controls over Direct Investment
	Outward Foreign Direct Investment
	Inward Direct Investment
V.	Controls over Direct Investment Liquidation
VI.	Controls over Real Estate Transaction
	Residents purchase overseas
	Non-residents purchase within borders
	Non-residents sale within borders
VII.	Controls over Individual Capital Flow
	1. Loan
	Residents offer for non-residents
	Non-residents offer for residents
	2. Gift, Donation, Bequest and Legacy
	Residents offer for non-residents
	Non-residents offer for residents
	3. Foreign Immigrants' overseas Debt Settlement
	4. The Transfer of Assets
	Immigrants transfer assets to foreign countries
	Immigrants transfer assets to home countries
	5. The transfer of gambling and lottery income

Chapter 8

Path to RMB Internationalization

Currency Internationalization means that the sovereign currency of a country can carry out the general functions such as being a store of value, medium of exchange and unit of account in international markets. Both Chinese and foreign scholars have deeply explored the functions which an international currency should perform. Chinn and Frankel (2005) hold that the official functions of an international currency include being an international reserve, acting as a vehicle currency to intervene in the foreign exchange market and serving as an anchor currency pegged to the home currency. Further, an international currency's private usage include replacing local currency in circulation and acting as an accounting currency and invoicing currency in international trade and international financial transactions. All these official and private uses can in fact be generalized under the concept of a "vehicle currency". According to the definition given in the *The New Palgrave Dictionary of Money and Finance*, a vehicle currency is a medium currency for pricing, conducting foreign trade and making international capital transactions. It has three functions of a traditional currency: being a unit of measure, a medium of exchange and a store of value. In fact, the internationalization of the RMB is the process of gradually making the RMB a vehicle currency commonly used in the world.

In my opinion, the internationalization of the RMB can be achieved in four phases. Firstly, the RMB (as circulating currency) can be used abroad in the form of cash or quasi-cash (debit and credit cards). Secondly, the RMB (as a settlement currency) can be used as a tool for pricing and payment in international trade. Thirdly, the RMB (as investment currency) can be used in international investment. Fourthly, the RMB (as a reserve currency) can be held in the foreign reserves of the International Monetary Fund (IMF) and various countries. This chapter will discuss the path of RMB internationalization from a circulating currency, to an investment currency and finally to a reserve currency.

8.1 The RMB as a Circulating Currency

8.1.1 *Uses of RMB in Overseas Circulation*

Although every freely convertible currency can circulate in regions and countries outside its home country (acting as a circulating currency), in fact the major circulating currency in the world is the US Dollar. According to the estimates of Goldberg (2010), by the beginning of 2009, about USD$580 billion in cash was circulating outside of the US (65% of the total US Dollar cash in circulation). Before the creation of the Euro, the Deutschemark also had a large circulation outside of Germany, but mainly in European countries. Now the Euro also mainly circulates in European countries. Currencies of other countries have very limited overseas circulation.

At present, while the RMB is not yet freely convertible, RMB overseas circulation can be realized in the following five ways. Firstly, in trade, the RMB can be used for payment in import border trade. Secondly, in travel and consumption, the RMB can be used by domestic travelers abroad to pay for goods and services. Thirdly, in investment, the RMB can be used in foreign investment in government projects and in companies' FDI where the trading partners agree to accept RMB for purchasing equipment and paying labor fees. Fourthly, in currency swaps, the PBOC (People's Bank of China, the country's central bank) has reached agreements with other countries' central banks to exchange RMB with foreign currencies within certain amounts when necessary. Fifthly, the RMB can be used in illegal channels such as smuggling, drug trafficking and "stall banks" (i.e., unofficial financing operations, large and small).

8.1.2 *The Status Quo of RMB Overseas Circulation*

8.1.2.1 *Turnover in RMB Overseas Circulation*

Since the middle and late 1990s, the RMB has been used as a circulating and invoicing currency in border trade between China and its neighboring countries and regions. After 2000, the scale of RMB invoicing in neighboring countries and regions steadily expanded. Some Chinese scholars have assessed the status quo of the RMB's overseas circulation. Wang *et al.* (2002) made a comparative analysis of the status quo, listing reasons for RMB usages and circulation in neighboring countries and regions. Li (2002) found that the RMB has been widely accepted as a payment currency in countries such as Vietnam, Thailand, Burma, North Korea, Mongolia, Russia, Pakistan and Nepal. In addition, countries and regions like Bangladesh, Malaysia, Indonesia, the Philippines, Singapore and South Korea have accepted RMB deposits and other business. According to Jiang and Zhu (2004), the accumulated export of RMB by 2003 had reached RMB200 billion. An investigation by the State Administration of Foreign Exchange (2009) estimated that, by the end of 2007, among the 14 adjacent countries to China, seven countries (including Russia, Mongolia, North Korea, Kazakhstan, Vietnam, Burma and Nepal) had set up settlement accounts in Chinese banks in border trade areas. The investigation further found that the yearly settlement reached USD$22.348 billion, a year-on-year increase of 53.5%. With the expansion of RMB settlement, the scale of RMB outflows to neighboring countries is also increasing. The RMB has already become an actual circulating currency in Mongolia, and is praised there as "the second US Dollar". In the year 2007 alone, the income of Chinese bank accounts through Mongolia's banks was RMB3.55 billion, expenditures were RMB4.07 billion, and RMB in cash transported to Mongolia accumulated to RMB1.4 billion. That same year, in Vietnam, the stock of RMB cash reached RMB1.8 billion. Besides neighboring countries, the circulation destinations of RMB also include Hong Kong, China. By 2012, the RMB deposits in Hong Kong increased to RMB603 billion — nearly double the RMB319 billion at the end of 2010. Although there are differences in the figures of total RMB circulated abroad between direct and indirect estimations, they all generally show that the scale of RMB cross-border circulation has been constantly expanding over the last 20 years. RMB inflows and outflows, total circulation and oversea deposits are all expanding. However, due to China's large trade surplus, there are also huge RMB backflows. Moreover, because of the RMB settlement accounts set up in banks of both countries, cash transactions are decreasing. Therefore, the increasing scale of RMB oversea circulation may trend downwards.

8.1.2.2 *Areas of RMB Overseas Circulation*

On July 2, 2009, six regulators in China jointly announced the "Measures for the Administration of Pilot RMB Settlement in Cross-Border Trade", which signaled the official launch of China's pilot RMB settlement in cross-border trade. On June 22, 2010, the PBOC announced an expansion of the pilot to 20 provinces, autonomous regions and municipal cities. At the same time, it lifted restrictions on oversea regions. The pilot's business scope was clearly defined as including "RMB settlement in cross-border goods trade, service trade and other current accounts". This provided further support for RMB circulation abroad.

To the extent that the RMB's overseas circulation has been accepted, the circulation areas can be categorized into three kinds (Feng, 2008).

The first category is Hong Kong and Macao, China. Due to the close economic connections between Hong Kong, Macao and the mainland, the RMB is widely used in the first two. On February 25, 2004, the PBOC further opened the RMB business in Hong Kong by increasing the scope and quota of the RMB cash exchanges to Hong Kong Dollars, and allowing Hong Kong residents' personal RMB checking to have a daily, per-account quota of RMB80,000 (to be spent in Guangdong Province). Many hotels, malls and retailers in Hong Kong and Macao accept RMB according to the exchange rate. Since the Hong Kong Dollar can be exchanged freely with the US Dollar, in fact the RMB can also be exchanged freely at any time (via US Dollars) in Hong Kong. At present, there are more than 100 regular RMB currency exchange shops in Hong Kong, and over 30 banks have opened RMB exchange services. It is very convenient for the RMB to be exchanged with the Hong Kong Dollar in Hong Kong and Macao, and the RMB's circulation in these places is second only to the Hong Kong Dollar. At first, the RMB business in Hong Kong mainly covered personal banking business, including deposits, exchange, remittances, debit and credit cards and checking. However, since 2007, mainland financial institutions has successively issued bonds in Hong Kong, and the cross-border RMB settlement pilot was launched in 2009 (and then expanded in 2010). With the enlargement of a beneficial policy framework, banks and other financial institutions in Hong Kong now provide comprehensive RMB services, including deposit, exchange, remittance, trade financing and wealth management. To support the operation of the RMB business, the RMB settlement system in Hong Kong was updated to the RMB Real Time Gross Settlement (RTGS) system in June 2007 (Hong Kong Monetary Authority, 2013).

The second category includes some neighboring countries and regions that have great dependence on China's economy such as Vietnam, Laos, Cambodia, North Korea, Mongolia, Russia, Pakistan and Nepal. The RMB is widely used in the cross-border trade between China and these countries, and even circulates nationwide in some of them. In Vietnam for example, the RMB has become the most popular foreign currency. Over 90% of border exports to Vietnam out of Guangxi are settled in RMB. In its capital Hanoi, many Vietnamese are professionally engaged in the RMB exchange business (concentrated by the river in the downtown area). Generally speaking, the RMB mainly circulates in the northern provinces of Vietnam, especially in the border area, and less so the southern areas. Similarly, in the northern part of Burma and Laos (especially the border area), the RMB is the main transaction currency. In Chiang Mai, a city in northern Thailand, there are many RMB free exchange agencies. In Cambodia, the RMB began circulating in the black market very early. Prime Minister Hun Sen of Cambodia labeled the RMB as the most stable currency in Asia at the beginning of 2002, and called for Cambodians to use RMB more frequently. In North Korea, the RMB is a currency in almost all border cities for loan settlement, goods trade and hard currency reserves. The goods in North Korean shops are priced in North Korean won, RMB and euros. The RMB is named as "the second US Dollar" there as well. In Mongolia, around 90% of the currency circulated in the border area is RMB. Even all over Mongolia, over 50% of the currency in circulation is RMB.

The third category includes nearby countries and regions that many Chinese travelers visit, such as Singapore, Malaysia, Thailand and South Korea. Following Chinese tourists travelling and shopping, the RMB circulates in these areas. Many RMB exchange agencies are set up and many banks also conduct RMB exchange business. Major travel service providers, such as shopping malls and hotels, provide direct exchange rates between the RMB and the local currency. Most commercial banks provide exchange services between RMB and the local currency, alongside RMB exchange for US Dollars.

The RMB's overseas circulation area has become larger and larger. In the early phase, the RMB only circulated in border ports and markets, but now it has become widely used all over many countries. With the increasing number of Chinese travelling abroad, consumption through China UnionPay enables RMB to be used in more areas. By the beginning of 2013, China UnionPay can be used in 141 countries and regions. Data from the Society for Worldwide Interbank Financial Telecommunication (SWIFT) shows that the RMB exceeded the Russian ruble in January 2013 to become the 13th most common international payment currency.

8.1.3 *Problems for the RMB as a Circulating Currency*

8.1.3.1 *Exchange Rates in Black Markets Determine the Overseas RMB Exchange Rate*

At a time when the RMB exchange rate is not fully marketized, the overseas RMB exchange rate is usually set by stall banks in neighboring countries and regions. Such an exchange rate is based on the cross exchange rate in the black market. Thus the RMB price is not stable, and this prevents further increases in the RMB's circulation area. Take Vietnam as an example. In the northern part of the country, the RMB has become accepted by the local citizens as a free circulating currency. This, in the first place, is related to the development of stall banks, but the determination mechanism of the exchange rate, on the other hand, prevents the further expansion of RMB in circulation. In Vietnam, the exchange rate in every RMB exchange center is not like the uniform quote in banks. Instead, the exchange rate between RMB and Vietnam's Dong varies greatly across different regions: The price is the highest in the border area, and lower in the south. Therefore, Vietnamese who hold RMB or investors in Vietnam will exchange RMB to Dong as much as possible in the border area, preventing the expansion of RMB circulation.

8.1.3.2 *Risks of RMB Overseas Circulation*

The more freely convertible a currency is, the smaller the risk said currency brings its holder, and the more possibilities a foreigner has to use it. Therefore, a prerequisite for RMB circulation abroad is that currency exchange is basically not subject to controls. Yet the RMB circulation in neighboring countries and regions is spontaneously formed in the market without bilateral agreement (and thus sans legal guarantees). This increases the risks of RMB in overseas circulation, and limits increases in the scale and volume of RMB in circulation. Indeed, stall banks — as the major centers of RMB exchange abroad — are underground private financial institutions. Their credit and operations are not subject to the supervision of their national institutions, and thus they increase the risk of holding and using RMB abroad.

8.1.4 *The Path of RMB Overseas Circulation*

RMB overseas circulation is mainly driven by border trade and travel consumption. At present, RMB circulation abroad is relatively small, but the RMB enjoys a high reputation in neighboring countries and regions. Against this background, the Chinese government needs to actively learn from past experiences in managing RMB cross-border circulation and take good opportunities to deal with all the problems in RMB circulation abroad. This will help realize the regionalization of the RMB.

8.1.4.1 *RMB Overseas Circulation Should Be Included in the Standard Financial Services System*

At present, the major exchange agencies for overseas RMB are stall banks, which prevent RMB overseas circulation from expanding. Including existing RMB overseas circulation into the standard financial services system would not only gradually replace the dominant position of stall banks, but also reduce the risks brought to dealers in black market transactions. At the same time, standard regulations can gather more accurate information on RMB supply and demand abroad, improving the monitoring of changes in RMB overseas circulation. In terms of specific measures, the bilateral cooperation of banks will play a crucial role in the circulation size and scope of the RMB in neighboring countries. Therefore, it is necessary to promote standard RMB banking businesses in neighboring countries, so as to convert the current spontaneous RMB regional circulation into a conscious, active policy.

8.1.4.2 *Comprehensive Management of RMB Overseas Circulation*

Apart from regulations for the financial system, a host of parties should cooperate in order to form a long-term strategy for regional economic and financial development. These include domestic customs departments, tax administrations, economic and trade authorities, banks, travel administrations and diplomatic authorities. Cooperation can remove political hindrances in regional cross-border regulation. Meanwhile, more high-level governmental exchanges and mutual visits should be promoted to lay a foundation for mutual trust. It is also necessary to conduct RMB business with neighboring countries and regions, and to conduct RMB personal consumption business in countries and regions where the RMB widely circulates.

8.1.4.3 *Standardizing Statistical and Monitoring Systems for the RMB's Overseas Circulation*

With the increasing volume and scale of RMB in overseas circulation, it is necessary to standardize statistics and monitoring of RMB circulation abroad, so as to crack down on illegal activities such as money laundering. This will provide substantial guarantees for the long-term development of RMB internationalization, and play an important role in China's implementation of future monetary policy and financial stability. In particular, financial authorities in Hong Kong, Macao and the mainland should set up a coordinated mechanism for bilateral data exchange and statistical monitoring to improve rapid response to emergencies. In international balance of payments statistics, the principle of discerning between the trade of Chinese citizens and non-Chinese citizens should be observed, and international trade with RMB settlement should be included in statistics, so as to improve China's monitoring and early warning regarding international balance of payments issues.

8.2 The RMB as a Settlement Currency

8.2.1 *Literature Review on the Choice of Settlement Currency*

International Trade Currency Choice Theory proposes that, when trade goods are products have significant differences, the producer is in a advantageous position and has the power to set prices. Thus in that situation the price is usually denominated in the currency of the export country, which is called Producer Currency Pricing (PCP). However when the goods are primary commodities that are similar in both countries, the price is usually denominated in the currency of the import country, which is called Local Currency Pricing (LCP). Through an empirical study of Denmark's and Sweden's different choices of invoicing currency in international trade, Grassman (1973) found that, when developed and developing countries are choosing an invoicing currency for international trade between them, the currency of developed countries is usually used for settlement. Particularly in the manufacturing industry, developed countries would like to use a local currency for settlement. This is called Grassman's Law in international trade.

Fluctuations in the exchange rate will also influence the choice of invoicing currency. Friberg (1998) found that if the fluctuation of the exchange rate between a third currency and the currency of a trading partner is smaller than that between the local currency and the currency of said trading partner, then traders would tend to choose the third currency for invoicing. Devereux and Engel (2001) built a dynamic general equilibrium model of two countries in an open economy. After making different assumptions about the risks of the international financial market, they found that both the exporter and the importer prefer to choose the currency from the country with the most prudent monetary policy as for invoicing. When the local monetary policy is stable, the exporter will choose the currency of the export county for pricing (i.e., PCP), and the foreign importer will choose LCP. When there is great change in the local monetary policy, exporters will choose LCP, whereas importers PCP.

The choice of invoicing currency in international trade is also affected by transactions in the financial market. Swoboda (1968) believed that only when there is a developed financial market and plenty of transactions in the foreign market — and when the local country has tremendous currency for international trade — can the currency become "medium of exchange".

The scale of a country's economy also affects the choice of settlement currency. In their studies, Hartmann (1998), Fukuda and Ono (2006) believe that larger economies not only increase exporters' international influence, but also influence importers' acceptance of a foreign currency. The larger the country's economy, the more ability it has to choose its local currency as a settlement currency. International political influences also affect the degree of a currency's internationalization. Bergsten (1975) held that for a currency to be an international currency, it needs both political and economic conditions. Politically, it needs a powerful position and international support; economically, it needs external and internal conditions. Exterior conditions refer to an exchangeable currency, reasonable capital mobility and a healthy international balance of payment. Internal conditions include stable economic growth, stable commodity prices, certain economies of scale, a developed financial market, a well-fledged financial system, etc.

8.2.2 *The Status Quo of RMB Settlement*

8.2.2.1 *Cooperation in International Currency*

The main purpose of currency swap is to provide short-term mobility support for two countries, as well as to provide financing for the commercial banks branches in the other country (promoting bilateral trade).

Since 2009, to promote bilateral trade and investment and to enhance trust in China's financial stability, the PBOC has signed bilateral currency swap agreements with the currency authorities of 19 countries and regions including South Korea, Hong Kong China, Malaysia, Belarus, Indonesia, Argentina, Iceland and Singapore (Table 8.1). At present, the scale of currency swaps has reached RMB1671.2 billion (Figure 8.1).

Table 8.1: Currency Swap Agreements

Time	Country	Type	Scale
December 2008	Bank of Korea	Bilateral currency swap agreement	RMB180 billion/ 38 trillion Won
December 2008	Hong Kong Monetary Authority	Currency swap agreement	RMB200 billion/ 227 billion Hong Kong Dollar
February 2009	Bank Negara Malaysia	Bilateral currency swap agreement	RMB80 billion/40 billion Ringgit
March 2009	National Bank of the Republic of Belarus	Bilateral currency swap agreement	RMB20 billion/8 trillion Belarusian Ruble
March 2009	Bank Indonesia	Bilateral currency swap agreement	RMB100 billion/ 175 trillion Rupiah
April 2009	Central Bank of Argentina	Bilateral currency swap agreement	RMB70 billion/38 billion Argentine Peso
June 2010	Central Bank of Iceland	Bilateral local currency swap agreement	RMB3.5 billion
July 2010	Monetary Authority of Singapore	Bilateral local currency swap agreement	RMB150 billion/about 30 billion Singapore Dollar
April 2011	Reserve Bank of New Zealand	Bilateral local currency swap agreement	25 billion Yuan
April 2011	Central Bank of the Republic of Uzbekistan	Bilateral local currency swap agreement	RMB0.7 billion
May 2011	Bank of Mongolia	Bilateral currency swap agreement	RMB5 billion
June 2011	National Bank of the Republic of Kazakhstan	Bilateral currency swap agreement	RMB7 billion
June 2011	Central Bank of the Russian Federation	New bilateral local currency settlement agreement	Sino-Russia local currency settlement expanded from cross-border trade to general trade, and covers more regions. The agreement stipulates that economic entities can decide on their own to use free exchange currency, RMB and Rouble in goods and

(*Continued*)

Table 8.1: (*Continued*)

Time	Country	Type	Scale
			service settlement and payment. It further enhances the financial cooperation between China and Russia, and promoting bilateral trade and investment.
October 2011	Bank of Korea	Renewing of sino-south Korea bilateral local currency swap agreement	The scale of currency swap increased from RMB180 billion/ 38 trillion Won to RMB360 billion/ 64 trillion Won
Novermber 2011	Hong Kong Monetary Authority	Renewing pf currency swap agreement	The scale of currency swap increased from RMB200 billion/227 billion Hong Kong Dollar to RMB400 billion/ 490 billion Hong Kong Dollar
December 2011	Bank of Thailand	Bilateral local currency swap agreement	RMB70 billion/320 billion Thai Baht
December 2011	State Bank of Pakistan	Bilateral local currency swap agreement	RMB10 billion/140 billion Rupee
January 2012	Central Bank of the United Arab Emirates	Bilateral local currency swap agreement	RMB35 billion/20 billion Dirham
February 2012	Bank Negara Malaysia	Renewing of bilateral local currency swap agreement	The scale of currency swap increased from RMB80 billion/ 40 billion Ringgit to RMB180 billion/ 90 billion Ringgit
February 2012	Central Bank Of The Republic Of Turkey	Bilateral local currency swap agreement	RMB10 billion/3 billion Turkish Lira
March 2012	Bank of Mongolia	Supplementary agreement to the bilateral local currency swap agreement	The scale of currency swap increased from RMB5 billion/1 trillion Tughrik to RMB10 billion/ 2 trillion Tughrik

(*Continued*)

Table 8.1: (*Continued*)

Time	Country	Type	Scale
March 2012	Reserve Bank of Australia	Supplementary agreement to the bilateral local currency swap agreement	RMB200 billion/30 billion Australian Dollar
June 2012	National Bank of Ukraine	Supplementary agreement to the bilateral local currency swap agreement	RMB15 billion/19 billion Hryvnia

Data source: Website of the PBOC.

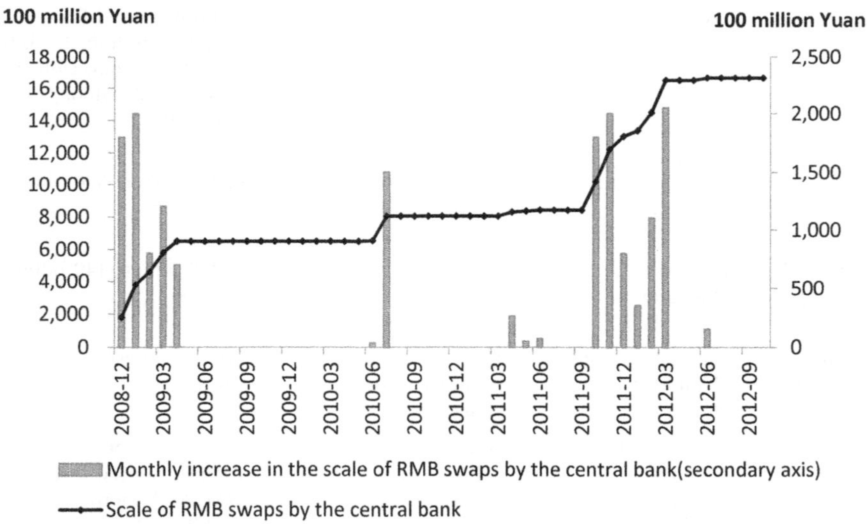

Figure 8.1: RMB Swap Scale

Data source: Wind Database.

8.2.2.2 *RMB Settlement in Cross-border Trade*

The executive meeting of the State Council on April 8, 2009 decided to conduct a cross-border RMB settlement pilot in cities such as Shanghai, Guangdong, Shenzhen, Zhuhai and Dongguan. On August 23, 2011, the domestic region of the pilot was expanded nationwide.

8.2.2.2.1 Significance of RMB Settlement in Cross-border Trade

RMB settlement in cross-border trade is a crucial step in the RMB's internationalization. RMB international settlement is different from RMB pricing and settlement in cross-border trade. In cross-border trade, RMB settlement is mainly realized in cash (bank account transfers account for a small part). The trade in RMB settlement is mainly petty border trade or black market trade. After the establishment of the RMB settlement pilots, enterprises engaged in foreign trade will have opportunities to directly use RMB for trade settlement — not only greatly reducing their exchange fees and trade costs, but more importantly reducing risks in foreign exchange transactions.

1. From the Micro Perspective of RMB Dealers

   (1) It is beneficial for China's export companies to reduce trade costs and to increase capital efficiency.

   When using foreign currency in cross-border trade settlement, enterprises usually need two currency exchanges and cancel after verification. So these enterprises need to bear the costs of two currency exchanges, and pay commissions that are higher than those in RMB business. Moreover, the procedure is very complicated, taking a long time to transfer RMB with a foreign currency. RMB settlement in cross-border trade can remove one exchange, which reduces companies' financial expenses to some extent, shortens the period of capital settlement, increases the speed of capital turnover and improves capital efficiency.

   (2) It is beneficial for enterprises to reduce transaction fees of financial derivative products and related risks.

   In international trade with foreign currency settlement, many enterprises will use some financial derivatives tools to avoid risks, but also will have to pay high costs (usually around 3% of income). At the same time, there is big risk in financial derivatives tools, so companies need to have professionals who are familiar with derivative products.

   RMB settlement in cross-border trade can avoid risks in foreign exchange and no financial derivative products are needed. This reduces the fees from dealing with derivatives products.

2. From the Macro Perspective of the Nation

   (1) It is beneficial for elevating the status of RMB in neighboring countries and making it internationalized.

RMB settlement can increase the scale of RMB capital mobility and RMB deposits in neighboring countries, further enhancing the status of the RMB in these places. Moreover, it supports the RMB performing currency functions in larger areas, which is an important step towards internationalization and future change in the international monetary system.

(2) RMB settlement in cross-border trade is a prerequisite for RMB free convertibility under the capital account.

Free exchange under the capital account is a symbol of RMB internationalization. The premise for free exchange under the capital account is sufficient accumulation of RMB in foreign financial markets. The RMB accumulated abroad in the earliest phase mainly relied on the foreign payment of RMB in cross-border trade.

Only when RMB capital abroad increases to a sufficient amount can China begin free RMB exchange under the capital account. At the same time, with the enlargement in scope and scale of cross-border RMB settlement, foreign debt in RMB leads to investor demands for RMB finical products and all kinds of transaction demands related to RMB in the international market. This demand would promote the development of RMB-denominated financial products.

8.2.2.2.2 The Status Quo of RMB Cross-border Trade Settlement

The executive meeting of the State Council on April 8, 2009 decided to set up RMB cross-border trade settlement pilots in cities such as Shanghai, Guangdong, Shenzhen, Zhuhai and Dongguan. On June 22, 2010, the PBOC, Ministry of Commerce, General Administration of Customs, State Administration of Taxation, and China Banking Regulatory Commission jointly released the *Notification on Expanding Pilot Areas of RMB cross-border trade settlement*, which expands the pilot areas in China from Shanghai and four cities in Guangdong to 20 provinces (autonomous regions and municipal cities), including Beijing, and expands the area outside of the mainland from Hong Kong, Macao and ASEAN countries, to all countries and regions. It also clearly mentions that the business in pilot areas can include RMB settlement in cross-border goods trade, service trade and other current account transactions. On August 23, 2011, the RMB cross-border trade settlement program was expanded nationwide in China.

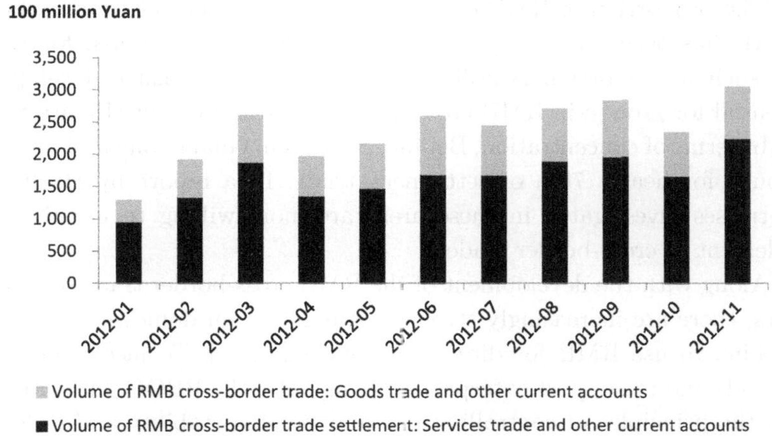

Figure 8.2: RMB Cross-border Trade Settlement (monthly)

Data source: Wind Database.

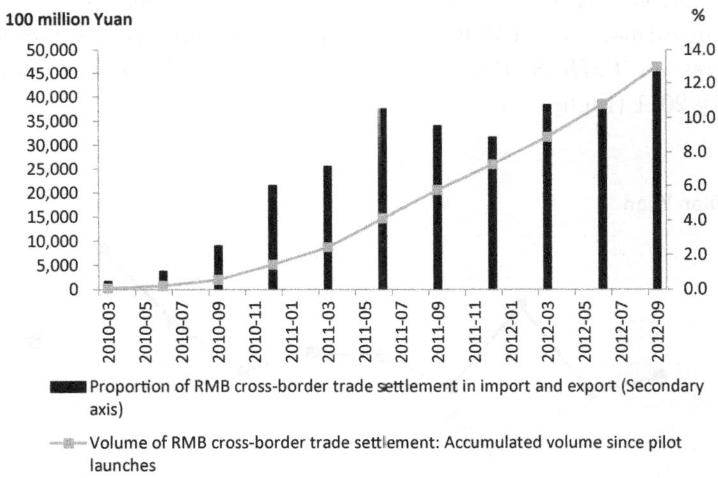

Figure 8.3: Proportion of RMB Cross-border Trade Settlement in Imports and Exports

Data source: Wind Database.

With the expansion of the RMB cross-border trade settlement, the total volume of RMB settlement has also increased. In November 2011, the monthly volume of RMB cross-border settlement reached RMB303.8 billion, and had accumulated to RMB4640.8 billion since its pilot. About two-thirds of this was from goods trade (Figures 8.2 and 8.3).

The proportion of RMB cross-border trade settlement in imports and exports has been increasing. By September 2012, it accounted for 12.6%. But such a proportion is still low, and there is extensive development potential for growth in RMB cross-border trade settlement (Figure 8.3).

In terms of concentration, Beijing, Shenzhen, Guangdong and Shanghai account for nearly 70% of settlement trade. In a report by HSBC, the enterprises investigated in these areas are more willing to use RMB for settlement in cross-border trade.

Along with the development of the RMB cross-border trade settlement pilots, there are increasingly stronger demands from domestic institutions in China to use RMB for direct investment abroad. To meet companies' demands and to support enterprises "going out", the PBOC, in accordance with the principles of controlling risk and keeping stability and order, set up pilots for RMB direct investment abroad in 2010. These proved very popular among companies and banks. To assist in the RMB settlement in cross-border trade pilot, and support financial banking institutions and domestic institutions in conducting RMB settlement of overseas direct investment, the PBOC issued and implemented the *Administrative Measures on RMB Settlement for Foreign Direct Investment (FDI)* on January 2011 (Figure 8.4).

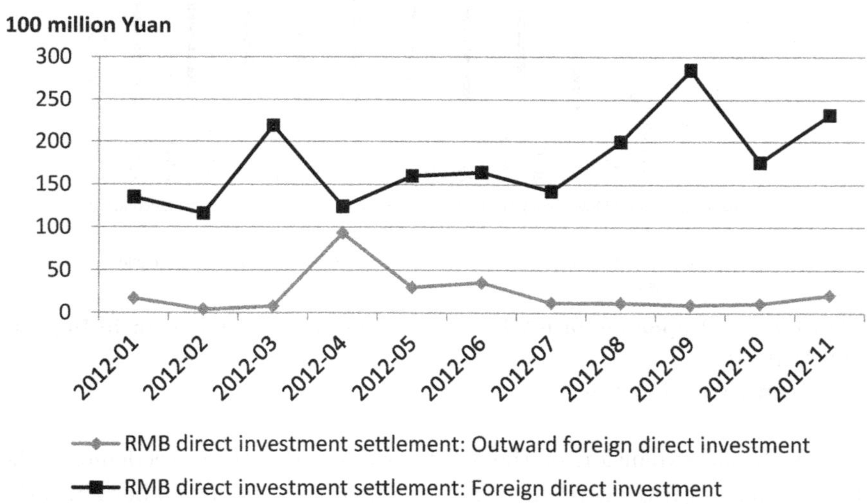

Figure 8.4: Scale of RMB-Denominated Settlement of Outward Foreign Direct Investment and of FDI

Data source: Wind Database.

Since its launch, RMB cross-border trade settlement has had great development. But national policies only take into consideration issues like the convenience of domestic enterprises' trade, settlement and investment. There is a lack of substantial measures related to the convenience of trade for companies abroad. Firstly, enterprises abroad have to bear the double costs of currency exchanges and the double risks of exchange rates. Secondly, the RMB they earn from trade settlement is difficult to invest in markets, so they cannot preserve or increase its value. Thirdly, they have very limited channels for sourcing RMB. Apart from trade settlement and bank exchange, the financing costs for RMB are higher than those for international currencies such as the US Dollar and the Euro. Moreover, in an environment without financial market tools, the enterprises have no way to hedge against interest rate risk.

In the face of such problems, China formulated some policies to solve the problem of overseas enterprises holding RMB. In November 2011, for the purposes of further expanding the use of RMB in cross-border trade and investment, as well as regulating banks and overseas investors in carrying out settlement for RMB-denominated foreign direct investment, the PBOC promulgated and implemented the *Administrative Rules on Settlement of RMB-denominated Foreign Direct Investment*. At present, FDI is increasing (Figure 8.4). In March 2013, to support the RMB settlement of cross-border trade pilot program and increase the avenues for RMB backflows, China allowed three types of institutions (including RMB clearing banks abroad) to set up pilot programs for investment in the interbank bond market with RMB funds. The three types of institutions include foreign central banks or monetary authorities, clearing banks for RMB business in Hong Kong and Macau and overseas participating banks for RMB settlement of cross-border trade.

The international payment ranking of RMB increased from 35th (by the end of 2010) to around 16th (by the end of 2012), and its global market share increased from 0.3% (July 2011) to 0.5% (September 2012), which was mainly realized in the Hong Kong market. Apparently, while the proportion of RMB payment is still small in the world, it has made great progress.

8.2.2.2.3 Case study of RMB settlement in Mainland-Taiwan Trade

With the ever increasing trade between the mainland and Taiwan, cross-strait trade is also increasing year by year. According to data from the

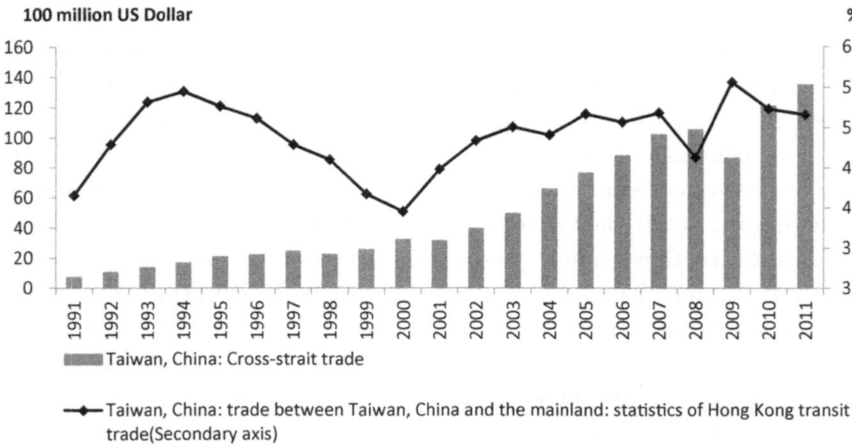

Figure 8.5: Cross-strait Trade Volume, 1991–2011

Data source: Wind Database.

Statistics Bureau of Taiwan, China, cross-strait trade by the end of 2011 had reached USD$13.4 billion, and Taiwan's imports and exports to the mainland accounted for over 5% (Figure 8.5).

Before 2002, due to strict controls over financial exchange, banks on both sides could only conduct "indirect banking" via a third party like Hong Kong, which brought high costs and low efficiency. It was very difficult to provide satisfying services for cross-strait banking, and it was also the most pressing issue for Taiwan-funded enterprises in the mainland at that time.

Thanks to the active promotion of cross-strait financial cooperation from the mainland, Taiwan authorities gradually formulated policies for cross-strait financial exchange and cooperation. In 2003, the Taiwan authorities passed the *Amendment to the Cross-Strait Relations Act*, which allows Taiwanese to hold some RMB when returning to Taiwan. In 2005, Taiwan offered pilot programs for RMB exchange business in Mazu and Jinmen. In 2008, the "legislature" of Taiwan passed the *Amendment to Cross-Strait People Relations Act*, which provides a legal basis for opening RMB exchanges. In June 2008, Taiwan passed *Measures on the Management and Clearing of RMB in Taiwan*. The "central bank" of Taiwan promulgated the list of "financial institutions and foreign currency agencies that offer RMB cash transaction". A total of 1,240 branches of 14 banks such as the Bank of

Taiwan and Taiwan Cooperative Bank, are allowed to offer RMB exchange business. A further 67 foreign currency agencies, including 46 hotels, 15 department stores, six temples and tourist spots, offer RMB purchasing business (but not selling) for only non-Taiwanese and overseas Chinese. Natural persons can exchange RMB with valid identity documents (ID card for Taiwan citizens, and passports for travelers and foreigners), each time in amounts less than RMB20,000. In the early phase, the service was only open to individuals, regardless of their identity and usages, but companies and legal person units are now included. By the end of 2010, RMB transactions in Taiwan had totaled RMB21.906 billion in sales and RMB11.552 billion in purchases. The Taiwan authorities opened two-way RMB exchange on Taiwan Island, which greatly promoted cross-strait currency exchange. This is not only beneficial for expanding the cross-strait financial exchange and cooperation, but also of great significance in cross-strait economic, trade and personal exchanges.

In terms of RMB transactions, at present, local banks in Taiwan can only conduct RMB transactions through Offshore Banking Units (OBUs). While the scale is gradually increasing, it is still very small: only RMB2.1 billion at the end of 2012 (Figure 8.6).

In the end of 2012, the monetary management institutions on both sides of the strait signed the *Memorandum on Cross-Strait Currency Clearing*

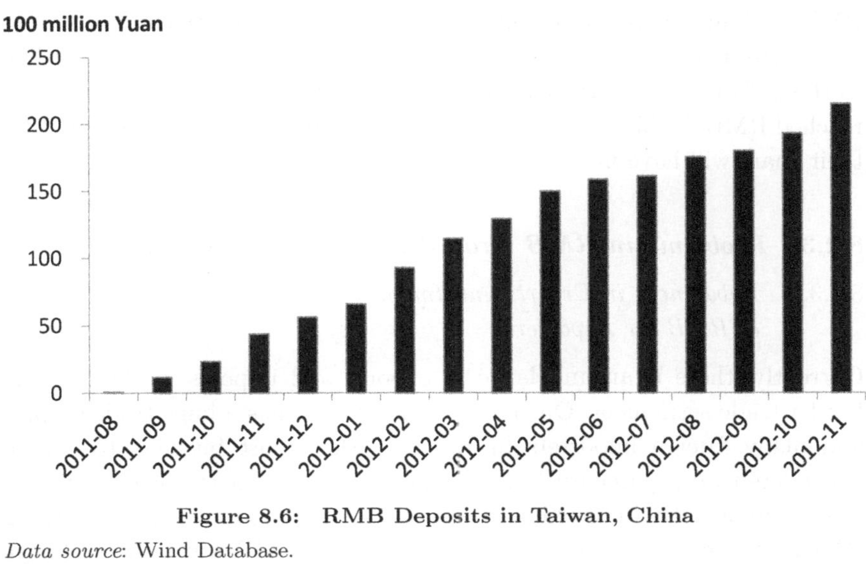

Figure 8.6: RMB Deposits in Taiwan, China

Data source: Wind Database.

Cooperation. Both sides agreed to select a currency clearing institution to provide clearing and settlement services in its own currency. The selected institutions are authorized to transport and deliver cash according to related laws and regulations. On December 11, 2012, the PBOC released a notice to authorize its Taipei Branch to act as a RMB clearing bank in Taiwan, signifying the official launch of the RMB market in Taiwan. It is predicted that there will be explosive growth in the scale of RMB settlement in cross-strait trade. With RMB settlement in cross-strait trade, people and companies on both sides of the strait can directly exchange RMB with the Taiwan Dollar without using US Dollars (lowering exchange costs). At the same time, cross-strait RMB settlement volumes and RMB deposits in Taiwan are expected to grow substantially. The Standard Chartered Bank announced that it completed much RMB settlement business for Taiwan companies.

The Standard Chartered Bank predicted in a research report released in late October that, once the Taiwan regulators allow RMB settlement in DBU accounts, there will be exponential growth in RMB trade settlement in Taiwan. SCB further predicted that between 2013 and 2015, RMB settlement of cross-strait trade will increase from RMB20 billion to over RMB160 billion, and its proportion in total cross-strait trade volumes will increase from 2.5% to 15%. Assuming that nearly one third of the cross-strait trade is settled in RMB, RMB settlement will double to RMB300 billion and 350 billion in 2016 and 2017, respectively.

There will also be fast growth in RMB deposit in Taiwan. According to the SCB report, by the end of 2013, RMB deposits in Taiwan will have reached RMB150 billion — about 2% of total deposits. By the end of 2015, their share will have increased to 5%.

8.2.3 *Problems in RMB Cross-border Trade Settlement*

8.2.3.1 *Imbalances in Exports and Imports and Limited Sources of RMB for Importers*

Currently, there is an imbalance in exports and imports in RMB cross-border trade settlement. On the one hand, China has a huge trade surplus and many foreign importers have very little export business to China. They often only purchase from China and sell in their home countries. More importantly, importers have very limited sources for acquiring RMB. At present, the two channels to source RMB are from exchange in China-foreign jointly funded commercial banks and through buying

RMB in Hong Kong. However, in contrast to Hong Kong, Macao and Southeast Asian areas, there is very little RMB in the commercial banks in Europe and America. Therefore, in China's exports and imports, even when the foreign importers agree to pay in RMB, the sourcing of RMB is a problem.

On the other hand, there are imbalances in the trade between China and other countries/regions. Again we take Taiwan as an example. Generally the mainland has a trade deficit with Taiwan (i.e., the imports of the mainland from Taiwan are larger than the exports). The proportion of RMB payments by mainland companies is higher among imports. At the same time, in imports from the mainland, Taiwan companies find it difficult to pay in RMB. Therefore, there is a demand imbalance between the Taiwan Dollar and the RMB. Such a demand imbalance results in huge amounts of RMB staying in Taiwan without investment channels, and hence decreases Taiwan companies' willingness to accept RMB payment.

The imbalance in RMB cross-border import and export settlement will cause the following problems:

(1) Foreign exporters gain the advantages of RMB appreciation.

Huge amounts of RMB are paid to foreign exporters and flow overseas. Although this increases RMB mobility in foreign markets and creates conditions for the RMB's internationalization, the advantages of RMB appreciation are also transferred from Chinese importers to foreign exporters. This is the Triffin Dilemma applied to RMB internationalization.

(2) Import payments are much more than export receipts, which results in increasing international reserves.

In RMB cross-border settlement of imports, the import payments that used to be paid in a foreign currency are now paid in RMB. This reduces the payment of foreign currency in China, and thus increases foreign reserves and adds pressure to the forex purchase position.

8.2.3.2 *Lack of Capital Backflow Channels*

In terms of present cross-border RMB business, the majority is import business — i.e., paying RMB to foreign countries and large amounts of RMB staying overseas. The RMB's capital account is not yet open and there are a lack of channels for RMB overseas investment. In the promotion of the Yen to become an international settlement currency, the

Japanese government adopted many methods including revising the *Foreign Exchange and Foreign Trade Law*, lowering the threshold for market access, and implementing the policy of permanent taxes. These were intended to loosen controls on the capital account, open the European market for the Yen, and build up the Tokyo offshore market. Japan also opened the short-term government bonds market, followed by the short-term discount treasury market. In the decade from 1980–1990, when Japan loosened its control over the capital account, the proportion of Yen settlement in Japan's imports and exports increased from 2.4% and 29.4% to 14.5% and 37.5% respectively.

At present, the PBOC has designed and gradually improved the RMB's backflow mechanism. First, RMB deposits in Hong Kong are transferred to the PBOC's branch in Shenzhen through clearing banks. Second, in August 2010, the central banks announced to allow three types of institutions (including foreign central banks or monetary authorities, clearing banks for RMB business in Hong Kong and Macau, and overseas participating banks for RMB settlement of cross-border trade) to invest in the interbank bond market. The investment capital can come from currency swaps between China's central bank and foreign central banks, or from RMB cross-border trade settlement. This is a natural progression for the development of cross-border RMB free settlement, and provides a backflow channel for overseas RMB. Third, each sum of money is approved, allowing the capital raised from RMB bonds by Chinese and foreign financial institutions and companies in Hong Kong to be transferred to the mainland.

8.2.3.3 *Chinese Companies Still Lack the Power to Choose the Settlement Currency*

In the choice of invoicing currency in international trade, especially in the manufacturing industry, developed countries like to use their local currencies for invoicing and settlement. As primarily low-end manufacturing enterprises, Chinese enterprises have great difficulties if they want to use RMB for invoicing and settlement in international trade. China's weak position in the international division of labor puts huge limitations on the status and scale of RMB settlement in international trade.

China's export goods are highly replaceable. Great changes have taken place in China's export structure after over 30 years of reform and opening up, with the proportion of primary goods decreasing from 66.7% in 1979 to 2.6% in 2012 and the proportion of mechanical and electrical transport products in manufactured goods accounting for 57.6%. However the proportion of deep processing, finished machining and high value-added products is still low. Therefore, China's export goods are highly replaceable.

At the same time, the proportion of foreign-funded enterprises is very high among China's export enterprises (about half). Most foreign funded enterprises are processing trade enterprises operating as original equipment manufacturers (OEMs). Processing trade accounts for a large proportion of China's export. China receives bonded imports of main raw materials and components from other countries' related companies, conducts processing and manufacturing locally and finally exports the finished goods all over the world. Such exports belong to various stages of supply chains bound together by transnational enterprises. Consequently, the invoicing currency tends to be the home currency of foreign-funded companies or a common currency in the international capital market.

8.2.3.4 *The Settlement Channel Lacks a Clearing Institution*

Bank settlement systems are the channels for capital flows and settlement. If a country has a developed global banking system, it can directly conduct its local currency's imports and exports, settlement and exchange. An expansive transaction network provides positive network externalities that can reduce transaction costs and increase economies of scale, further positively influencing the currency's internationalization. There is a lack of comprehensive clearing institutions and a uniform clearing platform for RMB settlement. The RMB's payment network is not large, giving it no economies of scale and hence burdening its users with high transaction costs. All these factors affect companies' willingness to use RMB for settlement.

8.2.4 ***International Experience***

8.2.4.1 *The Experience of the US Dollar Replacing the Pound to Become an International Settlement Currency*

Firstly, due to the industrial revolution and technological development, the US's trade volume accounted for around 25% or even one third of the world total. Driven by such large scale trade, the scaling effect of the US Dollar as settlement currency becomes more apparent. Trade costs were reduced to a large extent.

More importantly, the US overcame the limitations of a long-term trade surplus. With a long-term trade surplus, foreign currency income in the US was much greater than the expenditure of local currency. Under such circumstances, the US became the largest service trader and creditor in the world through its tremendous export of services and capital. Therefore, demand-oriented US Dollar holdings spontaneously formed in the international currency market, expanding the global mobility of the US Dollar.

Secondly, the US weakened the influence of the Pound through regionalization. By coming up with the Monroe Doctrine and Pan-Americanism, the US allied with over 20 Latin American countries to build the American Economic Community (or the so called "Dollar Bloc") to realize the regionalization of the US Dollar. Based on the "Dollar Bloc", the US Dollar gradually spread to surrounding areas, thus expanding its mobility and usage areas. As such, the US Dollar gradually became the international settlement currency in world trade.

8.2.4.2 *The Experience of the Yen as an International Settlement Currency*

In order to promote trade settlement in Yen, the Japanese government adopted many measures such as making full use of the competitive advantages of some industries, its export monopoly and its trade status to enhance Yen trade settlement. It revised the *Foreign Exchange and Foreign Trade Law*; built the Tokyo off-shore market and reformed its financial market to provide convenient channels for Yen export and backflow; established a government guarantee mechanism in financing credit to provide risk diversification and insurance for companies' Yen settlement and increase market trust in the Yen and created an electronic information trading exchange for a fast, continent-spanning exchange network to reduce the trade costs of Yen settlement. However, there were still many limitations of Yen settlement that impeded its advance towards an international settlement currency.

1. Japan is very dependent on the US in foreign trade. The US is the largest trading partner of Japan. Every year about one third of exports and a quarter of imports in Japan's foreign trade are with the US. But the Yen still cannot compete with the US Dollar, and trade with the US is mainly settled in dollars.

2. Japan has several flaws in its industrial structure. The focus of Japan's industrial structure changed from light and textile industries

after World War II, to heavy machinery industries. The proportion of technology-intensive products in Japan's export goods was increasing, which was positive for Yen settlement in exports. However, due to its small land and lack of natural resources, most of its agricultural goods, raw materials and mining resources are imported from foreign countries, and these are basically irreplaceable primary goods. According to the pricing currency choice theory, primary goods of the same quality in international trade are usually settled in the dominant international currency (i.e., the US Dollar).

3. The Yen experienced dramatic fluctuations in its exchange rate. According to the "Three-Country/Three Currency Model", there are three settlement currencies in international trade: the currency of the export country, the currency of the import country and the currency of a third country. If the exchange rate between the currencies of the two trading countries fluctuates dramatically, they will choose the relatively stable currency of a third country in which to settle. The Yen's exchange rate fluctuations are larger than those of the US Dollar and the Euro, which affects the Yen's share in import and export settlement.

8.2.5 *Suggestions on Promoting RMB Cross-border Settlement*

1. Improving overseas RMB backflow channels, and building RMB off-shore market.

   Currently, RMB cross-border trade settlement is conducted under the condition that the RMB is not fully freely exchangeable under the capital account. Further, RMB flowing abroad through trade cannot freely flow back to its home capital market. Therefore, it is necessary to develop a RMB off-shore market which makes possible overseas RMB circulation and transactions. Enterprises that hold RMB can gain a corresponding advantage so as to aid in promoting the development of RMB settlement.

   Therefore, relevant authorities may consider, in the near-term, gradually opening the long-term bond market and treasury market to provide more RMB investment channels.
2. Seeking opportunities for RMB cross-border trade settlement outside of Asia, rather than just in neighboring countries.

   Europe is the second largest trading partner of China, and there is huge strategic potential in RMB settlement there. Therefore, RMB settlement business should be gradually conducted in European countries where the Euro and US Dollar are weak. For example, not long ago there was a shortage of daily commodities in Iran due to the turmoil there, and the exchange rate fluctuated dramatically. Chinese enterprises can make use of this opportunity to export daily commodities to Iran. On the one hand, this caters to the strengths of China's export structure; on the other hand, China can use this kind of RMB settlement to expand the scope of RMB cross-border trade settlement.

3. Encouraging domestic financial institutions to "go out" to provide sourcing channels for RMB.

   Related authorities should establish cooperative banks to provide RMB sourcing channels for overseas companies. This would lay the foundation for further development of RMB cross-border trade settlement and the balancing of imports and exports. Meanwhile, it is also an excellent opportunity for China's financial institutions to "go out". This is not only good for the regional promotion of the RMB, but will also in turn benefit said companies by consolidating their competitiveness in the markets of these regions and increase their market shares in RMB business through the acceptance of RMB in these regions. Therefore, related authorities in China should encourage the implementation of the policy of domestic financial institutions "going out" and encourage the internationalization of the financial industry, so as to bring about the internationalization of the RMB.

8.3 The RMB as an Investment Currency

8.3.1 *The Status Quo of the RMB as an Investment Currency: A Denominating Currency for International Bonds*

8.3.1.1 *Off-shore RMB Bonds*

Since June 2007, when the PBOC allowed domestic financial institutions to issue RMB bonds in Hong Kong, the new issuance of off-shore RMB bonds reached RMB112.2 billion in 2012 (an increase of 4% compared with RMB107.9 billion in 2011). By the end of 2012, the balance of outstanding bonds had grown to RMB237.2 billion. As Table 8.2 shows, the issuers have expanded from domestic financial institutions to include (in 2009) China's Ministry of Finance and affiliated companies of the Bank of Hong Kong in the mainland, and (in 2010) also ordinary companies and international financial institutions.

Table 8.2: Off-Shore RMB Bonds Exchanged in Hong Kong

Unit: 1 billion Yuan

Date	Issuer	Nature	Scale	Rate of Return	Term Structure
July 2007	China Development Bank	Policy bank of China	5	3%	2 years
August 2007	Export–Import Bank of China	Policy bank of China	2	3.05%, 3.2%	2 years and 3 years
September 2007	Bank of China	State-owned commercial banks of China	3	3.15%, 3.35%	2 years and 3 years
July 2008	Bank of Communications	Joint-stock commercial bank of China	3	3.25%	2 years
August 2008	Export–Import Bank of China	Policy bank of China	3	3.4%	3 years
September 2008	China Construction Bank	State-owned commercial banks of China	3	3.24%	2 years
September 2008	Bank of China	State-owned commercial banks of China	3	3.25%, 3.4%	2 years and 3 years
June 2009	HSBC (China)	Chinese subsidiary of foreign bank	1	Floating interest rate	2 years
June 2009	Bank of East Asia (China)	Chinese subsidiary of foreign bank	4	2.8%	2 years
August 2009	China Development Bank	Policy bank of China	2	2.45%	2 years
August 2009	China Development Bank	Policy bank of China	1	Floating rate	2 years
September 2009	Ministry of Finance, China	China's ministry	6	2.25%, 2.7%, 3.3%	2, 3 and 5 years
July 2010	Hong Kong Hopewell Highway Infrastructure Limited	Hong Kong non-financial enterprise	1.38	2.98%	2 years
August 2010	McDonald's	US transnational enterprise	0.2	3%	3 years
September 2010	Bank of China	State-owned banks of China	5	2.65%, 2.9%	2 and 3 years

(*Continued*)

Table 8.2: (*Continued*)

Unit: 1 billion Yuan

Date	Issuer	Nature	Scale	Rate of Return	Term Structure
September 2010	Deutsche Bank (Hong Kong)	Chinese subsidiary of foreign bank	0.2	Semiannual rate: 2%	2 years
October 2010	Industrial and Commercial Bank of China (Hong Kong)	Hong Kong subsidiary of state-owned bank of China	0.17	2.3%, 2.65%	2 and 3 years
October 2010	China Development Bank	Policy bank of China	2	Floating rate	3 years
October 2010	Asian Development Bank	International financial institution	1.2	2.85%	10 years
October 2010	China Development Bank	Policy bank of China	3	2.7%, compounded semi-annually	3 years
October 2010	China National Heavy Duty Truck Group Co., Ltd	Domestic non-financial enterprises	2.7	2.95%, compounded semi-annually	2 years
November 2010	China Resources Power	Domestic non-financial enterprises	2	2.9%, 3.75%	3 years and 5 years
November 2010	China Merchants Holdings	Domestic non-financial enterprises	0.7	2.9%	3 years
November 2010	Ministry of Finance, China	Chinese ministry	5	1%, 1.8%, 2.48%	3, 5 and 10 years
November 2010	Export-Import Bank of China	Policy bank of China	5	2.65%, 1.95%	3 and 2 years
December 2010	Caterpillar	US non-financial transnational enterprise	1	2.25%	2 years
December 2010	VTB	Foreign bank	1	2.95%	3 years
December 2010	China Power International Development	Domestic non-financial enterprises	0.8	3.2%	5 years

(*Continued*)

Table 8.2: (*Continued*)

Unit: 1 billion Yuan

Date	Issuer	Nature	Scale	Rate of Return	Term Structure
December 2010	Galaxy Entertainment	Hong Kong non-financial enterprise	1.38	4.63%	3 years
December 2010	Ministry of Finance, China	Chinese ministry	3	1.6% (retail)	2 years
December 2010	Australia and New Zealand Bank (ANZ)	Foreign bank	0.2	1.45%	2 years
December 2010	Agricultural Bank of China	State-owned bank of China	1	1.2%, 1.4%	1 and 2 years
January 2011	Royal Bank of Scotland (RBS)	Foreign bank	0.1	1.8%	3 years
January 2011	China National Chemicals Import and Export Corporation	Domestic non-financial enterprises	3.5	1.8%	3 years
January 2011	World Bank	International financial institution	0.5	0.95%	2 years
Total	35	—	77.03	—	—

Data source: Cheung and Qin (2012).

As Table 8.2 shows, the main issuers of Hong Kong RMB off-shore bonds are Chinese financial institutions or government departments with background in domestic capital management. In contrast, foreign banks and non-banking financial enterprises generally have much lower issuance than domestic capital institutions. This fact suggests that the degree of this bond market's internationalization is not high — further hinting that neither is that of the RMB. There is still a long way to go for real development and maturity in the RMB bond market. The reason is that, due to international anticipation of RMB appreciation, there is an increasing risk (in the form of financing costs) for foreign institutions to issue RMB-denominated bonds. But, for domestic capital institutions, the off-shore market provides looser debit and credit conditions, better financial services, and lower borrowing costs.

8.3.1.2 *Panda Bonds*

A Panda bond is an RMB-denominated bond issued in China by international multilateral financial institutions. It is a foreign bond, i.e., a debt security issued by a foreign fundraiser from outside the country in whose currency the bond is denominated and in which the bond is sold. Many foreign bonds issued by foreign financial institutions are named after the country's most representative mascot (e.g., Yankee Bonds in the US, Samurai Bonds in Japan, Matador Bonds in Spain, etc.), so China named its RMB-denominated bond Panda bonds. According to statistics, by the end of 2010, China had only issued five Panda bonds, including four by international financial organizations with an amount of only RMB5 billion (far less than the scale of the Hong Kong off-shore bond market) and one by a Chinese subsidy of a foreign bank (Table 8.3). Similar to the situation in the Hong Kong off-shore bond market, and likewise due to the strong anticipation of RMB appreciation, foreign institutions are not keen on issuing RMB-denominated bonds in the mainland. Also, compared with the off-shore market, there is both greater supervision and control over RMB-denominated bonds and higher issuance costs in the mainland.

Table 8.3: Panda Bonds Issued by China

Unit: 1 billion Yuan

Time period	Issuer	Nature	Scale	Rate of Return	Term Structure
October 2005	Asian Development Bank	International financial institution	1	3.34%	10 years
October 2005	International Finance Corporation	International financial institution	1.13	3.4%	10 years
November 2006	International Finance Corporation	International financial institution	0.87	3.2%	7 years
December 2009	Asian Development Bank	International financial institution	1	4.2%	10 years
May 2010	Bank of Tokyo-Mitsubishi UFJ (China)	Chinese subsidy of foreign bank	1	Negotiated price	2 years

Data source: Cheung and Qin (2012).

8.3.1.3 *Opening the Interbank Bond Market*

On August 16, 2010, the Central Bank of China announced its permission for three types of institutions (including foreign central banks or monetary authorities, clearing banks for RMB business in Hong Kong and Macau and overseas participating banks for RMB settlement of cross-border trade) to invest in the interbank bond market. Their investment capital may come from currency swap arrangements between China's central bank and foreign central banks, or from RMB cross-border trade settlement. This is a natural development of RMB cross-border trade free settlement. In its early phase, policies only allowed increasing usage of RMB, but capital remained overseas. The opening of the interbank bond market means that China has opened convenient channels for overseas capital to flow back into mainland financial institutions. This will gradually establish the backflow mechanism for overseas RMB.

8.3.2 *Challenges for RMB in Becoming an Investment Currency*

8.3.2.1 *Depth and Width for the Development of the Financial Market*

For the RMB to become an investment currency, the prerequisites are that there are basically no controls on RMB convertibility, and that there is a wide, full-fledged financial market (and perhaps also related markets) for foreign RMB holders to freely and quickly enter and invest their holdings. A highly developed and open financial market can provide both quantity and variety in financial transaction tools, serving different interest groups and meeting the different demands from holders in terms of safety, mobility and returns. However, there are still strict controls on China's capital account, and its financial market development lags behind the offerings of developed countries. There is a huge gap between China and developed countries in terms of total capital volume, transaction scale, variety of financial products and financial creativity, etc.

8.3.2.2 *Stability of the RMB's Value*

Another premise for the RMB to become an investment currency is the stability of the RMB's value. The development of the RMB off-shore market and Panda bonds shows that anticipation of RMB appreciation has dampened the internationalization of the off-shore bond market. Due to such anticipation, there is a risk of increasing financing costs for foreign institutions that might issue RMB-denominated bonds. Fundamentally, only when a country's economic power is strong enough and its economy functions well, can it keep a stable currency value. Although China has maintained constant and rapid economic development, it is still a developing country with many problems — imbalanced industrial and economic structures, in particular. Therefore, the stability of currency value stands an important challenge for the RMB to become an investment currency.

8.3.2.3 *Multiple Controls over China's Financial Market*

There are many controls in China's financial market, so foreign institutions are not keen on issuing RMB-denominated bonds in China. At present, to issue a RMB-denominated bond, foreign institutions have to first go to the Ministry of Finance and other offices to submit application, which is then assessed by the Ministry of Finance, the PBOC, National Development and Reform Commission, and Securities and Futures Commission. Then the PBOC sets the interest rate of the bond and, finally, the Administration of Exchange Control manages the issuers' RMB special account and exchange settlement. Apart from all these steps, there is the problem of administrative licensing in approving the bond issuance. At present, foreign institutions have to refer to the financial bond approval project in the interbank bond market by the PBOC. Therefore, compared with the Hong Kong off-shore market, there are more controls and supervisions in mainland issuance of RMB-denominated bonds, making the overall cost higher. As a result, the multiple controls over the mainland's financial market are a huge challenge for the RMB to become a major international investment currency.

8.3.3 *The Choice of Path for RMB to Become an Investment Currency*

8.3.3.1 *Setting up the RMB Off-shore Financial Center*

While the RMB capital account is not yet open, China can first use Hong Kong as the RMB's off-shore financial center and as an indirect channel for free convertibility of the RMB under the capital account. Hong Kong is now the place where most RMB holdings stay, and with the ever-closer economic connection between Hong Kong and mainland, the free convertibility between RMB and the Hong Kong Dollar has made Hong Kong the premier RMB off-shore financial center. Thus China can make use of Hong Kong's status as international financial center to issue internationalized, RMB-denominated bonds and provide RMB trade credit. Before the RMB becomes a freely convertible international currency, Hong Kong will play an important role in setting up RMB accounts, developing RMB financial products, RMB exchanges, RMB market transactions and RMB cross-border settlement and clearing. At the same time, it is necessary to establish and improve the corresponding system, laws and regulations and mechanisms. This will both prevent risks and promote the development of RMB-denominated financial products and tools.

8.3.3.2 *Providing More RMB-denominated Assets*

An important reason for the US Dollar's rise as an international investment currency is that the US Dollar has enough mobility and a good investment environment (it dominants the global capital market). With the increase in overseas RMB holding, China has to provide RMB holders with more choices of assets. RMB cross-border mobility requires China to speed up opening the capital account and also to properly allow overseas RMB to buy Chinese government bonds, or to make direct investments in China. These options would allow China to achieve convertibility under some items in capital account.

8.4 The RMB as a Reserve Currency

The internationalization of RMB is the process of realizing RMB cross-border circulation, making the RMB both a settlement currency and a globally used invoicing currency, achieving investment settlement through further opening of the capital account and finally becoming a reserve currency. Only when the RMB becomes a global reserve currency — the final step in RMB internationalization — can the RMB become a real international currency. There has been great progress in RMB circulation and settlement, yet there is a long way to go for the RMB to become global reserve currency.

A reserve currency is an international circulating currency held by governments for international direct payment in international transactions. International reserves, representing a government's international liquidity, are a kind of reserve asset that governments use for international payment and to maintain the stability of their local currency exchange rate. According to IMF stipulations, a country's reserve currency may be composed of gold reserves, freely exchangeable currency, its reserve positions with the IMF, and its Special Drawing Rights (SDRs, also with the IMF).

Today the commonly used reserve currencies in the world are the US Dollar, Euro, Yen, Pound and Swiss Franc. The French Franc and German Deutschemark also used to be included in this elite group, but they were replaced by (and absorbed into) the Euro.

By the third quarter of 2012, the proportional holdings of the world's major reserve currencies were: the US Dollar accounting (61.81%), Pound (4.09%), Euro (24.14%), Yen (4.11%), Swiss Franc (0.34%) and others (5.52%).

8.4.1 *The International Experiences of the US Dollar and the Yen Becoming Reserve Currencies*

The historical background for the US Dollar becoming a reserve currency was very special. After two world wars, the US became the largest economy in the world, and the US Dollar began to circulate and be used globally. Due to the strong US economy, dollars rapidly exceeded pounds as the most internationalized currency. Further, the US established a global exchange rate system (the Bretton Woods system) to make the US Dollar the medium between the world's currencies and gold. Moreover, the post-war Marshall Plan, which promoted strong economic recovery in parts of Europe, rapidly increased the influence of the US Dollar in Western Europe and further contributed to its reputation and international status.

The path of the Yen becoming a reserve currency was different from that of the US Dollar. The post-war era witnessed fast economic growth and an increasing trade surplus in Japan. Since Japan kept its long-term trade surplus with the US, it gradually became the US's biggest creditor. In order to lower its deficit, the US constantly exerted pressure on the Yen exchange rate. Finally, the Plaza Accord formally depreciated the US Dollar, improving the competitiveness of US products and appreciating the Yen by a large margin. It was the substantial appreciation of Yen that struck Japan's export industry. Japan's economic development became stagnant and many enterprises began to seek development opportunities overseas, moving huge amounts of Yen out of Japan. The international

Table 8.4: Currency Composition of Official Foreign Exchange Reserves

	1995	1996	1997	1998	1999	2000	2001	2002	2003	2004	2005	2006	2007	2008
US Dollar	59.0%	62.1%	65.2%	69.3%	70.9%	70.5%	70.7%	66.5%	65.8%	65.9%	66.4%	65.7%	64.1%	64.0%
Euro	—	—	—	—	17.9%	18.8%	19.8%	24.2%	25.3%	24.9%	24.3%	25.2%	26.3%	26.5%
Deutschmark	15.8%	14.7%	14.5%	13.8%	—	—	—	—	—	—	—	—	—	—
Pound	2.1%	2.7%	2.6%	2.7%	2.9%	2.8%	2.7%	2.9%	2.6%	3.3%	3.6%	4.2%	4.7%	4.1%
Yen	6.8%	6.7%	5.8%	6.2%	6.4%	6.3%	5.2%	4.5%	4.1%	3.9%	3.7%	3.2%	2.9%	3.3%
French Franc	2.4%	1.8%	1.4%	1.6%	—	—	—	—	—	—	—	—	—	—
Swiss Franc	0.3%	0.2%	0.4%	0.3%	0.2%	0.3%	0.3%	0.4%	0.2%	0.2%	0.1%	0.2%	0.2%	0.1%
Other	13.6%	11.7%	10.2%	6.1%	1.6%	1.4%	1.2%	1.4%	1.9%	1.8%	1.9%	1.5%	1.8%	2.0%

Data source: IMF, European Central Bank, Wikipedia.

direct investment of Yen increased dramatically, and consequently the international status of the Yen also increased. In the 1990s, in order to escape a domestic economic downturn, Japan vigorously promoted financial reform to further internationalize the Yen. This made the Yen a global reserve currency, following the US Dollar and German Deutschmark.

From the experiences of the US Dollar and the Yen, it can be concluded that there are four factors for a currency to become reserve currency (Song, 2007): (1) Full currency convertibility; (2) a stable currency value; (3) a large number of international transactions using the currency; and (4) a developed domestic financial market and a full-fledged off-shore market.

8.4.1.1 *Full Currency Convertibility*

Full currency convertibility is a crucial factor in a currency's internationalization. Currency convertibility means that a currency can be converted to another reserve currency according to market exchange rates, for any reason. It can be broken down into two aspects: current account convertibility and capital account convertibility. China now has current account convertibility, but the capital account is not yet fully open. The US has had free convertibility since the creation of the Bretton Woods system, and Japan has had free convertibility since 1984, when it removed controls on non-residents' exchange.

8.4.1.2 *A Stable Currency Value*

For a currency to be global reserve currency, it has to hold a stable value. The RMB has to ensure a stable and reasonable value to become a reserve currency, because a stable value means a stable financial market, and is also a significant safeguard for economic development. Therefore, China should make it a primary goal in monetary policy to keep a stable currency value. While China is vigorously developing its economy, it also has to maintain the RMB's value. Only in this way can China consolidate and improve its economic development, and set up a healthy and stable financial market. As can be seen from the case of the Yen's internationalization, the dramatic fluctuation in its exchange rate caused great damage to Japan's economic development by greatly reducing its exports, and ultimately leading to a stagnant, even backward, economy.

8.4.1.3 *A Large Number of International Transactions Using the Currency*

Trade scale is an important factor that determines whether a currency can become a reserve currency. It is a prerequisite for a currency's "going out", and is the first step in a currency's internationalization. If a country has a large scale of trade, other countries will buy more goods from it more frequently, creating higher demand for its currency. Therefore, the transaction scale and volume will increase in a positive cycle: The local currency will be widely used by other countries in international trade, hence granting it ever higher degrees of internationalization. Due to the large war expenditures of many participating countries in the Second World War, the US Dollar quickly became the currency of large transactions in the world. After the war, the US launched the European Recovery Plan (usually called the Marshall Plan, due to its vigorous promotion by then American Secretary of State, Joe Marshall). This plan was aimed at providing economic aid for reconstruction to Western European countries that suffered greatly from the Second World War. The Marshall Plan lasted for four financial years from July 1947, and amounted to USD$13 billion. This huge injection of capital led to rapid economic recovery in Western European countries. At the same time, this "economic shot" greatly expanded the scale and volume of US Dollars in Europe, which helped rapidly internationalize the US Dollar. Moreover, the Marshall Plan also contributed to the elimination of trade barriers that had existed for a long time among European countries. For Japan, its rapid technological and economic development in the post-war era made it the world's second largest trading country (after the US). It had a yearly increasing trade surplus, dramatically increasing international transactions in Yen. Consequently, the international status of the Yen rose quickly, and it soon became a commonly used reserve currency in the world.

8.4.1.4 *A Developed Domestic Financial Market and a Full-fledged Off-shore Market*

The support and reliance of the internationalization of both the US Dollar and the Yen all come from a developed domestic financial market and a full-fledged off-shore market. With the internationalization of a currency, its home country will witness the establishment of a developed financial market or even a financial center. It is a developed financial market — such as New York or Tokyo — that provides a strong mobility guarantee for their countries' currencies. A full-fledged financial system is also an important basis and promoter of currency convertibility and the marketization of the exchange rate. Developed financial markets and full-fledged off-shore markets provide rich financial services and goods to market participants, so that those who hold such a currency can have lower trading costs and more investment channels. Moreover, the development of off-shore market can provide a buffer zone for a currency. This allows the currency to be used as a reserve currency for risk diversification. After the full convertibility of a currency, an off-shore market also connects domestic and international financial markets, further increasing the frequency and total volume of a currency's international settlement and its acceptance in the international market. Lastly, a full-fledged financial system is also an important steward of exchange rate stability and serves to increase the marketization of the exchange rate.

8.4.2 *The Status Quo of the RMB from the Perspective of Reserve Currency*

8.4.2.1 *The RMB Is not Yet Fully Convertible*

Full convertibility of the RMB means that it can be exchanged with other reserve currencies according to the market exchange rate, at any time. However, due to the controls on RMB exchange under the capital account, it is not yet fully convertible. China has already opened its current account, but its capital account is not yet fully open due to an undeveloped financial market and imperfect financial supervision. Although China introduced the Qualified Foreign Institutional Investors (QFII) program, which opened RMB exchange under the capital account to some extent, its scale is still small due to strict eligibility requirements. Guo Shuqing, Chairman of the China Securities Regulatory Commission, delivered a speech titled "On the Opening-up of China's Capital Market and RMB Convertibility" at the 37th International Organization of Securities Commissions (IOSCO) Annual Conference. He remarked that, among the 40 items of the capital account (as defined by the IMF), 14 items in China are convertible, accounting for 35% of the total. These are mainly concentrated in credit instruments trade, direct investment, direct investment liquidation, etc. A full 22 items are partially convertible, accounting for 55% (mainly in areas like bond market trade, stock market trade, real estate trade and personal capital trade). Lastly a mere four items are inconvertible, accounting for just 10%. These items are mainly in areas like non-citizens' participation in the domestic money market, trust fund market, and derivatives trade.

In terms of China's practical situation, five categories are basically convertible including direct investment, direct investment liquidation, credit business, real estate transactions and personal capital trade. Further some items are fully convertible.

8.4.2.2 *The Stable Value of RMB*

In a press conference for the Fifth Session of the 11th National People's Congress, then Premier, Wen Jiabao stressed that China's imports and exports in Sino-US trade were basically in balance. The Non-deliverable Forwards (NDF) market in the Hong Kong RMB off-shore market had two-way volatility, which means that the RMB exchange rate may be close to the equilibrium exchange rate. Therefore, this conclusion is well grounded, and is in accordance with the current economic development in China and the US.

8.4.2.3 *An Imperfect Financial Market in China*

The crucial condition for the RMB to become a reserve currency is to build strong mobility and accumulate a large number of RMB transactions in international trade. All these rely on a full-fledged financial market. Yet China's financial market is still under development, and its depth, width and efficiency cannot meet the demand for the RMB to become a reserve currency. At the same time, the development of the off-shore market is also an important condition for a currency to become a reserve currency. The RMB off-shore market development has just begun, and the available financial instruments are very simple with only a small issuance. Market regulations are yet to be fully developed. China still has a long way to go towards a full-fledged and mature off-shore market.

8.4.2.4 *The Ever-Increasing International Status of RMB*

Since 2009, when China began its RMB cross-border trade settlement pilot, the scale of RMB cross-border trade settlement has expanded over four years and the international status of the RMB has been increased. In the first half of 2012, RMB cross-border trade settlement reached RMB1251.9 billion, and RMB settlement in direct investment amounted to RMB110.5 billion. At the same time, China signed bilateral local currency swap agreements with Japan, South Korea, Malaysia, Thailand, Turkey, Australia and Mongolia. The scale of swap arrangements has been continually expanded. The PBOC has now signed more than 20 currency swap agreements with over ten countries and regions, representing a total volume of currency swaps of over RMB1.6 trillion. Hu, Deputy Governor of the PBOC, said at the 2012 Lujiazui Forum that the RMB had already become an official reserve currency in some countries and regions.

8.4.3 *The Choice of Path for the RMB to Become a Reserve Currency*

To become a reserve currency is the last and most important step among the four steps for RMB internationalization.

8.4.3.1 *Elevating the RMB's International Status to Make It a Regional Reserve Currency Sooner*

With China's economic development, the international status of the RMB and its usage in international settlement will increase. China exceeded Germany to become the second largest trading country in the world in 2009. In that same year it also became the largest exporter and second largest importer. Its overall trade volume in 2012 reached USD$3866.76 billion — exceeding the US whose trading volume was USD$3855.97 billion — and with this achievement it became the largest trading country in the world. The trade volume increased by 6.2% compared with that of 2011. By the end of 2012, China's foreign reserves totaled USD$3.31 trillion, ranking the first in the world, and 2.5 times those of Japan's. Meanwhile, since 2010, China has officially launched the RMB cross-border trade settlement and RMB investment settlement businesses. RMB cross-border trade settlement in 2011 was USD$2.08 trillion, accounting for about 10% of trade volume settled by other currencies, and the direct investment in RMB settlement was USD$100.87 billion. The fast development of foreign trade will be an important driver to escalate the RMB's international status. At present, China's surrounding countries and regions have a high acceptance of the RMB, and the RMB is widely used in border trade as a settlement currency and invoicing currency. Also, China has signed currency swap agreements with 14 countries and regions, which are helpful for expanding the usage of RMB in the world, increasing the usage frequency of RMB in trade and finance and making the RMB a regional reserve currency.

8.4.3.2 *Gradually Opening the Capital Account and Prudently Promoting Free Convertibility of RMB*

A necessary prerequisite for the RMB to become a reserve currency is to realize its convertibility under the capital account. Without free convertibility, the RMB cannot become reserve currency. China's Twelfth Five-Year Plan again proposed "gradual realization of free convertibility of RMB under capital account". China has to be prudent towards further opening of the capital account. It has to take into consideration the real situation and gradually expand the degree of openness towards foreign capital. While opening the capital account, China has to strengthen its supervision of RMB cross-border mobility. It has to better deal with the relationship between the real economy and the fictitious economy (in accordance with the principle that the latter should serve the former). China also has to encourage long-term and direct foreign investment, and investment in areas of the real economy. At the same time, it is necessary to strictly prevent hot money from flowing into China and to avoid the cross-border flow of hot money from affecting financial industries, causing market bubbles and creating imbalances in international payment. The absolute change of net error and omissions in China's balance of international payments is often related to the cross-border mobility of hot money. Therefore, the flow direction and scale of money can be basically inferred from changes in net error and omissions and its proportions in total import and export volume, as shown in Table 8.5 and Figure 8.7.

8.4.3.3 *Opening the Domestic Financial Market and Promoting the Development of the RMB Off-shore Market*

In order to increase the transaction scale and frequency of the RMB — in line with promoting the RMB as future international reserve currency — it is necessary to create a full-fledged financial market and RMB off-shore market. With the constant development of RMB cross-border trade settlement and direct investment RMB settlement, overseas RMB deposits are increasing. These deposits demand a matched off-shore market to increase the mobility of overseas RMB, to expand the RMB's international influence, and to reduce the influence of foreign capital flows on

Table 8.5: Proportions of Net Error and Omissions in China's Annual Balance of International Payments

Year	Total Volume of Imports and Exports (100 million US Dollar)	Net Error and Omissions (100 million US Dollar)	Proportion (%)
1997	3251.60	−169.5212	5.21
1998	3239.50	−12.83	0.40
1999	3606.30	−148.0434	4.11
2000	4742.90	−118.93073	2.51
2001	5096.50	−48.55572	0.95
2002	6207.70	77.94255	1.26
2003	8509.88	184.22347	2.16
2004	11545.50	270.45082	2.34
2005	14219.10	−167.66227	1.18
2006	17604.40	−128.77344	0.73
2007	21765.70	164.0223	0.75
2008	25632.55	−260.93843	1.02
2009	22075.35	−435.48382	1.97
2010	29739.98	−596.79682	2.01
2011	36418.60	−349.68771	0.96

Data source: GTA Database.

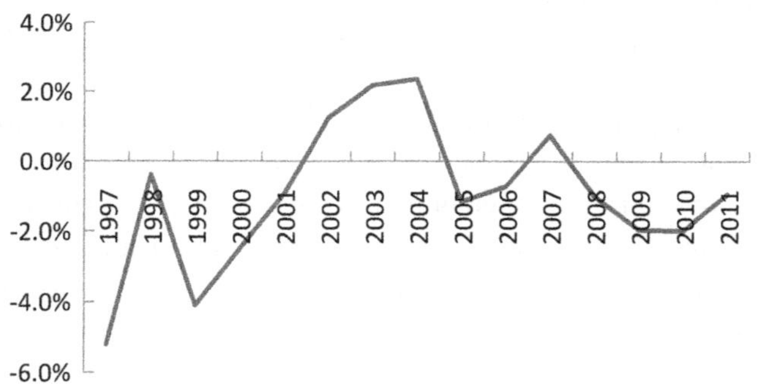

Figure 8.7: Changes in the Proportions of Net Error and Omissions
Data source: GTA Database.

the domestic financial market. At present, the Hong Kong RMB off-shore market has seen great development. The Ministry of Finance of China issued RMB20 billion in national debt in Hong Kong in 2011. Since August 1, 2012, banks in Hong Kong have started RMB services for non-Hong Kong residents, a measure that is good for attracting oversea RMB capital to flow to Hong Kong. By June 2012, RMB deposits in Hong Kong had reached RMB557.7 billion. Following Hong Kong, London initiated its RMB business center on April 18, 2012, becoming the second largest off-shore market. In addition, the establishment of the RMB clearing system in Taiwan suggests that there will be further developments in Taiwan's RMB off-shore market.

China will further open its financial market, such as increasing the number of RMB Qualified Foreign Institutional Investors (RQFII), properly lower the threshold of market access for qualified institutional investors, expand the investment scale of RQFII, and loosen investment controls on RQFII investment (so as to attract foreign capital). Also, the introduction and implementation of RMB Foreign Direct Investment (RFDI) will provide a new channel for RMB backflow.

Bibliography

In English

Bergsten C. F. (1975). *The Dilemmas of the Dollar: The Economics and Politics of the United States International Monetary Policy.* New York: New York University Press.

Chinn M. and Frankel J. (2005). Will the Euro Eventually Surpass the Dollar as Leading International Reserve Currency?. NBER Working Paper No. 11510.

Devereux M. B., Engel C., and Storgaard P. E. (2004). Endogenous Exchange Rate Pass-Through When Nominal Prices Are Set in Advance. *Journal of International Economics*, 63(2): 263–291.

Friberg R. (1998). In Which Currency Should Exporters Set Their Prices?. *Journal of International Economics*, 45(1): 59–76.

Fukuda S. I. and Ono M. (2006). On the Determinants of Exporters' Currency Pricing: History vs. Expectations. *Journal of the Japanese and International Economies*, 20(4): 548–568.

Goldberg L. S. (2010). Is the International Role of the Dollar Changing? *Current Issue in Economics and Finance*, 16(1): 1–7.

Grassman S. (1976). Currency Distribution and Forward Cover in Foreign Trade: Sweden Revisited, 1973. *Journal of International Economics*, 6(2): 215–221.

Hartmann P. (1998). Currency Competition and Foreign Exchange Markets: The Dollar, the Yen and the Euro. Cambridge: Cambridge University Press.

Hong Kong Monetary Authority (2013). Hong Kong: The Premier Offshore Renminbi Business Center. Available at http://www.hkma.gov.hk/media/eng/doc/key-functions/monetary-stability/rmb-business-in-hong-kong/hkma-rmb-booklet.pdf.

Swoboda A. K. (1968). The Euro-Dollar Market: An Interpretation. Essays in International Finance No. 64. Department of Economics, Princeton University.

In Chinese

Bi Y. J. (2005). Current Situation and Approaches of the Internationalization of RMB. *Journal of Shanxi Agricultural University* (*Social Science Edition*), 2: 119–121.

Chen L. (2008). *RMB Internationalization Strategy Research-Starting from East Asian Monetary Cooperation.* Nanjing: Nanjing University of Technology and Engineering.

Chen Y. L., Wang F. and Yang M. (2005). Currency Internationalization as a National Competitive Strategy: US Dollar's Empirical Evidence-and a Study on the Issue of Renminbi. *Economic Research Journal*, 2: 35–44.

Cheng S. W. (2009). *Economic Reform and Development in China.* Beijing: China Renmin University Press.

Cheung Y.-W. and Qin F. M. (2012). *RMB Exchange Rate: Past, Present and Future.* Beijing: China Finance Publishing House.

Chu H. (2009). RMB Internationalization Research. Fudan University Ph.D. dissertation.

Fang G. Z. (2008). The status and Strategy of RMB circulation in ASEAN. *South China Finance*, 5: 020.

Feng D. J. (2008). RMB Internationalization Issues Research of China's Neighboring Countries and Regions. Guangxi University Master's thesis.

Guo S. Q. (2012). The liberalization of China's Capital Market and the Convertibility of China's Capital Account. *Financial Regulation Research*, 6: 1–17.

Han K. H. (2000). On The Capital Account Liberalization in Developing Countries. University of International Business and Economics Master's thesis.

He F. (2009). The Realistic Choice of RMB Internationalization. *International Economic Review*, 4(7): 9–9.

He F. and Chen P. (2006). Active Management of Foreign Exchange Reserves: Singapore, Norway's' Experience and Enlightenment. *Studies of International Finance*, 6: 4–13.

Hu X. L. (2012). RMB has been Included in a Number of European Countries as Reserve Currency. China News Network.

Jiang B. K. and Zhang Q. L. (2005). Currency Internationalization: A Review of the Impact Conditions. *New Finance*, 8: 6–9.

Jiang B. K. and Zhu Y. G. (2004). On the Choice of Monetary Policy Regime under RMB's Capital Account Convertibility. *Fudan Journal (Social Sciences)*, 6: 40–48.

Kong K. P. (2010). The Selection of the Chinese Currency Reserves Constituted under the Global Financial Crisis. *Studies of International Finance*, 3: 64–72.

Li D. K. and Liu L. L. (2008). RMB Internationalization: Measurement Research and Policy Analysis. *Journal of Financial Research*, 11: 1–16.

Li H. (2002). The International Prestige of RMB Is Greatly Improved. *Shenzhen Commercial Daliy*, November 4.

Liu X. F. (2012). The Path of RMB towards an International Reserve Currency. *First Financial Daily*, 2012-06-26A07.

Liu X. M. (2009). The Impact of Capital Account Liberalization on China's Exchange Rate Formation Mechanism. Yunnan University of Finance and Economics Master's thesis.

Lu Q. J. (2010). U.S. Dollar Hegemony and International Monetary System Reform — On the Issue of RMB Internationalization. *Journal of Shanghai University of Finance and Economics*, 12(001): 61–69.

Luo L. P. (2011). Inspiration of RMB Internationalization Comes from Yen Internationalization *Securities & Futures of China*, 10: 138.

Shi J. (2008). The Realistic Choice RMB Internationalization Strategy. *Review of Economic Research*, 11: 1–16.

Song H. (2012). *The Choice of China's Exchange Rate Regime.* Beijing: China Financial Publishing House.

Song J. J. (2007). The Policy Options of RMB to Generate a Reserve Currency. *Research on Financial and Economic Issues*, 8: 10.

Song J. J. (2008). Changing Share of Yen in International Official Reserves and Implications for the Internationalization of RMB. *Contemporary Economy of Japan*, 5: 12–18.

State Administration of Foreign Exchange (2009). Chinese International Balance Report 2009.

Sun B. (2012). Capital Account Liberalization Order Research. Jilin University Ph.D. dissertation.

Sun H. X. (2011). The Study of International Monetary Conditions. Fudan University Ph.D. dissertation.

Tan Y. N. (2004). The Status and Recommendations of the Regional Development of RMB in the ASEAN. *South China Finance*, 9: 57–60.

The People's Bank of China. 2011 Report on Financial Statistics. Available at http://www.pbc.gov.cn/publish/goutongjiaoliu/2/2012/2012010103103021/2012010103103021_html.

Wang X. L. (2009). The Evolution of International Reserves and Its' Value Analysis of Reserve Currency. *Studies of International Finance*, 12: 40–48.

Wang Y. L. (2008). The Strategies and Processes of The Convertibility And Internationalization Of RMB Capital Account. *China Finance*, 10: 36–39.

Wang Y., Guan T., and Wen J. (2002). Towards the Convertibility of RMB: Practice of China Gradualism. Beijing: Economic Science Press.

Wu X. N., Wei X. H., and Liu J. (2005). Path Selection of RMB Internationalization Strategy. *Credit Reference*, 23(5): 82–84.

Xu X. H. (2006). Internationalization of the RMB: Theory and Evidence. Fudan University Ph.D. dissertation.

Yin L.Y. (2010). The Inspiration to RMB Internationalization from Yen Internationalization. *Academic Exchange*, 6: 117–119.

Zhang L. and Wang Z. H. (2010). Thinking of RMB Internationalization. *Modern Business Trade Industry*, 22(21): 172–173.

Zhang M. (2010). International Monetary System Reform: Background, Causes, Measures and China's Participation. *International Economic Review*, 1: 114–137.

Zhang R. H. (2012). The Thinking about RMB towards an International Reserve Currency. *China Finance*, 2012(9): 40–41.

Zhao Z. G. (2009). The way of International Monetary System Reform. *Finance and Economy*, 9: 13–14.

Zhou X. C. (2009). The Thinking on the Reform of the International Monetary System. *China Finance*, 7: 8–9.

Zhou X. J. (2009). The Status and Development Analysis of RMB Internationalization. *China Business and Trade*, 15: 148.

Index

Lightning Source UK Ltd.
Milton Keynes UK
UKOW06n1540240415

250293UK00005B/74/P

9 789814 644655